Data Visualization

Data Visualization

Principles and Practice

Alexandru Telea

A K Peters, Ltd.
Wellesley, Massachusetts

Editorial, Sales, and Customer Service Office

A K Peters, Ltd.
888 Worcester Street, Suite 230
Wellesley, MA 02482
www.akpeters.com

Library of Congress Cataloging-in-Publication Data

Telea, Alexandru C., 1972-
    Data visualization : principles and practice / Alexandru C. Telea.
        p. cm.
    Includes bibliographical references and index.
    ISBN-13: 978-1-56881-306-6 (alk. paper)
        1. Computer graphics. 2. Information visualization.
     3. Mathematics–Graphic methods–Data processing. I. Title.

T385.T452 2007
001.4′226028566--dc22

                                                2007027112

Cover image: Simplified vector field visualization via bottom-up clustering of a 3D field (Figure 6.26, p. 208).

Printed in India
11 10 09 08 07   10 9 8 7 6 5 4 3 2 1

To my mother

Contents

Chapter 1

Introduction

THE book is targeted at computer-science, mathematics, and engineering-sciences students in their last undergraduate years or early postgraduate phase. A second audience is practitioners in these fields who want to develop their own data-visualization applications but who have not had extensive exposure to computer graphics or visualization lectures. The book strives to strike an effective balance between providing enough technical and algorithmic understanding of the workings and often subtle trade-offs of the most widespread data-visualization algorithms while allowing the reader to quickly and easily assimilate the required information. We strive to present visualization algorithms in a simple-to-complex order that minimizes the time required to get the knowledge needed to proceed with implementation.

Data visualization is an extensive field at the crossroads of mathematics, computer science, cognitive and perception science, engineering, and physics. Covering every discipline that shares principles with visualization, ranging from signal theory to imaging and from computer graphics to statistics, requires in itself at least one separate book. Our goal is to provide a compact introduction to the field that allows readers to learn about visualization techniques. Hence, several visualization algorithms and techniques have been omitted. On one hand, we have chosen to focus on those techniques and methods that have a broad applicability in visualization applications, occur in most practical problems in various guises, and do not

1

demand a specialized background to be understood. On the other hand, we have also included a number of less mainstream research-grade visualization techniques. With these methods, we aim to give the reader an idea of the large variety of applications of data visualizations, illustrate the wide range of problems that can be tackled by such methods, and also emphasize the strong connections between visualization and related disciplines such as imaging or computer graphics.

Whenever applicable, existing commonalities of structure, principles, or functionality between the presented visualization methods are emphasized. This should help the reader better understand and remember a number of underlying fundamental principles and design issues that span the visualization field. These principles allow one to design and use visualization applications for a problem domain or data type much easier than if one had to learn the required techniques anew. Secondly, this helps students understand the nature of such cross-domain principles as sampling, interpolation, and reconstruction, and design issues such as optimizing the trade-off between speed, memory consumption, and data representation accuracy. We believe this approach of understanding mathematics and software design by seeing their concrete application in a practical domain may benefit computer-science students, in particular, who have a less extensive mathematical background.

Throughout the book, we illustrate algorithmic and software design issues by providing (pseudo)code fragments written in the C++ programming language. The reader is assumed to have an average understanding of the language, i.e., be familiar with the language syntax and have basic knowledge of data structures and object-oriented programming. Whenever possible, the examples are described in terms of plain structured programming. Object-oriented notation is used only when it simplifies notation and helps understand the described algorithms. No particular software toolkit, library, or system is used to support this description. There is a single exception to this rule: in a few instances, we make use of a small set of concepts present in the OpenGL programming library, such as graphics operations and data types, to illustrate some visualization techniques. OpenGL is one of the best-known and most well-supported graphics libraries in use, has a quite easy learning curve, and provides a compact and concise way to express a wide range of graphical operations. Knowledge of OpenGL is not required to follow the material in this book. However, the provided code fragments should allow and encourage readers who are interested in implementing several of the presented techniques to get a quick start. For both a quick start in programming OpenGL applications as well as an in-depth reference to the library, we strongly recommend the classics, also known as the Red Book [Shreiner et al. 03] and the Blue Book [Shreiner 04].

We have decided to follow a toolkit-independent exposition of visualization principles and techniques for several reasons. First, we believe that understanding the main principles and working of data-visualization algorithms should not be intermixed with the arduous process of learning the inevitably specific interfaces and assumptions of a software toolkit. Second, we do not assume that all readers have the extensive programming knowledge typically required to master the efficient usage of some visualization software toolkits in use nowadays. Finally, different users have different requirements and work in different contexts, so the choice of a specific toolkit would inevitably limit the scope of the presentation.

Last but not least, designing a complete visualization system involves many subtle decisions. When designing a complex, real-world visualization system, such decisions involve many types of constraints, such as performance, platform (in)dependence, available programming languages and styles, user-interface toolkits, input/output data format constraints, integration with third-party code, and more. Although important for the success of a system design, such aspects are not in the realm of data visualization but of software architecture, design, and programming. All in all, we believe that presenting the field of data visualization in a manner as independently as possible from a toolkit choice makes this book accessible to a broader, less specialized audience.

1.1 How Visualization Works

The purpose of visualization is to get insight, by means of interactive graphics, into various aspects related to some process we are interested in, such as a scientific simulation or some real-world process. There are many definitions of visualization. Following Williams et al., visualization is "a cognitive process performed by humans in forming a mental image of a domain space. In computer and information science it is, more specifically, the visual representation of a domain space using graphics, images, animated

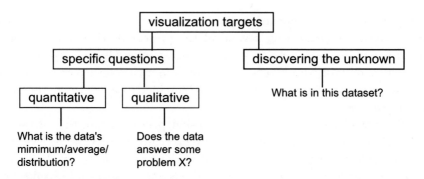

Figure 1.1. Types of questions targeted by the visualization process.

sequences, and sound augmentation to present the data, structure, and dynamic behavior of large, complex data sets that represent systems, events, processes, objects, and concepts" [Williams et al. 95].

In most applications, the path from the given process to the final images is quite complicated and involves a series of elaborate data-processing operations. Ultimately, however, the visualization process produces one or several images that should be able to convey insight into the considered process. In the words of pioneers in the field, visualization is "the use of computers or techniques for comprehending data or to extract knowledge from the results of simulations, computations, or measurements" [McCormick et al. 87].

The term "insight" is used very frequently in visualization-related disciplines and texts. However, what exactly does insight mean in this context? Visualization can help obtain several types of insight by answering several types of questions (see Figure 1.1). In the current context, we use the word "insight" to describe two types of information we get from a visualization application:

1. *answers* to concrete questions about a given problem;

2. *facts* about a given problem that we were not aware of.

In the first case, we have some concrete questions about a given phenomenon, process, or dataset.[1] The purpose of visualization in this context

---

[1]By *dataset*, we mean a collection of data values that describe some given process. A more formal definition of a dataset is given in Chapter 3.

is to answer these questions as well, and as quickly, as possible. Such questions can be *quantitative*, e.g., "given a 2D land map, how high are the highest points?" In this case we are interested in a measurable answer on a given scale of reference, e.g., "the highest peak is 2500 meters above sea level." A sample list of quantitative questions targeted by visualization applications includes:

- which are the minimum, maximum, or outliers of the values in a dataset, and for which data points do they occur?

- what is the distribution of the values in a dataset?

- do values of different datasets exhibit correlations, and how much?

- do values in a dataset match a given model or pattern, and how closely do they match?

At this point, readers may ask themselves why we need visualization to answer concrete questions such as what is the maximum value of a dataset, when a simple textual display would suffice. There are, indeed, many cases when this is true and when simple tools such as a text-based query-and-answer system work the best. However, there are also many cases when visualization works better for answering concrete, quantitative questions. In these cases, the answer to the question is not a single number but typically a set of numbers. For example, whereas the question "what is the value of a function $f(x)$ at a given point x" can be answered by printing the value, the question "what are the values of $f(x)$ for all x in a given interval" is best answered by plotting the graph of $f(x)$ over that interval. Distributions, correlations, and trends of several values are also best understood when depicted visually. Clearly, in some situations, task performance is better using visual representations, whereas in others, text-based representations are more efficient. An early study by Larkin and Simon [Larkin and Simon 87] on the effectiveness of visual representations on human task performance outlined two ways in which visual representations can outperform text-based ones:

- by substituting (rapid) perceptual inferences for difficult logical inferences;

- by reducing the search for information required for task completion.

Although not exhaustive, their research gives some theoretical underpinning to the intuitive appeal of using visualization to comprehend information.[2]

In addition to quantitative questions, a large number of questions targeted by visualization are of a *qualitative* nature, e.g., "given a medical scan of a patient, are there any anomalies that may indicate clinical problems?" A typical answer to this question would involve the discovery of patterns that have particular characteristics in terms of shape, position, or data values, which a human expert such as a medical doctor would classify as anomalous, based on his previous clinical experience. In such cases, it is quite hard, if not impossible, to answer the questions using fully automatic means, given the vague definition of the question and the high variability of the input data. The decisional input of the human expert, supported by interactive visualizations, is indispensable.

In scientific and engineering practice, questions typically range between extremely precise ones and very vague ones. Visualization is useful for both types of questions. Although it can be argued that precise questions can be answered with simple search-like queries that do not need any visual support, it can also be argued that displaying the answer of such queries in a visual manner makes them simpler to assimilate. Moreover, the visual support can provide additional information that may not be explicitly requested by the question but that can open broader perspectives on the studied problem. For example, displaying the highest peak on a land map both by indicating the peak's height as a number and also its position on a 3D elevation visualization shows not only the absolute height value but also how that value relates to the average height on the map (how high it is compared to the overall landscape, how many land points are at or close to the maximal height, and so on). This information, although not directly requested, can help formulate subsequent questions, which ultimately help the user to acquire a deeper understanding of the data at hand. This is one of the meanings of the term "insight."

In the second case, we may have no precise questions about our process at hand. However, we are interested in (literally) looking at, or examining, the information that this process provides. Why, one might ask, should we look at some data if we have no concrete questions to ask about it? There

---

[2]The title of their work, "Why a diagram is (sometimes) worth 10000 words," is emblematic for the well-known saying "A picture is worth a thousand words."

are several reasons for this. First, we may have had similar data in the past that was interesting, helpful, or critical for a given application, and we may want to find out if the current data is of the same kind. Second, we may have the feeling that, by examining a certain piece of data, we can acquire information on the process that produced it that we simply cannot obtain by other means. This role of visualization closely matches the perspective of a researcher who is interested in studying a phenomenon in order to find out novel facts and establish unexpected correlations. This is a second meaning of the term "insight."

The two types of questions are not separated in practice but rather serve two types of complementary scenarios. In the first scenario type, one has a number of precise questions to answer and is quite familiar with the type of data and application. This scenario is best targeted by fine-tuned visualizations answering those precise questions. However, after answering such questions, one may discover that some fundamental problem is still not solved, because the questions were too precise. In this situation, switching to the more exploratory, open-ended visualization scenario is a good continuation. This scenario follows a typical bottom-up pattern, going from precise to more general queries. In the second scenario type, the user receives a dataset that he is largely unfamiliar with. In this case, the best approach is to start with some exploratory visualization that presents a general overview of the data. After the general impression is formed, the user can decide, based on particularities discovered in the general view, which more specific, detailed visualization to use next, and thus which more precise question to answer. This scenario follows a top-down pattern, going from an overview to a detailed investigation. In the visualization field, this type of investigation is sometimes referred to as the *visualization mantra* of "overview, zoom, and details-on-demand," as coined by Shneiderman [Card et al. 99, Bederson and Shneiderman 03].

Finally, an important drive for visualizing data is sheer curiosity. Visualization methods often produce unexpected and beautiful imagery from many exotic types of data. Such images are intriguing and interesting to the eye. When examined in more detail, they can lead researchers to discover unexpected and valuable things about the processes and datasets at hand.

A further fundamental feature of visualizations is their *interactive* aspect. The visualization process is rarely a static one. In most applications,

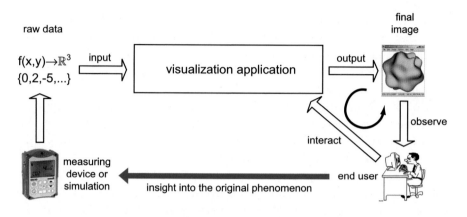

Figure 1.2. Conceptual view of the visualization process.

there is a need to visualize a large amount of data that would not directly
fit on a single screen, a high-dimensional dataset containing a large number
of independent data values per data point, or both. In such cases, displaying a static image that contains all the data is not possible. Moreover,
even when this is possible, there usually are many ways of constructing
the data-to-image mapping, which the user might like to try out in order
to better understand the data at hand. All these aspects benefit from the
use of interactive visualizations. Such applications offer the possibility of
modifying several parameters, ranging from the view angle, zoom factor,
and color usage to the type of visualization method used, and observing the
changes in the produced image. If the interact-visualize-observe feedback
loop (see Figure 1.2) is performed quickly enough, the user effectively gets
the sensation of "navigating" through the data, a feature which strongly
encourages and supports the exploration process.

What type of insight can we expect from a visualization application,
and what should we not expect? How can we measure how much insight a
given image provides us into a certain process? And how can we construct
visualization applications that provide us with the most insight into a problem or dataset of a given nature? To answer such questions, we must first
understand how to construct a visualization application, how to represent
the various types of data involved in the visualization process, how to set
the various parameters of this process, and how to interpret the results.
These are the topics of the following chapters.

1.2   Book Structure

The organization of this book follows a bottom-up structure. We assume that the reader has a minimal familiarity with computer graphics principles and techniques and is interested in starting from this basis and working to understand and eventually develop visualization methods. We introduce visualization techniques and principles gradually. We start with the simplest ones, which require just a minimal computer graphics and programming background. As the book unfolds, more complex mathematical and algorithmic notions are introduced to help readers understand the workings and trade-offs of advanced visualization techniques. Each chapter covers one separate visualization topic by presenting a number of visualization methods and algorithms for that topic. Just as the chapters themselves, the algorithms in a chapter are introduced in an increasing level of difficulty and specificity. We conclude several chapters by presenting a selection of the most recent advances in the field of visualization, in the form of one specialized, research-level algorithm or method.

We begin, in Chapter 2, with a simple example that introduces data visualization to the reader: drawing the graph of a function of two variables using a height plot. We use this well-known example to introduce several essential ingredients of data visualization, such as sampling and the dataset concept, and also make a comparison between visualization and computer graphics. These concepts are illustrated by easy-to-follow C++ code fragments.

In Chapter 3, we continue our presentation of the dataset concept by describing the most frequently used types of datasets in visualization. For each dataset type, we describe its particular advantages, as well as its specific requirements. We use the running example of the function height plot visualization introduced in Chapter 2 to illustrate the various differences between the presented dataset types. After completing this chapter, the reader should have a good understanding of the various trade-offs that exist between different dataset types, be able to choose the right type of dataset for a given visualization problem at hand, and understand several aspects related to efficiently implementing datasets in software.

Chapter 4 presents the visualization pipeline, the popular data-driven architecture used to construct most visualization applications nowadays.

This chapter has two goals. At a conceptual level, the reader is introduced to the various data processing stages that form the visualization process: data acquisition, data filtering or enrichment, data mapping, and rendering. At an implementation level, the architecture of a visualization application, seen as a set of data processing algorithms interconnected by the datasets they read and write, is explained. After completing this chapter, the reader should understand the various steps involved in the construction of a particular visualization application, ranging from the conceptual data processing stages up to an actual high-level software architecture specified in terms of interconnected algorithms and datasets. Readers interested in implementing visualization applications can use the practical information provided here as a guideline on how to structure the high-level architecture of their applications in terms of computational modules with decoupled functionality.

In the next seven chapters of the book (Chapter 5 up to Chapter 11), we present the main visualization methods and algorithms that are used in practice in visualization applications. The first three chapters in this group (Chapters 5, 6, and 7) discuss visualization methods for the most common data types in the visualization practice, ordered in increasing level of difficulty, i.e., scalars, vectors, and tensors, respectively. Chapter 8 presents domain modeling techniques, which encompass those visualization methods that manipulate both the data attributes and the underlying domain sampling, or grid, these live on.

Chapter 9 is an overview of image visualization methods and discusses the particularities of image data, i.e., scalars sampled on uniform two-dimensional grids. Here, specific techniques for image data are discussed, such as edge detection, histogram normalization, and skeletonization. Following this, Chapter 10 discusses volume visualization techniques, which target three-dimensional scalar fields sampled on uniform grids. Although the image and volume techniques presented in Chapters 9 and 10 can be seen as particular forms of scalar visualization, we discuss them separately, as image and volume visualization are, by themselves, vast research and application fields, which have developed many particular techniques suited to their specific data and goals.

Chapter 11 switches the focus from the visualization of scientific datasets, which typically come from the sampling of continuous functions over compact spatial domains, to the visualization of information, or *infovis*.

The infovis field targets the visual understanding of more general datasets such as text, database tables, trees, and graphs. As such datasets need not be the result of a sampling process of some continuous signal defined over some spatial domain, many specific visualization methods have been developed to cope with the increased level of abstraction of the data. Given the sheer size of this field, as well as the focus of this book on the visualization of scientific datasets, Chapter 11 provides only a brief incursion in the field of infovis. Several differences between scientific and information visualization are highlighted in order to give the reader some insight on the particular challenges that the infovis field is confronted with.

Finally, Chapter 12 concludes the book, outlining current development directions in the field of visualization.

Appendix A provides an overview concerning the design of visualization software systems. First, we present a classification of the different types of visualization systems from a software architecture perspective (Section A.1). The purpose of this classification is to emphasize some important choices that influence the construction of visualization systems. Next, a selection of representative visualization software systems is presented in the areas of scientific visualization, imaging, and information visualization (Sections A.2–A.4). Although not exhaustive, this overview should give the interested reader a starting point to search further for existing software that best matches a given set of requirements for a given application domain.

After completing this book, the reader should have a good impression of the palette of existing techniques for visualizing the various types of datasets present in the scientific visualization practice, the various trade-offs involved with each technique, and some of the main issues involved in the efficient implementation of the presented techniques into actual software. More advanced readers should, at this point, be able to implement functional, albeit simple, versions of several of the visualization algorithms discussed in this book. However, this book is not about implementing visualization algorithms. Readers interested in this topic should consult the specialized literature describing the design and use of visualization software toolkits [Schroeder et al. 04, Kitware, Inc. 04]. The aim of this book is to present an overview of data-visualization methods and teach the reader about the various trade-offs involved in the design of such methods, ranging from modeling issues to visual presentation and software design. But

above all, we feel that this book has reached its goal if it inspires the reader
to further study and explore the exciting world of visualization.

1.3   Notation

Throughout the book, we shall use the following notation conventions.
Variables and position vectors are denoted using italics, e.g., x, y. Direction vectors are denoted using bold, e.g., $\mathbf{p}$, $\mathbf{q}$. Continuous domains,
such as surfaces in 3D, are denoted by calligraphic letters, e.g., $\mathcal{S}$. Discrete
domains, such as datasets containing data sampled on grids, are denoted
by uppercase letters, e.g., S. Finally, pseudocode and C++ code fragments
are written using computer font, e.g., `printf`.

Chapter 2

From Graphics
to Visualization

$\mathbf{F}$OR many readers of this book, data visualization is probably a new
subject. In contrast, computer-graphics techniques, or at least the
term "computer graphics," should be familiar to most readers. In both
visualization and graphics applications, we take as input some data and,
ultimately, produce a picture that reflects several aspects of the input data.
Given these (and other) similarities, a natural question arises: what are the
differences between visualization and computer graphics? We shall answer
this question in detail in Chapter 4. For the time being, it is probably easier
to see the similarities between visualization and computer graphics. This
will help us answer the following question: what is the role of computer
graphics techniques in visualization?

This chapter introduces data visualization in an informal manner and
from the perspective of computer graphics. We start with a simple problem
that every student should be familiar with: plotting the graph of a function
of two variables $f(x, y) = z$. We illustrate the classical solution of this
problem, the *height plot*, in full detail. For this, we shall use code fragments
written in the C++ programming language. For the graphics functionality,
we shall use the popular OpenGL graphics library.

This simple example serves many functions. First, it illustrates the complete visualization process pipeline, from defining the data to producing a

rendered image of the data. Our simple example will introduce several important concepts of the visualization process, such as datasets, sampling, mapping, and rendering. These concepts will be used to build the structure of the following chapters. Second, our example introduces the basics of graphics rendering, such as polygonal representations, shading, color, texture mapping, and user interaction. Third, the presented example will make the reader aware of various problems and design trade-offs that are commonly encountered when constructing real-life visualization applications. Finally, our small application illustrates the tight connection between data visualization and computer graphics.

After reading this chapter, the reader should be able to construct a simple visualization example using just a C++ compiler and the OpenGL graphics library. This example can serve as a starting point from which the reader can implement many of the more advanced visualization techniques that will be discussed in later chapters.

2.1   A Simple Example

We shall start our incursion in the field of data visualization by looking at one of the simplest and most familiar visualization problems: drawing the graph of a real-valued function of two variables. This problem is frequently encountered in all fields of engineering, physics, mathematics, and business. We assume we have a function $f : D \to \mathbb{R}$, defined on a Cartesian product $D = X \times Y$ of two compact intervals $X \subset \mathbb{R}$ and $Y \subset \mathbb{R}$, $f(x, y) = z$. The graph of the function is the three-dimensional surface $S \in \mathbb{R}^3$, defined by the points of coordinates (x, y, z). In plain words, visualizing the function f amounts to drawing this surface for all values of $x \in X$ and $y \in Y$. Intuitively, drawing the surface S can be seen as warping, or elevating, every point (x, y) inside the two-dimensional rectangular area $X \times Y$ to a height $z = f(x, y)$ above the xy plane. Hence, this kind of graph is also known as a warped plot, height plot, or elevation plot. Most engineering and scientific software packages provide built-in functions to draw such plots.

However simple, this visualization yields several questions: How should we represent the function f and the domains X and Y of its variables? How should we represent the surface S to visualize? How many points are there to be drawn? What kind of graphics primitives should we use to do the drawing? Essentially, all these questions revolve around the issue of representing *continuous* data, such as the function f, surface S, and variable domains X and Y, on a computer. Strictly speaking, to draw the graph, we should perform the warping of $(x, y, 0)$ to $(x, y, f(x, y))$ for all points (x, y) in D. However, a computer algorithm can perform only a finite number of operations. Moreover, there are only a finite number of pixels on a computer screen to draw. Hence, the natural way to generate an elevation plot is to draw the surface points $(x_i, y_i, f(x_i, y_i))$ that correspond to a given finite set of *sample points* $\{x_i, y_i\}$ in the variable domain D. Figure 2.1 shows the pseudocode of what is probably the most-used method to draw an elevation plot. We sample the function definition domain $X \times Y$ with a set of N_x points placed at equal distances dx in X, as well as N_y points placed at equal distances dy in Y. Figure 2.1 shows the elevation plot for the Gaussian function $f(x, y) = e^{-(x^2+y^2)}$, defined on $X \times Y = [-1, 1] \times [-1, 1]$, using $N_x = 30$, $N_y = 30$ sample points. The sample domain is drawn framed in red under the height plot.

Using equally spaced points, regularly arranged in a rectangular grid, as the pseudocode in Listing 2.1 does, is an easy solution to quickly create

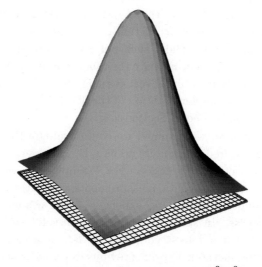

Figure 2.1. Elevation plot for the function $f(x, y) = e^{-(x^2+y^2)}$ drawn using 30×30 sample points.

```
float  X_min,X_max;                //X = [X_min,X_max]
float  Y_min,Y_max;                //Y = [Y_min,Y_max]
int    N_x,N_y;
float  dx = (X_max−X_min)/N_x;     //
float  dy = (Y_max−Y_min)/N_y;     //
float  f(float, float);            //the function to visualize

for(float  x=X_min;x<=X_max−dx;x+=dx)
  for(float  y=Y_min;y<=Y_max−dy;y+=dy)
  {
      Quad q;
      q.addPoint(x,y,f(x,y));
      q.addPoint(x+dx,y,f(x+dx,y));
      q.addPoint(x+dx,y+dy,f(x+dx,y+dy));
      q.addPoint(x,y+dy,f(x,y+dy));
      q.draw();
  }
```

Listing 2.1. Drawing a height plot.

a height plot. This samples the function domain D uniformly, i.e., uses the same sample point density everywhere. In addition to its simplicity, the uniform sampling permits us to approximate the graph of the function, the surface $\mathcal{S}$, with a set of four-vertex polygons, or quadrilaterals, constructed by consecutive sample points in the x and y directions, as shown in Listing 2.1. This serves us well, as virtually every modern graphics library provides fast primitives to render such polygons. Our pseudocode uses a simple C++ class Quad to encapsulate the rendering functionality. To draw a Quad, we first specify its four 3D vertices using its addPoint method, and then we draw() it. An implementation of the Quad class using the OpenGL graphics library is presented in Section 2.3.

In our visualization, we assumed we could evaluate the function f to visualize at every desired point in its domain D. However, this assumption might be too restrictive in practice. For example, the values of f may originate from experimental data, measurements, simulations, or other data sources that cannot be or are too expensive to be evaluated during the visualization process. In such cases, the natural solution is to explicitly store the values of f in a data structure. This data structure is then passed to the visualization method. For our previous example, this data structure needs to store only the values of f at our regularly arranged sample points. For this, we can use a simple data structure: a matrix of real numbers.

```
float  X_min,X_max;
float  Y_min,Y_max;
int    N_x,N_y;
float  dx = (X_max−X_min)/N_x;   //
float  dy = (Y_max−Y_min)/N_y;   //
float  data[N_x][N_y];           //the dataset to visualize

for(int  i=0;i<N_x−1;i++)
  for(int  j=0;j<N_y−1;j++)
  {
      float  x = X_min+i*dx,  y = Y_min+j*dy;
      Quad  q;
      q.addPoint(x,y,data[i][j]]);
      q.addPoint(x+dx,y,data[i+1][j]);
      q.addPoint(x+dx,y+dy,data[i+1][j+1]);
      q.addPoint(x,y+dy,data[i][j+1]);
      q.draw();
  }
```

Listing 2.2. Drawing a height plot using a sampled dataset.

The modified visualization method that uses this data structure as input, instead of the function f, is shown in Listing 2.2.

The data generation, i.e., the construction of the matrix *data*, and visualization, i.e., the algorithm in Listing 2.2, are now clearly decoupled. This allows us to use our height-plot visualization with any algorithm that produces a matrix of sample values, as described previously. The matrix *data*, together with the extra information needed for drawing, i.e., the values of X_{min}, X_{max}, Y_{min}, Y_{max}, N_x, and N_y forms a fundamental concept in data visualization, called a *dataset*. A dataset represents either a sampling of some originally continuous quantity, like in the case of our function $f(x, y)$, or some purely discrete quantity. An example of the latter is a page of text, which can be represented by a vector, or string, of characters, i.e., a char data[N_x], a spreadsheet, or a database table containing, e.g., non-numerical attributes. These attributes can in turn be represented as a matrix char data[N_x][N_y] of objects of type T, where T models the attribute type. Various data types, such as temperature and pressure fields measured by weather satellites or computed by numerical simulations; 3D medical images acquired by magnetic resonance imaging (MRI) and computed tomography (CT) scanners; and multidimensional tables emerging from business databases are represented by different types of datasets. Datasets form the input and output of the algorithms used in data visualization, like the function sampling and elevation-plot algorithms discussed in our simple function visualization example. These aspects are discussed in detail in Chapters 3 and 4.

Let us go back to our elevation plot. The numbers of samples to be used, i.e., N_x and N_y, are parameters to be chosen by the user. The question arises: what are optimal values for these parameters? By using more samples, the quality of the discrete representation, the data matrix, and subsequently the quality of the visualization, can only increase, reaching the continuous case in the limit when N_x and N_y tend to infinity. However, this poses increasing storage requirements for the dataset (the data matrix) and computing power requirements for the visualization method. On the other hand, choosing too few samples yields a fast, low-memory, but also low-quality visualization. Figure 2.2 illustrates this with a visualization of the same function as before, this time with N_x=10 and N_y=10 samples.

Comparing this image with the previous one (Figure 2.1), we see that reducing the sample density yields a worse approximation of the surface $\mathcal{S}$.

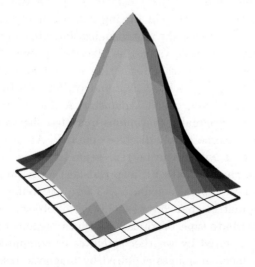

Figure 2.2. Elevation plot for the function $f(x, y) = e^{-(x^2+y^2)}$. A coarse grid of 10×10 samples is used.

This is especially visible close to the center point $x = y = 0$. Basically, our rendered surface approximates the continuous one with a set of quadrilaterals determined by the sample point locations and function values. The quality of this approximation is determined by how close this *piecewise-linear approximation*, as delivered by our set of rendered quadrilaterals, is to the original continuous surface $\mathcal{S}$. The question is thus how to choose the sample locations so that we achieve a good approximation with a given sample count, i.e., given memory and speed constraints. The answer is well known from signal theory [Ambardar 06]: the sampling density must be proportional to the local *frequency* of the original continuous function that we want to approximate. In practice, this means using a higher sample density in the areas where the function's higher-order derivatives have higher values.

To emphasize the importance of choosing a good sampling density, let us consider now a different function

$$g(x, y) = \sin\left(\frac{1}{x^2 + y^2}\right).$$

The speed of variation, or frequency, of this function increases rapidly as we approach the origin $x = y = 0$.[1] Figure 2.3 a shows the elevation plot of

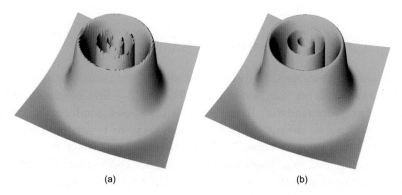

(a)   (b)

Figure 2.3. Elevation plot for the function $f(x, y) = \sin\left(\frac{1}{x^2+y^2}\right)$, rendered using (a) a uniform grid of 100×100 samples and (b) an adaptively sampled grid.

---

[1] We shall ignore, for simplicity, the fact that the function is not defined for the point $x = y = 0$.

this function constructed from a grid of 100 by 100 samples. Even though this plot has roughly 10 times more sample points than the one shown in Figure 2.1 for the Gaussian function, the resulting quality is clearly poor close to the origin. There are two solutions to alleviate this problem. First, we can increase the sampling density everywhere on the grid. However, this wastes samples points in the smooth areas, i.e., far away from the origin.

A better solution is to make the sampling density variable, for example, inversely proportional to the distance from the origin. Figure 2.3(b) shows the result of the nonuniform sampling density. Although we use as few samples as in the low-density, uniform-sampling approach (Figure 2.3(a)), the quality of the result is now visibly much higher in the central area. However, this quality comes at a price. It is now no longer possible to determine the sample point positions from the function domain extents and sample counts, as the density is nonuniform. Hence, we must explicitly store the sampling point positions together with the function samples in the dataset.

As we shall see in Chapter 3, several types of datasets permit the creation of such nonuniformly sampled grids, which offer different trade-offs between the freedom of specification of the sample positions, the storage costs, and the implementation complexity.

2.2   Graphics-Rendering Basics

In the next section, we shall discuss how we actually render the height plot constructed from our sampled dataset. For this, we first briefly cover the basics of graphics rendering in this section. Computer graphics is an extensive subject whose theory and practice deserves to be treated as a separate topic, and in a separate book. In this section, we shall sketch only the basic techniques used in a simple computer graphics application. Fortunately, these techniques are sufficient to illustrate and even implement a large part of the data-visualization algorithms discussed in this book, starting with our height plot visualization example. In later chapters, we shall introduce several more advanced computer graphics techniques, such as the use of transparency and textures, when presenting specific visualization methods that require them in their implementation.

Graphics rendering generates computer images of 3D scenes, or data-sets. The ingredients of this process are a 3D scene, a set of lights, and a viewpoint. Essentially, the process can be described as the application of a *rendering equation* at every point of the given dataset. For a given point, the rendering equation describes the relationship between the incoming light, the outgoing light, and the material properties at that point. In general, the rendering equation has a complex form [Foley et al. 95]. Solving the rendering equation computes the outgoing light, or illumination, for every point of a 3D scene, given the scene, light set, and viewpoint.

In practice, several rendering equations are used, which can approximate lighting effects to various degrees of realism. Two known approximations are the *radiosity* methods, which are good at producing soft shadows [Foley et al. 95, Sillion 94], and *ray-tracing* methods, which are good at simulating shiny surfaces, mirror-like reflections, and precise shadows [Foley et al. 95, Shirley and Morley 03]. However, both radiosity and ray-tracing methods are relatively expensive to compute, even for simple 3D scenes. The reason behind this is that the rendering equations used by such methods relate the illumination of a given point to the illumination of several, potentially many, other points in the scene. For this reason, such methods are also called *global illumination* methods. Hence, solving for the complete scene illumination amounts to solving a complex system of per-point rendering equations.

A more efficient approach is to simplify the rendering equation to relate the illumination of a given scene point only, and directly, to the light set. Such approaches are called *local illumination* methods, since the rendering equation solves for the illumination locally for every scene point. We shall present a local illumination method that is implemented by the rendering back-ends of most visualization systems nowadays, such as the OpenGL library. This method, also known as the *Phong lighting* method, assumes the scene to be rendered to consist of opaque objects in void space, illuminated by a point-like light source. Hence, the lighting has to be computed only for the points on the surfaces of the objects in the scene. Phong lighting is described by Equation (2.1):

$$I(p, \mathbf{v}, \mathbf{L}) = I_l \left(c_{\text{amb}} + c_{\text{diff}} \max(-\mathbf{L} \cdot \mathbf{n}, 0) + c_{\text{spec}} \max(-\mathbf{r} \cdot \mathbf{v}, 0)^\alpha \right). \quad (2.1)$$

Here, p is the position vector of the surface point whose lighting we compute, $\mathbf{n}$ is the surface normal at that point, $\mathbf{v}$ is the direction vector from p

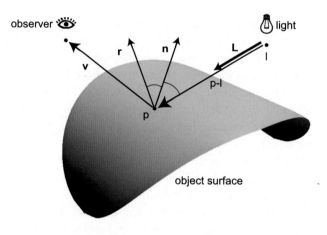

Figure 2.4. The Phong local lighting model.

to the viewpoint we look at the scene from, I_l is the intensity of the light, **L** is the direction the scene light illuminates p from, and r is the *reflection vector* (see also Figure 2.4):

$$\mathbf{r} = \mathbf{L} - 2(\mathbf{L} \cdot \mathbf{n})\mathbf{n}. \qquad (2.2)$$

Depending on the light source model, **L** takes different values. For a light source placed infinitely far away from the scene objects, also called a *directional light*, **L** is simply a direction vector. For an infinitely small light source located at some point l, equally shining in all directions, also called a *point-like light*, **L** is the unit-length vector in the direction $p - l$.

The lighting model in Equation (2.1) is a linear combination of three components: ambient, diffuse, and specular, whose contributions are described by the weighting coefficients c_{amb}, c_{diff}, and c_{spec}, respectively, which are in the range $[0, 1]$. Ambient lighting is essentially a constant value. This is a rough estimate of the light reflected at the current point that is due to indirect illumination, i.e., light reflected onto the current point by all other objects in the scene. Diffuse lighting, also known as *Lambertian reflection*, is proportional to the cosine of the angle between the light direction $-\mathbf{L}$ and the surface normal **n**, or the vector dot product $-\mathbf{L} \cdot \mathbf{n}$. This models the equal scattering of incoming light in all directions around the surface normal. Diffuse lighting simulates the appearance of plastic-like, matte surfaces, and does not depend on the viewpoint. Finally, specular, or mirror-like, lighting is proportional to the cosine of the angle between the reflected light direction $\mathbf{r}$ and view direction $\mathbf{v}$, raised to a specular power α. This models the scattering of the incoming light in directions close to the perfect mirror reflection direction $\mathbf{r}$. Specular lighting simulates the appearance of shiny, or glossy, surfaces, such as polished metal, and is viewpoint-dependent.

There is, so far, no *color* introduced in the lighting equation (2.1). This equation describes the interaction of light of a given color, or wavelength, with a surface. In other words, the factors c_{amb}, c_{diff}, c_{spec}, and I_l are all functions of the color. As we shall see next in Section 2.3, color can be modeled as a set of three intensities R, G, and B, corresponding to the red, green, and blue wavelengths respectively. Hence, in practice, Equation (2.1) is applied three times, so each of its factors will have three values, e.g., $c_{\text{amb}\ R}$, $c_{\text{amb}\ G}$, $c_{\text{amb}\ B}$, and similarly for the other factors.

Ideally, the rendering equation should be applied at every point of every object surface in a given scene. However, as we shall see in the next section, it might be more practical and/or efficient to evaluate the rendering equation only at a few surface points and use faster methods to compute the illumination of the in-between points.

2.3   Rendering the Height Plot

Rendering the datasets discussed in Section 2.1 using the height-plot method relied upon our `Quad` class, which draws a 3D quadrilateral, specified by its four vertices. We can implement this class easily using the OpenGL graphics library, following the basic rendering model presented in Section 2.2. The implementation is shown in Listing 2.3.

As explained in Section 2.2, OpenGL applies the rendering equation at a subset of the points of a given surface and uses the resulting illumination values to render the complete surface. The simplest, and least expensive, rendering model provided by OpenGL is *flat shading*. Given a polygonal surface, flat shading applies the lighting model (Equation (2.1)) only once for the complete polygon, e.g., for the center point, and then uses the resulting color to render the whole polygon surface. The polygon normal can be computed automatically by OpenGL from the polygon vertices.

```
class  Quad
{
public :

        Quad ( )
        {   glBegin (GL_QUADS} ;    }

void  addPoint ( float  x , float  y , float  z )
        {   glVertex3f ( x , y , z ) ;    }

void  draw ( )
        {   glEnd ( ) ;    }
} ;
```

Listing 2.3. Drawing a quadrilateral using OpenGL.

The polygon is assumed to be a flat surface, so its normal is constant. This implies a constant shading result following Equation (2.1), hence the name "flat shading." In OpenGL, the flat shading mode is selected by the function call

```
glShadingMode ( GL_FLAT ) ;
```

Several results of flat-shaded height plots using quadrilaterals implemented by the Quad class were shown in the previous section.

In order to apply Phong lighting (Equation (2.1)), we must specify the ambient, diffuse, and specular coefficients c_{amb}, c_{diff}, and c_{spec}. OpenGL offers a rich set of mechanisms to specify these coefficients, which we shall not detail here. The simplest way to control the appearance of a drawn object is to set its *material color*. If we use the default white light provided by OpenGL, this is equivalent to setting the diffuse factor c_{diff} in Equation (2.1). Setting the material color is accomplished by the function call

```
glColor3f ( r , g , b ) ;
```

where the color is specified by the RGB model using three floating-point values r, g, b in the range $[0, 1]$. The RGB color model is described in detail in Section 3.6.3. Note that the color specified by glColor3f affects all drawing primitives issued after that moment and until a new color spec-

ification is issued. Hence, to create the height plot shown in Figure 2.1, it
is sufficient to issue a single `glColor3f` call before all the quads are drawn.
The green color shown in the figure corresponds to the setting $r = 0.3$,
$g = 0.8$, $b = 0.37$.

Besides specifying the object color, we must specify the light intensity
and direction, i.e., the parameters I_l and $\mathbf{L}$ in Equation (2.1). In OpenGL,
lights are specified by a number of function calls. First, OpenGL must
be set up to use the Phong lighting equation, by enabling the lighting
mechanism. OpenGL supports several light sources (most implementations
provide at least eight of them). The next step is to enable one of the light
sources, say the first one. These two operations are accomplished by the
function calls

```
glEnable (GL_LIGHTING );
glEnable (GL_LIGHT0 );
```

After lighting and the desired light(s) are enabled, we can specify the
light intensity. As explained in the previous section, OpenGL uses a three-
component light model, so the Phong lighting model (Equation (2.1)) is
applied three times. Moreover, OpenGL allows us to separately specify
the amount of light that interacts with the ambient, diffuse, and specular
material components. Putting it all together, the lighting equations used
by OpenGL are

$$I^R(p, \mathbf{v}, \mathbf{L}) = I^R_{\text{amb}} c^R_{\text{amb}} + I^R_{\text{diff}} c^R_{\text{diff}} \max(-\mathbf{L} \cdot \mathbf{n}, 0)$$
$$+ I^R_{\text{spec}} c^R_{\text{spec}} \max(-\mathbf{r} \cdot \mathbf{v}, 0)^\alpha,$$

$$I^G(p, \mathbf{v}, \mathbf{L}) = I^G_{\text{amb}} c^G_{\text{amb}} + I^G_{\text{diff}} c^G_{\text{diff}} \max(-\mathbf{L} \cdot \mathbf{n}, 0)$$
$$+ I^G_{\text{spec}} c^G_{\text{spec}} \max(-\mathbf{r} \cdot \mathbf{v}, 0)^\alpha, \tag{2.3}$$

$$I^B(p, \mathbf{v}, \mathbf{L}) = I^B_{\text{amb}} c^B_{\text{amb}} + I^B_{\text{diff}} c^B_{\text{diff}} \max(-\mathbf{L} \cdot \mathbf{n}, 0)$$
$$+ I^B_{\text{spec}} c^B_{\text{spec}} \max(-\mathbf{r} \cdot \mathbf{v}, 0)^\alpha.$$

Here, the superscripts R, G, and B denote the color components. The
triplet $(I^R_{\text{amb}}, I^G_{\text{amb}}, I^B_{\text{amb}})$ specifies the amount (intensity) of light that interacts with the ambient material component $(c^R_{\text{amb}}, c^G_{\text{amb}}, c^B_{\text{amb}})$, and is specified by the function call

```
glLightfv (GL_LIGHT0,  GL_AMBIENT,  I);
```

Here, $I = (I_{amb}^R, I_{amb}^G, I_{amb}^B)$ is a vector of three floating-point values. The same function can be used to specify the diffuse and specular light intensities for all lights by replacing GL_AMBIENT with GL_DIFFUSE and GL_SPECULAR, respectively, and replacing GL_LIGHT0 with the desired light name.

Finally, we must specify the direction and position of the light (see Section 2.2). This is achieved by the function call

```
glLightfv (GL_LIGHT0,GL_POSITION,p);
```

Here $p = (p_x, p_y, p_z, p_w)$ is a vector of four floating-point values. If the fourth value p_w is zero, the light is directional with the direction $\mathbf{L} = (p_x, p_y, p_z)$. If p_w is not zero, the light is point-like, its position being given by $(p_x/p_w, p_y/p_w, p_z/p_w)$.

However attractive, this rendering of the surface approximation has several limitations. Probably the most salient one is the "faceted" surface appearance, due to its approximation by flat-shaded quadrilaterals. This artifact is visible even when we use a relatively densely sampled dataset, such as the one in Figure 2.2. When using flat-shaded polygons, removing this visual artifact completely for a height plot of an arbitrary function implies rendering polygons with a size of one pixel. In our setup, this implies, in its turn, using a prohibitively high sampling density. Just to give an impression of the costs, on a screen of 640×480 pixels, this strategy would require rendering over a hundred thousand polygons, and computing and storing a dataset of over a hundred thousand sample points, i.e., a memory consumption of a few hundred kilobytes, all for a simple visualization task.

We can easily improve on this by using *Gouraud shaded*, or smoothly shaded, quads. Gouraud shading assumes the surface represented by the quad to have a non-constant normal—specifically, every quad vertex can have a distinct normal vector. This is a simple approximation of a real smooth surface, whose normal would, in general, vary at every surface point. Gouraud shading applies the lighting model (Equation (2.1)) at every quad vertex, using the respective vertex normal, yielding potentially four different colors. Next, all quad pixels are rendered with a color that smoothly varies between the four vertex colors resulting from the shading,

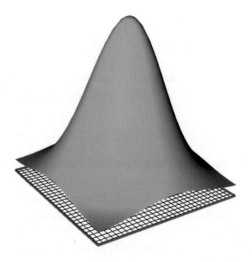

Figure 2.5. Elevation plot for the function $f(x, y) = e^{-(x^2+y^2)}$ (Gouraud shaded).

using a technique called *interpolation*. Interpolation is described in greater detail in Chapter 3. Figure 2.5 shows the result of Gouraud shading applied to the same dataset rendered in Figure 2.1 with flat shading. In OpenGL, the smooth shading mode is selected by the function call

```
glShadingMode(GL_SMOOTH);
```

To perform Gouraud shading, we must add vertex normal information to our `Quad` class. This is easily done by adding an extra method to this class:

```
void Quad::addNormal(float* n)
    {   glNormal3f(n[0],n[1],n[2]);   }
```

which specifies a normal vector $\mathbf{n} = (n_x, n_y, n_z)$ for every quad vertex. In OpenGL, specifying a vertex normal should be done together with the specification of the vertex itself. In our case, `addNormal()` should be called right after `addVertex()` for that respective vertex.

The next step is to compute the actual vertex normals for our surface. The computing method depends on how the surface is specified. If the surface is specified analytically, e.g., by a function, we can proceed as follows. From analysis, we know that a vector normal to the graph of f, i.e., to our surface, is given by

$$\mathbf{n} = \left(-\frac{\partial f}{\partial x}, -\frac{\partial f}{\partial y}, 1\right). \tag{2.4}$$

The vector $\mathbf{n}$ is related to another important mathematical concept called the *gradient*. Given a function $f : \mathbb{R}^2 \to \mathbb{R}$, the gradient of f, denoted ∇f, is the vector

$$\nabla f = \left(\frac{\partial f}{\partial x}, \frac{\partial f}{\partial y}\right). \tag{2.5}$$

For functions with more variables, the gradient is defined analogously. Intuitively, the gradient of f is a vector that indicates, at every point in the domain of f, the direction in the domain in which f has the highest increase at that point. We shall encounter numerous applications of the gradient in the following chapters.

In our example, $f(x,y) = e^{-(x^2+y^2)}$, so the vector $\mathbf{v} = (-2xf, -2yf, 1)$ has the same direction as the normal, though not the same length. We can thus compute the normal $\mathbf{n}$ by normalizing $\mathbf{v}$:

$$\mathbf{n} = \left(-\frac{2xf}{\sqrt{4x^2f^2 + 4y^2f^2 + 1}}, -\frac{2yf}{\sqrt{4x^2f^2 + 4y^2f^2 + 1}}, 1\right). \tag{2.6}$$

We can now draw the Gouraud-shaded height plot in Figure 2.5 using the code in Listing 2.4. Here, n is a function that computes the normal $\mathbf{n}$ of the original function f at a given point (x, y), i.e., implements Equation (2.6). This method works for any function for which we can compute its partial derivatives analytically, as in Equation (2.4). However, as discussed in Section 2.1, our function may not be specified analytically, but as a sampled dataset. Still, in practice, we can perform Gouraud shading of sampled (e.g., polygonal) datasets using a simple technique called *normal averaging*. For every sample point p_i, denote by $P_1..P_N$ all polygons that have p_i as a vertex. We define the vertex normal $\mathbf{n}_i$ at p_i as the average of all polygon normals $\mathbf{n}(P_j)$ that have p_i as a vertex:

$$\mathbf{n}_i = \frac{\sum_{P_j} \mathbf{n}(P_j)}{N}. \tag{2.7}$$

Intuitively, Equation (2.7) says that the direction of the vertex normal $\mathbf{n}_i$ is somewhere between the normals of the polygons P_j that share that vertex. For our height plot example, the resulting Gouraud shading obtained using

```
float    f(float ,float );      //the function to visualize
float* n(float ,float );        //the normal of f at (x,y)

for ( float  x=X_min; x<=X_max−dx ; x+=dx )
  for ( float  y=Y_min; y<=Y_max−dy ; y+=dy )
  {
      Quad  q ;
      q. addNormal( n( x , y ) ) ;
      q. addPoint ( x , y , f ( x , y ) ) ;
      q. addNormal( n( x+dx , y ) ) ;
      q. addPoint ( x+dx , y , f ( x+dx , y ) ) ;
      q. addNormal( n( x+dx , y+dy ) ) ;
      q. addPoint ( x+dx , y+dy , f ( x+dx , y+dy ) ) ;
      q. addNormal( n( x , y+dy ) ) ;
      q. addPoint ( x , y+dy , f ( x , y+dy ) ) ;
      q. draw ( ) ;
  }
```

Listing 2.4. Drawing a Gouraud-shaded height plot.

a normal vertex computed by averaging is practically identical to the one shown in Figure 2.5, which uses analytically computed normals.

Sometimes, however, averaging the polygon normals does not produce good results. The averaging in Equation (2.7) makes every polygon normal $\mathbf{n}(P_j)$ contribute equally to $\mathbf{n}_i$. However, some surfaces can contain polygons of highly variable sizes in the same neighborhood, e.g., sharing the same vertex. In this case, a more natural shading effect can be obtained by making the influence of a polygon on the vertex normals, and thus on the Gouraud shading of the surface, proportional to the polygon size. This can be easily achieved by using an area-weighted normal averaging, i.e.,

$$\mathbf{n}_i = \frac{\sum_{P_j} A(P_j)\mathbf{n}(P_j)}{\sum_{P_j} A(P_j)}, \tag{2.8}$$

where $A(P_j)$ is the area of polygon P_j.

In Section 3.9.1, we shall elaborate further on the connection between normal averaging and data resampling.

2.4 Texture Mapping

Extra realism can be added to rendered 3D models by using a technique called *texture mapping*. The flat-shaded rendering mode described so far

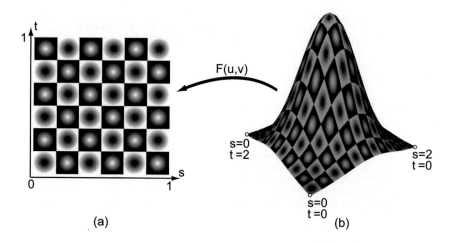

Figure 2.6. Texture mapping. (a) Texture image. (b) Texture-mapped object

assigns a single color to a polygon. The Gouraud-shaded mode assigns to
every polygon pixel a color that is linearly interpolated from the polygon
vertex colors. Such techniques are limited in conveying the large amount of
small-scale detail present in real-life objects, such as surface ruggedness or
fiber structure that are particular to various materials, such as wood, stone,
brick, sand, or textiles. Texture mapping is an effective technique that can
simulate a wide range of appearances of such materials on the surface of
a rendered object. As we shall see later in Chapters 6 and 9, texture
mapping is at the core of the implementation of a variety of visualization
techniques.

To illustrate the basic principle of texture mapping, let us look at a
simple example. Figure 2.6(a) shows a 2D texture. This is a simple 2D
monochrome image. Figure 2.6(b) shows the effect of mapping the texture
onto the 3D surface of our Gaussian height plot discussed earlier in this
chapter. The texture mapping process works as follows. First, imagine
that the texture image is defined in a 2D coordinate system (s, t). Usually,
s and t range between 0 and 1 and span the complete texture image, as
indicated in the figure. Hence, we can describe a monochrome texture as a
function $\text{tex}(s, t) : [0, 1] \times [0, 1] \rightarrow [0, 1]$. Next, we define, for every vertex of
the rendered polygons, two texture coordinate values s and t. Intuitively,
the polygon vertex texture coordinates specify a part of the texture im-

age that is warped to match the size and shape of the polygon and then is drawn on the polygon. When a polygon is rendered, its vertex texture coordinates are interpolated at every pixel, similarly to the color interpolation performed by Gouraud shading. The pixel is next rendered using a combination of the polygon color and texture color $\text{tex}(s, t)$. Putting it all together, we can see the texture mapping as a function T that maps a pixel from the surface of the rendered object to another pixel in the texture image.

The simple texture-mapping functionality described here and illustrated in Figure 2.6 can be implemented in OpenGL by the following steps. First, we must define a 2D texture. The easiest way to do this is to start from a monochrome image stored as an array of unsigned chars, which can be e.g., read from a file or defined procedurally. The following code fragment creates an OpenGL texture from the image **image** that has **width** × **height** pixels. First, we enable texture mapping in OpenGL. The parameter **GL_TEXTURE_2D** specifies that we shall use a two-dimensional texture. Next, we use the **glTexImage2D** OpenGL function to transfer the **width** × **height** bytes of **image** in the graphics memory and create a corresponding 2D texture. The **GL_LUMINANCE** parameter specifies that we define a monochrome texture, also called a *luminance* texture. The **glTexParameteri** function specifies how to treat texture coordinates s, t that fall outside the range $[0, 1]$, a feature that will be described later in this section. Finally, we use the **glTexEnvf** function to specify how the polygon color is going to be combined with the texture color. Here, we selected the **GL_MODULATE** mode, which multiplies the two values to yield the final pixel color. After the texture has been defined, we only have to associate texture coordinates with the vertices of the rendered polygons, and OpenGL will perform the texture mapping operation automatically. To assign texture coordinates, we add a new method to our **Quad** class

```
void Quad::addTexCoords(float s, float t)
    {   glTexCoord2f(s,t);   }
```

To render the texture-mapped height plot, we now simply add texture coordinates to every rendered polygon with the code fragment in Listing 2.6. Here, we have omitted the **addNormal** calls present in Listing 2.4 for conciseness. In this example, the texture coordinates are identical to

```
unsigned char* image;        //the image data
int width,height;            //the image size

glEnable(GL_TEXTURE_2D);
glTexImage2D(GL_TEXTURE_2D,  0,  GL_LUMINANCE,  width,  height,
             0,  GL_LUMINANCE,  GL_UNSIGNED_BYTE,  image);
glTexParameteri(GL_TEXTURE_2D,  GL_TEXTURE_WRAP_S,  GL_REPEAT);
glTexParameteri(GL_TEXTURE_2D,  GL_TEXTURE_WRAP_T,  GL_REPEAT);
glTexEnvf(GL_TEXTURE_ENV,  GL_TEXTURE_ENV_MODE,  GL_MODULATE);
```

Listing 2.5. Defining a 2D texture.

the height plot's x, y coordinates scaled to the range $[0, 2]$. Since we specified GL_REPEAT as value for the GL_TEXTURE_WRAP_S and GL_TEXTURE_WRAP_T OpenGL parameters (Listing 2.5, lines 6–7), the texture coordinates that fall outside $[0, 1]$ will be "wrapped" on this range. All in all, this produces the effect shown in Figure 2.6(b), where the texture seems to be projected from the xy plane to the height plot surface and replicated twice in every direction, as visible from counting the checkerboard squares in the texture image and the textured height plot.

By defining different texture coordinates, a multitude of texture mapping effects can be obtained, such as stretching, compressing, or rotating the texture image in a different way for every rendered polygon. The example presented here only briefly sketches the many possibilities offered by texture mapping, such as linear (1D) and volumetric (3D) textures, antialiased texture rendering, color and transparency textures, and multitexturing. A complete discussion of all possibilities of texture mapping is not possible here. For more details, as well as a complete description of the OpenGL texturing machinery and associated API, see the OpenGL reference and developer literature [Shreiner et al. 03, Shreiner 04].

2.5   Transparency and Blending

In the rendering examples discussed so far, we have used only fully opaque shapes. In many cases, rendering half-transparent (translucent) shapes can add extra value to a visualization. For instance, in our height plot running example, we may be interested in seeing both the gridded domain and the height plot in the same image and from any viewpoint. We can achieve

```
float   f(float,float);      //the function to visualize
float  sx = (X_max−X_min)/2;
float  sy = (Y_max−Y_min)/2;

for(float  x=X_min;x<=X_max−dx;x+=dx)
  for(float  y=Y_min;y<=Y_max−dy;y+=dy)
  {
      Quad q;
      q.addTexture(x/sx,y/sy);
      q.addPoint(x,y,f(x,y));
      q.addTexture((x+dx)/sx,y/sy);
      q.addPoint(x+dx,y,f(x+dx,y));
      q.addTexture((x+dx)/sx,(y+dy)/sy);
      q.addPoint(x+dx,y+dy,f(x+dx,y+dy));
      q.addTexture(x/sx,(y+dy)/sy);
      q.addPoint(x,y+dy,f(x,y+dy));
      q.draw();
  }
```

Listing 2.6. Drawing a texture-mapped height plot.

this effect by first rendering the grid graphics, followed by rendering the height plot, as described previously, but using half-transparent primitives.

In OpenGL, a large class of transparency-related effects can be achieved by using a special graphics mode called *blending*. To use blending, we must first enable it using the following function call:

```
glEnable(GL_BLEND);
```

Once blending is enabled, OpenGL will combine the pixels of every drawn primitive, such as polygons or lines, with the current values of the frame buffer (displayed image) at the locations drawn. In OpenGL terminology, the drawn primitive is called the *source*, whereas the frame buffer the primitive is drawn on is called the *destination*. Blending is performed independently for every source pixel drawn on a destination. If we denote the colors of the source and destination pixels by src and dst, respectively, the final value dst′ of the destination pixel is given by the expression

$$\text{dst}' = s_f * \text{src} + d_f * \text{dst}. \tag{2.9}$$

Equation (2.9) is essentially a weighted combination of the source and destination colors using the source and destination weight factors s_f and s_d

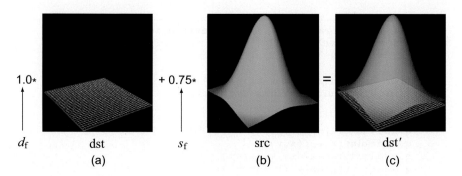

Figure 2.7. The height plot in (b) is drawn on top of the current screen contents in (a) with additive blending to obtain the half-transparent plot result in (c).

respectively, which are both real values in the range $[0, 1]$. This equation is applied independently for every color component (R, G, and B). The blending weights s_f and d_f, also called *blending factors*, can be specified in a variety of ways. In the following, we show how to specify these factors to achieve a simple transparency effect that combines the grid and plot rendering in our height plot example. The final result is shown in Figure 2.7(c). To obtain this result, we proceed as follows. First, we clear the screen to black. The reason for using black instead of the usual white background will become apparent soon. The frame buffer is cleared by the following sequence of OpenGL function calls:

```
glClearColor(0,0,0,0);              //specify the clear color
glClear(GL_COLOR_BUFFER_BIT);       //clear the frame buffer
```

Next, we draw the grid structure. We do not use any blending, since we want the grid itself to be fully opaque. The result is shown in Figure 2.7(a). The final step is to draw the half-transparent height plot on top of this grid. For this, we first enable blending, as described previously. Next, we specify the blending factors s_f and d_f. A half-transparent plot is achieved by using a source factor $s_f < 1$. To draw the height plot with this transparency on top of the grid currently present in the frame buffer, we can simply use a destination factor $d_f = 1$. This combination is achieved by the OpenGL code

glBlendFunc (GL_SOURCE_ALPHA, GL_ONE);
glColor4f(r,g,b,s_f);

For the result shown in Figure 2.7(c), the colors r,g,b have the same values as for the example discussed in Section 2.3 and s_f has a value of 0.7.

The function `glBlendFunc` takes two parameters that specify the source and destination blending factors. These parameters are symbolic constants rather than being the blending factors themselves, and specify how the actual blending factors s_f and d_f will be computed. The most commonly used values of these constants are as follows. The constant GL_ONE sets the value of the respective blending factor to 1. The constant GL_SOURCE_ALPHA specifies that the source factor s_f will be taken from the *fourth* component, also called the *alpha* component, of the color of the drawn primitives. Hence, if we next set the color using `glColor4f`(r, g, b, s_f), s_f will be the actual source blending factor used. The constant GL_ONE_MINUS_SOURCE_ALPHA sets the respective blending factor to $1 - s_f$, where s_f is the alpha value of the drawn primitives, as specified previously.

These parameters allow us to obtain various transparency effects. Using `glBlendFunc(GL_SOURCE_ALPHA,GL_ONE)` followed by drawing primitives that have the desired alpha values set via `glColor4f` starting with a black frame buffer effectively adds up the primitives' colors, weighted by their respective alpha values. We can achieve the same effect by using `glBlendFunc(GL_ONE,GL_ONE)`, i.e., setting $s_f = d_f = 1$, and factoring the source blending factor in the color by using `glColor3f`(rs_f ,gs_f ,bs_f). Using `glBlendFunc(GL_SOURCE_ALPHA,GL_ONE_MINUS_SOURCE_ALPHA)` realizes the convex combination

$$\text{dst}' = s_f * \text{src} + (1 - s_f) * \text{dst}. \tag{2.10}$$

The value of dst' is always clamped to one by OpenGL, so it is a good idea to use blending factors that will sum up to one when all primitives are drawn. This is achieved automatically if we use the blending factors as set by the convex combination in Equation (2.10).

Finally, there is a fourth constant GL_ZERO, which sets the respective source or destination blending factor to zero. Hence, calling the function `glBlendFunc(GL_ONE, GL_ZERO)` is equivalent to having blending disabled,

Figure 2.8. The height plot drawn half-transparently on top of the domain grid using a white background.

i.e., the source color will simply overwrite the destination (frame buffer) color.

Figure 2.8 shows the height plot drawn with the same transparency value of 0.7 on top of the domain grid, this time using a white background, obtained by setting `glClearColor(1,1,1,0)`. We leave the construction of the actual OpenGL blending code that achieves this image as an exercise for the reader.

Besides transparency, blending can be used to obtain many other graphical effects that are useful in visualization applications. Volume visualization, described in Chapter 10, fundamentally relies on blending to display volumetric datasets. Another use of blending is demonstrated in Section 6.6, for the construction of animated flow textures for visualizing vector fields. Yet another application of blending is described in Section 9.4.4, for the computation of distance fields in image data.

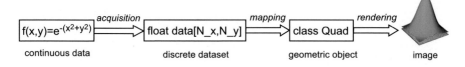

Figure 2.9. Structure of the visualization process for the elevation plot.

2.6 Conclusion

In this chapter, we introduced the basic structure of the visualization process, using as an example the simple task of visualizing a two-variable real-valued function. The process can be summarized as follows (see also Figure 2.9):

- *acquire* the data of interest into a discrete dataset;

- *map* this dataset to graphics primitives;

- *render* the primitives to obtain the desired image.

The presented example can be, and actually is many times, regarded as a pure graphics application rather than a data-visualization application. However, if we think of the primary goal of this example, conveying insight to the user about the values and variation of a real-valued function defined over a two-dimensional domain, we discover the visualization aspect. Moreover, this simple example allows us to encounter the fundamental concepts and building bricks of the visualization process: datasets, mapping, rendering, and the visualization process, or pipeline. *Datasets*, the elements used to store and represent data, are discussed further in Chapter 3 together with their main operations: sampling and interpolation. *Mapping*, the process that produces viewable geometric objects from the abstract datasets, is discussed further in its various guises from Chapter 5 onwards. *Rendering*, the process that displays a geometric set of objects, has been already discussed in this chapter. Finally, the complete chain of operations and concepts that constitutes the visualization process is discussed in Chapter 4.

Chapter 3

Data Representation

I N Chapter 2, we used a simple application, the visualization of a two-variable function using a height plot, to introduce several main concepts of data visualization, such as datasets, sampling, and rendering. Our discussion revolved around the dataset as a key concept for approximating a continuous signal by means of a discrete representation.

In this chapter, we expand this discussion on discrete data representation and approximation. First, we detail the notions of continuous data sampling and reconstruction. We introduce basis functions, discrete meshes, and cells, as a means of constructing piecewise continuous approximations from sampled data. These notions are illustrated using the simple example of visualizing a two-variable function with a height plot, introduced in Chapter 2. Next, we present the various types of datasets commonly used in the visualization practice and detail their relative advantages, limitations, and constraints. We also discuss several aspects related to efficiently implementing the dataset concept. After completing this chapter, the reader should have a good understanding of the various trade-offs involved in the choice of a dataset model, and be able to decide which is the most appropriate dataset for a given visualization application.

3.1 Continuous Data

The main goal of visualization is to produce pictures that enable end users get insight into data that describe various phenomena or processes, including both natural and human-controlled phenomena. Examples are the circulation of air in the atmosphere due to weather conditions; the flow of water in oceans and seas; convection of air in closed spaces such as buildings due to temperature differences caused by heating and cooling; the deformation, electrostatic charging, vibration, and heating of mechanical machine parts subjected to operational stress; and the magnetic and electrostatic fields generated by electrical engines.

Such phenomena are modeled in terms of various physical quantities. These quantities can be either directly measured or computed by software simulations. From the point of view of data representation, these quantities can be classified in two fundamentally different categories: intrinsically continuous and intrinsically discrete ones. Well-known examples of continuous quantities are pressure, temperature, position, speed, density, force, color, light intensity, and electromagnetic radiation. Examples of intrinsically discrete data are the hypermedia, e.g., text and image, contents of web pages; software source code; plain text, as found in documents of various types; and various kinds of database records.

For the sake of brevity, we shall from now on refer to intrinsically continuous data as "continuous data" and to intrinsically discrete data as "discrete data." Continuous data are usually manipulated by computers in some finite approximative form. To avoid confusion, we shall refer to this as "sampled data." Sampled data are also discrete, in the sense that they consist of a finite set of data elements. However, in contrast to what we call intrinsically discrete data, sampled data always originates from, and is intended to approximate, a continuous quantity. As we shall see in Section 3.2, we can always go from sampled data back to a continuous approximation of the original continuous data. In contrast, what we call intrinsically discrete data has no counterpart in the continuous world, as is the case of a page of text, for example. This is a fundamental difference between continuous (or sampled) data and discrete data. As we shall see throughout this book, this difference causes many, often subtle, constraints and choices in designing effective and efficient visualization methods.

Intrinsically continuous data, whether coming in its original continuous representation or represented by some sampled approximation, is the subject of a separate branch of data visualization. This branch is traditionally called *scientific visualization*, or *scivis*. The name reflects the fact that continuous data usually measure physical quantities that are studied by various scientific and engineering disciplines, such as physics, chemistry, mechanics, or engineering. Intrinsically discrete data, which has no direct continuous counterpart, is the subject of a relatively younger visualization branch, called *information visualization*, or *infovis*. This book mainly focuses on scivis methods and techniques, with the exception of Chapter 11, which performs a short overview of a few main infovis topics. Consequently, the remainder of this chapter will discuss solely the representation of continuous and sampled (scivis) data.

Mathematically, continuous data can be modeled as a function

$$f : D \rightarrow C,$$

where $D \subset \mathbb{R}^d$ is the function domain and $C \subset \mathbb{R}^c$ is the function codomain, respectively. In a related terminology, f is called a d-dimensional, or d-variate, c-value function. In other words, if we write $f(x) = y$, where $x \in C$ and $y \in D$, this actually means $f(x_1, \ldots, x_d) = (y_1, \ldots, y_c)$. In visualization applications, f or its sampled counterpart, introduced in Section 3.2, is sometimes called a *field*. Mathematically, f is continuous if for every point $p \in C$ the following holds:

$$\forall \epsilon > 0, \exists \delta > 0 \text{ such that if } \|x-p\| < \delta, x \in C \text{ then } \|f(x)-f(p)\| < \epsilon. \quad (3.1)$$

This continuity criterion is known as the *Cauchy criterion*, after the French eighteenth-century mathematician who proposed it, or the $\epsilon - \delta$ criterion, a name that follows from its formulation.

What does continuity mean in the intuitive sense? In plain terms, a function is continuous if the graph of the function is a connected surface without "holes" or "jumps." Furthermore, we say that a function f is

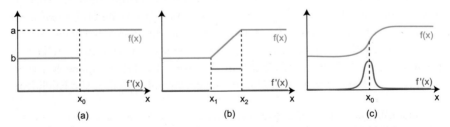

Figure 3.1. Function continuity. (a) Discontinuous function. (b) First-order C^0 continuous function. (c) High-order C^k continuous function.

continuous of order k if the function itself and all its derivatives up to and including order k are also continuous in this sense. This is denoted as $f \in \mathcal{C}^k$. Figure 3.1 illustrates the continuity concept for the case of a one-dimensional function $f : \mathbb{R} \to \mathbb{R}$, whose graph is displayed in green. The first image (Figure 3.1(a)) shows a function having a discontinuity at the points x_0. Clearly, if we evaluate the jump of f around the point x_0, i.e., evaluate $f(x_0 - \delta)$ and $f(x_0 + \delta)$, the jump $|f(x_0 + \delta) - f(x_0 - \delta)|$ will always have the fixed value $b - a$, regardless of how small the value δ is, i.e., how close we sample the function to the point x_0. The derivative $f'(x)$ is shown in red in the figure. Note that $f'(x)$ is not defined for the discontinuity point x_0.[1]

Figure 3.1(b) shows a continuous function $f \in \mathcal{C}^0$. Here, f consists of three linear components. The graph of f shows no holes or jumps, so clearly Equation (3.1) holds. In contrast, its first derivative f' is of the same type as the function f shown before in Figure 3.1, i.e., it is discontinuous. However, if we take the three intervals delimited by the two points x_1 and x_2 and ignore the points x_1 and x_2 themselves, the derivative f' is continuous for every interval. Functions f whose derivatives are continuous on compact intervals as in this example are also called *piecewise continuous*. Such functions will play an important role in approximating sampled data later in Section 3.2. A final example is shown in Figure 3.1(c). Here, both the function and its derivative are continuous, so $f \in \mathcal{C}^k$, where $k \geq 1$. Some functions, such as the Gaussian used in Chapter 2, are themselves and all their derivatives continuous. We denote this by $f \in \mathcal{C}^\infty$.

The triplet $\mathcal{D} = (D, C, f)$ defines a continuous dataset. In the following, we shall use the notation $\mathcal{D}$ to refer to a dataset and the notation D to refer to a domain. The dimension d of the *space* $\mathbb{R}^d$ into which the function domain D is embedded, or contained, is called the *geometrical dimension*. The dimension $s \leq d$ of the function domain D *itself* is called the *topological dimension* of the dataset. Understanding the difference between spatial and topological dimensions is easiest by means of an example. If D is a plane or curved surface embedded in the usual Euclidean space $\mathbb{R}^3$, then we have $s = 2$ and $d = 3$. If D is a line or curve embedded in the Euclidean

---

[1]Informally, we can say that $f'(x_0)$ is equal to infinity, as it has a finite jump at a point, which can be seen as an infinitely small interval. However, a numerical function (and hence its derivatives, too) is usually defined to take finite values, hence we call f not derivable, or discontinuous, in x_0.

space $\mathbb{R}^3$, then we have $s = 1$ and $d = 3$. You can think of the topological dimension as the number of independent variables that we need to represent our domain D. A curved surface in $\mathbb{R}^3$ can actually be represented by two independent variables, like latitude and longitude for the surface of the Earth. Indeed, we can describe such a surface by an implicit function $f(x, y, z) = 0$, which actually says that only two of the three variables x, y, and z vary independently. Similarly, a curve's domain can be described implicitly by two equations $f(x, y, z) = 0$ and $g(x, y, z) = 0$, which means that just one of the variables x, y, and z varies independently. Finally, another concept frequently used in describing functions and spaces is the *codimension*. Given the previous notation, the codimension of an object of topological dimension s and geometrical dimension d is the difference $d - s$.

To simplify implementation-related aspects, virtually all data visualization applications fix the geometrical dimension to $d = 3$. This makes application code simple, uniform, yet sufficiently generic. Hence, the only dimension that actually varies in visualization datasets is the topological dimension s. In practice, s is one, two, or three, which corresponds to the curve, planar, or volumetric datasets, respectively. Since the topological dimension is the only variable one, in practice it is also called the *dataset dimension*. In the remainder of this book, when we talk about a dataset's dimension, we mean its topological dimension, and implicitly assume that the geometric dimension is always three. Topological dimension is going to be important when we talk about sampled datasets and grid cells in Section 3.2.

In practice, dataset dimensions model spatial or temporal components. So, one may ask, what if we want to model a time-dependent volumetric dataset? This would require $s = 4$ dimensions, which would in turn ask for $d = 4$ geometric dimensions. Most visualization applications do not support such datasets explicitly, since they are relatively infrequent and supporting them would require working with more than three geometrical dimensions. In practice, time-dependent volumetric datasets are often represented as sequences of three-dimensional datasets where the sequence number represents the time dimension.

The function values are usually called dataset *attributes*. The dimensionality c of the function codomain C is also called the *attribute dimension*. The attribute dimension c usually ranges from 1 to 4. Attribute types are discussed later in Section 3.6. For the time being, let us assume for the simplicity of the discussion that $c = 1$, i.e., our function f is a real-valued function.

3.2   Sampled Data

Scientific visualization aims at displaying various properties of functions, as introduced in the previous section. However, we do not always avail of data in its continuous, functional, representation. Moreover, several operations on the data—including processing, such as filtering, simplification, denoising, or analysis, and rendering—are not easy, nor efficient, to perform on continuous data representations. For these reasons, the overwhelming majority of visualization methods works with sampled data representations, or sampled datasets. Two operations relate sampled data and continuous data:

- sampling: given a continuous dataset, we have to be able to produce sampled data from it;

- reconstruction: given a sampled dataset, we have to be able to recover an (approximative) version of the original continuous data.

Sampling and reconstruction are intimately connected operations. The reconstruction operation involves specifying the value of the function between its sample points, using the sample values, using a technique called *interpolation*. We have seen, in Chapter 2, a simple illustration of sampling and reconstruction for a two-dimensional dataset containing a scalar attribute: the surface representing the graph of a two-variable function. We sampled this dataset using two strategies, i.e., a uniform and a nonuniform sample point density. Next, we reconstructed (and rendered) the surface using a set of quadrilaterals determined by our sample points. This simple example illustrated a correlation between the sample-point density and distribution and the quality of the result of the polygon-based surface rendering. The conclusion was that the reconstruction quality is a function of the amount and distribution of sample points used. In the following, we shall analyze this relationship for the general case of a dataset represented as a d-variate, c-value function.

To be useful in practice, a sampled dataset should comply with several requirements: it should be *accurate*, *minimal*, *generic*, *efficient*, and *sim-*

ple [Schroeder et al. 04]. By *accurate*, we mean that one should be able
to control the production of a sampled dataset $\mathcal{D}_s$ from a continuous one
$\mathcal{D}_c$ such that $\mathcal{D}_c$ can be reconstructed from $\mathcal{D}_s$ with an arbitrarily small
user-specified error, if desired. By *minimal*, we mean that $\mathcal{D}_s$ contains the
least number of sample points needed to ensure a reconstruction with the
desired error. As we saw in Chapter 2, minimizing the sample count favors
a low memory consumption and high data processing and rendering speed.
By *generic*, we mean that we can easily replace the various data processing
operations we had for the continuous $\mathcal{D}_c$ with equivalent counterparts for
the sampled $\mathcal{D}_s$. By *efficient*, we mean that both the reconstruction operation and the data processing operations we wish to perform on $\mathcal{D}_s$ can be
done efficiently from an algorithmic point of view. Finally, by *simple*, we
mean that we can design a reasonably simple software implementation of
both $\mathcal{D}_s$ and the operations we want to perform on it.

Let us first consider the reconstruction of a continuous approximation
from the sampled data. We define reconstruction as follows: given a sampled dataset $\{p_i, f_i\}$ consisting of a set of N sample points $p_i \in D$ and
sample values $f_i \in C$, we want to produce a continuous function $\tilde{f} : D \to C$
that approximates the original f. The reconstructed function should equal
the original one at all sample points, i.e., $\tilde{f}(p_i) = f(p_i) = f_i$. One way to
define the reconstructed function that satisfies this property is to set

$$\tilde{f} = \sum_{i=1}^{N} f_i \phi_i, \tag{3.2}$$

where $\phi_i : D \to C$ are called *basis functions* or *interpolation functions*. In
other words, we have defined the reconstruction operation using a weighted
sum of a given set of basis functions ϕ_i, where the weights are exactly our
sample values f_i. Since we want that $\tilde{f} = f_j$ for all sample points p_j, we
get

$$\sum_{i=1}^{N} f_i \phi_i(p_j) = f_j, \forall j. \tag{3.3}$$

Equation (3.3) must hold for any function f. Let us consider a function g
that is overall zero, except at p_j, where $g(p_j) = 1$. Replacing the expression
for g in Equation (3.3) we obtain that

$$\phi_i(p_j) = \begin{cases} 1, & i = j, \\ 0, & i \neq j. \end{cases} \tag{3.4}$$

Equation (3.4) is sometimes referred to as the *orthogonality* of basis functions. Let us now consider the constant function $g(x) = 1$ for any $x \in D$. Replacing g in Equation (3.3), we obtain that $\sum_{i=1}^{N} \phi(p_j) = 1$ for all p_j, i.e., the sum of all basis functions is 1 at all sample points. However, if we enforce that this sum is 1 at all points $x \in D$, i.e.,

$$\sum_{i=1}^{N} \phi_i(x) = 1, \forall x \in D, \tag{3.5}$$

then we can exactly reconstruct g everywhere in D. The property described in Equation (3.5) is called the *normality* of basis functions or, in some other texts, the partition of unity. Basis functions that are both orthogonal and normal are called *orthonormal*. Most basis functions used in practice in data approximation are of this kind.

To reconstruct a sampled function, we can use different orthonormal basis functions. These offer different trade-offs between the continuity order of the reconstruction, on the one hand, and complexity of the functions, thus the evaluation efficiency of Equation (3.3), on the other hand. To be able to explain the different choices one has for basis functions, we must now introduce the notions of sample grids and grid cells.

A *grid*, sometimes also called a *mesh*, is a subdivision of a given domain $D \in \mathbb{R}^d$ into a collection of *cells*, sometimes also called *elements*, denoted c_i. The most commonly used cells are polygonal simplices, e.g., sets of connected lines in $\mathbb{R}$ (also called polylines), polygons in $\mathbb{R}^2$, polyhedra in $\mathbb{R}^3$, and so on. Moreover, the union of the cells completely covers the sample domain, i.e., $\bigcup_i c_i = D$, and the cells are nonoverlapping, i.e., $c_i \cap c_j = 0, \forall i \neq j$. In other words, a grid is a tiling of the domain D with cells. The vertices of these cells are usually the sample points $p_i \in \mathbb{R}^d$, though this is not required, as we shall see.

We can now define the simplest set of basis functions, the *constant basis functions*. For a grid with N cells, we define the basis functions ϕ_i^0 as follows:

$$\phi_i^0(x) = \begin{cases} 1, & x \in c_i, \\ 0, & x \notin c_i. \end{cases} \tag{3.6}$$

In Equation (3.6), the superscript 0 denotes that our basis functions are constant, i.e., of zero-order continuity. Clearly, these basis functions are orthonormal. If we now imagine our sample points are inside the grid cells,

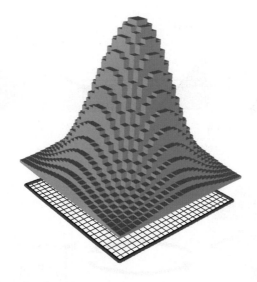

Figure 3.2. Gaussian function reconstructed with constant basis functions.

e.g., at the cell centers, then these basis functions approximate a given function $\tilde{f} = \sum_i f_i \phi_i^0$ by the piecewise, per-cell, constant sample values f_i. For a simple grid with equal cells, such as one created by the uniform sampling discussed in Chapter 2, this interpolation is equivalent to assigning to every point $x \in D$ the sample value of the nearest cell center. For this reason, the piecewise constant interpolation is also called *nearest-neighbor interpolation*. As an example, Figure 3.2 shows the reconstruction of the Gaussian function discussed in Chapter 2 with constant basis functions.

Constant basis functions are simple to implement and have virtually no computational cost. Also, they work with any cell shape and in any dimension. However, constant basis functions provide a poor, staircase-like approximation $\tilde{f}$ of the original f. Over every cell i, $\tilde{f}$ is piecewise constant, equal to the sample value f_i in that cell, but has discontinuities at the cell borders, as visible in our example (see Figure 3.2).

We can provide a better, more continuous reconstruction of the original function by using higher-order basis functions. The next-simplest basis functions beyond the constant ones are the *linear basis functions*. To use these, however, we need to make some assumptions about the cell types used in the grid. Let us consider a single quadrilateral cell c having the

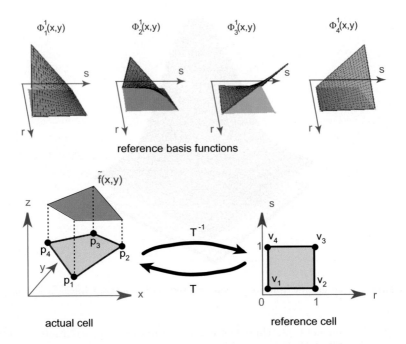

Figure 3.3. Basis functions, interpolation, and coordinate transformations for the quad cell.

vertices (v_1, v_2, v_3, v_4), where $v_1 = (0,0)$, $v_2 = (1,0)$, $v_3 = (1,1)$, and $v_4 = (1,1)$, i.e., an axis-aligned square of edge size 1, with the origin as first vertex. We call this the *reference cell* in $\mathbb{R}^2$. In the following, to distinguish coordinates given in the reference cell $[0,1]^d$ from coordinates given in the function domain $D \in \mathbb{R}^d$, we denote the former by $r_1, \ldots, r_d$ (or r, s, t for $d = 3$) and the latter by $x_1, \ldots, x_d$ (or x, y, z for $d = 3$). Coordinates in the reference cell are also called reference coordinates. For our reference cell, we define now four local basis functions Φ_1^1, Φ_2^1, Φ_3^1, and Φ_4^1, $\Phi_i^1 : [0,1]^2 \to \mathbb{R}$ as follows (see also Figure 3.3):

$$
\begin{aligned}
\Phi_1^1(r,s) &= (1-r)(1-s), \\
\Phi_2^1(r,s) &= r(1-s), \\
\Phi_3^1(r,s) &= rs, \\
\Phi_4^1(r,s) &= (1-r)s;
\end{aligned}
\tag{3.7}
$$

We denoted these local basis functions using capital letters (e.g., Φ) to distinguish them from global, gridwise ones, which are denoted with lowercase letters (e.g., ϕ). These basis functions are indeed orthonormal. For any point (r, s) in the reference cell, we can now use these basis functions to define a linear function $\tilde{f}(r, s) = \sum_{i=1}^{4} f_i \Phi_i^1(r, s)$, as in Equation (3.2). Since $\tilde{f}$ is a sum of linear basis functions, it is a first-order continuous reconstruction of the four sample values f_1, f_2, f_3, f_4 defined at the cell vertices. We would like now to perform exactly the same reconstruction as previously for any quadrilateral cell $c = (p_1, p_2, p_3, p_4)$ of some arbitrary grid, such as our height plot. In general, such cells are not axis-aligned unit squares located at the origin, but arbitrarily quadrilaterals in $\mathbb{R}^3$. How can we then use Equation (3.7) on such cells? The answer is relatively simple: for every such arbitrary quadrilateral cell c, we can define a coordinate transformation $T : [0, 1]^2 \rightarrow \mathbb{R}^3$ that maps our reference cell to c.

What should such a transformation T look like? First, we want to have a simple expression for T that works for any cell type. Second, we want to map the reference cell vertices v_i to the corresponding world cell p_i, so $T(v_i) = p_i$. Finally, we would like to have a linear transformation T, for simplicity and computational efficiency. All this suggests that we can design T using our reference basis functions. We do this as follows: given any cell type having n vertices $p_1, \ldots, p_n$ in $\mathbb{R}^3$, we define the transformation T that maps from a point r, s, t in the reference cell coordinate system to a point x, y, z in the actual cell to be

$$(x, y, z) = T(r, s, t) = \sum_{i=1}^{n} p_i \Phi_i^1(r, s, t). \tag{3.8}$$

In other words, T is a linear combination of the basis functions Φ_i^1 of the given cell, evaluated at the desired location r, s, t in the reference cell, weighted with the world cell vertex coordinates p_i. If T maps the reference cell to the world cell then its inverse T^{-1} maps points x, y, z in the world cell to points r, s, t in the reference cell, where our basis functions Φ_i^1 are defined. Using T^{-1}, we can rewrite Equation (3.2) for our quad cell c as

$$\tilde{f}(x, y) = \sum_{i=1}^{4} f_i \Phi_i^1(T^{-1}(x, y)). \tag{3.9}$$

To compute the inverse transformation T^{-1}, we must invert the expression given by Equation (3.8). Since this inversion depends on the actual cell type, we shall detail the concrete expressions for T^{-1} later in Section 3.4.

We now have a way to reconstruct a piecewise linear function $\tilde{f}$ from samples on any quad grid: for every cell c in the grid, we simply apply Equation (3.9). We can now finally define our piecewise linear reconstruction in terms of a set of global basis functions ϕ, just as we did before for the piecewise constant reconstruction (Equation (3.6)). Given a grid with sample points p_i and quad cells c_i, we can define our gridwise linear basis functions ϕ_i^1 as follows:

$$\phi_i^1(x, y) = \begin{cases} 0, & \text{if } (x, y) \notin \text{cells}(p_i), \\ \Phi_i^1(T^{-1}(x, y)), & \text{if } (x, y) \in c = \{v1, v2, v3, v4\}, \text{where } v_j = p_i, \end{cases}$$
(3.10)

where $\text{cells}(p_i)$ denotes the cells that have p_i as a vertex.

In other words, Equation (3.10) says that every basis function ϕ_i^1, corresponding to sample point p_i, equals the transformed local basis function Φ_j^1 of the corresponding cell vertex $v_j = p_i$, for all points in the cells that have p_j as vertex, and is zero everywhere outside these cells. We can verify that $\{\phi_i^1\}$ are orthonormal. Moreover, they are continuous of order 1, by definition. Hence, a reconstruction of a sampled dataset (Equation (3.2)) using these basis functions is piecewise linear, i.e., has piecewise constant derivatives. For this reason, the basis functions (3.10) are also sometimes called linear interpolation functions. For our height plot visualization, using these basis functions means that we approximate the function graph surface with a set of linear surface elements, that is, *planes*. Hence, all visualizations shown in Section 2.1 that rendered our height plot using a set of quads are nothing else but reconstructions of the function graph surface with linear basis functions. Luckily, we do not have to program this linear interpolation ourselves when doing rendering. For a number of cell types, such as lines, triangles, and quads, virtually all rendering engines nowadays (such as OpenGL) provide efficient interpolation implementations as rendering primitives.

The complete sampling and reconstruction process is illustrated schematically in Figure 3.4 for a 1D signal. Sampling the continuous signal f produces a set of samples f_i. Multiplying the samples by the global basis functions ϕ_i obtained from the reference basis functions Φ_j via the transform T, we obtain the reconstructed signal $\tilde{f}$.[2]

---

[2]Note the two special basis functions located at the two endpoints of the considered 1D interval (Figure 3.4(c)). The dashed lines indicate that the basis functions are of the same type as used inside the domain, but their support falls only partly in the domain.

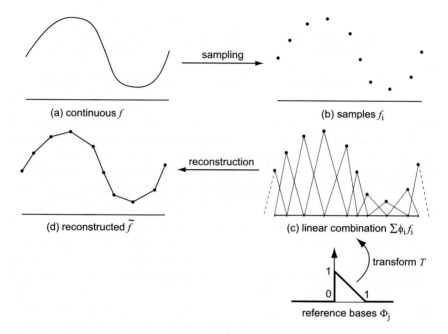

Figure 3.4. Overview of sampling and reconstruction.

The sampling and reconstruction mechanisms described so far can be applied to more data attributes than surface geometry alone. Let us consider, for example, surface shading. Shading, as introduced in Chapter 2, can be seen as a function $s : \mathbb{R}^3 \times \mathbb{R}^3 \to \mathbb{R}$ that yields the light intensity, given a surface point position $p \in \mathbb{R}^3$ and surface normal $\mathbf{n} \in \mathbb{R}^3$. We have seen how we can approximate the geometry of a surface given a set of surface sample points, using constant or linear basis functions, yielding a staircase (e.g., Figure 3.2) or polygonal (e.g., Figure 2.1) representation respectively. The question is now: can we apply the same reconstruction mechanisms for the surface shading too? And if so, what are the trade-offs?

Using our basis-function machinery, the answer is now simple. Given a polygonal surface rendering, flat shading, introduced in Chapter 2, assigns the intensity value $\tilde{s}$ computed using the lighting equation (Equation (2.1)) at every polygon center, to all polygon points. Clearly, this is nothing more than interpolation of the illumination function $\tilde{s}$ using piecewise basis functions (Equation (3.6)). Putting it together, a flat-shaded polygonal surface,

	constant geometry	linear geometry
constant lighting	staircase shading	flat shading
linear lighting	—	Gouraud shading

Table 3.1. Combinations of geometry and lighting interpolation types.

such as the height plot in Figure 2.1, is a reconstruction of the original continuous surface using piecewise linear interpolation for the geometry and piecewise constant interpolation for the illumination. What about the Gouraud, or smooth, shading introduced in Chapter 2? Recall that Gouraud shading evaluates the lighting equation (Equation (2.1)) at every polygon vertex v_i, using the corresponding vertex normal. For a quad, for example, this produces four illumination values s_i. Next, Gouraud shading produces a "smooth" illumination over the polygon by interpolating between these values s_i using piecewise bilinear basis functions. Putting it together, a Gouraud-shaded polygonal surface, such as the height plot in Figure 2.5, is a reconstruction of the original continuous surface using piecewise linear interpolation for both the geometry and illumination. The various combination possibilities of the geometry and lighting interpolation types are summarized in Table 3.1. Note that the combination of piecewise constant interpolation for geometry and piecewise linear interpolation for the lighting does not make sense, since the interpolated geometry is discontinuous.

3.3   Discrete Datasets

In the previous sections, we have described how to reconstruct continuous functions from sampled data provided at the vertices of the cells of a given grid. In brief, we can say that, given

- a grid in terms of a set of cells defined by a set of sample points,

- some sampled values at the cell centers or cell vertices,

- a set of basis functions,

we can define a piecewise continuous reconstruction of the sampled signal on this grid, and work with it (e.g., compute its derivatives or draw its graph) in similar ways to what we would have done with the continuous signal the samples came from.

In Section 3.1, we defined a continuous dataset for a function $f : D \to C$ as the triplet $\mathcal{D} = (D, C, f)$. In the discrete case, we replaced the function domain D by the sampling grid $(\{p_i\}, \{c_i\})$, and the continuous function f by its piecewise k-order continuous reconstruction $\tilde{f}$ computed using the grid, the sample values f_i, and a set of basis functions $\{\Phi_i^k\}$ (Equation (3.2)). Hence, the discrete (sampled) dataset counterpart of (D, C, f) is the tuple $\mathcal{D}_s = (\{p_i\}, \{c_i\}, \{f_i\}, \{\Phi_i^k\})$: grid points, grid cells, sample values, and reference basis functions. Visualization deals in the overwhelming majority of situations with discrete data, so discrete datasets are a fundamental instrument, both in theory and practice. When talking about *datasets* in the remainder of this book, we shall always refer to discrete datasets, as defined here.

In the previous sections, we have shown how to replace a continuous dataset $\mathcal{D}_c$ with its discrete counterpart $\mathcal{D}_s$. We have seen that this replacement means, from a mathematical point, working with a piecewise k-order continuous function $\tilde{f}$ instead of a potentially higher-order continuous function f. In this section, we turn our attention to the implementation aspects of discrete datasets. We recall the dataset requirements introduced in Section 3.1: a dataset should be *accurate, minimal, generic, efficient,* and *simple*. For a discrete dataset, these requirements translate to constraints on the number and position of sample points p_i, shape of cells c_i, type of reference basis functions Φ_i, and number and type of sample values f_i. These constraints determine specific implementation solutions, as follows. The cell shapes, together with the basis functions, determine different *cell types*. These are described next in Section 3.4. The number and position of sample points determine different *grid types*. These are described in Sections 3.5.1, 3.5.2, 3.5.3, and 3.5.4. Finally, the number and type of sample values f_i determine the *attribute types*. These are described in Section 3.6.

3.4 Cell Types

As explained in Section 3.2, a grid is a collection of cells c_i, whose vertices are the grid sample points p_i. Given some data sampled at the points p_i, the cells are used to define supports for the basis functions ϕ_i used to

interpolate the data between the sample points. Hence, the way sample
points are connected to form cells is related to the domain D we want
to sample, as well as the type of basis functions we want to use for the
reconstruction.

The dimensionality d of the cells c_i has to be the same as the topological
dimension of the sampled domain D, if we want to approximate D by the
union of all cells $\cup_i c_i$. For example, if D is a plane $(d = 2)$, we must use

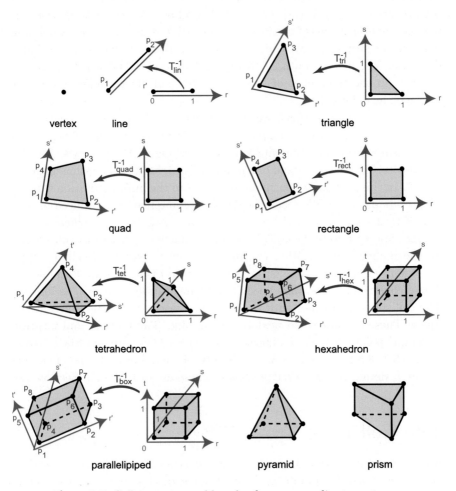

Figure 3.5. Cell types in world and reference coordinate systems.

planar cells, such as polygons. If D is a volume ($d = 3$), we must use volumetric cells, such as tetrahedra. In the following, we shall present the most commonly used cell types in data-visualization applications. Figure 3.5 shows, for each cell type, the shape of the cell, its vertices $p_0, \ldots, p_n$, and the shape of the reference cell in the reference coordinate system rst. For each cell type, we shall also present the linear basis functions it supports, as well as the coordinate transformation T^{-1} that maps from locations x, y, z in the actual (world) cell to locations r, s, t in the reference cell.

3.4.1   Vertex

We start with the simplest cell type of dimension $d = 0$. This cell is essentially identical to its single vertex, $c = \{v_1\}$. Following the normality property (Equation (3.5)), it follows that the vertex has a single, constant basis function:

$$\Phi_1^0(r) = 1. \tag{3.11}$$

Essentially, vertex cells are identical to, and provide nothing beyond, the sample points themselves. In practice, one does not make any distinction between sample points and vertex cells, so these cells can be seen more of a modeling abstraction than a practical element.

3.4.2   Line

The cell type of the next dimension is the line segment, or line. Line cells have dimension $d = 1$ and two vertices, i.e., $c = \{v_1, v_2\}$. Line cells are used to interpolate along any kind of curves embedded in any dimension, e.g., planar or spatial curves. Line cells allow linear interpolation. Given the reference line cell defined by the points $v_1 = 0, v_2 = 1$, the two linear basis functions are

$$\begin{aligned}
\Phi_1^1(r) &= 1 - r, \\
\Phi_2^1(r) &= r.
\end{aligned} \tag{3.12}$$

The transformation T^{-1} for line cells is simply the dot product between the position vector of the desired point in the cell $p = (x, y, z)$ with respect to the first cell's vertex p_1 and the cell vector $p_2 p_1$:

$$T_{\text{line}}^{-1}(x, y, z) = (p - p_1)(p_2 - p_1). \tag{3.13}$$

3.4.3 Triangle

We move now to the next dimension, $d = 2$. Here, the simplest cell type is the triangle, i.e., $c = \{v_1, v_2, v_3\}$. Triangles can be used to interpolate along any kind of surfaces embedded in any dimension, e.g., planar or curved surfaces. We can do linear interpolation on triangles. Given the reference triangle cell defined by the points $v_1 = (0,0), v_2 = (1,0), v_3 = (0,1)$, the three linear basis functions are

$$\begin{aligned}
\Phi_1^1(r, s) &= 1 - r - s, \\
\Phi_2^1(r, s) &= r, \\
\Phi_3^1(r, s) &= s.
\end{aligned} \tag{3.14}$$

The transformation T^{-1} for triangular cells is similar to the one for line cells. The coordinates r, s in the reference triangle are computed as dot products between the position vector $p - p_1$ of the point p in the world cell with respect to the world cell's first vertex p_1 and the world cell edges $p_2 p_1$ and $p_3 p_1$:

$$T_{\text{tri}}^{-1}(x, y, z) = (r, s) = ((p - p_1)(p_2 - p_1), (p - p_1)(p_3 - p_1)). \tag{3.15}$$

3.4.4 Quad

Another possibility to interpolate over two-dimensional surfaces is to use quadrilateral cells, or quads. We have seen examples of using quads for approximating curved surfaces since our first visualization example in Chapter 2, the height plot. Quads are defined by four vertices $c = (v_0, v_1, v_2, v_3)$ and have four corresponding basis functions. The reference quad, defined by the points $v_1 = (0,0), v_2 = (1,0), v_3 = (1,1), v_4 = (0,1)$, is an axis-aligned square of edge size 1. On this reference quad, the basis functions are

$$\begin{aligned}
\Phi_1^1(r, s) &= (1 - r)(1 - s), \\
\Phi_2^1(r, s) &= r(1 - s), \\
\Phi_3^1(r, s) &= rs, \\
\Phi_4^1(r, s) &= (1 - r)s.
\end{aligned} \tag{3.16}$$

A natural question arises whether to use quads or triangles when interpolating on surfaces. The answer is, in most cases, a matter of implementation convenience. Some operations on triangles with linear basis functions,

e.g., computing the intersection between the cell and a line or the distance
from a cell to a line, are relatively simpler (and possibly faster) to implement than on equivalent quads using bilinear basis functions. However,
rendering the same (large) grid using triangles might be slower than when
using quads, since roughly twice as many primitives have to be sent to the
graphics engine. When designing visualization software, a good practice is
to use as few cell types as possible. The same is true for any data processing operation that has to work on all the cells in a grid, e.g., computing
derivatives. A good trade-off between flexibility and simplicity is to support quad cells as input data, but transform them internally into triangle
cells, by dividing every quad into two triangles using one of its two diag-
onals. This simplifies and streamlines the overall software design, as only
triangle operations have to be further implemented.

The transformation T_{quad}^{-1} for a general quad cell is, unfortunately, not
as simple as for triangular cells. We cannot invert Equation (3.8) when
we deal with the bilinear basis functions of a quad cell (Equations (3.16)).
One solution for this problem is to numerically solve for r, s as functions
of x, y, z [Press et al. 02].

If our actual quad cells are rectangular instead of arbitrary quads, like
in a uniform or rectilinear grid, we can do better. In that case, the transformation T_{rect}^{-1} is practically identical to the one we used for triangle cells.
Given a quad cell with vertices p_1, p_2, p_3, p_4, we have

$$T_{\text{rect}}^{-1}(x, y, z) = (r, s) = ((p - p_1)(p_2 - p_1), (p - p_1)(p_4 - p_1)). \quad (3.17)$$

3.4.5 Tetrahedron

We now move to the next dimension, $d = 3$. Here, the simplest cell type
is the tetrahedron, defined by its four vertices $c = (v_1, v_2, v_3, v_4)$. On the
reference tetrahedron defined by the points $v_1 = (0, 0, 0), v_2 = (1, 0, 0), v_3 = (0, 1, 0), v_4 = (0, 0, 1)$, the four linear basis functions are

$$\begin{aligned}
\Phi_1^1(r, s, t) &= 1 - r - s - t, \\
\Phi_2^1(r, s, t) &= r, \\
\Phi_3^1(r, s, t) &= s, \\
\Phi_4^1(r, s, t) &= t.
\end{aligned} \quad (3.18)$$

Given a tetrahedral cell with vertices p_1, p_2, p_3, p_4, the transformation T_{tet}^{-1} follows the same pattern as T_{tri}^{-1} for triangular cells

$$T_{\text{tet}}^{-1}(x, y, z) = (r, s, t)$$
$$= ((p - p_1)(p_2 - p_1), (p - p_1)(p_3 - p_1), (p - p_1)(p_4 - p_1)).$$
$$(3.19)$$

Some applications use also *pyramid cells* and *prism cells* to discretize volumetric domains (see Figure 3.5). To limit the number of cell types we need to support in a concrete software implementation, pyramid and prism cells can be split into tetrahedral cells, similar to the way we split quad cells into two triangle cells.

3.4.6 Hexahedron

The next $d = 3$-dimensional cell type is the hexahedron, or hex, defined by its eight vertices $c = (v_1, \dots, v_8)$. The reference hexahedron is the axis-aligned cube of unit edge length, with v_1 at the origin. On this cell, the eight linear basis functions are

$$\begin{aligned}
\Phi_1^1(r, s, t) &= (1 - r)(1 - s)(1 - t),\\
\Phi_2^1(r, s, t) &= r(1 - s)(1 - t),\\
\Phi_3^1(r, s, t) &= rs(1 - t),\\
\Phi_4^1(r, s, t) &= (1 - r)s(1 - t),\\
\Phi_5^1(r, s, t) &= (1 - r)(1 - s)t,\\
\Phi_6^1(r, s, t) &= r(1 - s)t,\\
\Phi_7^1(r, s, t) &= rst,\\
\Phi_8^1(r, s, t) &= (1 - r)st.
\end{aligned}$$
$$(3.20)$$

Just as the tetrahedral cell in 3D is analogous to the triangle cell in 2D, hex cells are analogous to quad cells. Hence, the pros and cons of using hex cells instead of tetrahedra are similar to the 2D discussion involving quads and triangles, and so are the solutions. We can split hexahedral cells into six tetrahedra each, and then use only tetrahedra as 3D cell types, simplifying software implementation and maintenance.

Similar to quad cells, the transformation T_{hex}^{-1} for hexahedral cells cannot be computed analytically and must be determined using numerical methods. However, just as for quad cells again, we can do better in case our actual hex cells are parallelepipeds, i.e., their edges are orthogonal on each other (see Figure 3.5). These cells are also called *box cells*. In this case, T_{box}^{-1} can be computed just as we did for tetrahedra, by taking the dot product of the position vector $p - p_1$ with the cell edges. For a box cell with vertices $p_1 \dots p_8$, we obtain

$$T_{\text{box}}^{-1}(x, y, z) = (r, s, t)$$
$$= ((p - p_1)(p_2 - p_1), (p - p_1)(p_4 - p_1), (p - p_1)(p_8 - p_1)).$$
$$(3.21)$$

We have presented the most commonly used cell types in $d \in [0, 3]$ dimensions. As a closing remark, we mention that various authors and software packages sometimes offer more cell types, such as squares, pixels, triangle strips, polygons in 2D, and cubes and voxels in 3D. Such cells have similar (linear) interpolation functions and properties to the ones described here. Squares and pixels are essentially identical to our rectangle cell, except that they have equal-size edges, and pixels are usually thought to be aligned with the coordinate axes. Triangle strips [Shreiner et al. 03, Schroeder et al. 04] are not a different type of cell from an interpolation point of view, but just a more memory-efficient way to store sequences of triangle cells that share edges, so they can be seen as an implementation-level optimization. Cubes and voxels play the role in 3D that squares and pixels respectively have in 2D.

Finally, let us mention that the piecewise constant and linear basis functions, which we have described so far, are not the only ones used in practice. Some applications use *quadratic* cells, which are called so because they can support quadratic basis functions.[3] Quadratic cells are the equivalents of the cells presented here, but also contain the midpoints of cell edges and, for 3D cells, centers of cell faces, as shown in Figure 3.6 for a few cell types. Such cells can support quadratic basis functions and provide piecewise quadratic, hence smoother, reconstruction of data, which is C^2-continuous, and are often used in numerical simulation applications such as finite element methods [Reddy 93]. Figure 3.6 shows the quadratic interpolation $\tilde{f}_{\text{quad}}$ along a quadratic cell, which yields a parabola, and the equivalent linear interpolation $\tilde{f}_{\text{lin}}$ along the corresponding two linear cells obtained from splitting the quadratic cell.

However, few visualization applications support such cells. In practice, visualization applications usually convert datasets that contain quadratic

---

[3]Do not confuse *quadratic* cells, which support second-order basis functions, with *quadrilateral* (quad) cells, which are two-dimensional cells having four vertices.

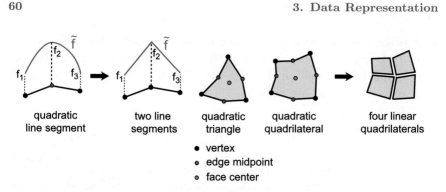

quadratic   two line   quadratic   quadratic   four linear
line segment   segments   triangle   quadrilateral   quadrilaterals

● vertex
● edge midpoint
○ face center

Figure 3.6. Converting quadratic cells to linear cells.

cells to the cell types we described previously by splitting the quadratic
cells at their midpoints into several linear cells, or even simply ignoring the
extra midpoints and their data. Besides the added complexity, quadratic
cells cannot be directly rendered by standard OpenGL, which supports
only linear (Gouraud) interpolation of colors over a polygon. Although
more recent additions, such as pixel shaders, allow simple implementations
to perform quadratic color interpolation at every pixel of a polygon, such
extensions are not yet commonly supported by visualization software.

As a general conclusion, when you have to implement and maintain a
specific visualization application, it is much simpler, faster, and less error
prone to support just the minimal number of cell types that are strictly
needed, rather than all possible variants. In general, you should add new
cell types to your application data representation only if these allow you
to implement some particular visualization or data processing algorithms
much more easily and/or efficiently than cell types your software already
supports.

3.5   Grid Types

Now that we have presented the cell types, we can describe the various
types of grids we can construct using these cells. Many types of grids exist
in the visualization practice. We shall describe the most widely used grid
types: uniform grids, rectilinear grids, structured grids, and unstructured
grids.

3.5.1 Uniform Grids

We start with the simplest grid type, the *uniform grid*. In a uniform grid, the domain D is an axis-aligned box, e.g., a line segment for $d = 1$, rectangle for $d = 2$, or parallelepiped for $d = 3$. We can describe this box as a set of d pairs $((m_1, M_1), \ldots, (m_d, M_d))$ where $(m_i, M_i) \in \mathbb{R}^2, m_i < M_i$ are the coordinates of the box in the ith dimension. On a uniform grid, sample points $p_i \in D \subset \mathbb{R}^d$ are equally spaced along the d axes of the domain D. If we denote by $\delta_1, \ldots, \delta_d \in \mathbb{R}$ the spacing, or sampling steps, along the d axes of D then a sample point on a uniform grid can be written as $p_i = (m_1 + n_1\delta_1, \ldots, m_d + n_d\delta_d)$, where $n_1, \ldots, n_d \in \mathbb{N}$. There are $N_i = (M_i - m_i)/\delta_i$ sample points on every axis. Hence, in a uniform grid, a sample point is described by its d integer coordinates $n_1, \ldots, n_d$. These integer coordinates are sometimes also called *structured coordinates*. A simple example of a uniform grid is a 2D pixel image, where every pixel p_i is located by two integer coordinates. The strong regularity of the sample points in a uniform grid makes their implementation simple and economical. We can uniquely order the sample points p_i in the increasing order of the indices, starting from n_1 to n_d, i.e.,

$$i = n_1 + \sum_{k=2}^{d} \left(n_k \prod_{l=1}^{k-1} N_l \right). \tag{3.22}$$

This numbering convention is sometimes called the *lexicographic order*, since it corresponds to a lexicographic (string-like) ordering of the strings $n_1, n_2, \ldots, n_d$ formed by concatenating the index values. If we use this numbering convention, we do not have to store explicit sample point coordinates for uniform grids, as these can be computed from the grid sizes and samples per dimension. Storing a d-dimensional uniform grid amounts, thus, to storing $3d$ values. For every dimension, we store (m_i, M_i, δ_i), i.e., the spatial extents and sampling step. Other schemes are also possible, such as storing the spatial extents and number of sample points per dimension (m_i, M_i, N_i). Moreover, this regular point ordering allows us to define the grid cells implicitly by using the point indexes. For example, let us consider a d-dimensional uniform grid using box-like cells, i.e., lines in 1D, quads in 2D, and hexahedra in 3D. In such a grid, we can compute the vertex indices v[] of the cell with index c using the function in Listing 3.1. In Listing 3.1, d is a constant indicating the grid dimension, i.e., 1, 2, or 3.

```
int getCell(int c,int* v)
{
    int C[d],j;                          //stores cell coordinates
    int P = ∏_{i=1}^{d-1} n_i;

    //compute cell coordinates  C[0],...,C[d-1]
    for(j = d-1; j>0; j--)
    {
        C[j] = c / P;
        c    -= C[j] * P;
        P    /= C[j-1];
    }
    C[0] = c;

    //now go from cell coordinates to vertex coordinates
    int i[d];
    for(i[0] = 0; i[0]>2; i[0]++)
        ...
        for(i[d-1] = 0; i[d-1]>2; i[d-1]++)
            v[j++] = lex(C[0]+i[0],...,C[d-1]+i[d-1]);

    return d;
}
```

Listing 3.1. Computing vertex indices from a cell index.

The idea of the algorithm is simple. First, we pass from the cell index c to the cell structured coordinates C[]. Next, we pass from cell structured coordinates to vertex structured coordinates. Finally, we pass from the vertex structured coordinates to the vertex indices. Here, the function lex($n_1, \ldots, n_d$) implements Equation (3.22). Similar cell index to vertex index translations are also derivable for other cell shapes, such as triangles in 2D and tetrahedra in 3D.

Our first visualization example (see Listing 2.1) used a 2D uniform grid to store the sample values of the two-variable function to be visualized. In the code, the grid was defined by its spatial extents X_min, X_max, Y_min, and Y_max and by the number of sample points per dimension N_x and N_y.

Figure 3.7 shows two examples of uniform grids, one for a 2D rectangular and the other for a 3D boxlike domain. The grid edges, that is, the cell edges whose vertices have one of the integer coordinates equal to zero, are drawn in red. The grid corners, i.e., the grid vertices whose integer coordinates are either minimal or maximal, i.e., equal to either 0 or N_i, are drawn in green.

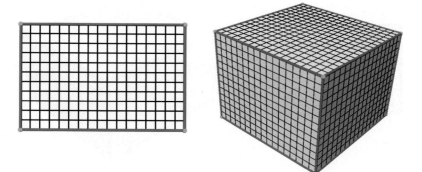

Figure 3.7. Uniform grids. 2D rectangular domain (left) and 3D box domain (right).

The major advantages of uniform grids are their simple implementation and practically zero storage requirements. Regardless of its size, storing a d-dimensional *grid* itself takes $3d$ floating-point values, i.e., only $12d$ bytes of memory.[4] Storing the actual sample *values* at the grid points takes storage proportional to the number of sample points. For example, storing one scalar value for each sample point, as in the case of our height plot visualization, requires $\prod_{i=1}^{d} N_i$ floating-point values. However, this is an issue concerning the data attributes themselves, not the grid, as described further in Section 3.6.

3.5.2 Rectilinear Grids

However simple and efficient, uniform grids have limited modeling power. Representing non–axis-aligned domain shapes requires framing them in an axis-aligned bounding box. Since this box is uniformly sampled, we waste memory for the sample values that fall outside the domain itself. A second problem was already illustrated in our first visualization example in Chapter 2. To accurately represent a function with a nonuniform variation rate, such as when drawing the graph of the function $e^{-(x^2+y^2)}$, we need either to use a high sampling density on a uniform grid (as in Figure 2.1), or use a grid with nonuniform sample density (as in Figure 2.3(b)).

---

[4]We assume in the following that the size of a floating-point number is four bytes, or 32 bits.

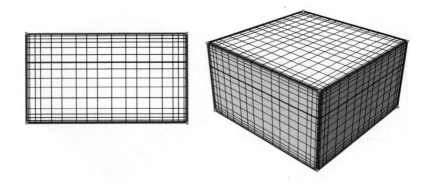

Figure 3.8. Rectilinear grids. 2D rectangular domain (left) and 3D box domain (right).

Rectilinear grids are a first step in this direction. They still keep the axis-aligned, matrixlike point ordering and implicit cell definition used by the uniform grids (Equation (3.22) and Listing 3.1), but they relax the constraint of equal sampling distances for a given axis. Instead, rectilinear grids allow us to define a separate sample step δ_{ij} for each row of points that shares a coordinate n_i in every dimension $j \in [1, d]$. A sample point on a rectilinear grid can be written as $p_i = (x_1, \ldots, x_d)$, where $x_i = m_i + \sum_{j=0}^{n_i-1} \delta_{ij}$. Figure 3.8 shows a rectilinear grid.

Implementing a rectilinear grid implies storing the grid origins (m_i, N_i) and sample counts for every dimension d, as for the uniform grid. Additionally, we must store $\delta_{ij}, i \in [1, d], j \in [1, N_i]$ sample steps. In total, the storage requirements are $2d + \sum_{i=1}^{d} N_i$ values, where we assume floating-points and integers to have the same size.

Figure 3.8 shows two examples of rectilinear grids. The grid edges and grid corners are colored in red and green, respectively, just as for the uniform grids presented in Section 3.5.1. These grids are similar to the uniform ones shown in Figure 3.7, except that the distances δ_{ij} between the sample points are now not equal along the grid axes. The 2D rectilinear grid (see Figure 3.8 (left)) is actually a slice extracted from the 3D grid (see Figure 3.8 (right)). Slicing is discussed in detail in Section 8.1.2.

3.5.3 Structured Grids

However useful, rectilinear grids do not remove the two constraints inherent to uniform grids. The sampled domain is still a rectangular box. The sample point density can be changed only one axis at a time. For our height plot visualization of the exponential function, for example, rectilinear grids do not allow us to place more sample points only in the central peak region, where we need them. To do this, we need to allow a free placement of the sample point locations.

Structured grids serve exactly this purpose. They allow explicit placement of every sample point $p_i = (x_{i1}, \ldots, x_{id})$. The user can freely specify the coordinates x_{ij} of all points. At the same time, structured grids preserve the matrix-like ordering of the sample points, which allows an implicit cell construction from the point ordering. Intuitively, a structured grid can be seen as the free deformation of a uniform or rectilinear grid, where the points can take any spatial positions, but the cells, i.e., grid topology, stay the same. Implementing a structured grid implies storing the coordinates of all grid sample points p_i and the number of points $N_1, \ldots, N_d$ per dimension. This requires a storage space of $3 \prod_{i=1}^{d} N_i + d$ values.

Structured grids can represent a large set of shapes. Figure 3.9 shows several examples. As shown in Figure 3.9 (left), structured grids can represent domains having a smooth, cornerless border, such as the circular domain in the image. The surface of our familiar function graph intro-

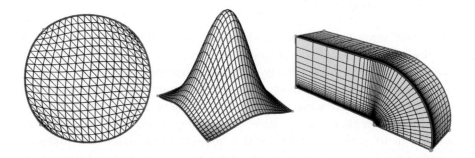

Figure 3.9. Structured grids. Circular domain (left), curved surface (middle), and 3D volume (right). Structured grid edges and corners are drawn in red and green, respectively.

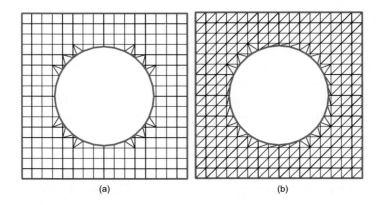

Figure 3.10. A domain consisting of a square with a hole in the middle cannot be represented by a structured grid. The domain border, consisting of two separate components, is drawn in red. Unstructured grids can easily model such shapes, whether using (a) a combination of several cell types, such as quads and triangles, or (b) a single cell type, such as, in this case, triangles.

duced in Chapter 2 is also best represented by a structured grid (see Figure 3.9 (middle)). Figure 3.9 (right) shows a 3D structured grid that has hexahedral cells. The grid edges and corners are drawn in red and green, respectively, just as for the uniform and rectilinear grid examples discussed in the previous sections.

3.5.4   Unstructured Grids

Structured grids can be seen as a deformation of uniform grids, where the topological ordering of the points stays the same, but their geometrical position is allowed to vary freely. There are, however, shapes that cannot be efficiently modeled by structured grids. For example, consider a domain consisting of a square with a circular hole in the middle (see Figure 3.10). We cannot cover this domain with a structured grid, since we cannot deform a rectangle to match a rectangle with a hole—the two shapes have different topologies.[5] A second limitation of all grid types described so far concerns the specification of grid cells. For uniform, rectilinear, or structured grids,

---

[5]The two shapes are distinguished by their *genus*. The plain square is said to be of genus 0, while the square with hole is of genus 1.

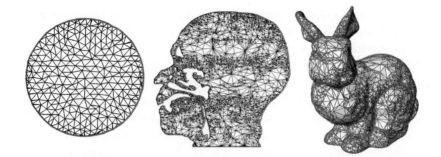

Figure 3.11. Unstructured grids. Circle (left), head slice (middle), and 3D bunny surface (right).

cells are *implicitly* specified, e.g., by always connecting grid points in the same order. This can be too restrictive in many cases.

These problems are solved by using unstructured grids. Unstructured grids are the most general and flexible grid type. They allow us to define both their sample points and cells explicitly. An unstructured grid can be modeled as a collection of sample points $\{p_i\}, i \in [0, N]$ and cells $\{c_i = (v_{i1}, \ldots, v_{iC_i})\}$. The values $v_{ij} \in [0, N]$ are called *cell vertices*, and refer to the sample points $p_{v_{ij}}$ used by the cell. A cell is thus an ordered list of sample point indices. This model allows us to define every cell separately and independently of the other cells. Also, cells of different type and even dimensionality can be freely mixed in the same grid, if desired. If cells share the same sample points as their vertices, this can be directly expressed. This last property is useful in several contexts. First, storing an index, usually represented by an integer, is generally cheaper than storing a d-dimensional coordinate, such as d floating-point values. Second, we can process the grid geometry, i.e., the positions of the sample points p_i, independently of the grid topology, i.e., the cell definitions.

Implementing an unstructured grid implies first storing the coordinates of all grid sample points p_i, just as for the structured grid, and next storing all vertex indices for all cells. These indices are usually stored as integer offsets in the grid sample point list $\{p_i\}$. If we use different cell types in the grid then we must either store the cell size, i.e., number of vertices, for every cell, or alternatively organize the cells in separate lists, where each list contains only cells of a given type. In practice, it is preferable to use unstructured grids containing a single cell type, as these are simpler to implement and also can lead to significantly faster application code. The costs of storing an unstructured grid depend on the types of cells used and the actual grid. For example, a grid of C d-dimensional cells with V vertices per cell and N sample points would require $dN + CV$ values.

Figure 3.11 shows several examples of unstructured grids. The first grid (Figure 3.11 left) shows the same circular domain as in Figure 3.9, but now sampled on an unstructured grid. The domain boundary is drawn in red. The second example (Figure 3.11 middle) shows a more complex 2D domain, obtained by slicing a 3D uniform dataset containing an MRI scan with a plane. Slicing is treated in detail in Section 8.1.2. The boundary of the domain is drawn in red, for clarity. It is clearly difficult, if not impossible, to sample domains with such complex and irregular boundaries using structured grids. The unstructured grid has no problem representing such a domain, however. The third example (Figure 3.11 right) shows an unstructured grid representing a 3D surface of a bunny, with the grid edges drawn in red for clarity. As in the previous example, unstructured grids can represent such shapes with no problem.

3.6　Attributes

So far, we have described three of the four ingredients of a discrete dataset $\mathcal{D}_s = (\{p_i\}, \{c_i\}, \{f_i\}, \{\phi_i^k\})$: the grid consisting of sample points p_i and cells c_i, and the reference basis functions Φ_i^k. This section discusses the sample values f_i in more detail.

As we said in the beginning of our discussion on data representation, visualization data can be modeled by some continuous or discrete function with values in a domain $C \in \mathbb{R}^c$. Hence, the sample values f_i are c-dimensional points. In visualization, the set of sample values of a sampled dataset is usually called *attribute data*. Attribute data can be characterized by their dimension c, as well as the semantics of the data they represent. This gives rise to several *attribute types*. These are described in the following sections.

3.6.1　Scalar Attributes

Scalar attributes are $c = 1$ dimensional. These are represented by "plain" real numbers. Scalar attributes can encode various physical quantities, such as temperature, concentration, pressure, or density, or geometrical measures, such as length or height. The latter is the case for our function $f : \mathbb{R}^2 \rightarrow \mathbb{R}$ visualized in our elevation plot example.

3.6.2   Vector Attributes

Vector attributes are usually $c = 2$ or $c = 3$ dimensional. Vector attributes can encode position, direction, force, or gradients of scalar functions. Usually, vectors have an orientation and a magnitude, also called length or norm. If only the magnitude is relevant then we actually have a scalar, rather than a vector, attribute. If only the orientation is relevant, we talk about *normalized* vectors, i.e., vectors of unit length. When these vectors represent the gradient of a function whose graph is a 2D curve or 3D surface, these unit vectors are called also *normals*, as described in Chapter 2. Some authors regard vectors and normals as two different attribute types. However, in practice there is no structural difference between the two. In particular, in most visualization software, normals are also stored using the same number of components as vectors, i.e., $c = 2$ for 2D curve normals and $c = 3$ for 3D surface normals, as this considerably simplifies the implementation.

3.6.3   Color Attributes

Color attributes are usually $c = 3$ dimensional and represent the displayable colors on a computer screen. The three components of a color attribute can have different meanings, depending on the color system in use. One of the most-used color systems is the well-known RGB system, where the three color components specify the amount, or intensity, of red, green, and blue that a given color contains. Usually, these components range from 0 (no amount of a given component) to 1 (component is at full brightness). The RGB system is an *additive* system. That is, every color is represented as a mix of "pure" red, green, and blue colors in different amounts. Equal amounts of the three colors determine gray shades, whereas other combinations determine various hues.

The RGB color space is usually represented as a *color cube* with one corner at the origin, the diagonally opposite corner at location $(1, 1, 1)$, and the edges aligned with the R, G, and B axes (see Figure 3.12(a)). Every point inside the cube represents one of the displayable colors. The

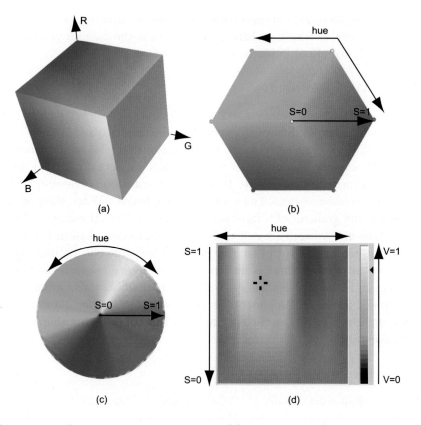

Figure 3.12. Color-space representations. (a) RGB cube. (b) RGB hexagon. (c) HSV color wheel. (d) HSV color widget (Windows).

cube's main diagonal connecting the points $(0,0,0)$ and $(1,1,1)$ is the locus of all the grayscale values. Brighter colors are located closer to the cube's outer faces (visible in the figure) whereas darker colors are located closer to the origin. RGB color representations are handy from an implementation perspective, as most graphics software, such as OpenGL and image storage formats, manipulate colors in this way.

However, manipulating a 3D cube representation of a color space can be difficult in practice. Moreover, since we cannot see "inside" the RGB cube, it may be handy to visualize only the outer surface of the cube. If we view the cube along the main diagonal using an orthographic projection, we see a 2D hexagon, as shown in Figure 3.12(b). The cube corners, the *primary colors*, are shown as small spheres. As we shall see next, this represents the space of all colors having a luminance equal to one. Moreover, all other colors situated inside the RGB cube are just darker versions of these colors.

Another popular color representation system is the HSV system, where the three color components specify the hue, saturation, and value of a given color. The advantage of the HSV system is that it is more intuitive for the human user. *Hue* distinguishes between different colors of different wavelengths, such as red, yellow, and blue. *Saturation* represents the color "purity." Intuitively, this can be seen as how much the hue is diluted with white or how far the color is from a primary color. A saturation of 1 corresponds to the pure, undiluted color, whereas a saturation of 0 corresponds to white. *Value* represents the brightness, or luminance, or a given color. A value of 0 is always black, whereas a value of 1 is the brightest color of a given hue and saturation that can be represented on a given system. For this reason, the HSV system is sometimes also called HSB, where "B" stands for brightness. The HSV color space is often represented using a *color wheel* (see Figure 3.12(c)). Every point p inside the color wheel represents an HSV color whose hue is given by the angle (scaled to the $[0,1]$ range) made by the vector $p - o$ with the horizontal axis, where o is the wheel's center, and whose saturation is given by the length $|p - o|$ of the same vector. Value is not explicitly represented by the color wheel. Hence, the color wheel shows all possible hues and saturations for a given value. The HSV color wheel is quite similar to the RGB color hexagon in terms of color arrangement. Compared to the hexagon, the color wheel has the advantage that the hue parameter is mapped to a visual attribute that varies smoothly, i.e., the wheel angle. For example, a curve of constant saturation is a circle and a hexagon, respectively, in these two representations.

As we shall see next, the value (or luminance) component of an HSV color is equal to the maximum of the R, G and B components. Hence, all colors shown by an HSV color wheel for a given value $V \in [0,1]$ are equivalent to all points on the outer faces of a cube similar to the whole RGB cube but of edge size V. Such an equal-value surface for $V = 0.5$ is shown in Figure 3.13 inside the RGB cube. As we shall see in Section 5.3, such a constant-value surface is called an *isosurface*.

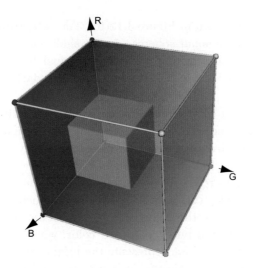

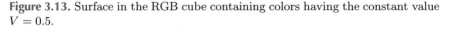

Figure 3.13. Surface in the RGB cube containing colors having the constant value $V = 0.5$.

In practice, there exist many other visual representations of color spaces. For example, the color selector widget in the Windows operating system uses a different representation, shown in Figure 3.12(d). This widget is similar to the HSV color wheel in the sense that it maps the hue and saturation components to a 2D surface, in this case a square instead of a circle. The value component is explicitly represented as a separate color bar at the right of the colored square, and shows all colors having the H and S components specified by the selected point in the color square and values $V \in [0, 1]$. The color square can be thought of as a "cut-out" of the color wheel along the horizontal positive half-axis followed by a stretch of the resulting shape to a square. Whereas the color wheel maps equal changes of the H and S parameters to unequal changes of position on the wheel by compressing the colors with low S components into a relatively small area around the center, the color square maps the HS space isometrically to the square area. This lets users specify low S colors potentially more easily than with the color wheel.

Since HSV color specification is often more convenient for the end user while RGB specification is required by various software, it is important to know how to map colors from the HSV to the RGB space. Listing 3.2

```
void rgb2hsv ( float    r , float    g , float    b ,
               float& h , float& s , float& v )
{
   float  M = max( r , max( g , b ) ) ;
   float  m = min( r , min( g , b ) ) ;
   float  d = M-m;
   v = M;                         //value = max( r , g , b )
   s = (M>0.00001)? d/M:0;  //saturation
   if  ( s==0) h = 0;             //achromatic case , hue=0 by convention
   else                          //chromatic case
   {
      if  ( r==M)        h =      ( g-b)/d;
      else  if  ( g==M) h = 2 +  ( b-r )/d;
      else              h = 4 +  ( r-g)/d;
      h /= 6;
      if  ( h<0) h += 1;
   }
}
```

Listing 3.2. Mapping colors from RGB to the HSV space.

provides a simple C++ function that converts from the RGB to the HSV
space. In this code, both RGB and HSV colors are represented as arrays
of three floating-point values, with the respective color components in the
natural array order. The largest RGB component gives the value, or luminance. The saturation represents the ratio between the largest and smallest
RGB component (normalized to $[0, 1]$), i.e., how much the color differs from
a grayscale value. Finally, the hue is given as the difference between the
medium and smallest RGB components. A special case takes place when
the saturation S equals zero. This corresponds to a grayscale, for which
the hue H cannot be determined uniquely. In this case, we set $H = 0$ by
convention.

Listing 3.3 shows the implementation of the inverse mapping from HSV
to RGB. The code distinguishes six cases, which correspond to sectors of 60
degrees of the color wheel. Within each sector, saturated colors are created
as a linear interpolation between two primary colors, for example red and
yellow for the first sector ($H \in [0, 1/6]$), as a function of H. The final
result is produced by linearly interpolating between the saturated color
and white, as a function of S.

Structurally speaking, color attributes can be also seen as vector attributes. However, color is often thought of, and also implemented as, a

```
void hsv2rgb(float   h,float   s,float   v,
             float& r,float& g,float& b)
{
   int    hueCase = (int)(h*6);
   float  frac    = 6*h-hueCase;
   float  lx      = v*(1 - s);
   float  ly      = v*(1 - s*frac);
   float  lz      = v*(1 - s*(1 - frac));
   switch (hueCase)
   {
     case 0:
     case 6: r=v;  g=lz; b=lx; break;   // 0<hue<1/6
     case 1: r=ly; g=v;  b=lx; break;   // 1/6<hue<2/6
     case 2: r=lx; g=v;  b=lz; break;   // 2/6<hue<3/6
     case 3: r=lx; g=ly; b=v;  break;   // 3/6<hue/4/6
     case 4: r=lz; g=lx; b=v;  break;   // 4/6<hue<5/6
     case 5: r=v;  g=lx; b=ly; break;   // 5/6<hue<1
   }
}
```

Listing 3.3. Mapping colors from HSV to the RGB space.

separate attribute in most data visualization software systems, for a number of reasons. First, operations on color are quite different than operations on general vectors. For example, it makes sense to decrease the saturation of a color, or compute its complementary color or its grayscale value, but these operations have no natural counterpart on vector data. Conversely, computing the angle between two vectors is a far more common operation on vector attributes, although it could be also performed on colors. Second, the three color components of a color attribute are usually represented as positive normalized real values in $[0, 1]$ or, in case of a discrete color model, as 8-bit integers in $[0, 255]$, whereas vector components usually are arbitrary real numbers. All in all, it follows that it is more natural, less confusing, and possibly also more efficient from an implementation point of view to represent colors and vectors as different attribute types.

3.6.4 Tensor Attributes

Tensor attributes are high-dimensional generalizations of vectors and matrices. Tensor data can most easily be explained by means of an example. Here, we consider measuring the curvature of geometric objects.

Consider first a planar curve C. For every point x_0 on C, let us take a local coordinate system xy such that x is tangent to the curve and y is

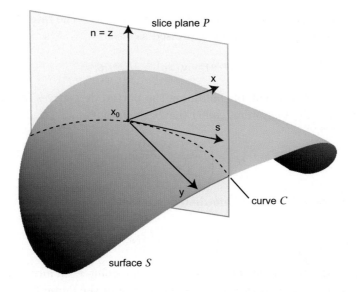

Figure 3.14. Curvature of two-dimensional surfaces.

normal to the curve in x_0. In this system, the curve can be described as $y = f(x)$ in the neighborhood of x_0, where $f(x_0) = 0$. The curvature is then defined as $\partial^2 f / \partial x^2(x_0)$. The curvature describes how small movements on C change the curve's normal or, alternatively, how the curve deviates from the tangent line at a given point. The more the normal changes, the more the curve differs from its tangent line, and the higher its curvature is.

Consider now a two-dimensional surface S (see Figure 3.14). For every point x_0 on S, take a local coordinate system xyz such that x and y are tangent to the surface and z coincides with the surface normal $\mathbf{n}$ in x_0. Around x_0, the surface can be described as $z = f(x, y)$, with $f(x_0) = 0$. Similar to the planar case, *curvature* describes how small movements along S result in changes to the surface normal or, in other words, how the surface deviates, at some given point, from its tangent plane at that point. However, there is a problem. Whereas movements around a point on a curve can happen only in two directions, and so can be described by a single number, movements around a point on a surface can happen in an infinite number of directions, so they cannot be described by a single number. To solve this problem, consider the gradient of the surface $\mathbf{g}$. The gradient $\mathbf{g}$

of the surface is in the direction of the surface normal. The rate of variation of $\mathbf{g}$ in some direction $\mathbf{s}$ can be expressed as

$$\mathbf{g}(x_0 + \mathbf{s}) = \mathbf{g}(x_0) + H(x_0)\mathbf{s}, \tag{3.23}$$

where H is a 2×2 matrix containing the partial derivatives of $f(x, y)$ in the *local* coordinate system, called the *Hessian* of f:

$$H = \begin{pmatrix} \frac{\partial^2 f}{\partial x^2} & \frac{\partial^2 f}{\partial x \partial y} \\ \frac{\partial^2 f}{\partial y \partial x} & \frac{\partial^2 f}{\partial y^2} \end{pmatrix}. \tag{3.24}$$

From Equation (3.24), we immediately see that

$$\frac{\partial^2 f}{\partial s^2}(x_0) = \mathbf{s}^T H \mathbf{s}. \tag{3.25}$$

This gives the curvature of our surface at some point x_0 in any given direction $\mathbf{s}$. This value is identical to the curvature of the curve $\mathcal{C}$ determined by the intersection of the surface with a plane that contains the vectors $\mathbf{n}$ and $\mathbf{s}$ (see Figure 3.14) and is also known as *normal curvature*. However, to use Equation (3.25), we have to build our local coordinate system every time we want to compute the curvature of some point.

We can simplify this procedure as follows. Consider that our surface $\mathcal{S}$ is given in global coordinates instead of local ones, for example as an implicit function $f(x, y, z) = 0$. We can then express the rate of change of the surface normal as

$$\frac{\partial^2 f}{\partial s^2}(x_0) = \mathbf{s}^T H \mathbf{s}. \tag{3.26}$$

where H is the 3×3 Hessian matrix of partial derivatives of $f(x, y, z)$ in the *global* coordinate system:

$$H = \begin{pmatrix} \frac{\partial^2 f}{\partial x^2} & \frac{\partial^2 f}{\partial x \partial y} & \frac{\partial^2 f}{\partial x \partial z} \\ \frac{\partial^2 f}{\partial y \partial x} & \frac{\partial^2 f}{\partial y^2} & \frac{\partial^2 f}{\partial y \partial z} \\ \frac{\partial^2 f}{\partial z \partial x} & \frac{\partial^2 f}{\partial z \partial y} & \frac{\partial^2 f}{\partial z^2} \end{pmatrix}. \tag{3.27}$$

Using Equation (3.27), we can compute the curvature of a surface given in global coordinates, without the need of constructing a local coordinate system.

Summarizing, we can compute the curvature of a planar curve using its second derivative $\partial^2 f/\partial x^2$, and the curvature of a 3D surface in a given direction using its Hessian matrix H of partial derivatives. The Hessian matrix is also called the *curvature tensor* of the given surface.

Besides curvature, tensors can describe other physical quantities that depend on direction, such as water diffusivity or stress and strain in materials. Tensors are characterized by their *rank*. Scalars are tensors of rank 0. Vectors are tensors of rank 1. The Hessian curvature tensor is a rank 2 symmetric tensor, since it is expressed by a symmetric, rank 2 matrix. In general, tensors of rank k are k-dimensional real-valued arrays.

In the visualization practice, two-dimensional symmetric tensors are the most common. We shall discuss tensor data in more detail in Chapter 7, when we present tensor visualization methods.

3.6.5 Non-Numerical Attributes

All the attribute types presented to far were real-valued, i.e., points in some space $\mathbb{R}^c$. The question arises whether attribute types that are not represented by real numbers can be also used. From a purely implementation perspective, the answer is simple: we can use any data type as an attribute type in a discrete dataset, by storing the data values, i.e., instances of the desired data type, at the grid points. Examples of possible non-numerical attribute types are text, images, file names, or even sound samples.

However, when doing this, an essential question immediately arises: what is the meaning of such a dataset? We defined a *sampled*, or discrete, dataset as the tuple $\mathcal{D}_s = (\{p_i\}, \{c_i\}, \{f_i\}, \{\Phi_i^k\})$, consisting of grid points $p_i \in D$, grid cells c_i, sample values $f_i \in C$, and reference basis functions $\Phi_i^k : D \to \mathbb{R}$. The main property for $\mathcal{D}_s$ was to permit us to reconstruct some piecewise, k-order continuous function $\tilde{f} : D \to C$, given its sample values $f_i \in C$. If our attribute types are real values, i.e., $C \subset \mathbb{R}^c$, we have seen how to construct our basis functions to interpolate between the sample values. The situation is quite different when we use non-numerical attribute types. First, what should the meaning of the multiplication between sample values f_i and real-valued basis functions Φ_i and of addition of the sample values in Equation (3.9) be? For instance, what should multiplication of a string with a real value and addition of two strings mean? It is, of course, always possible to define such operations for non-numerical data types such that the reconstruction equation can be applied. However, the deeper question is: what is the relationship between what we reconstruct in this way, i.e., our $\tilde{f}$, and what we had originally sampled into the f_i values, i.e., f?

In many cases, such a relationship is hard to find, or even nonexistent for non-numerical attributes. Conversely, if the sample values in some discrete dataset have indeed come from the sampling of a continuous function f, it is always possible to define its reconstruction $\tilde{f}$, regardless of the attribute type. It is always technically possible to store non-numerical attributes in a discrete dataset, such as at the points on a grid. However, this should only be seen as an implementation convenience for some particular purpose, and *not* as defining a sampled dataset. Remember that the notion of a sampled dataset implies the existence of meaningful basis functions on the grid, which can interpolate between the sample values of a given type. If we cannot interpolate the attribute type in the sample values, the semantics of the sample points, cells, and sample values in our discrete dataset is not that of a sampled dataset.

As mentioned in Section 3.1, scientific visualization, or SciVis, is the branch of data visualization that works with sampled datasets, and is the main topic of this book. Purely discrete datasets, which may include points, cells, and attribute values, but no basis functions, are the domain of information visualization, or infovis. Infovis techniques are briefly covered in Chapter 11.

3.6.6   Properties of Attribute Data

The main purpose of attribute data is to allow a reconstruction $\tilde{f}$ of the sampled information f_i (see Equation (3.2)). There are more operations possible on attribute data. In general, these operations can be associated with manipulations one wants to do on the reconstructed function $\tilde{f}$. For example, given a function $v : \mathrm{D} \to \mathbb{R}^3$ that represents some vector quantity, and its reconstruction $\tilde{v}$ using the vector attributes v_i, we can compute a reconstruction $\tilde{f}$ of the "vector magnitude" function $f : \mathrm{D} \to \mathbb{R}, f(x) = |v(x)|$, by simply setting $f_i = |v_i|$. That is, we have replaced the "vector magnitude" operation on the continuous functions with an equivalent operation on their sample values that creates scalar attributes f_i from the vector attributes v_i.

Attribute data in sampled datasets have several general properties. First, attribute data, i.e., the sample values f_i, must be defined for all sample points p_i of a dataset $\mathcal{D}_s$. Indeed, if samples are missing at some points p_j, it is not possible to apply Equation (3.2) over the cells that share these points p_j, i.e., reconstruct $\tilde{f}$ over those cells. In practice, we may, however, lack sample values f_j over some subset of points $M \subset \{p_i\}$ of our sampling domain, for various reasons. In such cases, several solutions are possible. First, we can completely remove p_j from the grid, since we have no data at those locations. However, this implies repairing the grid, i.e., replacing all cells that originally used any of the p_j by new cells that do not use p_j but still represent a tiling of the domain D (see Section 3.2). This operation can be rather complex when many points p_j lack data, and also can change the grid type from the uniform, rectilinear, or structured types to the more complex unstructured grid type (see Sections 3.5.1–3.5.4). A second solution is to define the missing values f_j in some way. The simplest way is to replace them by some special "default" value, e.g., zero. This is simple to do, and also allows us to distinguish these points from the regular points in the subsequent visualizations. Finally, we can define the missing values $f_j \in M$ using the existing values $f_i \notin M$ using some more complex interpolation scheme, as described in Section 3.9. Note that, in case our grid carries attribute data for which no interpolation scheme is defined (see Section 3.6.5), we have no constraint that attributes must be defined at all sample points, since Equation (3.2) does not apply.

A second property of attribute data is that any cell type can contain any number of attributes, of any type, as long as these are defined for all sample points, as discussed previously. Indeed, all cell types presented in Section 3.4 define their own basis functions and thus allow reconstruction following Equation (3.2). The reader may have noticed that, given c real-valued data attributes defined over the same domain D, it is possible to think of these either as a single function $f : D \rightarrow \mathbb{R}^c$ or as c separate functions $f_i \rightarrow \mathbb{R}$ for $i \in [1..c]$. In other words, we can choose whether we want to model our data as a single c-value dataset or as c one-value datasets. Of course, other combinations are possible, too. The answer to this choice is to consider all attributes that have a related meaning as a single higher-dimensional attribute, and to separate attributes with different meanings. For example, consider a two-dimensional ($d = 2$) image dataset, which has an RGB color $c = 3$ defined at every point in $D \subset \mathbb{R}^2$. We could model this either as a single function $f : D \to \mathbb{R}^3$, where the value of f at some point x yields the color (R, G, B) of that point, $f(x) = (R, G, B)$. Alternatively, we could use three functions $r : D \to \mathbb{R}$, $g : D \to \mathbb{R}$, and $b : D \to \mathbb{R}$, where every function yields one color component, i.e., $r(x) = R$, $g(x) = G$, $b(x) = B$. The first representation is more natural, as the color components have a related meaning. Moreover, operations on color attributes must consider all color components simultaneously.

Some data visualization applications classify attribute data into *node* or *vertex attributes* and *cell attributes*. Node attributes are defined at the vertices of the grid cells, hence they correspond to a sampled dataset that uses linear, or higher-order, basis functions. Cell attributes are defined at the center points of the grid cells, hence they correspond to a sampled dataset that uses constant basis functions. Vertex attributes can be converted to cell attributes and conversely by resampling, as described in Section 3.9.1.

A final word must be said about interpolation of higher-dimensional attribute data. From the reconstruction formula (see Equation (3.2)) and the definitions of our basis functions $\Phi_i : D \to \mathbb{R}$ for all our cell types (see Section 3.4), it follows that reconstruction of a $c > 1$-dimensional function from a c-dimensional attribute data $f_i \in \mathbb{R}^c$ is done by reconstructing all its c components separately from the respective components of f_i. This happens for color attributes, where we interpolate the three R, G, B color components separately. However, the attribute components are sometimes related by some constraint. This happens for normal attributes $\mathbf{n} \in \mathbb{R}^3$ where the three components n_x, n_y, n_z are constrained to yield unit length normals, i.e.,

$$|\mathbf{n}| = \sqrt{n_x^2 + n_y^2 + n_z^2}. \tag{3.28}$$

Depending on the choice of the basis functions, interpolating the three components n_x, n_y, n_z separately as scalar values may *not* preserve the unit length property on the interpolated normal $\mathbf{n}$. This is simple to verify when, e.g., using linear basis functions Φ^1. There are several solutions to this problem. The easiest is to interpolate the components separately, using whatever basis functions we like, and then enforce the desired constraint on the result by normalizing it, i.e., replacing $\mathbf{n}$ with $\mathbf{n}/|\mathbf{n}|$. This gives good results when the sample values do not vary too strongly across a grid cell. However, enforcing the constraint on the interpolated result can fail. For example, imagine a line cell (a, b) having the normals $n_a = (-1, 0, 0)$ and

$n_b = (1, 0, 0)$ at its end points. In the middle, the interpolated normal is the null vector, which cannot be renormalized to unit length. An answer to this problem is to represent the constraint *directly* in the data attributes, rather than enforcing it after interpolation. For normal attribute types, this means representing 3D normals as two *independent* orientations, e.g., using polar coordinates α, β, instead of using the three x, y, z components, which are *dependent* via the unit length constraint. We can now interpolate the normal orientations α, β using the desired basis functions, and will always obtain the correct result.

3.7 Computing Derivatives of Sampled Data

For the same polygonal surface, Gouraud shading usually produces better-looking, easier-to-understand results than flat shading. Since both flat and Gouraud shading are highly optimized nowadays by rendering engines and graphics cards, choosing between the two is not really a matter of optimizing performance. We saw in Chapter 2 that Gouraud shading requires surface normals to be available, in some way, at the polygon vertices. Also, we saw how to compute surface normals using the derivatives of the data, in case these are a continuous function. In this section, we address the problem of computing derivatives when we have a sampled dataset.

One of the requirements mentioned in the previous section for a sampled dataset $\mathcal{D}_s$ was that it should be generic, i.e., that we can easily replace the various data processing operations available for its continuous counterpart $\mathcal{D}_c$ with equivalent operations on the $\mathcal{D}_s$. We saw, also, that computing derivatives is such an operation. Derivatives of data are needed for a wide range of processing tasks, ranging from the simple normal computation for Gouraud shading to more complex data filtering and smoothing and feature detection tasks, as described in Chapters 5 and 9.

How should we compute data derivatives in case all we have is a sampled dataset $\mathcal{D}_s = (p_i, c_i, f_i, \Phi_i)$? Since we replaced our continuous signal f with $\tilde{f}$, a logical answer is to compute derivatives of the reconstructed signal $\tilde{f}$ and use them instead of the derivatives of the original signal f. We know how to reconstruct $\tilde{f}$ from $\mathcal{D}_s$ using a given set of basis functions: $\tilde{f} = \sum_{i=1}^{N} f_i \phi_i$ (see Equation (3.2)). Remember, f is a d-dimensional function, i.e., $f : D \in \mathbb{R}^d$. We can now compute the derivative of $\tilde{f}$ with respect to its ith variable x_i as

$$\frac{\partial \tilde{f}}{\partial x_i} = \sum_{j=1}^{N} f_j \frac{\partial \phi_j}{\partial x_i}. \tag{3.29}$$

This is a linear combination of the derivatives of the basis functions in use. However, this expression is not very convenient to use, since the actual basis functions ϕ_j are quite complex on a general grid (see Equation (3.10)). We can simplify the the computation of the derivatives of $\tilde{f}$ using the expressions of the reference basis functions Φ_j, since these look the same on all cells of a given type in a given grid. Using Equations (3.9) and (3.29), we get

$$\frac{\partial \tilde{f}}{\partial x_i} = \sum_{j=1}^{N} f_j \frac{\partial \Phi_j}{\partial x_i}(r). \tag{3.30}$$

We now use the derivation chain rule and obtain

$$\frac{\partial \Phi}{\partial x_i} = \sum_{j=1}^{d} \frac{\partial \Phi}{\partial r_j} \frac{\partial r_j}{\partial x_i} \tag{3.31}$$

to obtain

$$\frac{\partial \tilde{f}}{\partial x_i} = \sum_{j=1}^{N} f_j \sum_{k=1}^{d} \frac{\partial \Phi_j}{\partial r_k} \frac{\partial r_k}{\partial x_i}. \tag{3.32}$$

Finally, we can rewrite Equation (3.32) in a convenient and easy-to-remember matrix form, as follows:

$$\begin{pmatrix} \frac{\partial \tilde{f}}{\partial x_1} \\ \frac{\partial \tilde{f}}{\partial x_2} \\ \cdots \\ \frac{\partial \tilde{f}}{\partial x_d} \end{pmatrix} = \sum_{j=1}^{N} f_j \underbrace{\begin{pmatrix} \frac{\partial r_1}{\partial x_1} & \frac{\partial r_2}{\partial x_1} & \cdots & \frac{\partial r_d}{\partial x_1} \\ \frac{\partial r_1}{\partial x_2} & \frac{\partial r_2}{\partial x_2} & \cdots & \frac{\partial r_d}{\partial x_2} \\ \cdots & & & \\ \frac{\partial r_1}{\partial x_d} & \frac{\partial r_2}{\partial x_d} & \cdots & \frac{\partial r_d}{\partial x_d} \end{pmatrix}}_{\text{inverse Jacobian matrix } J^{-1}} \begin{pmatrix} \frac{\partial \Phi_j}{\partial r_1} \\ \frac{\partial \Phi_j}{\partial r_2} \\ \cdots \\ \frac{\partial \Phi_j}{\partial r_d} \end{pmatrix}. \tag{3.33}$$

The matrix in Equation (3.33), containing the derivatives of the reference cell coordinates r_i with respect to the global coordinates x_j, is called the *inverse Jacobian matrix* $J^{-1} = (\partial r_i / \partial x_j)_{ij}$. As the name suggests, this matrix is indeed the inverse of the *Jacobian matrix* $J = (\partial x_i / \partial r_j)_{ij}$. In Section 3.2, we introduced a coordinate transform $T : [0, 1]^d \rightarrow \mathbb{R}^d$ that maps points from the reference cell to the actual cells, i.e., $T(r_1, \ldots, r_d) = (x_1, \ldots, x_d)$, and its inverse $T^{-1}(x_1, \ldots, x_d) = (r_1, \ldots, r_d)$. Section 3.4 presented concrete forms of T^{-1} for various cell types. Using T^{-1}, we can rewrite the inverse Jacobian as

$$J^{-1} = \left(\frac{\partial T_i^{-1}(x_1, \ldots, x_d)}{\partial x_j} \right)_{ij}, \qquad (3.34)$$

where T_i^{-1} denotes the ith component of the function T^{-1}.

Putting it all together, we get the formula for computing the partial derivatives of a sampled dataset $\tilde{f}$ with respect to all coordinates x_i:

$$\left(\frac{\partial \tilde{f}}{\partial x_i} \right)_i = \sum_{k=1}^{N} f_k \left(\frac{\partial T_i^{-1}}{\partial x_j} \right)_{ij} \left(\frac{\partial \Phi_k}{\partial r_i} \right)_i. \qquad (3.35)$$

To use Equation (3.35) in practice, we need to evaluate the derivatives of both the reference basis functions Φ_k and the coordinate transform T^{-1} at the desired point x. We have analytic expressions or numeric methods to compute Φ_k and T^{-1} for every cell type (see Section 3.4), so the procedure is straightforward. Alternatively, we can evaluate the Jacobian matrix instead of its inverse, using the reference-cell to world-cell coordinate transforms T instead of T^{-1}, then numerically invert J, and finally apply Equation (3.33). We can make another important observation. For all cells described in Section 3.4, the coordinate transformations T^{-1} are linear functions of the arguments x_i, so their derivatives are constant. Hence, the derivatives of $\tilde{f}$ are of the same order as those of the basis functions Φ_k we choose to use.

Let us see what this means for our shaded polygonal surface example. We have seen that this is a piecewise linear (order 1) surface reconstruction. Normals are computed using the surface derivatives (see Equation (2.4)). Hence, surface normals for a polygonal surface are piecewise constant, which is exactly what flat shading does. In other words, flat shading is the mathematically "correct" shading for a polygonal surface.

For uniform and structured datasets, Equation (3.35) for computing partial derivatives is actually quite simple. For example, consider an uniform grid with cell size $(\delta_1, \ldots, \delta_d)$, as described in Section 3.5.1. For an axis-aligned, box-like cell having the lower-left corner $(p_1, \ldots, p_d)$ and the upper-right corner $(p_1 + \delta_1, \ldots, p_d + \delta_d)$, the coordinate transformation is

$T^{-1}(x) = ((x_1 - p_1)/\delta_1, \ldots, (x_d - p_d)/\delta_d)$. Hence, the derivatives of T^{-1} are

$$\left(\frac{\partial T_i^{-1}}{\partial x_j}\right)_{ij} = \left\{ \begin{array}{ll} 1/\delta_i, & i = j, \\ 0, & i \neq j. \end{array} \right. \tag{3.36}$$

Let us now consider some concrete cell and its basis functions, such as the 2D quad and its bilinear basis functions given in Section 3.4.4. By computing the derivatives $\partial \Phi_i / \partial r$ and $\partial \Phi_i / \partial s$ for all the four basis functions Φ_1, Φ_2, Φ_3, and Φ_4 and substituting these in Equation (3.36), we get the expression of the derivatives $\partial \tilde{f}/\partial x$ and $\partial \tilde{f}/\partial y$ for our reconstructed function $\tilde{f}$ over the given cell

$$\begin{array}{ll} \frac{\partial \tilde{f}}{\partial x} & = (1-s)\frac{f_2 - f_1}{\delta_1} + s\frac{f_3 - f_4}{\delta_1}, \\ \frac{\partial \tilde{f}}{\partial y} & = (1-r)\frac{f_4 - f_1}{\delta_2} + r\frac{f_3 - f_2}{\delta_2}, \end{array} \tag{3.37}$$

where f_1, f_2, f_3, and f_4 are the sample values at the four cell vertices corresponding to basis functions Φ_1, Φ_2, Φ_3, and Φ_4. In other words, this means that the partial derivatives of $\tilde{f}$ inside a given cell are computed by linearly interpolating the 1D derivatives of $\tilde{f}$ along opposite cell edges. A similar result can be obtained for rectilinear grids, as well as for hexahedral cells.

Computing derivatives of discrete datasets is a delicate process. If the dataset is noisy, the computed derivatives tend to exhibit even stronger noise that the original data. Care must be used when interpreting information contained in the derivatives. A relatively simple method to limit these problems is to prefilter the input dataset in order to eliminate high-frequency noise, using methods such as the Laplacian smoothing described in Section 8.4. However, one must be aware that smoothing may also eliminate important information from the dataset together with the noise.

3.8   Implementation

In this section, we present an implementation of the dataset concept. The proposed implementation follows several of the requirements for datasets introduced in Section 3.2. First, it allows subsequent application code to treat all dataset types uniformly, by defining a generic `Grid` interface that is implemented in particular ways by the various concrete grid types. Second, it provides a reasonable balance between implementation simplicity and memory and speed efficiency, making it useful in practical applications. We stress that this implementation is not an optimal one. Higher efficiency can be achieved, both in terms of speed and smart storage schemes that minimize data duplication and copying when working with multiple datasets. For readers interested in studying an efficient and effective implementation of the dataset concept, we strongly recommend a study of [Schroeder et al. 04, Kitware, Inc. 04]. However, describing such a dataset implementation in detail, with all the design issues involved, is beyond the scope of this book.

3.8.1 Grid Implementation

We begin by defining a `Grid` interface that declares all operations all our grid types should support as shown in Listing 3.4.

The methods `numPoints` and `numCells` return the number of grid points and cells, respectively. In a grid, both points and cells are identified by unique integer IDs. For uniform, rectilinear, and structured grids, these IDs usually correspond to the lexicographic ordering of the grid elements (see Equation (3.22)). Given an id, the methods `getPoint` and `getCell` return the point coordinates and the cell vertex IDs for the point or cell specified by the passed id argument. The method `findCell` returns the cell id for the cell that contains a given location given in world coordinates, or an invalid cell id, such as -1, if the location falls outside the grid. Finally, the method `world2cell` implements the inverse transformation from

```
class Grid
{
public:
        virtual          ~Grid() {}
        virtual int      numPoints()          = 0;
        virtual int      numCells()           = 0;
        virtual void     getPoint(int, float*) = 0;
        virtual int      getCell(int, int*)   = 0;
        virtual int      findCell(float*)     = 0;
        void             world2cell(int, float*, float*);
};
```

Listing 3.4. Grid implementation.

```
class UniformGrid : public Grid
{
public:
        UniformGrid(int N1_, int N2_, float m1_, float m2_,
                    float M1, float M2)
        :N1(N1_),N2(N2_),m1(m1_),m2(m2_),
        d1((M1-m1)/N1_),d2((M2-m2)/N2_) { }
    int    numPoints()
           { return N1*N2; }
    int    numCells()
           { return (N1-1)*(N2-1); }
    void   getPoint(int i, float* p)
           { p[0]=m1+(i%N1)*d1; p[1]=m2+(i/N1)*d2; }
    int    getCell(int i, int* c);
           //see Listing 3.1
    int
    int    getDimension1()
           { return N1; }
    int    getDimension2()
           { return N2; }

protected:

    int      N1,N2;
    float    m1,m2;

private:

    float    d1,d2;
};
```

Listing 3.5. Uniform grid implementation.

world coordinates to cell parametric coordinates, i.e., the transform T^{-1} described in Section 3.4. Specifically, world2cell(c,world,cell) maps from the 3D world coordinates world to the 3D parametric coordinates cell for the cell with the id c. In the case of 2D or 1D cells, this method will ignore the extra coordinates. This method does not depend on the actual grid type but on the cell type, so it can be implemented in the base class. The world2cell method does *not* check whether the world point is indeed contained in the given cell—this is the job of the findCell method. If the world point is in the specified cell then the resulting parametric coordinates are in the $[0, 1]$ range. If not then at least one of the resulting parametric coordinates falls outside this range.

```
int findCell(float* p)
{
  int C[2];

  //compute cell coordinates C[0],C[1]
  C[0] = int((p[0]-m1)*N1/d1);
  C[1] = int((p[1]-m2)*N2/d2);

  //test if p is inside the dataset
  if (C[0]<0 || C[0]>=N1-1 || C[1]<0 || C[1]>=N2-1)
    return -1;

  //go from cell coordinates to cell index
  return C[0] + C[1]*N1;
}
```

Listing 3.6. Implementing `findCell` for uniform grids.

Since we are going to subclass `Grid`, we implement a dummy virtual destructor. This ensures that application code can safely delete `Grid` subclasses via references or pointers—the `virtual` specifier ensures that the appropriate subclass destructor gets invoked [Stroustrup 04]. Next, we implement the different grid types described in the previous sections by subclassing the `Grid` interface. To simplify the presentation, we shall consider only the case of 2D grids with quad cells. However, the implementation shown here can be easily generalized to other dimensions and cell types. For the same reasons, we skip the implementation of the attribute interpolation using basis functions and the coordinate transformations. These can be programmed by following their description in Sections 3.4 and 3.6.

Listing 3.5 shows the implementation of a `UniformGrid`, which is a straightforward mapping of the structure presented in Section 3.5.1. For uniform grids, the implementation of `findCell` is quite simple, as the grid topology is regular. Listing 3.6 exemplifies this for 2D uniform grids. First, we compute the cell coordinates from the point world coordinates. Next, we compute the cell id from the cell coordinates.

Let us now consider the rectilinear grid. We can simplify its implementation by subclassing it from `UniformGrid`. We can inherit most methods except `getPoint()`, since rectilinear and uniform grids share the same topology but not the same geometry.

```
class  RectilinearGrid  :  public  UniformGrid
{
public :
        RectilinearGrid ( vector <float >* d_ , float  m1 , float  m2)
        : UniformGrid ( N1 , N2 , m1 , m2 , 0 , 0 )
        {  d[0]=d_[0];  d[1]=d_[1];  }
    void  getPoint ( int  i , float * p)
        {  p[0]=m1+d[0][ i%N1 ];  p[1]=m2+d[1][ i /N1 ];  }

private :

        vector <float > d [ 2 ];
};
```

Listing 3.7. Rectilinear grid implementation.

In Listing 3.7, we store the 2D grid point x- and y-coordinates in float arrays d[0] and d[1] implemented using the Standard Template Library (STL) class std::vector<float>. Here and in the following, we omit the namespace qualification std:: for brevity. In actual code, either prefix all STL symbols with this namespace (e.g., write std::vector<float>) or specify using namespace std; in every file before making use of these symbols. STL provides a versatile and expressive set of programming building blocks, such as basic data containers and algorithms. Using STL to implement the various aspects of datasets massively simplifies the overall implementation and reduces the code size and the chance for errors such as memory leaks. Moreover, recent STL implementations are carefully optimized for memory and speed, so using STL containers incurs a negligible overhead as compared to classical arrays, for example.

For rectilinear grids, implementing findCell is also quite simple. First, we compute the cell coordinates from the point world coordinates, similar to the uniform grid. However, this process requires two searches (for 2D grids) in order to determine in which intervals [d[0][i], d[0][i+1]] (for the x-axis) and [d[1][j], d[1][j+1]] (for the y-axis) does the target point fall. These intervals can be found either via linear searches on the two axes, yielding a complexity of $\max{(O(N1), O(N2))}$. Or, if we explicitly store the vectors of grid coordinates $(0, d[0][1], \ldots, \sum_{i=1}^{N1} d[0][i])$ and $(0, d[1][1], \ldots, \sum_{i=1}^{N2} d[1][i])$, we can use binary search instead, yielding a complexity of $\max{(O(\log N1), O(\log N2))}$. Given its relative simplicity, we leave the actual implementation as an exercise for the reader.

```
class  StructuredGrid  :  public  UniformGrid
{
public :
            StructuredGrid ( int  N1, int  N2, float  m1, float  m2,
                              float  M1, float  M2)
            : UniformGrid (N1 , N2 , m1 , m2 , M1 , M2)
            { points . resize (2*N1*N2 );  }
    int     numPoints ()
            { return  points . size ()/2;  }
    void    getPoint ( int  i , float * p)
            { p[0]= points [2* i ];  p[1]= points [2* i +1];  }
    void    setPoint ( int  i , float * p)
            { points [2* i]=p [0];  points [2* i+1]=p [1];  }

private :

        vector <float > points ;
};
```

Listing 3.8. Structured grid implementation.

Structured grids have the same topology as uniform and rectilinear grids, but a different geometry than rectilinear grids. Hence, we derive our `StructuredGrid` class from `UniformGrid` as seen in Listing 3.8.

Since structured grids allow us to set the coordinates of every point independently, we provide a `setPoint` method to this end. Finally, structured grids do not have a regular geometry that can be exploited to implement a fast and simple version of the `findCell` method. Since the vertex coordinates can be arbitrary, `findCell` must perform an actual search that identifies in which cell our target point falls. Iterating over all cells is clearly too slow. An acceptable solution is to use a *spatial search structure*.

Several types of structures allow fast location of the closest point, or N closest points, of a given point set to a given candidate point. Such structures typically subdivide the convex hull or bounding box of the point set hierarchically in disjoint cells that can be tested quickly. Finding the closest point(s) to the candidate point is done by traversing the spatial subdivision tree starting from the root cell (which contains the complete point set, i.e., the complete grid in our case) and following the path of cells that contain the candidate until a leaf cell is reached. If the leaf cell contains several points, a simple linear search is used to determine the closest one(s). Several spatial search structures exist. A first notable

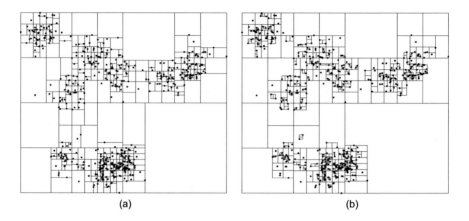

(a)   (b)

Figure 3.15. Spatial subdivision of a 2D point cloud using (a) kd-trees and (b) bd-trees.

example is *octrees*, which use axis-aligned boxes as cells and split every cell into four (in 2D) or eight (in 3D) smaller cells of equal size. More efficient examples are *kd-trees* [Bentley 90, Friedman et al. 77] and box decomposition trees, *bd-trees* [Arya et al. 98]. These use also axis-aligned cells, but every cell is now split into two subcells. The splitting direction and the splitting line (in 2D) or plane (in 3D) are determined by a number of rules in order to balance the tree optimally. In addition, kd-trees can split a cell into a shrunken version of the cell and the space outside, which creates less-deep trees for highly clustered point sets, hence improving the search time.

A very efficient, simple-to-use open-source software package for spatial search providing kd-trees and bd-trees is the Approximate Near Neighbors (ANN) package written in C++ [Mount 06]. ANN works efficiently even beyond 3D, supports N-nearest-neighbor search with a user-specifiable N, is simple to install and call, and uses preprocessing time and space linear in the point set size and the dimension. Another open-source package that offers efficient spatial search structures such as kd-trees is the Gnu Triangulated Surface (GTS) library [GTS 06]. Figure 3.15 shows the generated kd-tree (left) and bd-tree (right) respectively for a 2D point set.

Spatial search structures such as octrees, kd-trees, and bd-trees work best for point sets. To use them for implementing the `findCell` operation, we insert the complete set of grid vertices in the data structure and search for the closest *vertex* to the given point candidate. Once this is found, we test the cells that use this vertex to see which one actually contains the candidate. If none does, which can happen in some special configurations, we search for the second-closest vertex and repeat the procedure until the containing cell is found. An extra speed-up that can be used is based on the heuristic that, in practice, application algorithms search for cells starting from a geometrically coherent set of points. In other words, consecutive calls to findCell will return the same cell, cells that are neighbors, or other cells that are close to each other in the dataset. We can exploit this in the implementation of findCell by caching the previously returned cell and, in subsequent calls, first testing whether the searched location falls in this cell. If so, the function completes without any search. If not, the existing spatial search structure is used.

```
class  UnstructuredGrid  :  public  Grid
{
public :
          UnstructuredGrid(int  P, int  C)
          {  points . resize (2∗P);   cells . resize (3∗C);   }
    int    numCells ()
          {  return  cells . size ()/3;  }
    int    numPoints ()
          {  return  points . size ()/2;  }
    int    getCell (int  i , int∗  c)
          {
            c[0]= cells [3∗ i ];   c[1]= cells [3∗ i +1];
            c[2]= cells [3∗ i +2];  return  4;
          }
    void   getPoint (int  i , float∗  p)
          {  p[0]=points [2∗ i ];   p[1]=points [2∗ i +1];  }
    void   setCell (int  i , int∗  c)
          {  cells [3∗ i ]=c [0];   cells [3∗ i +1]=c [1];
            cells [3∗ i +2]=c [2];  }
    void   setPoint (int  i , float∗  p)
          {  points [2∗ i ]=p [0];   points [2∗ i +1]=p [1];  }

private :
      vector <int>    cells ;
      vector <float > points ;
};
```

Listing 3.9. Unstructured grid implementation.

One limitation of spatial search structures is that they take relatively long to build as compared to the search time. This is not a problem in case of a grid with fixed geometry. If the grid's geometry changes frequently compared to the number of searches, it can be faster to use a brute-force linear search instead of a spatial search structure.

We now turn our attention to unstructured grids. Unstructured grids have the same geometry as structured grids but have a different topology. Yet, we cannot derive a `UnstructuredGrid` class from `StructuredGrid`, since the latter also inherits a regular topology from `UniformGrid`. Hence, we derive `UnstructuredGrid` directly from the `Grid` interface as seen in Listing 3.9.

Unstructured grids allow us to set the vertices that constitute the cells independently. To this end, we provide the `setCell` method. Finally, unstructured grids can use the same `findCell` implementation based on spatial search structures as the structured grids.

3.8.2   Attribute Data Implementation

Now that we have the grid functionality, we must implement the data attributes. In Section 3.2, we discussed two interpolation methods for attribute data, constant and linear. Both methods work in a piecewise fashion: you provide the world coordinates x_j of a point in a given cell. From these, parametric cell coordinates r_j are computed, using the transformation T^{-1}, and these are used to evaluate the cell's reference basis functions Φ_i weighted by the cell's attribute values f_i at its sample points (see Equation (3.9)).

An ideal interface for a dataset would let us evaluate its reconstruction function $\tilde{f}$ at any coordinates x_j inside the sampled domain, i.e., treat the dataset as a truly (piecewise) continuous function. However, since we use piecewise reconstruction, this would imply finding the cell the desired point is in, as described previously. This is an expensive operation, which can potentially be needed many times if we need to evaluate $\tilde{f}$ on many cells. Luckily, many data-processing algorithms do not need to evaluate the dataset at purely random locations. In practice, most data-processing algorithms work on a cell-by-cell basis, instead of requiring evaluation of the reconstruction function at random locations.

The data attribute evaluation functionality can be easily added to our dataset class. To do this, we make some design decisions. First, we shall support only piecewise constant and linear interpolations, both for all cell types. This may seem restrictive at first. However, the overwhelming majority of visualization applications use only these interpolation methods, in practice, since they are simple to implement and quick to compute. Second, we shall enforce that attribute values f_i are defined for all sample points i. As explained in Section 3.6.6, this is a natural property if we think of reconstructing signals over the whole domain. Third, we must decide which attribute types of those described in Section 3.6 we want to store in our dataset, and how many of each type. In general, we would like to store a user-defined number of each type, and also allow for user-defined attribute types. In the following sample implementation, however, we shall include only a single scalar attribute and leave the extension to several instances of several attribute types as an exercise for the reader. Finally, in the example presented here, we limit ourselves to 2D grids, as in the previous code examples shown earlier in this section.

In practice, we need attribute data for all grid types we have defined. Hence, we shall provide attribute support by adding extra code to the base class `Grid`. For piecewise constant interpolation, this is done with the following simple code:

```
public:

    float& getC0Scalar(int i)
            { return c0_scalars[i]; }
    float   getC0Scalar(int c,float x,float y)
            { return getC0Scalar(c); }

protected:

    vector<float> c0_scalars;
```

Given a cell index `i`, the first method `getC0Scalar(int)` returns the corresponding cell scalar attribute. Cell attributes are stored as a `vector` of floats. The second method `getC1Scalar(int,float,float)` performs the piecewise constant interpolation of the scalar data, given a cell index and a location within that cell. This basically amounts to returning the cell scalar value. Similar methods can be implemented for vector data. For a dataset

```
public :

    float& getC1Scalar(int  i)
           { return c1_scalars[i];  }

    float   getC1Scalar(int  c, float* p)
           {
               int  cell[MAX_CELL_SIZE];
               int  C = getCell(c, cell);
               float  q[3], f=0;
               world2cell(c,p,q);
               for(int  i=0;i<C;i++)
                  f += getC1Scalar(cell[i])*Phi(i,q[0],q[1]);
               return f;
           }

protected :

    vector<float> c1_scalars;
```

Listing 3.10. Implementing linear interpolation for scalar data.

having N cells, one typically allocates a `vector<float>` c0_vectors having $3N$ float elements such that the vector $\mathbf{v} = (v_x, v_y, v_z)$ for cell i is stored at locations $3i, 3i+1, 3i+2$ in the container. In pure object-oriented fashion, it is tempting to consider manipulating vectors via some `Vector` class and thus storing vector attributes as a `vector<Vector>` c0_vectors instead of a "plain" float array. However, most visualization application implementations will not use this model, since it complicates the code significantly. Also, frequent operations on attributes, such as iteration, creating and copying attribute arrays, and reading and writing components of such an array will become slower when using the extra structuring level implied by a `Vector` class instance.

For piecewise linear interpolation, we add the code shown in Listing 3.10 to the `Grid` class. The first method `getC1Scalar(int)` returns the sample value stored at a given grid vertex sample point, i.e., implements what is usually called *vertex data*. As for the cell data, we made this function return a reference, so one can both read and write the vertex scalar attributes. The second method `getC1Scalar(int,float*)` performs the piecewise linear interpolation of the scalar data, given a cell index and a world coordinate location (given as a 2-float vector) within that cell, i.e., it implements Equation (3.9). In this function, the `MAX_CELL_SIZE` constant represents

```
public :

float* getC1Vector(int i)
         { return &(c1_scalars[3*i]); }

void    getC1Vector(int c, float* p, float* v)
         {
           int cell[MAX_CELL_SIZE];
           int C = getCell(c, cell);
           float q[3];
           world2cell(c,p,q);
           v[0]=v[1]=v[2]=0;
           for(int i=0;i<C;i++)
           {
             float* vi = getC1Vector(cell[i]);
             v[0]      += vi[0]*Phi(i,q[0],q[1]);
             v[1]      += vi[1]*Phi(i,q[0],q[1]);
             v[2]      += vi[2]*Phi(i,q[0],q[1]);
           }
         }

protected :

    vector<float> c1_vectors;
```

Listing 3.11. Implementing linear interpolation for vector data.

the maximum number of vertices in a cell, which is eight for the cells discussed here. The method `world2cell` performs the transformation from world coordinates p to parametric coordinates q. Finally, the function `Phi` models the per-vertex basis functions of the considered cell.

Similar methods can be implemented for vector data as in Listing 3.11. Just as for cell vector attributes, vertex vector attributes are best stored consecutively component-wise in a float array `c1_vectors`. The first method `getC1Vector(int)` returns a pointer to the first component v_x of a cell's vector attribute. The second method `getC1Vector(int,float*,float*)` performs the piecewise linear interpolation of the vector data over a cell, similar to the analogous `getC1Scalar` method for scalar data, and returns the interpolated vector in a user-provided float array v.

In actual production code, a dataset needs to support several instances of all the attribute types. This requires an interface by which the user can specify which of the instances of a certain attribute type is to be used. A simple and effective solution is to store the attribute vectors in an associative array that can be addressed by a unique name. With STL, this can be done for scalar attributes by using a `map<string,vector<float>*>`, for example. Given an attribute name as a `string` (for example, "temperature"), the `map` class returns a reference to the corresponding `vector<float>` that stores the actual data, or null if there is no such attribute. Similar associative arrays can be constructed for every attribute type.

3.9   Advanced Data Representation

In the preceding sections, we have seen how to reconstruct piecewise constant and piecewise linear functions from sampled datasets, represented on grids with various cell types, using constant and linear basis functions. For the vast majority of data visualization applications, these representations are sufficient. However, there are situations when more advanced forms of data manipulation and representation are needed. In this section, first, we will describe the task of data *resampling*, which is used in the process of converting information between different types of datasets that have different sample points, cells, or basis functions (Section 3.9.1). Then we will describe the process of interpolating data provided as a set of scattered points, in case we do not have cell information (Section 3.9.2).

3.9.1   Data Resampling

In our height-plot visualization example in Chapter 2, we saw several instances of reconstructing functions from a sampled dataset. We used piecewise linear interpolation for the polygonal surface itself. We used piecewise constant interpolation for the flat shading and piecewise linear interpolation for the Gouraud shading, respectively. Finally, we used piecewise constant interpolation for the surface normals. We saw in Chapter 2 that we need normal values at the polygon vertices, the vertex normals, to do the Gouraud shading of the surface. However, piecewise constant normals, i.e., the polygon normals themselves, are discontinuous at the polygon vertices—actually, over the complete polygon edges—so we cannot use them as approximations for the vertex normals. How can we compute vertex normal values from the known polygon normals?

The answer to this question is provided by a more general operation on discrete datasets, called *resampling*. Consider a *source* dataset $\mathcal{D} =$

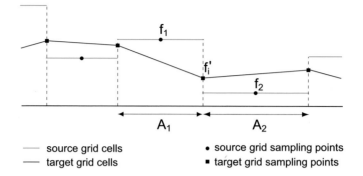

Figure 3.16. Converting cell to vertex attributes. The vertex value f_i' equals $\frac{A_1 f_1 + A_2 f_2}{A_1 + A_2}$, the area-weighted average of the cell values using vertex i.

$(\{p_i\}, \{c_i\}, \{f_i\}, \{\Phi_i\})$ and a *target* dataset $\mathcal{D}' = (\{p_i'\}, \{c_i'\}, \{f_i'\}, \{\Phi_i\})$, which approximate both the same continuous function $f : D \to C$, but where the source grid $(\{p_i\}, \{c_i\})$ differs from the target grid $(\{p_i'\}, \{c_i'\})$. Resampling computes the values f_i' of the target dataset as function of the values f_i of the source dataset. For simplicity, we assume that both datasets use the same set of basis functions Φ_i, although this is not a strict requirement.

Let us now consider a common resampling operation in data visualization: converting cell attributes (f_i) to vertex attributes (f_i'). Cell attributes imply the use of constant basis functions Φ_i, as discussed in Section 3.2. Vertex attributes, in contrast, imply the use of higher-order basis functions, such as linear ones. On the other hand, we want the sample points of the target grid cells (which are the target grid vertices) to be identical to the source cell vertices for the two grids to match, as shown in Figure 3.16 for a one-dimensional grid.

A desirable property of resampling a function $\tilde{f}$ is that it should lead to a function $\tilde{f}'$ that is close to $\tilde{f}$ over the whole domain D. Mathematically, this can be expressed as

$$\int_{c_i'} \tilde{f}' ds \approx \int_{c_i'} \tilde{f} ds, \quad \forall \text{ cells } c_i' \in \mathcal{D}'. \tag{3.38}$$

That is, the integrals of the original function $\tilde{f}$ and the resampled function $\tilde{f}'$ are equal over all cells c_i' of the target grid. Using the normality property of the basis functions (see Equation (3.5)), we obtain after some computations that

$$f'_i = \frac{\sum_{c_j \in \text{ cells}(p_i)} A(c_j) f_j}{\sum_{c_j \in \text{ cells}(p_i)} A(c_j)}, \tag{3.39}$$

where $A(c_j)$ is the area of source grid cell c_j and cells(p_i) are all cells that have point p_i as vertex. In other words, vertex data is the area-weighted average of the cell data in the cells that use a given vertex. Equation (3.39) is identical to Equation (2.8) used in Section 2.2 to compute vertex normals for Gouraud shading from the polygon normals. Using similar reasoning, we can compute the conversion formula from vertex attributes (f'_i) to cell attributes (f_i) as being

$$f_i = \frac{\sum_{p_j \in \text{ points}(c_i)} f'_j}{C}, \tag{3.40}$$

where points(c_i) denotes all points p_j that are vertices of cell c_i and $C = |\text{points}(c_i)|$ is the number of vertices of cell c_i. In other words, cell attributes are the average of the cell's vertex attributes.

In conclusion, we can always convert between cell attributes and vertex attributes. However, this does not mean that a dataset with cell attributes is *identical* to one with vertex attributes. As explained previously, cell attributes imply using piecewise constant interpolation, whereas vertex attributes imply a higher-order interpolation, such as linear. Resampling data from, e.g., cells to vertices increases the assumed continuity. If our original sampled data were indeed continuous of that order, no problem appears. However, if the original data contained, e.g., zero-order discontinuities, such as jumps or holes, resampling it to a higher-continuity grid also throws away discontinuities which might have been a feature of the data and not a sampling artifact. An example of this delicate problem is given in Section 9.4.6. In contrast, resampling from a higher continuity (e.g., vertex data) to a lower continuity (e.g., cell data) has fewer side effects—overall, the smoothness of the data decreases globally.

Data resampling is not limited to converting between cell and vertex samples. Two other frequently used resampling operations are *subsampling* and *supersampling*. Subsampling is a resampling operation that reduces the number of sample points. Subsampling is useful when we are interested in optimizing the processing speed and memory demands of a visualization application by working with smaller datasets. In most cases, the subsampled dataset uses the same basis functions as the original dataset and its points are actually a subset of the original dataset points. However, this is not mandatory. After eliminating a certain number of sample points, subsampling operations can choose to redistribute the remaining points in order to obtain a better approximation of the original data in terms of the integral criterion defined earlier. Subsampling implementations can take advantage of the dataset topology. For example, on uniform, rectilinear, and structured grids, an often-used subsampling technique is to keep every kth point along every dimension and discard the remaining ones. This technique, called *uniform subsampling*, is simple to implement and quite effective when the original dataset is densely sampled with respect to the data variation. However, uniform subsampling makes no assumptions about the spatial data variation, so it might discard important features, such as regions where the data changes rapidly, together with less important, constant regions. Given the way most interpolation functions (such as constant and linear) reconstruct the data, a desirable property of subsampling is to keep most samples in the regions of rapid data variation and cull most samples from the regions of slow data variation. In Section 8.4, we shall present several subsampling methods applicable to both structured and unstructured datasets.

Supersampling (also called *refinement*) is the inverse of subsampling. Here, more sample points are created from an existing dataset. Similar to subsampling, the supersampled dataset usually includes all the original dataset points and uses the same basis functions, although this is not mandatory. Supersampling is useful in several situations when we need to manipulate or create information on a dataset at a level of detail, or scale, that is below the one captured by the sampling frequency, or density, of that dataset. In that case, we introduce more points by supersampling, and then use these to encode the desired detail information. The counterpart of uniform subsampling is *uniform supersampling*, which introduces k points into every cell of the original dataset. Similar to subsampling, an efficient supersampling implementation usually inserts extra points only in those spatial regions of the dataset where we need to further add extra information. We shall discuss several supersampling methods in Section 8.4.

3.9.2   Scattered Point Interpolation

So far, our definition of a sampled dataset has been based on a grid of cells that represent a tiling of the data domain (see Section 3.2). However, there are situations when we would like to avoid constructing or storing such a grid. Such a case occurs when you have measured some data at some given points that have a complex spatial distribution, and you have no explicit cell information that would connect the points into a tiling of some domain. A classical example is 3D surface scanning, where laser devices are used to measure the position of a set of points on the surface of a 3D object. For complex object surfaces, this process delivers a scattered 3D point set, also called a *point cloud*, with optional surface normal and surface color per-point attributes. Hence all the data we have to work with are the points and their corresponding data values $\{p_i, f_i\}$. For the scanning example, the data values f_i are the surface normals and/or colors measured by the scanner device.

Remember, the goal of a dataset is to allow reconstructing some continuous signal $\tilde{f}$ from a sampled representation. In our surface scanning example, how can we reconstruct a smooth surface $\tilde{f}$ if all we are given is the point set $\{p_i, f_i\}$, where f_i are surface normals? Recalling the reconstruction formula (see Equation (3.2)), we need to define some basis functions ϕ_i at the sample points p_i. There are several ways to do this.

Constructing a grid from scattered points. First, we can construct a grid from the point set. The way this is done depends on the meaning of the point samples p_i. If these points come from the sampling of some supposedly smooth 3D surface, we can construct an unstructured grid with 2D cells, e.g., triangles, which have p_i as vertices, and which approximate a smooth surface as much as possible. Several *triangulation methods* exist to do this. We shall describe such method in more detail in Section 8.3. Once we have this grid, we can use the constant or linear interpolation functions described earlier in this chapter.

Gridless interpolation. A second way is to avoid constructing a grid altogether. This has several advantages. Constructing unstructured grids from large, complex 3D point clouds can be a delicate process. Storing the grid can be a high burden for very large datasets. As described in Section 3.5.4, storing the cell information can double the amount of memory required in the worst case. Moreover, our point set can change in time, because it represents some moving object or because we would like to process it with geometric modeling operations such as editing, filtering, or deformations. Triangulating the point set to compute a grid every time the points change can be a very costly operation. Finally, if we have a large point set representing a complex 3D surface, visualizing it by rendering the corresponding triangulation may not be the fastest option. In such cases, we can do better by using a gridless point representation.

How can we reconstruct a continuous function from a scattered point set without recurring to an explicit grid? What we need is a set of gridless basis functions, which should respect the properties in Equations (3.4) and (3.5) as much as possible. There are several ways to construct such functions. A frequently used choice for gridless basis functions is *radial basis functions*, or RBFs. These are functions $\Phi : \mathbb{R}^d \rightarrow \mathbb{R}_+$, which depend only on the distance

$$r = |x| = \sqrt{\sum_{i=1}^{d} x_i^2} \tag{3.41}$$

between the current point $x = (x_1, \ldots, x_d) \in \mathbb{R}^d$ and the origin. Moreover, RBFs smoothly drop from one at their origin ($r = 0$) to a vanishing value for large values of the distance r.

In practice, we would like to limit the effect of a basis function to its immediate neighborhood. This is computationally efficient. To do this, we specify a radius of influence R, or support radius, beyond which Φ is equal to zero. In this setup, a common RBF is the Gaussian function

$$\Phi(x) = \begin{cases} e^{-kr^2}, & r < R, \\ 0, & r \geq R, \end{cases} \quad \text{where } r = |x|. \tag{3.42}$$

The parameter $k \geq 0$ in Equation (3.42) controls the decay speed, or the shape, of the radial basis functions. Setting $k = 0$ yields constant cylinder-shaped radial functions, which are equivalent to the constant basis functions we used for grid-based datasets. Higher values of k yield faster-decaying functions. For $d = 2$, that is, on a 2D domain, the graph of such a radial basis function looks like our visualization running example introduced in Chapter 2. Besides Gaussian functions, we can use other radial basis functions too. Another popular choice are inverse distance functions defined as

$$\Phi(x) = \begin{cases} \frac{1}{1+r^2}, & r < R, \\ 0, & r \geq R, \end{cases} \quad \text{where } r = |x|. \tag{3.43}$$

In practice, we would like to make the support radius R variable for each sample point p_i. The radius values R_i control the influence of the sample data value of a point p_i. Higher values of R_i yield smoother reconstructions $\tilde{f}$, since more RBFs overlap at a given point. However, this has a higher computational cost. Lower values of R_i yield less-smooth reconstructions, but higher performance. In the limit, setting $R_i = 0$ for all points yields the scattered point set where $\tilde{f}$ coincides with the sample values f_i at the sample point locations and is zero everywhere else. In practice, setting R_i to the average interpoint distance in the neighborhood of point p_i gives a good balance between interpolation smoothness and computational efficiency. For uniformly sampled point sets, we can set $R_i = 1/\sqrt{\rho}$, where ρ is the surface point density, measured in points per surface unit area.

Using the reference RBF Φ and the per-point support radius values R_i, we can define the global RBFs $\phi_i(x) = \Phi(T_i^{-1}(x))$, just as we did for the grid-based interpolation. The inverse transform T^{-1} that maps from the world space to the reference RBF space is just a translation from the current sample point p_i to the origin and a scaling of the distance r with a factor of R/R_i.

Performance issues. Once we have our global RBFs ϕ_i, we can reconstruct our function $\tilde{f}$ just as with grid-based approaches (see Equation (3.2)). Given a point p, we shall sum only those basis functions ϕ_k that are nonzero at p. In the case of a grid-based interpolation, finding these basis functions was trivial, as they were the functions associated with the vertices of the cell that contained p. In the case of radial basis functions, we must find the k nearest sample points $p_1, \ldots, p_k$ to p so that $|p - p_k| < R_k$, since only the basis functions ϕ_k have a nonzero contribution at p. One way to accomplish this is to store all sample points p_i in a spatial search structure such as a kd-tree [Bentley 75, Samet 90, Mount 06]. Given a point p, we search the k nearest neighbors p_k to p so that $|p - p_k| < R(p)$, where $R(p)$ is the average value of R in a neighborhood of p, and use the RBFs ϕ_k to evaluate Equation (3.2). For $R(p)$, we can use the average interpoint distance in the neighborhood of point p.

Spatial search structures provide efficient retrieval of the k nearest neighbors at any given location. A good, scalable implementation of such a search structure is provided by the Approximate Nearest Neighbor (ANN) library [Mount 06]. In some sense, such a data structure plays the role of a grid, i.e., it lets us find which are the sample points that affect a given spatial region. And just as when using grids, we must update our search data structure when our point set changes by reinserting the sample points that have moved. This is an operation that can be done efficiently [Mount 06, Clarenz et al. 04].

Radial basis functions with compact support are an efficient and effective way to smoothly interpolate scattered point data. However, unless extra constraints are set on the support radius values R_i and function shape parameter k, these functions are not by definition orthonormal, as the constant and linear basis functions defined on a grid were. This means that the reconstruction $\tilde{f}$ may not exactly interpolate the sample values f_i at the sample point locations p_i. Overly large values for R_i yield an overestimated $\tilde{f}$ that exceeds the sample values f_i, as well as an oversmoothed reconstruction. Conversely, overly small values for R_i yield a good fit between $\tilde{f}$ and f_i, but the signal $\tilde{f}$ may exhibit a characteristic "wavy" appearance due to the violation of the partition of unity property (see Equation (3.5)). For computing RBFs that respect the partition of unity property and also yield smooth reconstructions, we recommend studying the references at the end of this section.

A simple solution that offers a second-best alternative to orthonormal basis functions is to constrain the results of the interpolation to lie in the range of the sample values f_i, as follows. Given k nearest neighbors $p_1, \ldots, p_k$ of some point p with sample values f_i, we compute $\tilde{f}(p)$ as

$$\tilde{f}(p) = \frac{\sum_{i=1}^{k} f_i \phi_i(p)}{\sum_{i=1}^{k} \phi_i(p)}. \qquad (3.44)$$

When using the inverse distance basis functions (see Equation (3.43)), this method is called Shepard's interpolation method [Shepard 68]. Shepard's interpolation method produces results which are very similar with Gaussian RBF methods.

Summarizing, we can represent data purely as scattered point sets carrying the data samples (p_i, f_i). Some visualization texts call such representations unstructured point datasets. However, if the function of a dataset is to provide a (piecewise) continuous reconstruction of its data samples using some variant of Equation (3.2), we need to specify also a choice for the basis functions Φ_i to have a complete dataset (p_i, f_i, Φ_i). Several such functions can be used in practice, such as radial basis functions. To efficiently perform the reconstruction, searching methods are needed that return the sample points p_i located in the neighborhood of a given point p.

Scattered data interpolation and approximation is an extensive subject. More information on this can be found in specialized references such as the recent book by Wendland [Wendland 06]. For a shorter, but still rigorous mathematical treatment of meshless interpolation methods, see [Belytschko et al. 96].

3.10   Conclusion

In this chapter, we have presented the fundamental issues involved in representing data for visualization applications. Visualization data is produced, in many cases, by sampling a continuous signal defined over a compact spatial domain. The combination of the signal sample values, the discrete representation of the signal domain, and the mechanisms used to reconstruct a (piecewise) continuous approximation of the signal is called a *dataset*. Virtually all data-processing operations in the visualization process involve using the discrete representation provided by the dataset. Hence, having generic, efficient, and accurate ways to represent and manipulate datasets is of utmost importance.

In practice, the signal domain is discretized in a grid that contains a set of cells defined by the sample points. The data samples, also called *data attributes*, are stored at these points, and can be of several types. The most used are numerical types which permit interpolation: scalar, vector, color, and tensor. Together with these cells, basis functions are provided for signal reconstruction. The most-used basis functions in practice are constant and linear, given the simplicity of implementation and direct support in the graphics hardware.

Several types of grids provide different trade-offs between representation flexibility and storage and computational costs. The most-used types in practice are uniform, rectilinear, structured, and unstructured grids. Finally, gridless interpolation methods exist as well. These provide signal reconstruction from the sample point avoiding the construction and storage of cells altogether. To provide this extra flexibility, special spatial search data structures are required for fast location of neighbor points.

Visualization data can also originate from different sources than sampling a continuous signal. Data attributes such as text, images, or relations are purely discrete, and often not defined on a spatial domain. Such datasets form the target of information visualization applications, and are separately described in Chapter 11.

In the following chapters, we shall see how the various aspects described in this chapter (sampling and reconstruction, interpolation and basis functions, grids and cells) will be reflected in the construction of different types of visualization applications.

Chapter 4

The Visualization Pipeline

I N Chapter 2, we showed the basic steps of a visualization application and also sketched a simple data representation for the function graphing problem. In Chapter 3, we described in detail how to represent discrete, sampled data. We introduced several dataset types that offer different trade-offs between representation flexibility and storage and implementation requirements. At this point, we should have a good understanding of how to represent the data we are interested in visualizing. The focus of this chapter is to present the structure of a complete visualization application, both from a conceptual and a practical perspective.

We begin our discussion with a conceptual description of the structure of visualization applications (Section 4.1), which presents the four main ingredients of such an application: data importing, data filtering and enrichment, data mapping, and data rendering. Next, we describe several implementation considerations of this conceptual structure (Section 4.2). Section 4.3 discusses a classification of the various algorithms used in the visualization process. Finally, we conclude our analysis on the structure of visualization applications (Section 4.4).

4.1 Conceptual Perspective

As explained in Chapter 1, the role of visualization is to create images
that convey various types of insight into a given process. The process is
illustrated conceptually in Figure 1.2. The visualization process consists
of the sequence of steps, or operations, that manipulate the data produced
by the process under study and ultimately deliver the desired images. On
both the conceptual and the design level, this divide-and-conquer strategy in designing visualizations allows one to manage the complexity of the
whole process. On the implementation level, this strategy allows us to
construct visualizations by assembling reusable and modular data processing operations, much as in other fields of software engineering. Given this
modular decomposition, the visualization process can be seen as a *pipeline*
consisting of several stages, each modeled by a specific data transformation
operation. The input data flows through this pipeline, being transformed
in various ways, until it generates the output images. Given this model,
the sequence of data transformations that take place in the visualization
process is often called the *visualization pipeline.*

The visualization pipeline typically has four stages: data importing,
data filtering and enrichment, data mapping, and data rendering. These
are illustrated schematically in Figure 4.1. We shall detail all these steps
of the visualization pipeline.

In order to better understand the various operations that take place
in the visualization pipeline, we can use a functional description of this
process. Conceptually, we can see the visualization pipeline as a function
Vis that maps between $\mathbb{D}_I$, the set of all possible types of raw input data,

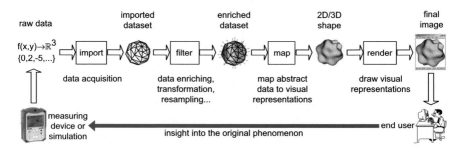

Figure 4.1. The visualization pipeline.

and the set $\mathbb{I}$ of produced images:

$$\text{Vis} : \mathbb{D}_I \to \mathbb{I}. \tag{4.1}$$

By examining the produced image, whether by interactive means or not, users should be able to obtain insight into the original raw data and answer questions about phenomena captured by this data. Conceptually, we can also model this process by a function Insight that maps from the output image to the input data, in inverse direction to the Vis function:

$$\text{Insight} : \mathbb{I} \to \mathbb{D}_I. \tag{4.2}$$

For simplicity and conciseness, we have described Insight as a function mapping from images to raw data. In reality, Insight maps from the produced images to the actual questions the user has about the raw data, which are not necessarily one-to-one with the data itself. We shall detail this point further in Section 4.1.3. For the time being, it is sufficient to understand that the process of getting insight goes in an inverse direction to the visualization pipeline itself.

Let us also mention that the user's feedback that connects the images with the original problem (the blue arrow in Figure 4.1) is not limited to insight only. When visually monitoring a life process that generates data, the user may want to *steer* the process in a given direction by changing its parameters. Applications that provide such facilities effectively close the loop between the visualization output and the application's inputs. If the complete round trip is executed in (sub)second time, the user effectively steers the process at hand by means of visual feedback. This process, called *computational steering*, is implemented by several visualization software applications, such as SciRUN [SCIRun 07], CUMULVS [CUMULVS 07, Geist et al. 97], and CSE [van Liere et al. 07, van Liere and van Wijk 96].

Clearly, not all Vis functions of the type sketched in Equation (4.1) are equally relevant for our goal of getting insight into, or understanding, the desired aspects of our dataset. Moreover, for real-world, complex application scenarios, it is quite plausible that we cannot construct the desired visualization function in a single step. The various steps of the visualization pipeline shown in Figure 4.1 correspond to specific functions, each taking care of a specific concern. The concatenation, or composition, of these functions yields the desired visualization. The functional model of the visualization pipeline is shown in Figure 1.2.

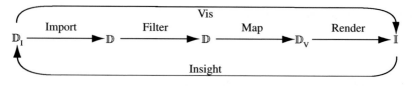

Figure 4.2. The visualization process seen as a composition of functions.

Figure 4.2 shows a necessarily simplified view of the actual complex interactions that involve the user, visualization application, input data, and produced images by this application, as well as the obtained insight. Many other factors are of importance in establishing qualitative and quantitative dependencies between these elements, such as the actual domain-specific knowledge of the user; the way insight builds up by executing the visualization process described in Figure 4.1 repeatedly for the same, or different, inputs; and the type of user interaction that allows various parameters of this process to be interactively tuned, to name just a few. Different models for the way visualization works have been presented, which incorporate these factors up to different extents and in different ways [Schroeder et al. 04, van Wijk 05].

In the following sections, we shall detail the four steps of the visualization pipeline presented in Figure 4.1 and, at the same time, discuss the desirable properties of their corresponding functions.

4.1.1   Importing Data

First, we have to be able to *import* our input data into the visualization process. Conceptually, this implies finding a representation of the original information we want to investigate in terms of a dataset, be it continuous or discrete. In functional terms, importing the input data maps the raw information $\mathbb{D}_I$ that is available at the beginning of the visualization process to a dataset $\mathcal{D} \in \mathbb{D}$, such as the ones described in Chapter 3. Here, $\mathbb{D}$ represents the set of all supported datasets of a given visualization process. If we consider the data representation given in Chapter 3, $\mathbb{D}$ consists of uniform, rectilinear, structured, and unstructured datasets. Importing data can be described by the function

$$\text{Import} : \mathbb{D}_I \to \mathbb{D}. \tag{4.3}$$

Practically, importing data means choosing a specific dataset implementation and converting the original information to the representation implied by the chosen dataset. Ideally, this is a one-to-one mapping or data copying, which usually involves reading the input data from some external storage, such as a file or a database, or from a live data source, such as a measuring device, a scanner, or an analog-to-digital converter. A direct mapping can happen only if the chosen dataset can directly represent the input data. In practice, data importing can imply translating between different data storage formats, resampling the data from the continuous to the discrete domain, like we did in Section 2.1, or from one resolution and/or grid type to another, as discussed in Section 3.9.1. For our height-plot example introduced in Section 2.1, our input data is a continuous function $f(x, y) \to \mathbb{R}$, and the import operation involves sampling it on the desired dataset, such as a regular grid.

It is important to realize that the choices made during data importing determine the quality of the resulting images, and thus the effectiveness of the visualization. For example, if the imported data is incorrect, incomplete, or the importing method throws away information from the original data, it is in general very hard (and sometimes impossible) to completely restore the data quality later in the visualization pipeline. For this reason, the data importing step should try to preserve as much of the available input information as possible, and make as few assumptions as possible about what is important and what is not. Concerns such as simplifying or filtering the data should be addressed in the next steps of the visualization process. We illustrated these considerations in Chapter 2 by showing how the quality of the height plot is affected by the choice of the grid type and sampling density.

4.1.2 Data Filtering and Enrichment

Once we have imported the data, we must decide which are its important aspects, or features, we are interested in. In most cases, the imported data is not one-to-one with the aspects we want to get insight into. This is inherent to our choice of importing data "as is." Usually, raw data do not model directly the aspects targeted by our questions. If it were so, we would not need visualization at all, as we could just directly query the input data and get the desired answers. Visualization is useful when the subject of our questions involves more complex features than directly modeled by the input data. Hence, we must somehow distill our raw dataset into more appropriate representations, also called *enriched datasets*, which encode our features of interest in a more appropriate form for being analyzed and visualized. This process is called *data filtering* or *data enriching*, since it performs two tasks. On one hand, data is filtered to extract relevant information. On the other hand, data is enriched with higher-level information that supports a given task. In the literature, these two operations are typically not discussed separately, but amalgamated in a single stage of the visualization pipeline. Given this, we shall use in the the terms "filtering" and "enrichment" interchangeably, unless specified otherwise explicitly in the context.

Data filtering can be described by the function

$$\text{Filter} : \mathbb{D} \to \mathbb{D}. \qquad (4.4)$$

Both the input (domain) and output (co-domain) of the filtering function are datasets, since the filtering function is strictly a data manipulation operation. This is in contrast to the data importing function and, as we shall see shortly, to the mapping and rendering functions as well.

Let us give some examples of data filtering. Usually, we are not interested in the properties of the complete input dataset, but only in those of a specific *subset of interest* that is significant for a given goal. For example, medical specialists are usually interested in seeing only specific anatomical structures related to a certain condition, which are a subset of the entire dataset they obtain from scanning devices such as CT or MRI scanners. Financial analysts may want to focus on the behavior of only a small subset of companies of interest, given a large set of stock exchange data containing the stock prices of thousands of companies. Selecting a subset of interest can be done in the spatial domain, in the attribute value domain, or in a combination of both. For our height-plot example, computing derivatives of the sampled dataset, as described in Section 3.7, is an example of a filtering operation.

Another reason for data filtering is the fact that input datasets can be overwhelmingly large. This makes efficient processing difficult, which can be a serious problem when our users require interactive visualization applications. A more fundamental problem related to size is the limited output resolution of the typical computer screens used by visualization applications. Think of the simple example of displaying a 2D colored image. This is an instance of visualizing a 2D dataset that has color attributes specified per cell (or pixel). If the input datasets exceed a certain size, the visualization will produce output images that no longer fit a given screen. One solution used in practice is *zooming*, i.e., subsampling the input image and displaying only a subset of its pixels that captures the overall characteristics of the complete dataset. The complementary solution, *panning*, i.e., selecting a subset of the input image at its original resolution, can also be seen as a form of data filtering.

A final reason for data filtering is convenience. It is very hard, if not practically impossible, to describe the large palette of data processing operations involved in the visualization process in terms of a single data representation or dataset type. Hence, datasets are usually transformed from one form to the other during the visualization process, such that they fit the data model required by the processing operations we want to apply. Practically, this implies working with different types of datasets that have different dimensionalities, cells, grids, interpolation functions, and attribute values.

4.1.3 Mapping Data

The filtering operation produces an enriched dataset that should directly represent the features of interest for a specific exploration task. Once we have this representation, we must map it to the visual domain. We do this by associating elements of the visual domain with the data elements present in the enriched dataset. This step of the visualization process is called *mapping* and can be modeled by the function

$$\text{Map} : \mathbb{D} \to \mathbb{D}_V. \tag{4.5}$$

This function takes a dataset $\mathcal{D} \in \mathbb{D}$ and maps it to a dataset of *visual features* $\mathcal{D}_V$. The easiest way to think of visual features is to imagine them as subsets of a visual domain $\mathbb{D}_V$, i.e., $\mathcal{D}_V \in \mathbb{D}_V$. The visual domain is a multidimensional space whose axes, or dimensions, are those elements that we perceive as quasi-independent visual attributes. Examples of these axes are shape, position, size, color, texture, illumination, and motion. Clearly, there are cases when these visual attributes are not independent, but overlap—think of texture, color, and illumination, for instance. However, the principle remains the same. Typically, a visual feature is a colored,

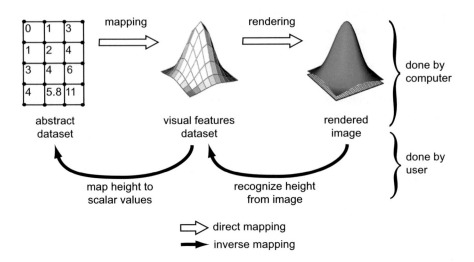

Figure 4.3. The direct and inverse mapping in the visualization process.

shaded, textured, and animated 2D or 3D shape. In rendering parlance, a visual feature dataset $\mathcal{D}_V$ is a 3D scene and the visual domain $\mathbb{D}_V$ is the set of all possible 3D scenes.

The actual visual features, thus the actual mapping function, used in a specific application depend very much on the purpose of the visualization, specifics of the data, and ultimately on the preference of the designer of that visualization. For our height-plot example, the mapping operation takes the sampled dataset that represents our function and constructs a set of polygons that represent a height surface. In this case, we *mapped* the actual dataset extent to the xy-coordinates of a polygonal surface, and the height attribute of the dataset points to the z-coordinate. The 3D coordinates of the polygonal surface are the visual features that encode our dataset extent and height scalar attribute (see Figure 4.3).

When we read this description of the mapping operation, one question arises frequently: why do not we directly map our dataset $\mathcal{D} \in \mathbb{D}$ to the final Image $\in \mathbb{I}$, i.e., what is the use of the intermediate visual feature dataset $\mathcal{D}_V$? And yet, this part of the visualization pipeline is usually split in two steps: mapping (discussed in this section) and rendering (discussed in the next section). There are several good reasons for this splitting, as follows:

- purpose: mapping encodes explicit design decisions about *what*, and *how*, we want to visualize. Mapping typically converts "invisible" data to "visible" representations. In contrast, rendering simulates the physical process of lighting a "visible" 3D scene. In other words, mapping specifies those visual attributes that encode actual data, whereas rendering specifies the remaining visual attributes that users can tune to their taste to examine the 3D scene. In our height-plot example, the plot's geometry encodes data, so it is specified at the mapping stage. However, the color of the plot, the viewpoint, and the lighting parameters do not encode actual data, so the user can tune them while examining the 3D scene. This is exactly what happens when the user rotates the 3D plot to view it from different angles, for example.

- modularity: both mapping and rendering operations are quite complex. In practice, they consist of numerous substeps that have elaborate implementations. Separating the two operation types (and their implementations) modularizes the visualization pipeline and favors a clean design based on separation of concerns and software reuse. In particular, many graphics methods and their implementations, such as 3D rendering libraries, can be readily (re)used in a visualization application once the rendering step is separated from the mapping step.

Data mapping is probably the operation in the visualization pipeline that is most characteristic for the visualization process. The other operations of the visualization pipeline largely overlap with techniques present in other disciplines as well. Importing and filtering data can be largely thought of in terms of resampling, projection, restriction, and various other signal processing operations, at least in the case of sampled (scivis) datasets. The rendering operation is basically nothing more than applying computer graphics techniques, such as coordinate transformations, lighting, texture mapping, and rasterization. In contrast, data mapping targets the quite-specific visualization task of making the invisible and multidimensional data visible and low-dimensional, respectively. To do this, the data mapping function Map should try to satisfy several desirable properties.

First, Map has to be *injective*. That is, different values $x_1 \neq x_2$ from the dataset $\mathcal{D}$ to be visualized should be mapped to different visual attribute values $\text{Map}(x_1) \neq \text{Map}(x_2)$ in the visual feature dataset $\mathcal{D}_V$. This property is essential for the design of an effective visualization. To understand this, think of how users interpret the images produced by visualization applications. When we look at such an image, we want to be able to make some judgments about the original data or parts of it. For example, when we look at the image of the height plot of a function $z = f(x, y)$, we want to be able to say which is the height z of any point (x, y) in the function domain. In other words, we must be able to mentally *invert* the function Vis (or a part of this function) that encoded the initial data into the image features (see Equation (4.1)). For this, we must be able to invert some of the components of this function: the rendering Render, mapping Map, filtering Filter, and data importing Import operations. In practice, Filter and Import may be not invertible. Moreover, we may not want to invert these components of the visualization pipeline, for example when the elements we are really interested in getting insight into are individualized only after the filtering step. Still, if Map and Render are invertible, we can make judgments about the enriched datasets $\mathcal{D}$ that model our problem domain, using the rendered images. However, if neither Map nor Render is invertible, it is hard to make discriminative judgments about the data looking at the final image.

Let us detail the process of inversion a bit further. For a 3D scene containing easily recognizable shapes and good lighting and viewing parameters, our human vision system should be able to invert the Render function; that is, we should be able to recognize which are the 3D visual features $\mathcal{D}_V$ which are rendered in the 2D image. Of course, this requires the visual feature dataset $\mathcal{D}_V$ to be rendered appropriately. For example, a 3D scene rendered from a bad angle and with low lighting will produce an image in which we may not recognize any of the 3D visual features present in the scene, hence an image which does not tell us anything *insightful*.

We are thus left with inverting Map. For this, we should be able to mentally associate data attribute values $x_i \in \mathcal{D}$ with the visual features $\mathcal{D}_V$ that we have recognized in the rendered images. For example, when we see a point with high *elevation* on our 3D function plot, we should infer the function has a high *value* there (see Figure 4.3). Similarly, when we see a *red* spot on a weather heat map, we should infer the temperature is *high* there. If the function Map is injective, it is invertible over its whole value range, which is what we want.

Nevertheless, having Map invertible from a purely mathematical point of view is sometimes not enough. We must know how, and be able, to do the inversion mentally when we look at the pictures. For this, we must first and foremost know the significance of the visual attributes used in the rendering. That is, we must know how color, shape, position, texture, and the other visual attributes used in the mapping relate to data attributes of interest. This knowledge can be implicit, encoded in well-established conventions that are assumed to be known by all our users. An example would be visualizations that map some attribute to an icon orientation, shape, and size, such as weather maps that use special icons to denote wind speed and direction, sun intensity, and type and strength of rainfall. Other widely spread conventions include the orientation of cartographic maps, where the north is usually placed at the top, and the specific colormaps used to indicate relief forms on these maps, with their typical shades of blue (water courses and lakes), green (fields), light brown (medium heights), dark brown (mountains), and white (peaks), and similarly for traffic signs.

This knowledge can be provided also explicitly. For example, most visualizations that map numerical attributes to colors display a *colormap*, or color bar, which shows how colors correspond to values, and effectively assists the user in doing the mental color-to-value inverse mapping. Colormaps are discussed in detail further in Chapter 5.

A stronger, and equally useful property used in many visualization applications, is that the function Map tries to preserve distances when mapping from the data to the visual domain. That is, the distance $d(x_1, x_2)$ between any two values x_1 and x_2 in the dataset $\mathcal{D}$ should suggest the distance $d'(\text{Map}(x_1), \text{Map}(x_2))$ in the visual feature dataset $\mathcal{D}_V$. The simplest way to do this is to use a direct proportionality relationship between the two. This is useful when we are interested in visually comparing relative values rather than assessing absolute attribute values. For example, looking at our 3D elevation plot, we can tell the relative function values of various data points in the domain by visually comparing their heights in the 3D plot, even though we may have no exact idea about their absolute values. In practice, visualization applications often use *linear* mapping functions to map between some numerical attribute value and some visual attribute, such as height, position, luminance, or hue. Linear functions are quite effective, since they are invertible, simple to understand, and also preserve distances quite well between the data and visual spaces. However, linear functions do not work well when the range of distances to be mapped is very large and the data values are not uniformly spread over this range, but clustered in small subranges thereof.

Mapping functions used in visualizations where data is to be measured are sometimes called *measurement mappings* [Lanza and Marinescu 06]. Following measurement theory, a measurement mapping function must fulfill the *representation condition*, which states that such a mapping must "map entities into numbers and empirical relations into numerical relations in such a way that the empirical relations preserve and are preserved by the numerical relations" [Pfleeger et al. 05].

Let us note that in practice, many Map functions are, strictly speaking, not invertible over their entire range, and also do not preserve distances. This is not a problem as long as the introduced deviations do not make users draw incorrect conclusions from what they see. As always, evaluations of the effectiveness of a mapping function can only be made with respect to a concrete application domain, task, and user group. To give just a simple example, a colormap that translates scalar values to hues that works perfectly for most people may be quite ineffective for colorblind users.

Related to the inversion process is the difference between *data* and *information*. Following the discussion of Spence [Spence 07], we state that the main task of visualization is to derive information, i.e., useful facts that lead to conclusions about a certain problem, from data, i.e., recorded figures such as the signal samples on a grid. The mapping function should allow retrieving information, and not just raw data, from the produced pictures.

4.1.4   Rendering Data

The rendering operation is the final step of the visualization process. Rendering takes the 3D scene created by the mapping operation, together with several user-specified viewing parameters such as the viewpoint and lighting, and renders it to produce the desired images:

$$\text{Render} : \mathbb{D}_V \to \mathbb{I}. \qquad (4.6)$$

In typical visualization applications, viewing parameters are considered part of the rendering operation. This allows users to interactively navigate and examine the rendered result of a given visualization by rendering the 3D scene without having to recompute the mapping operation. Indeed, if the viewpoint changes but the 3D scene produced by the mapping stays the same, all we have to do is render the scene anew with the new viewing parameters, which is a relatively cheap operation.

4.2   Implementation Perspective

Putting it all together, we can describe the visualization pipeline as a composition of functions that have dataset arguments and values. If we denote by $\mathbb{D}$ the space of all our datasets then we have

$$Vis = F_1 \circ F_2 \circ \cdots \circ F_n, \qquad \text{where } F_i : \mathbb{D} \to \mathbb{D}. \qquad (4.7)$$

The various functions F_i perform the data importing, filtering, mapping, and rendering operations, in that order. The input of F_1 is the application's raw data, and the output of F_n is the final image. This model allows us to decompose each of the four stages into as many subfunctions as we need. This has several purposes. First, it is conceptually easier to think of complex operations, such as filtering, in terms of a composition of simple filter-like atomic operations that each address a specific task. Secondly, this favors modular, reusable software design and allows us to assemble visualization applications from a set of predefined functional components. In practice, there is no clear-cut separation as to which functions should be considered in the data importing, filtering, mapping, and rendering stages. Different visualization application implementations make different choices here. From a purely implementation perspective, all data types used in the pipeline (raw data, sampled datasets, and images) can be considered as datasets, and all pipeline operations can be modeled as functions that read and write datasets.

The design of a visualization application has two main parts. First, we choose the right data-processing operations, or functions F_i, that are needed in the visualization pipeline of a given application (see Equation (4.7)). Second, we choose the right dataset implementations $\mathcal{D}_j \in \mathbb{D}$ to connect the pipeline functions F_i. We outlined in Chapter 3 how to implement the datasets $\mathcal{D}_j$. We now briefly discuss how to implement the data processing operations F.

```
class F
{
public :
    void             setInput ( Grid * , int );
    Grid *           getOutput ( Grid * , int );
    virtual  void    execute () = 0;
protected :
    vector <Grid*>  inputs ;
    vector <Grid*>  outputs ;
};
```

Listing 4.1. Visualization operation implementation.

If we use an object-oriented design, we can implement the functions F as classes that have three properties:

- they read one or more *input* datasets $\mathcal{D}_i^{\text{inp}}$;

- they write one or more *output* datasets $\mathcal{D}_j^{\text{out}}$;

- they have an `execute()` operation that computes $\mathcal{D}_j^{\text{out}}$ given $\mathcal{D}_i^{\text{inp}}$.

The choice of letting the function F have several datasets as input (arguments) and output (results) is purely a practical one. The actual number, type, and meaning of the inputs and outputs depends on the semantics of the function itself. In implementation terms, a function F with these properties can be modeled as a class F with three methods as shown in Listing 4.1. The `setInput()` and `getOutput()` methods are simple accessors to the input and output datasets $\mathcal{D}_i^{\text{inp}}$ and $\mathcal{D}_j^{\text{out}}$, respectively. These are represented by `Grid` subclasses, such as uniform or unstructured datasets, which have been detailed in Chapter 3. In a basic implementation, the accessors would simply store references to the input and output datasets in the local `inputs` and `outputs` vectors of the F class. Concrete visualization operations would inherit from the abstract class F in Listing 4.1 and implement the actual `execute()` operation, which would read and write the input and output datasets in the `inputs` and `outputs` containers of the base class.

Given this implementation, a visualization application can be seen as a network of function, or operation, objects F_i that are connected with each other by sharing input and output `Grid` datasets. Figure 4.4 depicts such a simple application consisting of four function objects and four datasets.

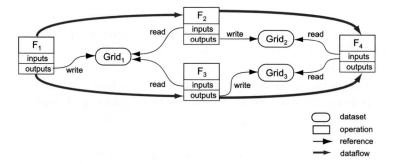

Figure 4.4. A visualization application as a network of objects.

The first operation F_1 has no input, as it imports the data into the pipeline from an external source. The operation F_4 has no output—we assume this is the rendering operation that produces the final image. Operations can have multiple inputs or outputs, and the same dataset can be read by multiple operations. Having the same dataset written by multiple operations is possible, too, but generally not recommended, as it complicates substantially both the implementation and the understanding of the design.

When we input new raw data into the pipeline, the application should first execute F_1, then F_2 and F_3 (in any order, since they do not depend on each other), followed by F_4. In the general case, consider the graph whose nodes are the operations F_i and edges are the data dependencies between operations, i.e., there is a directed edge F_i to F_j if F_i writes a dataset that is read by F_j. In Figure 4.4, this graph consists of four nodes $F_1 \cdots F_4$ and four edges (drawn in blue). If the application graph is acyclic, the execution is equivalent to calling the `execute()` method of all operations F_i in the order of the *topological sorting* of the graph [Cormen et al. 01]. This ensures that an operation is called only when all its inputs are available and up-to-date. Cyclic application graphs can also be accommodated but require more complex update mechanisms, for which reason they are less used in practice. The sequence of operation executions in this application model follow the "flow" of data from the importing operation to the final rendering operation. For this reason, this design is often called a *dataflow* application model.

Summarizing, a visualization application can be implemented as a network of operation objects that have dataset objects as inputs and outputs.

To execute the application, the operations are invoked in the dataflow order, starting with the data importing and ending with the rendering. However in principle sufficient, this model needs numerous additions to provide a scalable and efficient implementation for a visualization framework. Among the most notable additions, we mention reference counting and automatic memory management for the dataset and operation objects, typed inputs and outputs that ensure the dataset-operation compatibility, smart pipeline traversal methods that minimize the number of performed operation executions upon data changes, parallelization and distribution of execution on one or several machines, progressive update mechanisms that allow users to stop the pipeline execution at any desired moment, and serialization facilities for both the datasets and the application itself.

Several professional visualization frameworks implement these features and also provide hundreds of advanced data manipulation, mapping, and rendering operations.[1] Among these, we mention the Visualization Toolkit (VTK) [Schroeder et al. 04, Kitware, Inc. 04]. VTK is a professional visualization framework based on the previously discussed dataflow application model. VTK implements all the preceding advanced mechanisms, provides a huge set of visualization operations, has a highly efficient implementation in C++, and comes with bindings for several interpreted languages, such as Tcl, Java, and Python. Another major advantage of VTK is that it is an open-source product, which means it can be easily modified. As a consequence, VTK is used and continuously improved by a large developer community. However, it has to be noted that the great flexibility, genericity, and efficiency of the VTK toolkit come with a price in terms of complexity. Learning how to use VTK to develop visualization applications is an involved task that requires considerable programming experience. For readers interested in exploring the possibility of using VTK for their visualization applications, we refer to the several available books that describe both the principles and design of the toolkit [Schroeder et al. 04, Kitware, Inc. 04], as well as to the web resources containing the open source VTK software [Kitware, Inc. 06].

Building visualization applications is not restricted to programmers who write source code. Several more advanced methods offer simpler, more

---

[1]For more information on actual visualization software, see Appendix A.

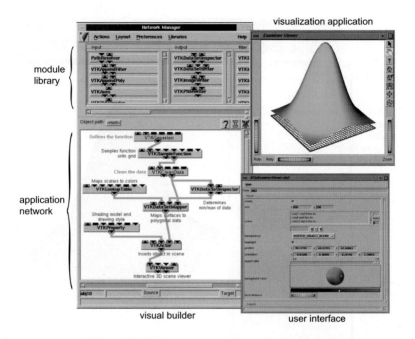

Figure 4.5. The height-plot application in the VISSION application builder [Telea and van Wijk 99].

intuitive application construction mechanisms. A popular development metaphor during the 1990s was visual application building, which has been implemented by several visual programming environments or visual application builders [AVS, Inc. 06, Walton 04, Telea and van Wijk 99]. In this paradigm, the end user constructs the dataflow application network by assembling iconic representations of the visualization operations. Icons describing the operations available in a number of module libraries are dragged onto a canvas workspace where their inputs and outputs are connected by means of mouse manipulations. Graphical user interfaces are provided by the environment to let users interactively control the parameters of the various visualization operations, thereby achieving the goal of interactive data exploration. When the user modifies such a parameter, the environment triggers a dataflow execution engine that updates the complete application network from the affected operations onward until a new image is rendered in the visualization window.

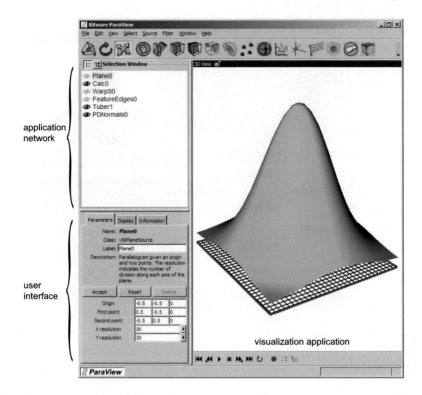

Figure 4.6. The height-plot application in the ParaView application builder [Henderson 04]

Figure 4.5 illustrates these concepts for the VISSION environment [Telea and van Wijk 99]. Many other visualization systems use a similar visual application construction model based on an underlying dataflow network. Figure 4.7 shows a snapshot from a different visualization application in the AVS visualization system [AVS, Inc. 06]. The main design elements, i.e., the module library, the application dataflow network, the user interfaces, and the actual visualization window, are easily recognizable.

A similar, albeit more recent type of visual application builder is illustrated in Figure 4.6 by the ParaView environment [Henderson 04]. Similar to VISSION in that they both use the VTK library and its underlying machinery to provide the actual implementation of visualization operations, ParaView features a more beginner-friendly end user interface. The free-

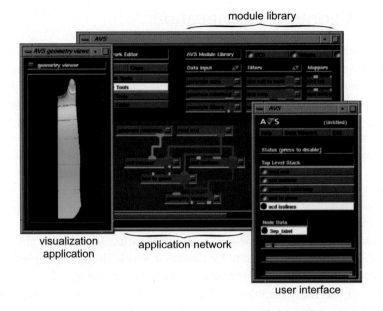

Figure 4.7. A visualization application in the AVS application builder [AVS, Inc. 06].

dom of constructing application networks of fully general graph topology by visual programming (present in VISSION) is traded in ParaView for a simpler application-building process using conventional GUI menus that is easier and faster to learn and use.

The main attraction of visual programming environments such as the ones illustrated in Figures 4.5 and 4.6 is that they allow rapid prototyping of visualization applications by users who have virtually no programming skills. However, such environments are less effective for the production of complex visualization applications. Many real-world visualization applications have typically hundreds of operations, contain an intricate control flow that cannot be easily modeled using the dataflow paradigm, and need complex custom code for their user interfaces. Moreover, the structure of such applications changes rarely after they have entered their mature development phase. All these factors make visual programming environments less suited for the creation of final applications, albeit they remain quite effective for the prototyping phase.

4.3   Algorithm Classification

At this point, we have all the theoretical and practical ingredients needed
to start learning about a number of specific visualization techniques, also
called *visualization algorithms*. The visualization practice of the last 15
years has generated a large number of visualization algorithms. If we look
at any general-purpose visualization software system, library, or framework, we find hundreds of such techniques. Clearly, we need a way to
organize these techniques so that we can learn them and refer to them
easily. There are several ways to classify visualization techniques. Most
existing classifications in use are based in some way or another on the
way the visualization techniques interact with each other as parts of the
same visualization pipeline. Any taxonomy is based on some commonality
that its elements share. In the case of visualization algorithms, they share
the input and output datasets by means of which they are coupled in the
visualization pipeline, as described earlier in this chapter.

One of the most intuitive and widespread taxonomies of visualization
techniques is based on the type of attributes these techniques work with.
Following the attribute terminology introduced in Section 3.6, we talk thus
about *scalar*, *vector*, and *tensor visualization methods*. These methods are
discussed in Chapters 5, 6, and 7, respectively. Readers may have noticed
that Section 3.6 introduced *color* attributes as a separate class. Color visualization methods are essentially either rendering methods, which we do
not discuss separately, or image processing methods, which we shall treat
separately in Chapter 9. Finally, the non-numeric attribute types, such as
text, graphs, or general data tables, are targeted by information visualization (infovis) methods, which we shall briefly overview in Chapter 11.

As in any taxonomy, there are elements that do not easily fit our
attribute-based classification of visualization methods. For example, there
are specific visualization methods that deal with the underlying sampling
domain representation rather than with the attributes. We classify these
methods in a special category called *domain modeling methods*. Examples
of such methods are grid warping techniques that change the location of
the sample points, cutting and selection techniques that extract a subset of
the sampling domain as a separate dataset, or resampling techniques that
change the cells and/or the basis functions used to reconstruct the data.
These methods form the subject of Chapter 8.

Alternative classifications exist as well. Schroeder et al. propose in a *structural* classification that groups visualization techniques by the type of dataset ingredient they change into *geometric* techniques (that alter the geometry, or locations, of sample points), *topological* techniques (that alter the grid cells), *attributes* techniques (that alter the attributes only), and *combined* techniques (that alter several of a dataset's ingredients) [Schroeder et al. 04]. Yet another type of classification was proposed by Marcus et al. in terms of a five-dimensional model containing the following dimensions [Marcus et al. 03]:

- task: what is the task to be completed?

- audience: which are the users?

- target: what is the data to visualize?

- medium: what is rendering (drawing) support?

- representation: what are the graphical attributes (shapes, colors, textures) used?

This classification is useful to describe not only visualization algorithms, but also entire visualization applications.

Besides the classifications discussed here, in practice, virtually every visualization software framework proposes its own classification that reflects either some user-centered aspect of the software interface or some implementation-oriented aspect. However, our practice has shown that many users naturally think of (scientific) visualization methods in terms of scalar, vector, tensor, and domain modeling algorithms. Hence, we shall use this classification in our presentation of the most widely used visualization techniques.

4.4 Conclusion

In this chapter, we have described the structure of the visualization process, or visualization pipeline, both from a conceptual and an implementation point of view. In this section, we shall try to draw several conclusions about this process.

First and foremost, although our aim has been to present the structure of a visualization application from a modular perspective, where every module in the pipeline has a clearly defined function, the situation in practice is often quite far from this model. There is no clear-cut separation of the visualization stages of data importing, filtering, mapping, and rendering. Still, the main separation point in the visualization pipeline takes place at the moment when the abstract data becomes potentially visible, i.e., after the mapping stage. This characteristic is present in all visualization applications. Further pipeline refinements, such as distinguishing data importing from data filtering, are less obvious. Actual applications can separate and structure the pipeline in different ways, depending on design and implementation considerations that go beyond the topic of this general discussion.

A second point of interest concerns the desirable properties of a given visualization pipeline structuring. From an implementation point of view, the elements that are assembled to form the pipeline should meet the usual requirements of software components: modularity, reusability, simplicity, extensibility, minimality, and generality. As in any software engineering domain, meeting all these requirements is clearly a daunting task and is in general not optimally possible, given the extremely wide range of possible visualization operations and datasets.

A third point of interest concerns the properties of the mapping function. The effectiveness of a given visualization is critically determined by this function. In general, the mapping function should be invertible, so we can grasp the data properties by looking at its visual mapping, and unambiguous, so we do not doubt about what we see. There is, however, no silver bullet in designing such mapping functions. Constructing a "good" data-to-image mapping is as much of a science as an art. From the scientific arena, we can reuse elements of sampling and signal theory, visual perception, computer vision, and cognitive sciences. Visualization is also a craft or an art, as such choices are not always deterministic. In this respect, aesthetics is essential to a good visualization, as its users must be attracted to spend effort to study and work with it.

In the remaining chapters, we shall present concrete instances of the visualization pipeline described in this chapter, in terms of several visualization methods for scalar, vector, tensor, image, volumetric, and abstract data.

Chapter 5

Scalar Visualization

$\mathbf{V}$ISUALIZING scalar data is frequently encountered in science, engineering, and medicine, but also in daily life. Recalling from Section 3.6, scalar datasets, or scalar fields, represent functions $f : \mathcal{D} \to \mathbb{R}$, where $\mathcal{D}$ is usually a subset of $\mathbb{R}^2$ or $\mathbb{R}^3$. There exist many scalar visualization techniques, both for 2D and 3D datasets. In this chapter, we present a number of the most popular scalar visualization techniques: color mapping, contouring, and height plots. We start in Section 5.1 with color mapping and then discuss the design of effective colormaps in Section 5.2. In Section 5.3, we discuss contouring in two and three dimensions. In Section 5.4, we present the height plots.

5.1   Color Mapping

Color mapping is probably the most widespread visualization method for scalar data. Putting it simply, color mapping associates a color with every scalar value. Using the visualization pipeline terminology introduced in Chapter 4, color mapping is a mapping function $m : \mathcal{D} \to \mathcal{D}_V$. The geometry of $\mathcal{D}_V$ is the same as $\mathcal{D}$, but with a color that depends on the scalar data defined on $\mathcal{D}$. In other words, this means that color mapping is not concerned with creating specific shapes to visualize data, but with coloring such shapes on which scalar data is defined to show the data values. For every point of the domain of interest $\mathcal{D}$, color mapping applies a function $c : \mathbb{R} \to$ Colors that colors that point with a color $c(s)$ which depends on the scalar value s at that point.

There are several ways to define such a scalar-to-color function c. We shall discuss two of the most common forms: color look-up tables and transfer functions. Color look-up tables are the simplest way to implement color mapping. Simply put, a color look-up table C, also called a *colormap*, is a uniform sampling of the color-mapping function c:

$$C = \{c_i\}_{i=1..N}, \quad \text{where} \quad c_i = c\left(\frac{(N-i)f_{\min} + if_{\max}}{N}\right). \quad (5.1)$$

In practice, Equation (5.1) is implemented as a table of N colors $c_1, \ldots, c_N$, which are associated with the scalar dataset values f, assumed to be in the range $[f_{\min}, f_{\max}]$. Knowing the scalar range is important, as it allows us to construct a color mapping with a clear and simple meaning: the colors c_i with low indices i in the colormap represent low scalar values close to $f_{\min}$, whereas colors with indices close to N in the colormap represent high scalar values close to $f_{\max}$. In practice, $f_{\min}$ and $f_{\max}$ can either be determined automatically by examining the sampled dataset values or be prescribed by the user. In the latter case, dataset values outside the prescribed range $[f_{\min}, f_{\max}]$ are clamped to this range to yield valid colors in the given colormap. Scaling the dataset values to their range works well when we can determine this range in advance of the visualization. However, imagine an application where we want to visualize a time-dependent scalar field $f(t)$ with $t \in [t_{\min}, t_{\max}]$. The typical solution is to visualize the color-mapped values of the scalar field $f(t)$ for consecutive values of t in $[t_{\min}, t_{\max}]$. However, if we do not know $f(t)$ for all values t before we start the visualization, we cannot compute the absolute scalar range $[f_{\min}, f_{\max}]$ to apply Equation (5.1). Moreover, even when this is possible, we may not want to do so. If the range $[f_{\min}(t_i), f_{\max}(t_i)]$ of a time step $t_i \in [t_{\min}, t_{\max}]$ is much smaller than the absolute range $[f_{\min}, f_{\max}]$, normalizing f to the absolute range will show little detail as we look at the individual frames. In such situations, a better solution might be to normalize the scalar range separately for every time frame $f(t)$. Of course, this implies drawing different color legends for every time frame as well.

Besides using a sampled scalar-to-color function to a discrete look-up table, one can also define the function c analytically, if desired. Since colors are usually represented as triplets in either the RGB or HSV color systems, this is usually done by defining three scalar functions $c_R : \mathbb{R} \to \mathbb{R}$, $c_G : \mathbb{R} \to \mathbb{R}$, and $c_B : \mathbb{R} \to \mathbb{R}$, whereby $c = (c_R, c_G, c_B)$. The functions c_R, c_G, and c_B are also called *transfer functions*. More on transfer functions will be presented in Chapters 9 and 10 when we discuss image and volume visualization. In practice, one uses predefined look-up tables when there is no need to change the individual colors at runtime and transfer functions when the investigation goals require dynamically changing the color-mapping function.

5.2   Designing Effective Colormaps

The main challenge for visualizations using color mapping is to design an *effective* colormap C. But what does it mean for a colormap to be effective? In terms of the mapping operation described in Section 4.1.3, a color-mapping visualization is effective if, by looking at the generated colors, we can easily and accurately make statements about the original scalar dataset that was color mapped. Different types of statements and analysis goals require different types of colormaps. For example, a common goal in scalar visualization is to tell the absolute values of a given dataset. To do this, we must be able to mentally invert the color-mapping function c; that is, look at a color of some point in the visual domain $\mathcal{D}_V$ and tell its scalar value f. To be able to do this, we must know the color-mapping function c. In practice, this is achieved by drawing a *color legend*. This is usually a color strip containing all the colors c_i in the colormap with associated labels that indicate the values f for all or a number of the depicted colors. By looking at an actual visualization and comparing its colors with the labeled colors in the colormap, we are able to infer the scalar values of the depicted dataset.

However, the preceding mechanism has some conditions to succeed. First, the color-mapping function c must be invertible, as explained in Section 4.1.3. This requires the function to be injective, meaning that every scalar value in the range $[f_{\min}, f_{\max}]$ is associated with a unique color. The colors used must be unique in the eye of the beholder. It is not sufficient that the colors have different numerical (e.g., RGB) values. We must also be able to easily perceive them *visually* as being different if we want to be

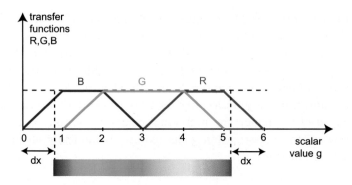

Figure 5.1. Construction of rainbow colormap.

able to map them to scalars using the color legend. Second, the spatial resolution of the visualized dataset must be high enough as compared to the speed of variation of the scalar data f that we are able to visually distinguish separate regions having different colors.

As already stated, different analysis goals pose different constraints on the colormap design. In some applications, we want to attract the attention of the user to certain value ranges or individual values. We can achieve this by designing a colormap that uses particularly salient colors for those values, such as bright, warm, saturated colors, and dull, cold, low-luminance colors for the remaining values. Colormap design can also be influenced by application or domain-specific conventions and traditions. For example, many engineering and weather forecast applications use a blue-to-red colormap, often called the *rainbow* colormap (see Figure 5.1). This colormap is based on the intuition that blue, a "cold" color, suggests low values, whereas red, a "hot" color, suggests high values. We can construct a rainbow colormap using three transfer functions R, G, B, shown in Figure 5.1. The rainbow colormap is constructed by the code in Listing 5.1. This constructs three trapezium-shaped transfer functions R, G, and B, ranging from zero to one. The functions are centered at different locations on the scalar value (horizontal) axis, which determines the blue-to-red colormap structure. The functions overlap almost everywhere, which makes the hues in the colormap vary smoothly. The parameter $dx \in [0, 1]$ controls the amount of pure blue and red used at the beginning and the end of the colormap, respectively, which gives more aesthetically

```
void c(float f, float& R, float& G, float& B)
{
    const float dx = 0.8;
    f = (f<0)? 0 : (f>1)? 1 : f;              //clamp f in [0,1]
    g = (6-2*dx)*f + dx;                      //scale f to [dx, 6 - dx]
    R = max(0,(3-fabs(g-4)-fabs(g-5))/2);
    G = max(0,(4-fabs(g-2)-fabs(g-4))/2);
    B = max(0,(3-fabs(g-1)-fabs(g-2))/2);
}
```

Listing 5.1. Rainbow colormap construction.

pleasing results than a colormap containing only mixed hues. In terms of the interpolation theory discussed in Chapter 3, these transfer functions can be seen as piecewise linear basis functions used to interpolate between their corresponding primary colors.

In some applications, we want to emphasize the variations of the data rather than absolute data values. This is useful when we are interested in detecting the dataset regions where data changes the most quickly or, alternatively, stays constant. For this goal, we can use a colormap containing two or more alternating colors that are perceptually very different. When the data values change, the colors change abruptly, yielding easily detectable band-like patterns in the visualization. Figure 5.2 illustrates this design. In the left image, we visualize a scalar function $f(x, y) = e^{-10(x^4+y^4)}$, whose shape is quite similar to the Gaussian shown in Figure 2.1. Instead of a height plot, we now use a grayscale colormap that maps the function value range $[0, 1]$ to 30 distinct shades of gray. The result is a smooth image (see Figure 5.2(a)). If we use now a colormap that maps the same value range to an alternating pattern of black and white colors, we obtain the zebra-like result shown in Figure 5.2(b). Thin, dense stripes indicate regions of high variation speed of the function, whereas the flat areas in the center and at the periphery of the image indicate regions of slower variation.

Many other colormap designs are possible. For example, geographical applications often encode landscape height using a particular colormap that contains colors which suggest the typical relief forms at different heights, including blue (sea, lowest), green (fields), beige (hills), brown (mountains), and white (mountain peaks, highest). In other applications, such as classical medical imaging, the simple luminance colormap already demonstrated

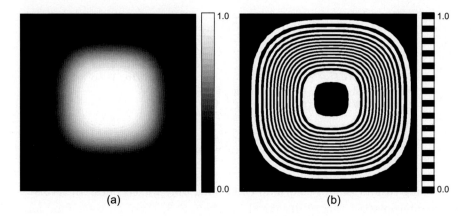

Figure 5.2. Visualizing the scalar function $e^{-10(x^4+y^4)}$ with (a) a luminance colormap and (b) a zebra colormap. The luminance colormap shows absolute values, whereas the zebra colormap emphasizes rapid value variations.

in Figure 5.2(a) works best. Figure 5.3 shows a color-mapped slice from an MRI volumetric dataset.[1] For the color mapping, we used both a gray value (luminance) scale and a rainbow colormap. Slicing is explained further in Section 8.1.2. Most medical specialists, but also nonspecialists, would agree that the grayscale produces a much easier-to-follow, less-confusing visualization on which details are easier to spot than when using the rainbow colormap.

The previous example brings up an important design element of colormaps. The rainbow colormap is based on the assumption that "warm" colors, such as yellow and red, are perceived as being associated with higher data values, whereas "cold" colors such as blue suggest low values. This assumption is based on the traditional interpretation of the rainbow colormap as a heat, or temperature, map. While this might be the intuitive perception for visualizing a temperature dataset, this association is much harder and more unnatural to do in case of, for example, a medical dataset. A good design rule is, hence, to use a colormap whose hue ordering is naturally coupled with the type of data and application domain the data stems

---

[1]More on MRI and medical visualization will be presented in Chapter 10.

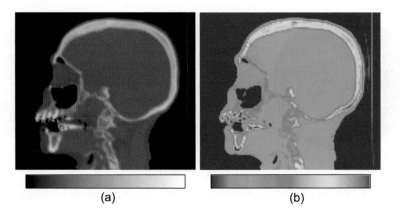

Figure 5.3. Medical visualization with luminance and rainbow colormaps.

from. For medical visualizations, for example, the black-to-white colormap can be more effective than the rainbow one, as these grayscales map intuitively to the ones visible in X-ray photographs.

Besides the invertibility requirement for colormaps, visualization applications often also require a *linearity* constraint to be satisfied. To explain this, assume, for example, that we visualize a linear function $f(x) = x$ with the rainbow colormap. The result of the visualization is actually identical to the color bar displayed at the bottom of Figure 5.3(b). It can be argued that this colormap, which essentially maps value to hue, is not linear. Some users perceive colors to change "faster" per spatial unit in the higher yellow-to-red range than in the lower blue-to-cyan range. Hence, a linear signal would be perceived by the user as nonlinear, with possibly undesirable consequences.[2]

Another important aspect of the color-mapping technique is the relationship between the colormap design, scalar data variation speed, and domain sampling frequency. Let us illustrate this by means of an example. Figure 5.4 shows a sphere geometry on which a periodic sine function is visualized with a rainbow colormap. The mesh is overlaid on top of the visualization to emphasize the sampling frequency. The periodic band structure of the function is clearly visible in Figure 5.4(a), where the sphere

---

[2]Note that the linearity requirement on colormaps is equivalent to an invertibility of the colormap's first derivative.

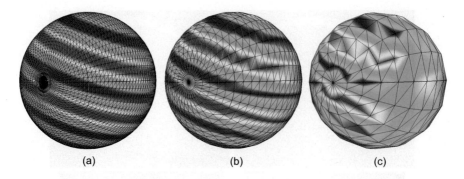

Figure 5.4. Texture-based color mapping. The sphere geometry is sampled with (a) 64 × 64 points, (b) 32 × 32 points, and (c) 16 × 16 points.

is sampled at a 64 × 64 resolution. However, the structure starts getting noisy as we decrease the sampling resolution (Figure 5.4(b), 32 × 32 samples). If the resolution is decreased further, we obtain a completely incorrect visualization (Figure 5.4(c)) that may suggest a completely different function than the actual one to the unprepared user. The problem here is caused by the way color mapping is implemented. In this example, the color mapping (see Equation (5.1)) is performed only at the grid vertices. For every vertex, the resulting index into the color look-up table is stored as a texture coordinate. Once these are computed, the surface cells are rendered as polygons textured with a 1D texture containing the colormap. 1D textures work similarly to the 2D textures described in Chapter 2, with the exception that they are described by a single texture coordinate and they are stored as a 1D image, i.e., a vector of colored pixels.

The advantage of the texture-based color mapping implementation described previously is that it produces reasonable results even for a sparsely sampled dataset. However, this technique requires rendering texture-based polygons, an option that may not be available on low-end graphics hardware or in situations when we want to use the available texture for other purposes. A second implementation of color mapping, presented next, does not require using texture. Just as in the previous case, color mapping (see Equation (5.1)) is performed only at the grid vertices. Instead of texture coordinates, the actual colors are now stored as color attributes for each vertex. Next, the surface cells are rendered as colored polygons. The color is interpolated at every pixel by the polygon rendering machinery.

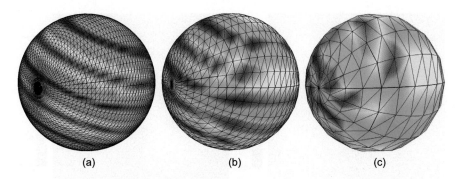

Figure 5.5. Vertex-based color mapping. The sphere geometry is sampled with (a) 64 × 64 points, (b) 32 × 32 points, and (c) 16 × 16 points.

This vertex-based color mapping implementation is probably the most widespread one due to its simplicity and direct support by even low-end graphics hardware. Figure 5.5 shows the result of this method for the same dataset and sampling resolution as in Figure 5.4. Although the vertex-based method is simpler to implement and less demanding in graphics resources than the texture-based method, it visibly produces more artifacts at the same sampling resolution as compared to the texture-based method. The reason for this resides in the fact the two methods interpolate two different quantities at every rendered polygon pixel. The texture-based method interpolates an *index* into the colormap and, thus, applies the index-to-color mapping, i.e., the function c in Equation (5.1), separately at every rendered pixel. The vertex-based method interpolates the mapped *color* itself and, thus, applies the index-to-color mapping only at the polygon vertices. Practically, the vertex-based method skips colors from the colormap if the scalar data varies too quickly over the dataset domain, whereas the texture-based method does not.

Another important aspect in colormap design is the choice of the number of colors N. Choosing a small N would inevitably lead to the *color banding* effect. This is well-known to any computer user who has tried to reduce the number of colors in a color image using image processing programs. Figure 5.6 demonstrates color banding on a simple scalar dataset. The scalar data ranges between -0.23 and 0.23. The dataset is visualized four times using the same rainbow look-up table, each time with fewer colors in the look-up table. As the number of different colors in the look-up

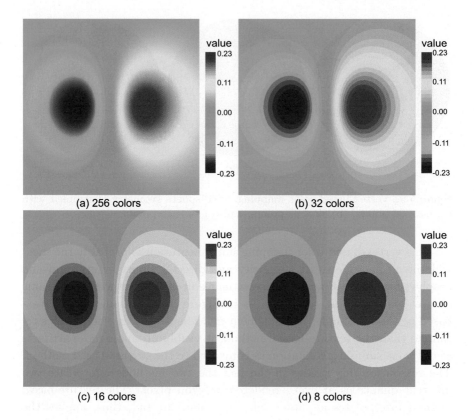

Figure 5.6. Color banding caused by a small number of colors in a look-up table.

table decreases, equal color bands become visible in both the image and the color legend. Mathematically, color banding produces artifacts identical to undersampling the scalar signal range. Indeed, when we use, for example, just 32 colors to visualize the dataset in Figure 5.6(b), the effect is practically the same as if we first undersampled our scalar signal to 5 bits, and then visualized it via a colormap with a high number of colors. When we visualize a continuous dataset, color banding is usually not desirable, as it creates discrete visual artifacts in the rendered image that do not reflect any discreteness of the input data. As demonstrated in Figure 5.6, color banding can be avoided by increasing the number of colors in the colormap and ensuring there are no sharp perceptual transitions in the colormap. The more quickly the data varies spatially, the smoother the colormap has to be to avoid color banding. Typical scalar visualization applications would use between 64 and 256 different colors in a colormap, the preference being for more rather than fewer colors.

Colormap design is also influenced by geometric factors. Not all colors are equally strongly perceived when displayed on surfaces that have the same area. Also, perceiving a color accurately is strongly influenced by the colors displayed in neighboring areas. In other words, densely packed colors are not perceived separately under a certain spatial scale, but blended together by the human eye. This becomes an issue when the areas in question are very small. In some cases, the eye will not even be able to separate individual colors as such. Whereas this situation is generally undesirable, a useful application of the limited power of separation of human vision is the RGB color mixing mechanism used by many devices such as computer displays and TV screens. Here, a large spectrum of colors is generated by displaying closely packed, small-scale dots colored in the primary red, green, and blue hues, with various intensities. A similar system is used by the dithering processes in the printing technology.

Another factor in colormap design is the user group. While most users would feel comfortable with colormaps containing a large variety of hues, 6 to 10 percent of all men would not be able to correctly separate red from green hues. This and other forms of colorblindness should be taken into account when designing colormaps in critical applications or applications intended to be used by a large public.

Yet another factor in colormap design is the medium used to present the visualization. Computer screens (CRT or LCD), printed materials (matte or glossy), and projectors have quite different ways of reproducing and displaying color. It is hard to design rich colormaps, containing more than a dozen colors, that look the same on all these devices. A very common mistake made in practice is to use hue-based colormaps, such as the rainbow colormap, and display the resulting visualizations on luminance-based devices, such as black-and-white printed material. A large amount of detail immediately disappears in such cases, such as red and green colors, which look quite different on a computer screen, becoming indistinguishable from a luminance point of view on a black-and-white printout.

Color mapping, as described previously, is a method that generates color values from scalar values by means of a colormap or color transfer

function. A related set of techniques involves modifying the gray values of
a grayscale image or colors of a color image in order to emphasize details
of interest. Although such techniques involve some common algorithmic
and design elements, they are of a fundamentally different nature, as they
work on a the colors of an existing image rather than in the process of
creating colors from scalars. We shall discuss such techniques separately in
the context of image processing (see Section 9.3.1).

Designing effective colormaps is a complex task that is as much a science
as an art. This involves knowledge of the application domain conventions,
typical data distribution, visualization goals, general perception theory, intended output devices, and the user preferences. There is no universally
effective colormap. For a concrete application, the best advice is to use the
typical colormaps accepted in practice for that given domain or industry.
Generally, for guidelines for designing colormaps, we refer to dedicated literature on perception in visualization [Ware 04], color science [Stone 03],
and the use of color in information visualization [Card et al. 99, Bederson
and Shneiderman 03]. A good starting reference for the various problems
and subtleties involved in the process of designing colormaps for visualizing scalar data is the paper of Bergman et al. [Bergman et al. 95], which
also describes a rule-based mechanism and tool for assisting users with
selecting effective colormaps for different types of datasets. For another
extensive discussion of issues involved in color mapping both continuous
and categorical attributes, see the book of Colin Ware on information visualization [Ware 04]. For a general discussion of color science, a good
starting point is the book of Stone on digital color [Stone 03]. For the
design of colormaps that have a few (5–10) different colors, one can use the
ColorBrewer tool resource [Brewer and Harrower 07]. Among other features, *ColorBrewer* can generate colormaps tuned for encoding sequential
and qualitative value types and optimized for different types of output,
such as monochrome or color printer, projector, laptop, and monitor.

5.3   Contouring

In the previous section, we described how 2D scalar fields can be visualized using the simple colormap technique. We also discussed how using
too few colors in a colormap leads to undesired color banding effects (see

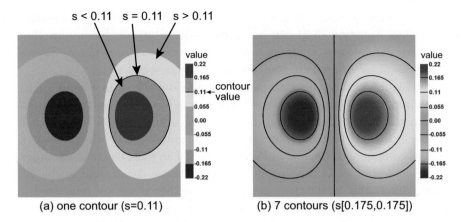

(a) one contour (s=0.11)   (b) 7 contours (s[0.175,0.175])

Figure 5.7. Relationship between color banding and contouring.

Figure 5.6). However, color banding is related to fundamental and widely used visualization technique called *contouring*. To understand contouring, think of the meaning of the sharp color transitions that separate the color bands in Figure 5.7(a).

Consider, for instance, the transition between the yellow and orange bands; that is, all points in the figure that are on the border separating two colors. As can be seen from the associated color legend, the points in the yellow band have scalar values s above 0.11, whereas the points in the orange band have scalar values s below 0.11 (see also Equation (5.1)). Hence, the points located on the transition itself have the scalar value $s = 0.11$. Note that, for this reasoning to hold, we must assume that our dataset does not exhibit a sudden "jump" localized exactly on the extent of the transition itself. This holds for all datasets that represent the sampling of a continuous signal.

The points located on such a transition, drawn in black in Figure 5.7(a), are called a *contour* line, or *isoline*. Formally, a contour line C is defined as all points p in a dataset $\mathcal{D}$ that have the same scalar value, or isovalue $s(p) = x$, or

$$C(x) = \{p \in \mathcal{D} | s(p) = x\}. \tag{5.2}$$

The name "isoline" also reflects this definition, as in Greek, *isos* means "the same" or "equal." The name "contour line" stems from one of the first applications of this technique in cartography. Contour lines are drawn on land maps to explicitly indicate all points that have the same altitude. Note that Equation (5.2) can be applied also in higher dimensions than two. For 3D datasets, contours are 2D surfaces called *isosurfaces*. Several examples of isosurfaces are provided later in this section.

In Figure 5.7(b), we show the same scalar dataset as in Figure 5.7(a), visualized with the same rainbow colormap. However, this time the colormap has 256 entries, instead of only eight as in Figure 5.7(a). This is visible in the fact that the color legend itself exhibits a smoother hue variation as compared to the one in Figure 5.7(a). The right image is smoother, which is desirable, as it helps us distinguish more detail than in the left image. Yet, this image does not help us further if we are interested in easily and quickly distinguishing which are the points that have a specific scalar value of interest, e.g., $s = 0.11$. This task was easily done on the left image, because the color map used there exhibited a clear hue transition from dark blue to cyan located precisely at this value. We can actually combine the advantages of contours and color mapping by simply drawing contours for all values of interest on top of a color-mapped image that uses a rich colormap. The result is shown in Figure 5.7(b), where we have drawn seven contours for scalar values equally spaced in $[-0.165, 0.165]$.

Besides indicating points where the data has specific values, contours can also tell us something about the data variation itself. Assume that we have a set of contours for scalar values that are equally spaced in the *scalar* domain, such as in Figure 5.7(b). Clearly, the contours themselves are not equally spaced in the *spatial* domain. Areas where contours are closer to each other, such as in the center of the image, indicate higher variations of the scalar data. Indeed, the scalar distance between consecutive contours (which is constant) divided by the spatial distance between the same contours (which is not constant) is exactly the derivative of the scalar signal.

Contours have a number of important properties. Consider Figure 5.8, which shows a two-variable function $z = f(x, y)$ with the familiar elevation plot technique. Over the function graph, three isolines are drawn, for three different values, v_0 (blue), v_1 (red), and v_2 (yellow). The isolines are translated on the vertical (z) axis above the xy plane with their corresponding values v, instead of being drawn in the dataset domain (xy plane) as in Figure 5.7. In this situation, the isolines correspond with the intersection of the function graph with horizontal planes $z = v_i$, $i \in \{0, 1, 2\}$.

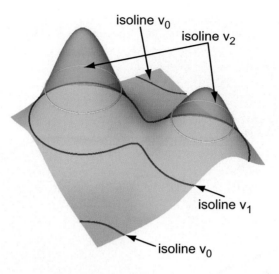

Figure 5.8. Isoline properties.

Several properties of isolines are noticeable in Figure 5.8. First, isolines can be either closed curves, such as the yellow isoline, or open curves, such as the blue and red isolines. Isolines never stop inside the dataset itself— they either close upon themselves, such as the yellow one, or stop when reaching the dataset border, such as the blue and red ones. Second, an isoline never intersects (crosses) itself, nor does it intersect an isoline for another scalar value. Hence, isolines for different values are "nested" inside each other, as we can see in Figure 5.7. These properties always hold for a (piecewise) continuous dataset as defined in Section 3.1. In other words, the scalar data does not have "jumps" between points that are close in the dataset domain. Finally, consider Figure 5.9, which shows the same scalar function and its isolines as in Figure 5.8, this time viewed from above along the z-axis. The vector field displayed in the image shows the gradient of the scalar function. This figure demonstrates an important property of the contours, namely that they are perpendicular to the gradient of the contoured function. This property is not surprising: the gradient of a function is the direction of the function's *maximal* variation, whereas contours are points of equal function value, so the tangent to a contour is the direction of the function's *minimal* (zero) variation. Another example

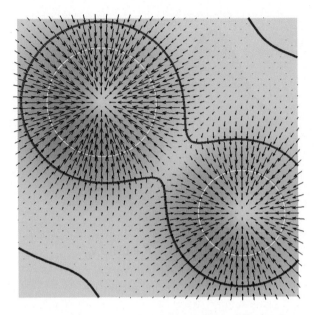

Figure 5.9. The gradient of a scalar field is perpendicular on the field's contours.

showing how the gradient of a scalar field is perpendicular to its isolines is given in Section 9.4.6.

How can we compute contours, given a discrete, sampled dataset $\mathcal{D}$? Since this dataset is defined as a set of cells carrying node or cell scalar data, plus additional basis functions (Chapter 2), it is natural to try to construct contours in the same discrete cell space. In the actual construction technique, presented next, we shall use an important property of isolines. We have seen in Section 3.1 that the reconstruction of a sampled dataset with piecewise linear basis functions is a piecewise linear function itself. The graph of this function is piecewise linear, too. Being the intersection of the function graph with a horizontal plane, the isoline of a discrete dataset is, therefore, piecewise linear. Since an isoline has topological dimension 2, this is a polyline.

The basic algorithm for constructing an isoline is quite simple. The principle is illustrated by the simple 5×5 cell grid in Figure 5.10, where we construct the isoline for the value $v = 0.48$. For every cell c of the dataset, we test whether the isoline intersects the respective cell, as follows. For

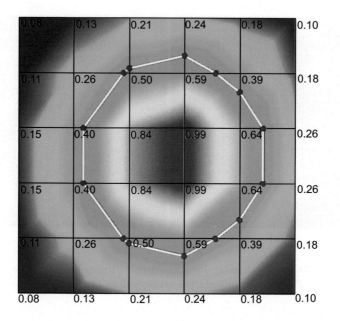

Figure 5.10. Constructing the isoline for the scalar value $v = 0.48$. The figure indicates scalar values at the grid vertices.

every edge e of the cell c, we test whether the isoline value v is between the scalar vertex attributes v_i and v_j corresponding to the edge end points p_i and p_j. If the test succeeds, the isoline intersects e at a point

$$q = \frac{p_i(v_j - v) + p_j(v - v_i)}{v_j - v_i}. \tag{5.3}$$

This result is obtained by expressing q as a linear interpolation of p_i and p_j with the same weights used to express v as a linear interpolation of v_i and v_j. We repeat the previous procedure for all edges of our current cell and finally obtain a set of intersection points $S = \{q_i\}$ of the isoline with the cell. For the sample dataset in Figure 5.10, these points are drawn in purple. The set S contains at least two points, since an isoline cannot enter a cell without exiting it, as discussed previously, and at most as many points as cell edges, since the dataset is linearly interpolated along every cell edge, so there can be at most one intersection point along every edge. Next, we must connect these points together to obtain the actual isoline.

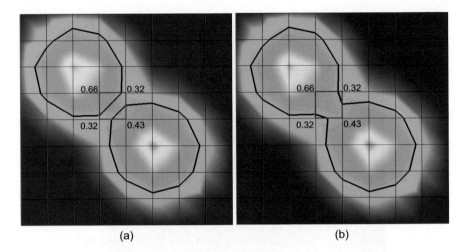

Figure 5.11. Contour ambiguity for a quad cell (drawn in red). The isovalue is equal to 0.37. The figures indicate the scalar values at the cell vertices.

Since we know that our isoline is piecewise linear over a cell, we can use line segments to connect these points. These lines are drawn in white in Figure 5.10. If S contains exactly two points, there is no problem. However, S can contain more points, as illustrated in Figure 5.11 for the quad cell marked in red, which has four intersection points.

In this case, exactly two possibilities exist for connecting the four intersection points, shown in the left and right images in Figure 5.11. Note that the other connection possibilities are invalid, as they would lead to intersecting contours. The first possibility (see Figure 5.11(a)) creates two separate contour loops, whereas the second possibility (see Figure 5.11(b)) creates a single contour loop. In practice, an implementation may choose either of the connection possibilities separately for each cell. If one has additional knowledge on the contour topology, e.g., that it must have a single connected component, this information can be used to discriminate between the two connection possibilities. When we use a triangular mesh, such ambiguities do not exist. This may suggest that we could eliminate ambiguities from quad meshes by splitting all quad cells into two triangles each. However, the ambiguity is now shifted to the quad-splitting process. For example, the isoline configuration inside the marked cell in

Figure 5.11(a) would be produced when using two triangles obtained by splitting the quad cell diagonally from the lower-left to the upper-right vertex. Similarly, the configuration in Figure 5.11(a) would be produced when using two triangles obtained by splitting the quad cell diagonally from the upper-left to the lower-right vertex.

It is now clear that contouring needs to have at least piecewise linear, C^1 datasets as input. This means that we cannot directly contour image data, for example, which is actually a uniform grid with piecewise constant (C^0) interpolation. Resampling image datasets to piecewise linear datasets can be easily done, as explained in Section 3.9.1. However, note that this has the hidden effect of changing the continuity assumptions on the dataset from piecewise constant to piecewise linear. While this should not pose problems in many cases, there are situations when such changes in assumptions can lead to highly incorrect visualizations. An example of such a situation is discussed in Section 9.4.6.

A final issue to be considered is the complexity of computing contours. If we make no specific assumptions about a dataset then a contour for a given isovalue can pass through every single cell of that dataset. For each cell, we must test whether the isovalue intersects every cell edge and, if so, compute the exact intersection location using Equation (5.3). Hence, it is important to reduce the number of operations done per cell. The most popular method that accomplishes this is the *marching squares* method, which works on 2D datasets with quad cells, and its *marching cubes* variant, which works on 3D datasets with hexahedral cells [Lorensen and Cline 87]. These methods are discussed next.

5.3.1   Marching Squares

The marching squares method begins by determining the *topological state* of the current cell with respect to the isovalue. A cell's topological state describes which of the cell edges are intersected by the contour and how these intersection points are to be connected with lines to yield the isoline fragments. To simplify the description, we shall say that a cell vertex p_i is *inside* the isoline if its scalar value v_i is smaller than the isovalue v, and *outside* the isoline if v_i is greater than v. The situation $v_i = v$ can be subsumed by either the inside or outside case. A quad cell has, thus, $2^4 = 16$ different topological states. The state of a quad cell can be represented by a 4-bit

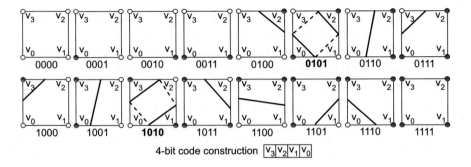

Figure 5.12. Topological states of a quad cell (marching squares algorithm). Red indicates "inside" vertices. Bold indices mark ambiguous cases.

integer index, where each bit stores the inside/outside state of a vertex. This integer can be used to index a *case table* (see Figure 5.12) that holds optimized code for every topological state. Optimizations include performing the edge-isovalue intersection computations (see Equation (5.3)) only on those edges that are known to be intersected for a specific topological state. The states 0101 and 1010 in the case table represent the ambiguous situations described previously for the example in Figure 5.11. That is, the method implementation can choose whether to create the full lines or the dashed ones.

Putting it all together, we obtain the marching squares implementation shown in Listing 5.2.

The marching squares algorithm constructs independent line segments for each cell, which are stored in an unstructured dataset type, given that

```
for each cell c_i of the dataset
{
    int index = 0;
    for (each vertex v_j of c_i)
        store the inside/outside state of v_j in bit j of index;
    select the optimized code from the case table using index;
    for (all cell edges e_j of the selected case)
        intersect e_j with isovalue v using Equation ~(5.3);
    construct line segments from these intersections;
}
```

Listing 5.2. Marching squares pseudocode.

isolines have no regular structure with respect to the grid they are computed on. An useful postprocessing step is to merge the coincident end points of line segments originating from neighbor grid cells that share an edge. Besides decreasing the isoline dataset size, this also creates a dataset on which operations such as computing vertex data from cell data via averaging (see Section 3.9.1) is possible.

5.3.2 Marching Cubes

The marching cubes algorithm operates similarly to marching squares, but accepts 3D instead of 2D scalar datasets and generates 2D isosurfaces instead of 1D isolines. Marching cubes begins just like marching squares does. Since a hex cell has eight vertices, marching cubes would need to treat $2^8 = 256$ different topological cases. In practice, this number is reduced to only 15 by using symmetry considerations.[3] The 16 different topological states used by marching cubes are sketched in Figure 5.13.

In contrast to marching squares, there are more ambiguous cases for marching cubes, i.e., cases when the intersection points of a cell can be connected in several ways with planar components. The six ambiguous cases for marching cubes are marked by bold indices in Figure 5.13. The ambiguous cases for marching cubes are cells whose faces are themselves

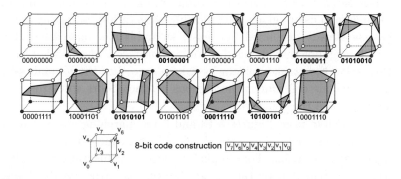

Figure 5.13. Topological states of a hex cell (marching cubes algorithm). Red indicates "inside" vertices. Bold indices mark ambiguous cases.

---

[3]The same reduction could be done for the 16 topological cases of marching squares. However, 16 is already a small number, so there is little need to further reduce the size of the case table.

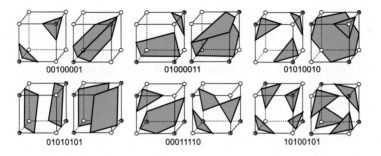

Figure 5.14. Ambiguous cases for marching cubes. Each case has two contouring variants.

ambiguous cases for marching squares, i.e., have two diagonal vertices "inside" and the other two "outside." There are several variants in which we can construct contours in these cells, as illustrated by Figure 5.14.

Unfortunately, in an ambiguous case, we cannot select the variant to use independently for every cell, as we did for marching squares. If we did so, there would be the risk that the constructed isosurface could exhibit artificial cracks. There are several ways to prevent this. First, we can replace every hex cell with three tetrahedra and use a marching tetrahedra algorithm instead of marching cubes. Marching tetrahedra has no ambiguous cases, just as marching triangles. Second, we can still use marching cubes with a small extension, given the following observation: an ambiguous hex cell has, as already explained, (at least) an ambiguous quad face. Hence, its hex cell neighbor that shares that ambiguous face is also ambiguous. We can thus solve the crack problem by taking care that the variants picked for an ambiguous cell *and* its ambiguous cell neighbors solve the shared *face* ambiguity in the same way.

As it is visible from Figures 5.13 and 5.14, marching cubes generates a set of polygons for each contoured cell, which includes triangles, quads, pentagons, and hexagons. For simplicity, most implementations would triangulate these polygons on the fly, or even directly generate the triangles from the various cases, and save the resulting 3D isosurface as an unstructured dataset. Just as for marching squares, a postprocessing pass is needed to merge the coincident end points of triangles originating from neighbor grid cells that share a face. An additional step needed for marching cubes is the computation of isosurface normals. These are needed for

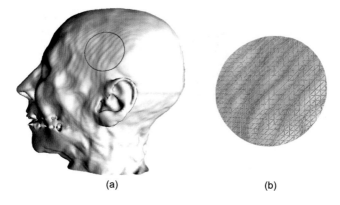

(a)   (b)

Figure 5.15. Ringing artifacts on isosurface. (a) Overview. (b) Detail mesh.

smooth shading, and can be computed by normal averaging, as explained in Section 2.3.

Interpreting the results of marching cubes must be done with care. Figure 5.15 shows an isosurface of an MRI scan uniform dataset of 128^3 voxels for an isovalue corresponding to the skin tissue. From the given viewpoint, the isosurface exhibits a "wavy" pattern that is clearly visible in the area marked in the image. This pattern is not an actual feature of the data but is caused by subsampling of the original signal on a low-resolution uniform grid. Figure 5.15(b) shows a zoomed in view with the isosurface grid overlaid on top of the shaded artifact area. The relation between the regular structure of the underlying 3D dataset and the unstructured triangle mesh of the isosurface is visible. Users should be familiar with their specific application data to avoid confusing the the presence of such artifacts with actual features in the data. This observation applies also to other artifacts, such as holes in the surface or small disconnected components. As a general rule, most isosurface details that are under or around the size of the resolution of the isosurfaced dataset can be either actual data or artifacts, and should be interpreted with great care.

We can draw more than a single isosurface of the same dataset in one visualization. Figure 5.16 shows two isosurfaces of a tooth scan dataset. The blue opaque isosurface corresponds to a high isovalue, which denotes a hard material such as the enamel present on the tooth upper surface. The beige isosurface corresponds to a lower isovalue, which denotes the softer

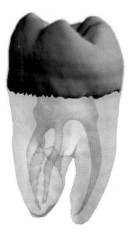

Figure 5.16. Two nested isosurfaces of a tooth scan dataset.

dentine material present inside the tooth. By making the latter isosurface semitransparent, we can see through it and discover the first opaque isosurface, and also see its internal surface, which corresponds to the tooth nerve chamber. The process of rendering several nested semitransparent isosurfaces that correspond to a discrete sequence of isovalues can be generalized to the continuous case, as we shall see with the volume rendering technique presented in Chapter 10.

Isosurfaces and isolines are strongly related, as the following example shows. Consider the same 3D dataset containing a human head MRI scan as used in Figure 8.2 (see Section 8.1.2). Let us construct an isosurface of this dataset for the isovalue that corresponds to the skin tissue (see Figure 5.17(d)). Consider now a 2D slice from the same dataset (Figure 5.17(b)) on which we construct an isoline for the skin isovalue (drawn in red in Figure 5.17(c)). Finally, let us slice the isosurface itself with the same slicing plane we used before. The result is shown in green in Figure 5.17(e). If we compare Figures 5.17(c) and 5.17(e), we see that the isoline is identical to the intersection of the slice plane and the 3D isosurface. In other words, we can say that the slicing and contouring operations are commutative. This observation is important, as it suggests that 3D isosurfaces (and other similar surfaces) can be constructed by assembling a set of 2D contours located on a set of parallel slice planes. If the set is

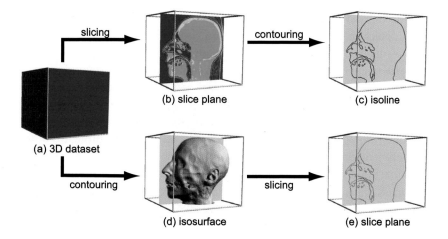

Figure 5.17. Isosurfaces, isolines, and slicing.

dense, i.e., the slice planes are close to each other, and the dataset does not exhibit too-sharp variations, we can connect points on an isoline with the closest points on the isolines from the previous and next slice and construct the 3D isosurface. This technique can be useful in several situations, for example when we do not have the original 3D volume to isosurface, but have a set of 2D contours on consecutive (near) parallel slices.

The marching squares and marching cubes algorithms have many variations and come in many flavors. In general, these variations try to address several requirements, such as genericity in terms of input dataset type, speed of execution, and quality of obtained contours. There exist similar algorithms to marching squares and marching cubes for all cell types, such as lines, triangles, and tetrahedra. These algorithms can treat all grid types, e.g., structured and unstructured, including grids with mixed cell types, as long as all encountered cell types are supported. All algorithm variants produce unstructured grids. If the input dataset has more vertex attributes than just the scalars used to contour, it is possible to interpolate all vertex attributes at the locations of the contour vertices and save them into the output contour dataset.

Isosurfaces can be also generated and rendered using point-based techniques. Point-based techniques exploit the observation that 3D surfaces can be rendered using large numbers of (shaded) point primitives. When the point density is high enough, there are no gaps in the rendering and the surface looks realistic. As we have seen, isosurfaces produced by marching cubes from uniform datasets have a quasiconstant point density, which makes them well suited for point-based rendering. On several graphics hardware configurations, point primitives can be considerably faster, and demand less memory, than polygonal ones. Moreover, rendering a dense set of points, also called a *point cloud*, eliminates the often costly stage of assembling polygonal primitives into a mesh, eliminating duplicate points, and computing vertex normals. Point-based techniques are detailed further in Section 8.3.2 in the context of scattered points interpolation.

A classical algorithm for generating and rendering isosurfaces using point sets is *dividing cubes* [Cline et al. 88]. Dividing cubes works for 3D uniform and rectilinear grids, i.e., grids that have box-shaped cells (see Section 3.5). Similar to marching cubes, dividing cubes iterates over all dataset cells and detects those intersected by the given isosurface by comparing the isovalue with the cell vertex values. For dividing cubes, however, it suffices to detect whether a cell has at least one inside and one outside vertex, which is cheaper than the full bit-coding done by marching cubes. The cells that pass the intersection test are next recursively subdivided into a $2 \times 2 \times 2$ lattice of smaller cells. The cell-isosurface intersection test and cell subdivision are recursively repeated until the cell size falls below a minimal size. The algorithm is similar to the one used when building octrees or similar spatial subdivision structures. For all resulting cells, the dividing cubes algorithm draws a shaded point primitive located at every cell center. In sampling terms, we can say that dividing cubes approximates the isosurface using constant basis functions, whereas marching cubes uses linear basis functions (see Chapter 3).

For dividing cubes, the ideal minimal cell size is that of a screen pixel, in which case every point primitive is of pixel size and there are no visual gaps or other rendering artifacts in the rendered isosurface. However, this may be costly, so the division can be stopped earlier, yielding larger cells. In this case, larger point primitives can be used, such as splats (see Section 8.3.2), in order to obtain a gap-free isosurface rendering. To prevent visual gaps when zooming in an isosurface rendered with dividing cubes, we can either dynamically recompute the isosurface, i.e., generate more point primitives, a slower but more accurate option, or simply increase the point primitive size, which is fast but can create visual artifacts when viewing close-ups.

5.4   Height Plots

Height plots, also called elevation or carpet plots, were introduced by our first visualization example in Section 2.1. Given a two-dimensional surface $\mathcal{D}_s \in \mathcal{D}$, part of a scalar dataset $\mathcal{D}$, height plots can be described by the mapping operation

$$m : \mathcal{D}_s \to \mathcal{D}, m(x) = x + s(x)\mathbf{n}(x), \forall x \in \mathcal{D}_s, \qquad (5.4)$$

where $s(x)$ is the scalar value of $\mathcal{D}$ at the point x and $\mathbf{n}(x)$ is the normal to the surface $\mathcal{D}_s$ at x. In other words, the height plot mapping operation "warps" a given surface $\mathcal{D}_s$ included in the dataset along the surface normal, with a factor proportional to the scalar values.

In their most common variant, height plots warp a planar surface $\mathcal{D}_s$. This type of height plot has been demonstrated several times in this book, starting with Chapter 2. However, we can produce height plots starting from different basis surfaces $\mathcal{D}_s$, such as the torus shown in Figure 5.18. The values of the scalar dataset on the torus surface are shown with a blue-to-red colormap in Figure 5.18(a). Figure 5.18(b) shows the height plot of these scalar values, done by warping the torus surface with the scalar values along the surface normal. In this image, both the height and the color encode the scalar value—in other words, the bumps are red, whereas the valleys are blue. The two visual cues strengthen each other to convey the scalar value information. If desired, one can encode two different scalar values with a height plot, one into the plot's height and the other into the plot's color.

(a)   (b)

Figure 5.18. Height plot over a nonplanar surface.

Height plots are a particular case of *displacement*, or *warped*, plots. Displacement plots are used to visualize vector datasets and are detailed in Section 6.4.

5.5 Conclusion

In this chapter, we have presented a number of fundamental methods for visualizing scalar data: color mapping, contouring, slicing, and height plots. Color mapping assigns a color as a function of the scalar value at each point of a given domain. Contouring displays all points within a given two- or three-dimensional domain that have a given scalar value. Height plots deform the scalar dataset domain in a given direction as a function of the scalar data. These techniques work on 1D, 2D, and 3D datasets of arbitrary topology. The main advantages of these techniques is that they produce intuitive results, easily understood by the vast majority of users, and they are simple to implement. However, such techniques have also a number of restrictions.

In their standard form, color mapping, contouring, and height plots take as input a one- or two-dimensional scalar dataset. This may be restrictive, for example, when we want to visualize a 3D scalar dataset. Additional techniques such as slicing can be used to extract a lower-dimensional subset, such as a 2D slice from a 3D volume, and display it using the visualization methods presented in this chapter. Slicing techniques are further elaborated in Chapter 8. In some other cases, however, we want to visualize the scalar values of *all*, not just a few, of the data points of a 3D dataset. Volume-rendering techniques, presented in Chapter 10, are an answer to this demand.

Besides these fundamental techniques, many different scalar visualization methods exist. For example, specific methods exist for the visualization of scalar data defined over images and volumes, i.e., two-dimensional and three-dimensional uniform grids with scalar attributes, respectively. These methods are discussed further in more detail in Chapter 9 (image visualization) and Chapter 10 (volume visualization).

Chapter 6

Vector Visualization

VECTOR data is as frequently encountered, and as important, as scalar data. Strictly put, a vector is a tuple of n scalar components $\mathbf{v} = (v_1, \cdots, v_n)$, $v_i \in \mathbb{R}$. An n-dimensional vector describes, for example, a position, direction, rate of change, or force in $\mathbb{R}^n$. However, the majority of visualization applications deal with data that describes physical phenomena in 2D or 3D space. As a consequence, most visualization software defines all vectors to have three components. 2D vectors are modeled as 3D vectors with the third (z) component equal to null. Although one could provide separate implementation-level support for 2D vectors, this would massively complicate the structure of visualization software, lead to code replication, and ultimately reduce performance.

Recalling from Section 3.6, vector fields are functions $f : \mathcal{D} \to \mathbb{R}^3$, where $\mathcal{D}$ is usually a subset of $\mathbb{R}^2$ or $\mathbb{R}^3$. Vector datasets are samplings of vector fields over discrete spatial domains. In this chapter, we shall discuss a number of popular visualization methods for vector datasets: vector glyphs, vector color coding, displacement plots, stream objects, texture-based vector visualization, and the simplified representation of vector fields.

A very important application domain for vector visualization is *computational fluid dynamics (CFD)*. CFD simulations are able to predict the time-dependent behavior of compressible 3D fluid flows consisting of several potentially interacting substances, or species, having different densities and pressures, over complex spatial geometries. The solution of a CFD simu-

lation consists of several datasets, each for a different time step. For each
time step, several attributes are computed and stored into the solution
dataset, such as velocity, pressure, density, flow divergence, and vorticity.
Since divergence and vorticity are fundamental concepts in understanding
the structure of vector fields and are used by many visualization methods
for vector data, we shall detail these notions first.

We begin our discussion by first describing a number of fundamental
mathematical operators that are used to analyze vector fields (Section 6.1).
Next, we present vector glyphs, one of the simplest and most popular techniques used to visualize such fields (Section 6.2). The use of scalar visualization techniques to depict vector fields is discussed in Section 6.3.
We then introduce the displacement plot technique for visualizing vector
data (Section 6.4). Section 6.5 presents stream objects, which use integral
techniques to construct paths in vector fields. Section 6.6 discusses the
use of textures for visualizing vector fields. Section 6.7 discusses a number of strategies for simplified representation of vector datasets. Finally,
Section 6.8 concludes this chapter.

6.1   Divergence and Vorticity

Divergence and vorticity are important quantities for vector field visualization, but also for the visualization and processing of other types of datasets,
such as meshes, images, and scalar and tensor fields. Given a vector field
$\mathbf{v} : \mathbb{R}^3 \to \mathbb{R}^3$, the *divergence* of $\mathbf{v} = (v_x, v_y, v_z)$ is the scalar quantity

$$\operatorname{div} \mathbf{v} = \frac{\partial v_x}{\partial x} + \frac{\partial v_y}{\partial y} + \frac{\partial v_z}{\partial z}. \tag{6.1}$$

Intuitively, if $\mathbf{v}$ is a flow field that transports mass, div $\mathbf{v}$ characterizes the
increase or loss of mass at a given point p in the vector field in unit time.

- A positive divergence at p denotes that mass would spread from
  p outward. Positive divergence points are called *sources* (see Figure 6.1(b)).

- A negative divergence at p denotes that mass gets sucked into p.
  Negative divergence points are called *sinks* (see Figure 6.1(c)).

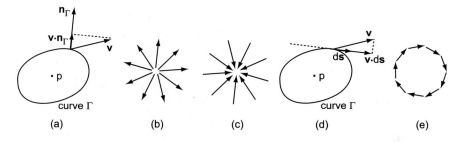

Figure 6.1. Divergence and curl in 2D. (a) Divergence construction. (b) Source point. (c) Sink point. (d) Rotor construction. (e) High-vorticity field.

- A zero divergence at p denotes that mass is transported without getting spread or sucked, i.e., without compression or expansion.

An equivalent definition of the divergence of $\mathbf{v}$ at a point p is

$$\operatorname{div} \mathbf{v} = \lim_{\Gamma \to 0} \frac{1}{|\Gamma|} \int_\Gamma (\mathbf{v} \cdot \mathbf{n}_\Gamma) \mathrm{d}s. \tag{6.2}$$

Here, Γ is a closed hypersurface (a curve for 2D vector fields and a surface for 3D vector fields) around the current point p, $|\Gamma|$ is the area (2D) or volume (3D) enclosed by Γ, and $\mathbf{n}_\Gamma$ is the outward normal of Γ (see Figure 6.1(a)). The integral in Equation (6.2) computes the flux that the vector field transports through the imaginary boundary Γ. The limit $\Gamma \to 0$ describes a curve that shrinks around the current point x until it becomes infinitesimally short.

Figure 6.2(a) shows the divergence of a 2D flow field using a blue-to-red colormap. The vector field is visualized with arrow glyphs for illustration purposes. Red areas indicate high positive divergence, or sources. Two such sources are clearly visible. Blue areas indicate high negative divergence, or sinks. Within the dark blue area, two pronounced sinks are visible. If we correlate the divergence and vector glyph visualizations, we get the image of a flow field that emerges from the sources and ends up in the sinks.

Given a vector field $\mathbf{v} : \mathbb{R}^3 \to \mathbb{R}^3$, the *vorticity* of $\mathbf{v}$, also called the *curl* or *rotor* of $\mathbf{v}$, is the vector quantity

$$\operatorname{rot} \mathbf{v} = \left(\frac{\partial v_z}{\partial y} - \frac{\partial v_y}{\partial z}, \frac{\partial v_x}{\partial z} - \frac{\partial v_z}{\partial x}, \frac{\partial v_y}{\partial x} - \frac{\partial v_x}{\partial y} \right). \tag{6.3}$$

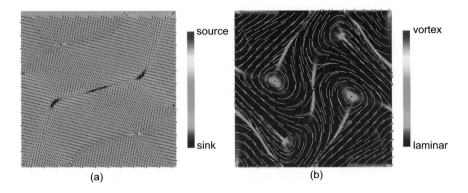

Figure 6.2. (a) Divergence of a 2D vector field. (b) Absolute value of vorticity of a 2D vector field.

The vorticity rot **v** of **v** is a vector field that is locally perpendicular to the plane of rotation of **v** and whose magnitude expresses the speed of angular rotation of **v** around rot **v**. Hence, the vorticity vector characterizes the speed and direction of rotation of a given vector field at every point. In some textbooks, the rotor is also denoted as curl **v**.

An equivalent definition of the vorticity of **v** at a point p is

$$\text{rot } \mathbf{v} = \lim_{\Gamma \to 0} \frac{1}{|\Gamma|} \int_{\Gamma} \mathbf{v} \cdot d\mathbf{s}. \qquad (6.4)$$

Here, Γ is a closed curve around the current point p that shrinks toward p (see Figure 6.1(d)) and $|\Gamma|$ is the area (2D) or volume (3D) enclosed by Γ. Vorticity signals the presence of vortices in vector fields. An informal definition of a vortex is a region where the vector field locally circles around a point called the *vortex center*. High-vorticity areas (such as in Figure 6.1(e)) indicate the presence of vortices. High vorticity and high divergence are complementary. For example, the divergence of the high-vorticity field in Figure 6.1(e) is zero and the vorticity of the high-divergence fields in Figures 6.1(b) and (c) is also zero. Generalizing, it can be shown that for a vector field **v**, it holds that div rot **v** = 0.

Figure 6.2(b) shows the absolute value of the vorticity of the MHD field used previously in this chapter using a blue-to-red colormap. The field itself is visualized with arrow-capped stream tubes, a technique detailed in Section 6.5. Blue areas indicate low-vorticity, laminar regions. Red areas

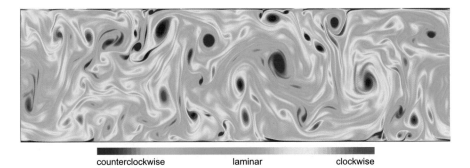

counterclockwise   laminar   clockwise

Figure 6.3. Vorticity of a 2D fluid flow field. Note the alternation between vortices with opposite spinning directions. (Image courtesy of I. Barosan, Eindhoven University, the Netherlands.)

indicate high-vorticity regions. We can see two types of such regions. Two small circular red spots indicate localized vortices, which are also outlined by the circling streamlines. Several elongated thin red strips indicate areas where the vector field quickly changes direction. Given the shape, these are not vortices, but separation lines that divide regions where the flow has opposite directions. If one is interested in locating such high-vorticity areas, a simple method of reasonable accuracy is to contour the vorticity field for high isovalues and select the data points inside such a contour.

Figure 6.3 visualizes the vorticity of a more complex turbulent 2D flow. Blue and red indicate counterclockwise and clockwise spinning vortices respectively. Green indicates low-vorticity, laminar regions. The image clearly conveys the high complexity of the flow. A typical pattern for such phenomena, which are also known as *turbulent flows*, is the high number of vortices and the alternation of their spinning directions. Such flows are encountered in the study of aerodynamics and fluid dynamics and can exhibit highly complex patterns. Understanding such patterns is one of the important ongoing challenges of scientific visualization.

The *streamwise vorticity* Ω of a field $\mathbf{v}$ is the scalar quantity equal to the projection of rot $\mathbf{v}$ along $\mathbf{v}$ itself:

$$\Omega = \frac{\mathbf{v} \cdot \text{rot } \mathbf{v}}{|\mathbf{v}||\text{rot } \mathbf{v}|}. \tag{6.5}$$

Intuitively, Ω describes how quickly $\mathbf{v}$ turns around itself.

Another quantity used to characterize vector fields is *helicity*. Helicity is defined as one-half the scalar product of the velocity and vorticity vectors. Intuitively, helicity describes the extent to which the vector field exhibits a corkscrew-like local motion. Helicity is a conserved quantity if the flow is inviscid and homogeneous in density. Helicity is useful in weather studies for understanding severe convective storms and tornadoes, since in strong updrafts, the velocity and vorticity vectors tend to be aligned, yielding high helicity [Majda et al. 01].

To compute divergence and vorticity, we need the partial derivatives of the vector field components. On a discrete dataset, these can be approximated using the formulas specific for every grid cell type given in Section 3.7. However, as with all discrete datasets, derivatives can be sensitive to noise, so the results of such computations must be interpreted carefully.

6.2   Vector Glyphs

Vector glyphs are probably the simplest, and fastest, and most popular technique for visualizing vector fields. The vector glyph mapping technique essentially associates a vector glyph, or *vector icon*, with every sample point of the vector dataset. Various properties of the icon, such as location, direction, orientation, size, and color, are adjusted to reflect the value of the vector attribute it represents. The name *glyph*, meaning "sign" in Greek, reflects this principle of associating discrete visual signs with individual vector attributes. Every glyph is a sign that conveys, by its appearance, properties of the represented vector, such as direction, orientation, and magnitude.

There are many variations of this framework for vector glyphs. Essentially, they propose various trade-offs between sampling density (how many glyphs we can display on a given screen area) and number of encoded attributes (how many attributes we can display per glyph). We shall present a number of vector glyphs, starting with the simplest one: the line. Lines essentially show the position, direction, and magnitude of a set of vectors. Given a vector dataset defined on a sampled domain D, we associate a line $l = (x, x + k\mathbf{v}(x))$ with every sample point $x \in D$ that has a vector attribute $\mathbf{v}(x)$. The parameter k represents the scaling factor used to map the vector magnitudes to the geometric domain. Oriented line glyphs are sometimes also called *hedgehogs*, due to the particularly spiky appearance of the visualization.

Figure 6.4 shows a line glyph, or hedgehog, visualization of a 2D vector field defined on a square domain. The vector field is a velocity field from a magnetohydrodynamic (MHD) simulation [Brandenburg 03]. The original

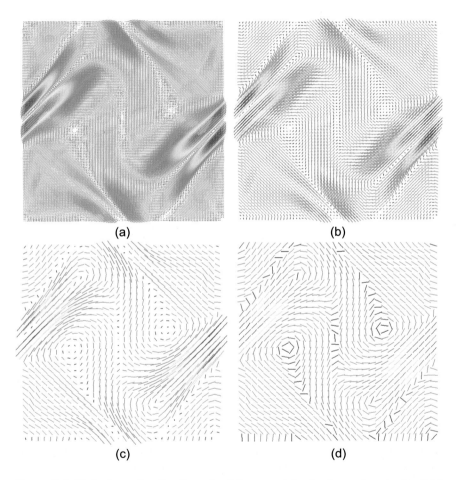

Figure 6.4. Hedgehog visualization of a 2D magnetohydrodynamic velocity field. (Data courtesy of Prof. Martin Rumpf, University of Bonn, Germany.)

uniform dataset has a resolution of 256×256 sample points. The images show the hedgehog visualization of the vector field uniformly subsampled in both x and y dimensions at a rate of 2 (see Figure 6.4(a)), a rate of 4 (Figure 6.4(b)), and a rate of 8 (Figure 6.4(c)). In all these images, the line glyphs are scaled proportionally to the vector field magnitude, the scaling factor k being proportional to the subsampling rate. In Figure 6.4(d), the vector field is uniformly subsampled at a rate of 4, but the line glyphs are all scaled to the same length. The glyphs are colored by color mapping the vector field magnitude scalar field to blue-to-red colormap. In this way, color cues strengthen (or replace) length cues to convey information about the vector magnitude. In many applications, color is used to show other scalar fields related to the vector field, such as pressure, temperature, or density.

Looking at Figure 6.4, we can make a number of important observations. First, it is clear that high-resolution vector datasets must be subsampled in order to be visualized with hedgehogs. Comparing Figures 6.4(a), (b), and (c), we can argue that it is easier to comprehend the vector field in the last image than in the first two, as the line glyphs are longer, hence their direction and orientation are easier to discern. The direction is even easier to follow in the last image (Figures 6.4(d)), where all glyphs the same, relatively large, size. Hence the clarity of hedgehog visualizations depends strongly on the glyph scaling factor. Ideally, a glyph should be as large as possible, since larger glyphs have an easier perceivable direction, but not too large, so it would not intersect neighboring glyphs. If we scale all glyphs to the same size, as in Figure 6.4(d), this constraint is easy to obey by scaling each glyph to the average cell size at its origin. This removes clutter, but eliminates the use of the glyph size (length) as a visual cue for the vector field magnitude. If we scale the glyphs to reflect the vector field magnitude, such as in Figures 6.4(a)–(c), eliminating clutter is more problematic. We could still use a unique glyph scaling factor k so that all glyphs are locally smaller than the cell size. Another option is to use a nonlinear term $k\mathbf{v}$, which, e.g., has constrained minimal and maximal values or has a logarithmic, instead of linear, variation with $|\mathbf{v}|$. This will prevent clutter and guarantee glyph visibility, but will drop the one-to-one relationship between vector magnitude and glyph length.

More complex shapes can be used for glyphs besides lines. Figure 6.5 shows the same 2D vector field as in Figure 6.4, this time visualized with

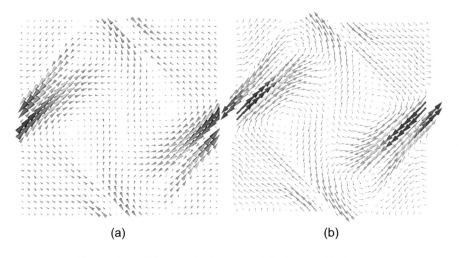

(a)   (b)

Figure 6.5. Different glyph types. (a) Cones. (b) Arrows.

3D cone and arrow glyphs. Such glyphs have the advantage of being able to convey direction and *orientation*, whereas lines convey direction only. However, these glyphs also take more space to draw, so they increase the clutter or require lower-resolution datasets. An interesting compromise between arrows and lines is to use Gouraud shaded lines. By shading the line glyph from full color (or full opacity) at the glyph origin to the background color (or full transparency) at the line tip, a visual effect similar to a thin arrow can be obtained without the need for extra screen space.

By using even more complex glyph shapes, we can encode more attributes than the vector field itself. This feature is needed in situations when one has to analyze not just the relative behavior of a single (vector) field in different spatial regions, but the correlations between several scalar and vector fields. Such situations occur frequently in computational fluid dynamics (CFD) simulations. A 3D CFD solution consisting of flow velocity, vorticity, divergence and material density, pressure, and temperature offers $3 + 3 + 1 + 1 + 1 + 1 = 10$ attributes per dataset point. To visualize all this information, we would need to design a glyph with 10 degrees of freedom. Such glyphs have been designed and used in the visualization of fluid flow [van Walsum et al. 96], albeit with limited effectiveness.

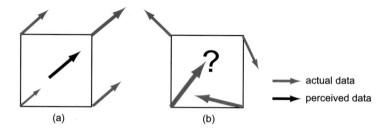

Figure 6.6. Visual interpolation of vector glyphs. (a) Small data variations are easily interpolated. (b) Large data variations create more problems.

6.2.1   Vector Glyph Examples

The trade-off between the power of expression of glyphs, or number of attributes they can encode, and minimal screen size needed by a glyph is an important characteristic of glyph-based visualizations. To understand this better, let us compare these for a moment with the color mapping visualizations discussed in Section 5.1. In both cases, the data attributes are available only at the discrete sample points of a dataset D. However, color mapping is typically applied at *every point* of the dataset D, either via texture-based interpolation or via the vertex-based color interpolation provided by the polygon rendering machinery. We say that color mapping produces a *dense* visualization, where every pixel represents an (interpolated) data value. In contrast, most glyph-based visualizations for vector data cannot have this freedom. Since a glyph takes more space than just a pixel, we cannot draw one glyph at every pixel of a given dataset. All glyph visualizations share this inherent discreteness, or sparseness, of the output. This affects the inverse image-to-data mapping (see Chapter 4) at the core of the visualization process.

Consider a zoomed-in detail showing a hedgehog plot over a single cell of a 2D vector field (see Figure 6.6). In the first case (see Figure 6.6(a)), the vector field variation over the displayed cell is quite small. We can easily interpolate *mentally* the displayed arrow glyphs and arrive at the conclusion that the vector field has an upper-right direction and orientation, and increases in magnitude in this direction. In the second case (see Figure 6.6(b)), the situation is more problematic. The vector field varies largely between the vertices of the considered cell, so it is harder to mentally interpolate between these four vector glyphs and get an idea of how the field actually behaves over the considered surface. Clearly, the interpretation can get very confusing when we have hundreds of cells in this situation.

This difference between scalar (color-mapped) visualizations and vector (glyph) visualizations can be explained in sampling terms. Scalar color mapping techniques such as the ones discussed in Section 5.1 produce a *piecewise linear* visualization. Glyph techniques produce a *purely discrete* visualization. In the first case, we do not have to mentally interpolate between drawn pixels, as the graphics hardware has done this task for us. In the second case, we only have visual indication at the sample points (e.g., cell vertices), so we must do this interpolation ourselves. When the visualized signal varies smoothly, like in Figure 6.6(a), this task is relatively easy. When this is not the case, like in Figure 6.6(b), we have a harder problem. The task is made more difficult when we have to interpolate between *directions* and *orientations*, as in the case of vector glyphs, since this is apparently not easily done by the human visual system.

Another problem of vector glyph visualizations is caused by the regular pattern of the sample points present in uniform and rectilinear grids. The problem is visible in the central area of Figures 6.4(c) and (d). In these regions, the perception of the diagonal orientation of the vector glyphs is weakened by the regular vertical pattern of the uniformly distributed sampling points. This problem affects dense visualizations to a much lesser degree. The regular subsampling problem is present also when the subsampling grid is not aligned with the original grid. Figure 6.7(a) shows an arrow glyph visualization of the same 2D vector field as in Figure 6.4, this time subsampled on a rectilinear grid rotated approximately 30 degrees with respect to the original dataset grid. The undesired visual interference between the grid lines and glyph directions is clearly visible. By subsampling the dataset using a randomly distributed (instead of regularly arranged) set of points, the problem can be alleviated. This is illustrated in Figure 6.7(b), where we use the same dataset and subsampling rate as before but a random point distribution instead of a regular one.

Vector glyphs can be used to visualize 3D vector fields, too. Figure 6.8 shows an arrow glyph visualization of a 3D vector dataset sampled on a uniform grid containing $128 \times 85 \times 42$ data points that describes the flow of water in a box-shaped basin that has an inlet, located upper-right,

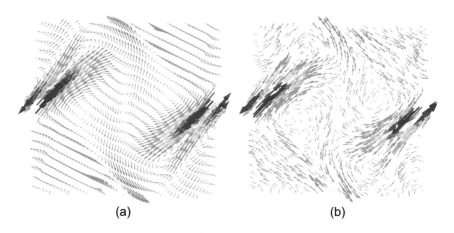

(a)   (b)

Figure 6.7. (a) Vector glyphs on a dataset regularly subsampled on a rotated sample grid. (b) Subsampling artifacts are alleviated by random sampling. Both visualization display 1200 glyphs.

an outlet, located lower-right, and two obstacles (not drawn in the figure) that cause the sinuous behavior of the flow. Visualizing such a dataset with vector glyphs at full resolution would produce a completely cluttered result. Randomly subsampling the dataset to 100,000 points and visualizing it with line glyphs produces the result shown in Figure 6.8(a). Besides the known problems of glyphs in 2D, an additional problem of 3D glyph visualization becomes apparent here: occlusion. Closer glyphs obscure further ones, which makes understanding the flow behavior deep inside the dataset quite difficult. Note that using arrow instead of line glyphs only increases the occlusion problem, as arrows have a larger screen area than lines.

We can alleviate the occlusion problem by further subsampling the dataset to only 10,000 data points (see Figure 6.8(b)). However, the dataset is now too sparse to be able to distinguish local details. A different way to tackle the occlusion problem is to draw the glyphs transparently. Figure 6.8(c) shows the same visualization as in Figure 6.8(a), but this time using line glyphs with a transparency of 0.15. Closer glyphs now cause less occlusion, allowing us to "see" deeper inside the dataset. An interesting visual effect is achieved by using monochrome, instead of color mapped, transparent line glyphs (see Figure 6.8(d)). Here, a single color (black) is blended, so the resulting visualization is easier to interpret. The high ve-

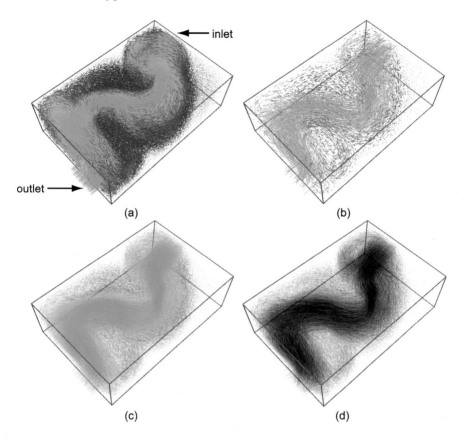

Figure 6.8. Glyph-based visualization of a 3D vector field. (Data courtesy of Prof. Martin Rumpf, University of Bonn, Germany.)

locity "flow core" located at the center of the fluid flow is now easily visible as a dark region. We shall investigate transparency-based techniques for visualizing 3D datasets in more detail later in Chapter 10, when discussing volume visualization methods.

In addition to 2D (planar) surfaces and 3D volumes, glyph-based visualization can be used on 3D surfaces embedded in volumetric datasets. The idea behind this technique is similar to the color-mapping technique on 3D surfaces presented for scalar fields in Section 5.1. First, we select a surface of interest from a given 3D dataset. Next, we draw vector glyphs

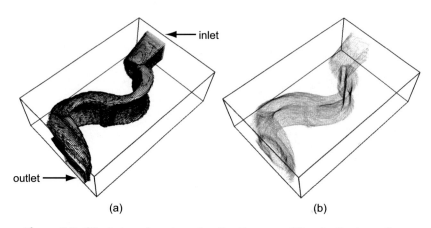
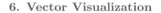

(a)   (b)

Figure 6.9. Glyph-based vector visualization on a 3D velocity isosurface.

at the sample points of the surface. Figure 6.9 illustrates this. The surface of interest is a velocity magnitude isosurface of the vector field itself. The selected isovalue isolates the flow core, i.e., the region where the velocity magnitude is equal to about half the maximal velocity over the whole dataset. The square shapes of the inlet and outlet are now visible. Figure 6.9(a) shows the isosurface and line glyphs rendered on the isosurface itself. The glyphs are not color mapped by velocity magnitude as before, since they all have the same length given the definition of the supporting surface. Figure 6.9(b) shows a variant of the previous visualization. Here, the support surface is not shown, which allows us to see the all the vector glyphs that were previously masked by the surface. To diminish occlusion, we use a transparency of 0.3 for the glyphs.

An important observation about vector glyph visualizations on surfaces is that the vectors do not have to be tangent to the surface. This condition holds only for a special type of surfaces called *stream surfaces*, which are discussed further in Section 6.5. Glyph visualizations on such surfaces are easier to understand, since the glyphs tend to stay on the surface, rather than on surfaces on which the field is not tangent, where the glyphs get visually entangled and cause more visual clutter.

Summarizing our discussion, the main advantages of glyph-based visualization of vector fields are the simple implementation and intuitive interpretation of glyphs such as arrows. However, as we have seen, these advantages are offset by several problems, such as occlusion, subsampling artifacts, and potentially difficult visual interpolation of directions. The interpretation difficulties caused by these problems can be partially overcome by techniques such as random subsampling, carefully setting glyph lengths, and, in the case of 3D glyph visualizations, by interactively investigating the result by 3D manipulation. In the following sections, we shall present several other visualization techniques for vector fields that try to alleviate these problems.

6.3   Vector Color Coding

As we have seen in the previous section, dense visualizations, such as color-mapped surfaces, have several advantages compared to sparse visualizations, such as glyphs. The natural question that arises is whether we can develop dense visualizations for vector fields, similar to the color-mapped surfaces used for scalar fields. One of the simplest techniques to produce such visualizations is *vector color coding*. Similar to scalar color mapping, vector color coding associates a color with every point of a given surface on which we have defined a vector dataset. The color is used to encode the vector orientation and direction attributes. Vector color coding can be easiest understood if we represent colors in the hue-saturation-value (HSV) system introduced in Chapter 2. Colors in the HSV system can be visualized using a so-called *color wheel*, such as the one shown at the right in Figure 6.10. Every distinct hue corresponds to a different angle of the color wheel: red is $0°$, magenta is $60°$, blue is $120°$, cyan is $180°$, green is $240°$, and yellow is $300°$. Saturation is represented as the distance from the wheel center to a given color point. Value is usually represented as a separate one-dimensional "luminance" parameter, since the color wheel can encode only two distinct parameters.

Vector color coding proceeds as follows. Assume we have a color wheel of unit radius and all vectors in the dataset are scaled so that the longest one has unit length. Under these conditions, every vector is represented by the color it points to if we place it at the center of the color wheel. The vector orientation is encoded in the hue and the vector length in the value. The saturation parameter is set to one, i.e., we use only fully saturated colors. The color coding process is applied for every point of the dataset, similarly to the scalar color coding, either via texture or polygon color interpolation (see Section 5.1).

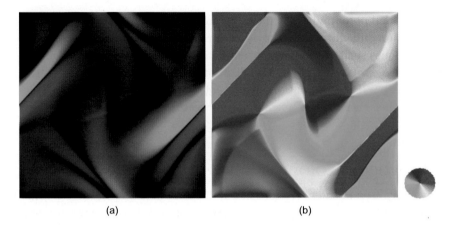

(a)   (b)

Figure 6.10. Vector color coding. (a) Orientation and magnitude. (b) Orientation only.

Figure 6.10(a) shows the vector color coding for the same 2D vector dataset as was used in the previous section. Clearly, this image does not suffer from the sampling problems discussed for glyph visualizations, which is a positive element. Low-vector-magnitude regions can be easily detected as dark (low value) areas, whereas high-vector-magnitude regions show up as brightly colored areas. However, in contrast to the intuitive arrow plots, this visualization is highly abstract. The inverse mapping from hue to vector orientation takes quite some time to be learned, so users have to be trained extensively to interpret such images.

Several variations of the basic idea exist. If we are interested only in the vector orientation and not the magnitude, we can set the value component to one, and we obtain the visualization shown in Figure 6.10(b). Here, the orientation patterns of the vector field are easier to distinguish than in Figure 6.10(a), since the image is brighter. Besides the standard color wheel containing all rainbow hues, other color wheels can be used to emphasize on certain orientations, similar to the various colormap manipulations described in Section 5.1 for scalar fields.

Besides the directional color coding, we can also directly encode the vector components v_x, v_y, v_z into colors. In this setting, a 3D vector field is visualized by three separate scalar color-mapped fields. Although this method is probably the simplest way, from a technical perspective, to produce a visualization of a vector field, it has limited effectiveness. The user must visually correlate the same locations in three color images to get insight into the vector data at that location. Even if the user were able to accurately identify the location of the same spatial point in three different images, mentally performing three separate color-to-scalar mappings independently is a very hard task. Furthermore, it is difficult to imagine the direction of a vector just by looking at three scalar fields representing its components. For a more involved discussion on the reasons to avoid this type of color coding, see Colin Ware's book on information visualization [Ware 04]. All in all, this method is seldom used, except in cases when users are very familiar with the vector field structure and domain shape, e.g., due to a low variability, and want to look for specific outlier-like details.

Vector color coding can also be applied to 3D surfaces. However, the mapping of a 3D orientation to hues on the color wheel is not as simple as in the 2D case. Although such mappings can be done, for example by using the hue channel to encode the x and y vector components and the value channel to encode the z component, performing the inverse mapping from hue to 3D orientation visually is generally a very challenging task. If we are interested in less than a general mapping, the problem becomes simpler to tackle. For example, let us again consider the 3D fluid flow dataset discussed in the previous section, which we have visualized in Figure 6.9 with a velocity magnitude isosurface. We may be interested in seeing how much the actual flow direction differs from the isosurface normal or, in other words, how far this isosurface is from a stream surface tangent to the flow. For this, we can color-code the angle α between the surface normal $\mathbf{n}$ and the vector data $\mathbf{v}$, which can be computed as

$$\alpha = \arccos\left(\frac{\mathbf{n} \cdot \mathbf{v}}{|\mathbf{v}|}\right). \tag{6.6}$$

The result, shown in Figure 6.11, is a scalar field that can be visualized with color mapping. On top of the colored isosurface, the vector field itself is visualized with semitransparent line glyphs. The large green areas indicate that the vector field is close to tangent to a large percentage of the given surface. The dark blue area in the upper-right part of the image indicates a region where the vector field "exits" the surface. This is the region where the inflow bounces straight against the upper obstacle inside

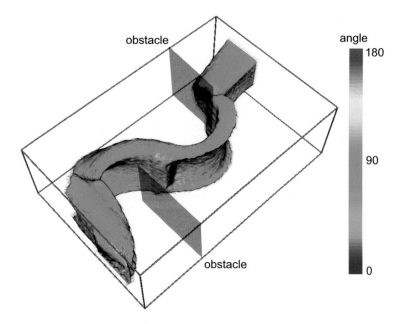

Figure 6.11. Color coding the tangency of a vector field to a given surface. The angle between the vector and surface normal is encoded via a rainbow colormap.

the box (drawn in light gray). In contrast, the red region in the middle of the image indicates a region where the vector field "enters" the surface. In this area, the flow starts being deflected by the lower obstacle in the box.

Summarizing, vector color coding solves many of the technical problems that glyph plots suffer from. However, its lack of intuitiveness makes it not so popular outside specialized areas.

6.4 Displacement Plots

Vector glyphs, described in the previous section, can be understood in terms of displaying trajectories. The vector glyph with the origin at some point p can be seen as the trajectory p would follow in $\mathbf{v}(p)$ over a short time interval Δt. The vector glyph shows both the start and end points of the trajectory, i.e., p and $p + \mathbf{v}(p)\Delta t$ respectively. Displacement plots take

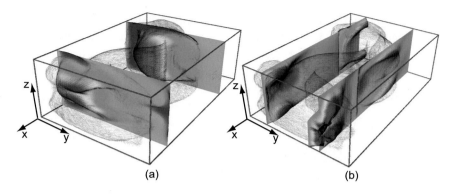

Figure 6.12. Displacement plots of planar surfaces in a 3D vector field.

a different approach by showing only the end points of such trajectories. Given a surface $S \in D$ inside the domain D of a vector field, where S is discretized as a set of sample points p_i, a displacement plot of S is a new surface S' given by the set of sample points

$$p'_i = p_i + k\mathbf{v}'(p_i). \tag{6.7}$$

In Equation (6.7), $\mathbf{v}'$ is a vector field that controls the displacement of the surface S and k is the displacement factor (analogous to Δt) that controls how pronounced the displacement is.

In the simplest case, we can set $\mathbf{v}' = \mathbf{v}$, and displace the surface S in the direction of the actual vector field itself. Figure 6.12 demonstrates the displacement plot technique for the 3D flow dataset introduced in Section 6.2 for two planar surfaces orthogonal to the x-axis (Figure 6.12(a)) and y-axis respectively (Figure 6.12(b)). Both examples use a displacement factor $k = 20$. In this example, the displacement plots are colored by the vector field component on which the input surface is perpendicular, i.e., $|\mathbf{v}_x|$ for Figure 6.12(a) and $|\mathbf{v}_y|$ for Figure 6.12(b). Blue shows the minimal (negative) displacement, red is the maximal (positive) displacement, and green indicates a nondisplaced point with vector value close to zero. The color mapping enhances the information provided by the displaced surface geometry. To ease the interpretation, the visualization is enhanced with semitransparent vector glyphs.

A natural interpretation of a displacement plot is to think of it as being the effect of displacing, or warping, a given surface in the vector field.

For this reason, displacement plots are sometimes also called *warped plots*. Displacement plots have the major advantage that they produce a visually continuous result—at least when they are applied on a continuous input surface. However, displacement plots produce a more abstract, less intuitive visualization than simpler methods such as vector glyphs. In Figure 6.12(a), for example, the red areas, warped forward in the direction of the x-axis, indicate regions where the fluid flow strongly follows the inlet-to-outlet direction (see Figure 6.9 for the position of the flow inlet and outlet). Blue regions are also interesting, as these indicate a *backward* flow that goes against the main stream. In such regions, phenomena such as vortices can occur. Figure 6.12(b) tells a similar story, but now from the perspective of the y-axis. Note, however, that the displacement plot technique presented here is not the same as the height plot technique described in Section 5.4. Height plots visualize a *scalar* field by warping a given surface along its normal. Displacement plots visualize a *vector* field by warping a given surface along the vector field itself. This is visible in Figure 6.12(b). Here, the front surface is warped outside the flow box-shaped domain in the area of the outlet. Similarly, the back surface is warped inside the flow domain in the area of the inlet. If we used height plots of, e.g., the velocity magnitude, these surfaces would have been warped in the direction of their normals, which would not have led to such effects. If, however, we set the warping direction $\mathbf{v}' = s\mathbf{n}$, where $\mathbf{n}$ is the surface normal and s is some scalar value, Equation (6.7) produces warped plots. In practice, we can project the vector field on the surface normal, i.e., use $\mathbf{v}' = \mathbf{v}\mathbf{n}$, in which case we obtain a height plot of the velocity magnitude.

Several elements control the quality of a displacement plot. First, the displacement factor k in Equation (6.7) must be carefully set. Values that are too large would warp the input surface too much, which can easily lead to self-intersecting surfaces. Even when self intersection does not occur, large warp factors shift the displaced surface far away from its actual location. This conveys incorrect insight to the user, as one will visually associate the warped surface with the actual location $p + k\mathbf{v}(p)$ it is drawn at, and not with the original location p the surface was intended to represent. Values that are too small, on the other hand, do not show the warping effect strongly enough so that it is recognizable in the visualization and it lets the users map it back visually to a displacement value. Just as for color mapping, nonlinear scaling and clamping techniques can be applied

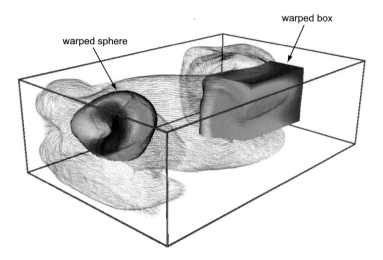

Figure 6.13. Displacement plots using a box and a spherical surface.

to control the mapping of the vector data to displacement values. A second important parameter is the shape and position of the surface to be warped. These parameters actually control the set of points at which we are interested in visualizing the vector field. Planar surfaces are often a popular choice for displacement plots. Since they are flat, displacement values are easiest to distinguish on them. However, even when using planar surfaces, some care is needed. The worst case takes place when the surface is (almost) tangent to the vector field to be visualized. In this case, the warped surface stays in the same plane as the original surface, so the actual goal of using the warping as a visual cue for the vector field is not reached. Moreover, such situations easily lead to self-intersecting polygons on the surface.

Besides planes, other geometric objects can be used to create displacement plots. In Figure 6.13, two displacement plots were created using a sphere (left) and a box (right) surface, both colored by the velocity magnitude. The visual difference between the expected shape of the original object and the perceived (deformed) shape serves as a cue for the vector magnitude. In addition to surfaces, 1D curves can be used too, if desired. In general, the choice of the object to deform should be correlated with the expected vector field behavior and meaning. For example, if we have

a force field describing material deformation in the 3D domain of some
mechanical assembly, we can use the assembly's own surface as input for
the displacement plot. The obtained visualization conveys the "natural"
meaning that the assembly's surface is being deformed by the force acting
on it.

6.5   Stream Objects

Both the vector glyph and displacement plot techniques visually relate the
actual position p of a sample point to its displaced position $p + \mathbf{v}\Delta t$ in the
vector field $\mathbf{v}$. We can think of vector glyphs as "trajectories" over a short
time Δt of imaginary particles released in the vector field at some desired
locations. Similarly, displacement plots can be seen as the end points of
the trajectory over a short time Δt of a given input surface. Hence, the
natural question arises whether we could use such trajectories, computed
for longer time intervals, to visualize a given vector field.

Stream objects are the answer to this question. Rather than a single
visualization technique, stream objects are more of a family of such techniques, related by the idea of visualizing the trajectory of some input object
in a vector field over a given time interval.

6.5.1   Streamlines

We shall start exploring the stream objects family with its simplest,
and probably most frequently used, member: the streamline. Before we
proceed, we must make a distinction between time-dependent and time-
independent vector fields. Time-dependent vector fields are quite common
in computational fluid dynamics, where they describe the flow of a fluid as
a function of both space and time. However, such fields are quite difficult
to visualize, given the high dimensionality (and also the sheer size) of the
involved data. For example, visualizing a 3D time-dependent vector field requires displaying four dimensions for every data point. Time-independent,
also called *stationary*, vector fields are a function only of space. Given this
terminology, a *streamline* is the curved path over a given time interval T of
an imaginary particle passing through a given start location or *seed* p_0, in a
stationary vector field over some domain D. A streamline can be described
as the integral of the vector field $\mathbf{v}$ over some interval T and starting from

the location p_0:

$$S = \{p(\tau), \tau \in [0, T]\}, p(\tau) = \int_{t=0}^{\tau} \mathbf{v}(p)dt, \quad \text{where } p(0) = p_0. \quad (6.8)$$

We have said that streamlines are defined for time-independent vector fields. Indeed, in Equation (6.8), the time t represents *integration* time and not the *physical time* of a time-dependent dataset. To eliminate confusion, it is useful to think about integration time as just a technical concept. In case of time-dependent vector fields, several different types of curves can be integrated in the vector field. *Streamlines* can be computed by fixing the physical time to a desired value and using Equation (6.8). *Particle traces* can be computed as the paths of a given set of seed points, or particles, in the time-dependent field $\mathbf{v}(t)$. In this case, the integration time from Equation (6.8) and the physical time that defines $\mathbf{v}(t)$ coincide, so the particle traces change direction as they advance while the flow changes in time. *Streaklines* are particle traces at a given time instant that have passed through a given location. Visualizing time-dependent vector fields with stream objects is an advanced topic that we shall not cover in further detail.

For a sampled vector dataset, we must solve Equation (6.8) using the definition of $\mathbf{v}$ given by the reconstruction equation (Equation (3.2)). In the case of piecewise linear basis functions, we remember that this reconstruction gives the vector field over every dataset cell as a linear combination of the vector field values at the cell vertices. For contours (defined by Equation (5.2)), we used this property of the reconstruction to represent contours as a set of piecewise linear primitives (lines or planes), one primitive per dataset cell. However, we cannot use the same per-cell construction strategy for streamlines. Since the interpolated vector direction usually changes within every cell, the streamline segments determined by each cell are not straight lines. Instead, we shall compute streamlines by discretizing the integration time t.

Several numerical methods solve Equation (6.8) approximately by discretizing the time t and replacing the integral with a finite sum. The simplest, but also least accurate, method is the Euler integration, given by the expression

$$\int_{t=0}^{\tau} \mathbf{v}(p)dt = \sum_{i=0}^{\tau/\Delta t} \mathbf{v}(p_i)\Delta t \quad \text{where } p_i = p_{i-1} + \mathbf{v}_{i-1}\Delta t. \quad (6.9)$$

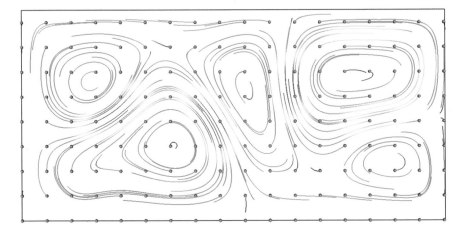

Figure 6.14. Streamlines in a 2D flow field. The small gray balls indicate the seed points.

The points p_i sample the streamline starting from the seed point p_0. The Euler integration considers the vector field $\mathbf{v}$ to be spatially constant and equal to $\mathbf{v}(p_i)$ between every sample point p_i and the next one p_{i+1}. Hence, the streamline will be approximated by a piecewise-linear curve, or polyline $p_0, \ldots, p_N$.

Figure 6.14 shows a first example of streamlines. Here, we trace $18*9 = 162$ streamlines in a 2D flow vector field. The seed points, indicated by gray ball glyphs, are equally spaced in the x and y directions and are obtained by regularly subsampling the dataset on a grid of 18 by 9 points. The streamlines are colored by the vector magnitude using a blue (low speed) to red (high speed) colormap. All streamlines are traced up to the same maximal time T, but have different lengths, since the vector field has large variations in speed, as indicated by the streamline colors.

The streamline tracing process is described by Listing 6.1 for a 2D vector dataset. The code in Listing 6.1 accepts a vector dataset **g** and traces a single streamline from a given location **p0** using the integration step **dt**. The streamline stops when it either exits the dataset, exceeds a maximal length **maxL**, or exceeds a maximal time **maxT**. The streamline is saved as a polyline into an unstructured grid **s**. In this example, we use Euler integration and piecewise linear vector interpolation, but different

```
void streamline(Grid& g,float* p0,float dt,float maxT,
                float maxL,UnstructuredGrid& s)
{
  float v[3],p[3],q[3];
  int   c = g.findCell(p0);              //find starting cell
  float t = 0, l=0;
  int   i = 0;

  for (;t+=dt,i++,p[0]=p0[0],p[1]=p0[1]) //trace streamline
  {
    if (c==-1 || t>maxT || l>maxL)
//stop criteria reached?
       break;
    s.setPoint(i,p0);                    //add streamline point
    if (i)
    {
      s.setCell(i-1,i-1,i);              //add streamline cell
      l += length(p,p0);                 //update length
    }
    g.getC1Vector(c,p0,v);
    p0[0] += v[0]*dt;                     //Euler integration
    p0[1] += v[1]*dt;
    g.world2cell(c,p0,q);                 //exit current cell?
    if (q[0]<0 || q[0]>1 || q[1]<0 || q[1]>1)
       c = g.findCell(p0);
//find newly entered cell
  }
}
```

Listing 6.1. Streamline tracing.

strategies can be used if desired. In terms of cost, an important factor is the use of the `Grid::findCell` method, which returns the cell id a given world point is into. As explained in Section 3.8, this operation can be quite costly on structured and unstructured grids, as it involves searching.

Within a cell, the vector field is interpolated using the `Grid::getC1Vector` method described in Section 3.8. To test whether the integration has exited the current cell, we transform the world coordinates p0 into parametric coordinates q using the `Grid::world2cell` method and check whether the parametric coordinates fall outside the $[0, 1]$ range. In actual production code, the search of the cell containing a given location can be done more efficiently than using the generic `findCell`, based on the heuristic that small integration steps potentially move the current point out of the current cell into one of its (direct) neighbor cells. Hence, the search can start checking these neighbors first. The `setPoint` and `setCell` methods add a point and a cell, respectively, to the streamline dataset (see Section 3.8). Specifically, the ith cell of the streamline is formed by the points i and $i + 1$ of the dataset. Finally, the `length` function computes the length of the line segment with endpoints p and p0.

Several technical considerations arise when computing streamlines. A first concern regards the accuracy of the integration method used. Euler integration has an error of $O(\Delta t^2)$, which means that halving the integration step Δt reduces the integration error by a quarter. However, numerical integration has the unpleasant property that it accumulates errors as the integration time τ increases, since positions along the streamline are computed incrementally. This means, in practice, that the "tails" of long streamlines tend to deviate from their actual correct locations. The accuracy of integration can be improved by using higher-order methods. A frequently used replacement for the Euler integration is the Runge-Kutta method. This method approximates the vector field $\mathbf{v}$ between two sample points p_i and p_{i+1} along a stream object with the average value $\frac{\mathbf{v}(p_i)+\mathbf{v}(p_{i+1})}{2}$. This method produces more accurate streamlines than the Euler method for the same time step Δt. This allows us to increase the time step Δt and maintain similar accuracy, which in turn decreases computation time. Many other numerical methods exist for approximating Equation (6.8) with various trade-offs between accuracy and computational complexity. We refer for further details to the specialized literature [Press et al. 02].

In contrast, methods such as marching cubes, for example, bound the error by the size of a cell, since they do not propagate information from cell to cell. Setting the integration step Δt to small values reduces such errors, but at additional costs: the integration takes more time, and the resulting streamline has more sample points, which need more storage and rendering time.

Finding optimal values for Δt is, in general, a difficult problem. These depend *locally* on the dataset cell sizes, vector field magnitude, vector field variation, desired streamline length, and desired computation speed. By "locally," we mean that it is often desirable to adapt Δt as the integration proceeds instead of using a constant Δt for the complete streamline. Although there is no silver bullet for setting Δt optimally, there are a few hints in this direction. Using a constant Δt is equivalent to a uniform sampling of the *integration time* dimension. For a vector field of varying magnitude, this obviously produces sample points p_i that are spaced irregularly along the streamline, or a nonuniform sampling of the *spatial* dimension. This is often undesirable. Even when using a small Δt, large vector field values generate large streamline steps $|\mathbf{v}|\Delta t$ that can skip several dataset cells, hence undersample the vector field. For a rapidly varying vector field, this can change the streamline direction dramatically, yielding a misleading visualization. A simple way to alleviate this problem is to adapt Δt locally to the vector field magnitude so that the spatial integration step $|\mathbf{v}|\Delta t$ has constant length. Setting Δt so that this length is smaller than the current cell size ensures that no vector samples are skipped during the integration. In practice, spatial integration steps of around one-third of a cell size should yield good results for most vector fields.

A second issue regards the integration stop criterion. A maximal time criterion, such as in Equation (6.8), is quite nonintuitive, as the total streamline length largely depends on the actual vector field values. A better, more intuitive stop criterion is to set a maximal length for the streamline. Also, the integration process should be stopped when the vector field magnitude becomes zero, since the trajectory comes to an end there. In practice, one would stop integrating when the vector field magnitude $|\mathbf{v}|$ drops under some small value ϵ.

Last but not least, a crucial issue for the effectiveness of streamline visualizations is the choice of the location and number of seed points. A streamline conveys information visually for the points on (or close to) its trajectory. However, when we choose a seed point, we don't know in advance which points of a dataset the streamline will go through. Setting the seed point answers only the question "show all points that are on the trajectory starting here," or "show where this point would be advected by the field." A variant of this question is "show all points on the trajectory ending here." This can be easily achieved by using negative Δt values, i.e., tracing the streamline upstream. By tracing both upstream and downstream streamlines, we can answer yet another variant of our question, i.e., "show all points on the trajectory passing through here." One way to use streamlines is to densely sample some area of interest, or "seed area" in the dataset with seed points and next trace streamlines until some stop criterion is met. However, even if the seed area is densely sampled, this does not guarantee the complete dataset will be densely covered by streamlines. Depending on the actual field, areas in the dataset can even remain completely unintersected by streamlines, so the user cannot tell anything about the vector field there from the visualization.

A second strategy for the seed point distribution is to densely sample the complete dataset instead of only some given area. The aim of this strategy is to produce visualizations that answer the question "show the complete dataset with streamlines." The resulting visualization should have several properties, as follows [Verma et al. 00]:

- coverage: every dataset point should be at a minimal (small) distance from some streamline, so that the user has some visual cue of what the field looks like close to that point. In a more relaxed setting, we can require that the streamlines should cover all important flow features. By important features, we mean all features of the vector field that are of interest for a given user in a given application context. Although task-specific, and thus hard to ensure in a unique manner, this is an important design principle. We can restate this also in terms of having streamlines sample the "feature space" densely enough, so that all items that are considered relevant features are reflected in the visualization.

- uniformity: the density of the streamlines in the final image should be confined between some minimal and maximal values. This translates into having a bounded streamline sampling density of the image plane. Indeed, if we have too many streamlines over a given area, cluttering will occur. If we have too few then undersampling occurs, i.e., we are not able to tell what the field looks like between two streamlines. This is relatively simple to ensure for 2D datasets, where the image space coincides with the geometric (dataset) space. For 3D visualizations, this is harder to do, as it requires either a view-dependent evaluation of the streamline density in image space or a more restrictive bounding of the volumetric streamline density.

- continuity: longer streamlines are preferred over short ones, as they produce less discontinuous, easier to interpret, visualizations. On a more subtle level, visual continuity across a streamline is related to the uniformity criterion mentioned previously.

Just as for the vector glyphs, several sampling strategies are possible to create dense streamline visualizations. The simplest solution is to distribute the seed points regularly or randomly in the domain and trace streamlines of some minimal length. This solution gives good coverage but can easily lead to cluttering. A better solution is to trace a streamline until it gets closer to any of the already traced streamlines or itself, thereby minimizing cluttering. We can combine this idea with an iterative insertion of seed points in the areas of the dataset that are undersampled, thereby maximizing coverage. Finally, we can discard streamlines that are too short and keep trying new seed points until the streamline length exceeds the desired threshold, thereby maximizing the streamline average length. A simple-to-implement and effective method for creating evenly distributed streamlines based on these ideas was proposed by Jobard and Lefer in [Jobard and Lefer 97]. A related, albeit more complex-to-implement method based on optimizing a quality energy-like functional based on the positions of the seed points and streamline characteristics was proposed by Turk and Banks in [Turk and Banks 96]. This method has been extended to structured curvilinear grids by Mao et al. [Mao et al. 98]. A different method for creating evenly distributed streamlines for 2D vector fields related to the previous techniques is the "farthest point streamline seeding" of Merbarki et al. [Mebarki et al. 05]. Methods that sample the dataset with streamlines that attempt to cover all topological patterns of interest in the vector field are proposed by Verma et al. [Verma et al. 00] for 2D fields and Ye et al. [Ye et al. 05] for 3D fields.

6.5.2 Stream Tubes

In addition to plain lines, we can use other graphical shapes to visualize the integral trajectories. A popular choice is *stream tubes*. These can be constructed by sweeping a circular cross-section along the streamline curve computed as described previously. At every streamline point, the cross-section is orthogonal to the streamline tangent vector. Additionally, we can use a vector glyph at the downstream end of the stream tube to indicate the vector field direction, which is not shown by the plain streamlines or stream tubes. Figure 6.15 demonstrates this technique on our familiar 2D MHD vector field. In both images, around 500 stream tubes capped with vector glyphs are drawn from a set of seed points obtained by regularly subsampling the domain in both directions. The difference between the two images relies in the way we cap the tubes.

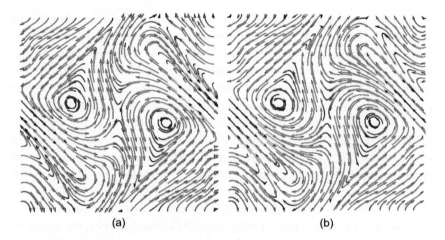

(a)   (b)

Figure 6.15. Stream tubes with arrow heads. The construction can ensure that either (a) the seed points or (b) the arrow heads are arranged on a regular grid.

In Figure 6.15(a), the stream tubes are integrated *forward* in the vector field and the caps are, hence, placed at the *downstream* end of the tubes. In this case, the tubes begin on a regular (uniform) grid and the arrow glyph ends exhibit an irregular behavior, subject to the vector field behavior. In Figure 6.15(b), the stream tubes are integrated *backward* in the vector field, so the caps are placed at the *upstream* end of the tube, i.e., the seed points themselves. The tubes appear to begin on an irregular grid (the set of end points of the backward integration trajectories) and they end, with arrow glyphs, on the regular seed point grid. Depending on the actual visualization task, as well as the aesthetic preference of the user, one image may be subtly better than the other.

The thickness, or radius, parameter of stream tubes can be also used to convey some extra information. For example, we can modulate the tube radius to map a scalar value along the stream tubes, such as temperature, density, viscosity, or pressure, but also flow-related quantities, such as vorticity. However, this degree of freedom has some limitations. The visual range of the radius is quite small. There is a lower bound imposed by the difficulty of distinguishing the actual radius of tubes that are too thin, and there is an upper bound beyond which stream tubes would take too much space and (self)intersect, just as the vector glyphs. An interesting effect

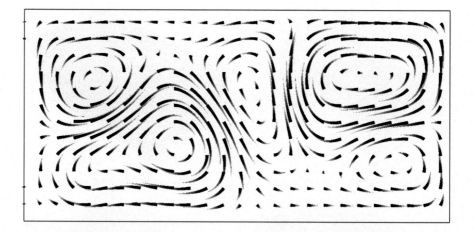

Figure 6.16. Stream tubes with radius and luminance modulated by normalized tube length.

can be obtained by modulating both the tube radius and color as functions of the normalized tube length (see Figure 6.16). We use here the same 2D flow dataset as our first streamline example (see Figure 6.14). For every seed point, obtained by regular domain subsampling, we trace a stream tube whose radius varies linearly from some maximum value R_{max} to 0 and whose luminance varies from black to white. The obtained effect resembles a set of curved arrow glyphs. The luminance and radius visual cues enhance each other to convey an arguably better insight than the plain streamlines of Figure 6.14.

6.5.3 Streamlines and Tubes in 3D Datasets

Choosing an appropriate sampling strategy that solves the coverage, density, and continuity issues well is more critical when tracing streamlines in 3D datasets as compared to 2D datasets. Figure 6.17 illustrates several sampling strategies and parameter settings for a 3D flow dataset. In all cases, we obtain the uniformly spaced seed points by undersampling the uniform dataset ($128 \times 85 \times 42$ points) at some given rate in all three dimensions. The streamlines are colored by the velocity magnitude using a blue-to-red colormap. First, we undersample at a rate of $10 \times 10 \times 10$ (see Figure 6.17(a)) and use a maximal streamline length of 100, which is close to

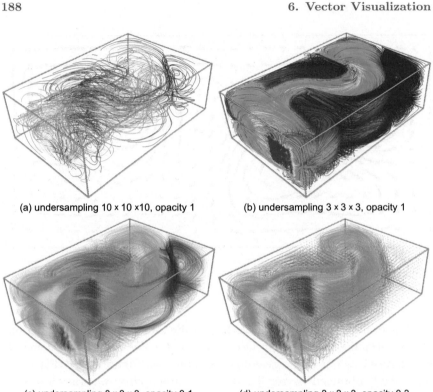

(a) undersampling 10 × 10 ×10, opacity 1   (b) undersampling 3 × 3 × 3, opacity 1

(c) undersampling 3 × 3 × 3, opacity 0.1   (d) undersampling 3 × 3 × 3, opacity 0.3

Figure 6.17. Streamlines in a 3D flow dataset.

the size of the domain's length. This avoids cluttering but creates a sparse visualization that fails to convey insight in many areas. We can improve coverage by decreasing the undersampling to a rate of $3 \times 3 \times 3$ and use the same maximal length (see Figure 6.17(b)). Due to the increased streamline density, the flow structure becomes easier to follow, at least in the outer zones. The relative spatial continuity in velocity magnitude, mapped to color hue continuity, helps us distinguish coherent flow patterns, such as the high-speed flow inner core (green) and the maximal speed zone located at the outflow (red). However, occlusion becomes a problem. We can solve the occlusion problem as we did for the vector glyphs, i.e., by lowering the transparency of the streamlines to 0.1 (see Figure 6.17(c)). Finally, as a comparison, we use the same $3 \times 3 \times 3$ undersampling rate but now trace

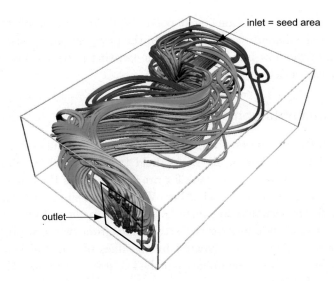

Figure 6.18. Stream tubes traced from a seed area placed at the flow inlet.

streamlines until a maximal time of 100 is reached (see Figure 6.17(d)). In this dataset, the velocity magnitude ranges between 0 and 2. However, as we see in Figure 6.17(d), we now obtain many very short streamlines in the low-speed flow areas. This lets us better visualize the flow's high-speed inner core. This image can be thought as generalizing the vector glyph visualization in Figure 6.8(c): the vector glyphs are actually very short streamlines computed with a single integration step.

Being 3D objects, stream tubes have the extra advantage of providing some shading and occlusion cues, which allow us to better determine their actual relative position and orientation in 3D vector visualizations, as compared to plain streamlines drawn as 1D curves. However, as it is already visible from Figure 6.17, stream tubes are thicker, so they take more screen space, which increases cluttering.

In case we are not interested in a dense coverage of the complete domain with stream objects, choosing the seed area must be done with the same level of care as in 2D and 3D datasets. Figure 6.18 illustrates this for the already familiar 3D flow dataset. Here, we densely sample a circular area close to the flow inlet with 200 stream tubes. The visualization clearly shows how the flow bounces against the invisible obstacle close to the inlet, gets deflected in all directions, next bends to avoid a second obstacle, and finally exits the domain via the outlet. In the last portion, we also detect a separation of the flow into two symmetric twisting patterns that get both sucked by the outlet.

6.5.4   Stream Ribbons

In Figure 6.18, we saw how a dense bundle of stream tubes can be used to gain insight into how a 3D vector field twists around its direction of advection. The visual cues to look for are stream tubes that twist around each other, yet stay close to each other. We can get a similar type of insight using a different visualization technique called *stream ribbons*. A stream ribbon is created by launching two streamlines from two seed points close to each other. The surface created by the lines of minimal length with endpoints on the two streamlines is called a stream ribbon. If the two streamlines stay relatively close to each other then the stream ribbon's twisting around its center curve gives a measure of the twisting of the vector field around the direction of advection.

Figure 6.19 shows two examples of stream ribbons. Both examples trace the ribbons from the inlet region of our familiar 3D flow dataset. In the left image, two relatively thick ribbons are traced. The left ribbon quickly enters a region of high vorticity, as indicated by its twisting. In

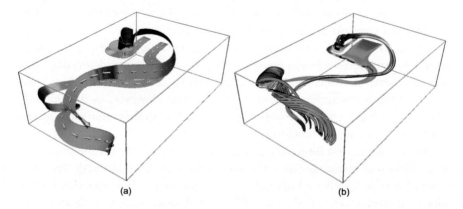

(a)   (b)

Figure 6.19. Stream ribbons in a 3D flow dataset. (a) Two thick ribbons. (b) 20 thin ribbons.

contrast, the right ribbon strays relatively untwisted until its last portion, where it shows evidence of some moderate vorticity. Both ribbons are colored with the streamwise vorticity using a classical blue-to-red colormap. The two streamlines that form the edge of each ribbon are visualized with stream tubes. As an extra element, vector glyphs are added on the central symmetry curve of each ribbon, to show the advancing direction of the flow. The vector glyphs are scaled to show the velocity magnitude. As we can see, the velocity magnitude is high in the low-vorticity areas and relatively low in the high-vorticity areas.

In the right image, 20 stream ribbons are traced from the same inlet region as in the previous case. In the first portion, the flow is laminar, so the stream ribbons stay connected to each other, forming a stream surface, as we shall see in the next section. This apparent surface is suddenly broken by the impact of the flow with the invisible obstacle situated in the domain. From this location, every stream ribbon evolves separately from the others, the complete set of ribbons being split into two main components. In the last portion, the ribbons exhibit the same general twist pattern that was shown by the stream tube visualization in Figure 6.18.

6.5.5   Stream Surfaces

We have seen in the previous section how stream ribbons, densely seeded on a given curve, can be used to visualize how that curve would be advected in the vector field. This technique can be generalized to compute so-called *stream surfaces* of the vector field. Given a seed curve Γ, a stream surface S_Γ is a surface that contains Γ and is everywhere tangent to the vector field. Given this definition, both stream ribbons and stream tubes can be seen as particular cases of stream surfaces. For stream tubes, the seed curve is a small closed curve such as a circle, whereas for the stream ribbons the seed curve is a short line. Stream surfaces have the intuitive property that the flow described by the vector field is always tangent to the surface, i.e., cannot cross it. Hence, stream surfaces whose seed curves intersect the flow domain boundary or are closed curves can be used to segment the flow domain into disjoint regions that exhibit noninterfering flow patterns. Finally, stream surfaces have the additional advantage, as compared to streamlines or stream ribbons, of being two-dimensional objects, which are easier to follow visually.

Stream surfaces can be constructed in several ways. A simple approach is to trace densely seeded streamlines from the seed curve. Next, the traced streamlines are connected to generate the stream surface. This can be done, for example, by connecting each vertex of the actual polylines that represent the streamlines with the closest vertex of any other such polyline. A different approach is to parameterize the streamlines by traveled distance. Points on all streamlines that have the same traveled distance value are next connected. Both approaches essentially parameterize the stream surface along two directions, one tangent to the (advected) seed curve, and one normal to it, in the direction of the flow. Sampling the two directions allows us to construct a stream surface as a quad mesh.

When constructing stream surfaces, one must be careful to correctly treat regions of high divergence, whether positive or negative. In such regions, the streamlines do not run parallel to each other. Detecting such regions can be done, for example, by comparing the distances between the advected seed curve points that are to be connected with a reference value. If the actual distance becomes too small then the streamlines converge, so it may be desirable to remove some of them from the tracing process to prevent too small polygons from being created, reduce computational costs, and increase performance. If the actual distance becomes too large then the streamlines diverge. Such a situation is easily visible in Figure 6.19 at a short distance from the inlet, where the flow, and hence the ribbons too, abruptly get split into two separate sets. In such a case, we must decide whether we want to explicitly model this as a flow split event or not. If so then the advected seed curve is split into two separate curves at this point, and these curves get advected separately, giving rise to two independent stream surfaces. This is useful if we want to explicitly visualize such flow split events. If we do not want to model such splits then extra seed points can be added along the advected seed curve segment whose length exceeds the reference value, in order to maintain a high streamline density, and the generation of the stream surface is continued as usual.

6.6   Texture-Based Vector Visualization

So far, most of the presented vector visualizations used discrete objects, such as vector glyphs, streamlines, or stream surfaces. By their very nature, discrete visualizations cannot convey information about every point of a given dataset domain, as we have seen on several occasions. The interpolation of attributes between these discrete objects must be done visually by the user. In contrast, dense visualizations such as color plots present the user with a (piecewise) continuous signal that can be easier to interpret. The question arises how we can do this for vector fields.

Texture-based visualizations are an answer. The idea is to create a texture signal that encodes the direction and magnitude of a vector field in the various texture parameters such as luminance, graininess, color, and pattern structure. The main challenge here is how to encode the vector direction in the texture parameters. An intuitive and effective idea is to use the texture graininess for this. Since their appearance at the beginning of the 1990s [van Wijk 91, Cabral and Leedom 93], several methods have used this principle to produce visualizations of vector fields.

To understand the basic principle, consider an input texture N consisting of small-scale black-and-white noise defined over the domain of the 2D vector field we want to visualize (see Figure 6.20). For each pixel p of this domain, we trace a streamline $S(p, s)$ upstream and downstream through p for some maximal distance L. Here, s parameterizes the streamline. Next, we set the value $T(p)$ of the output texture T at the current location p to be the weighted sum of the values of the input noise texture N measured along the streamline $S(p)$ that passes through p. As a weighting function

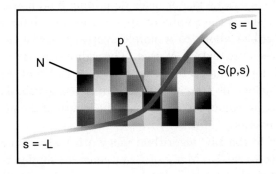

Figure 6.20. Line integral convolution principle. The color $T(p)$ of pixel p is given by integrating the colors of a noise texture N along the streamline $S(p, s)$ passing through p. The red color intensity along S shows the magnitude of the weight function $k(s)$.

$k(s) : \mathbb{R} \to \mathbb{R}_+$, we can use a Gaussian $k(s) = e^{-s^2}$, or other functions that are 1 at the origin and decay smoothly and symmetrically from the origin until they reach near-zero values at the maximal distance L.

The obtained value $T(p)$ is

$$T(p) = \frac{\int_{-L}^{L} N(S(p,s))k(s)ds}{\int_{-L}^{L} k(s)ds}. \tag{6.10}$$

The denominator in Equation (6.10) normalizes the weight factors for an arbitrary value of L.

Intuitively, we can think of this process as blurring, or filtering, the noise image along the streamlines with a set of filters $k(s)$ that are aligned with the streamlines. As we shall see in Chapter 9, the filtering operation described by Equation (6.10) can be seen as a convolution of the noise and filter functions N and k. Hence, this process is also known in the visualization field as *line integral convolution (LIC)* [Cabral and Leedom 93, Rezk-Salama et al. 99].

If we apply Equation (6.10) for all pixels using streamline lengths L of several tens of pixels, we obtain a texture T whose pixel colors exhibit little variation along a streamline, due to the strong blurring, but show strong variation between neighboring streamlines, due to the similar strong variation of the initial noise. Although they can be used for any vector field, texture-based vector visualization methods have been mainly developed in the context of visualizing vector fields describing fluid flows.

Figure 6.21 shows the results of applying the line integral convolution algorithm described above to a simple synthetic vector field.[1] The left image shows the noise texture N used. The right image shows the resulting LIC texture T for an integration length L equal to 5% of the domain size. Using smaller values for L creates textures increasingly similar to the input noise. Using larger values for L increases the length of the perceived snake-like texture patterns.

In addition to the LIC algorithm, many other algorithms use textures to visualize vector fields. Many of them generate similar textures to the LIC method, which are coherent along various types of flow lines, such as streamlines or streaklines, and show a high noise-like variation between

---

[1] The C code for generating these images is freely available with the SIGGRAPH '99 Course Notes [McReynolds and Blythe 99].

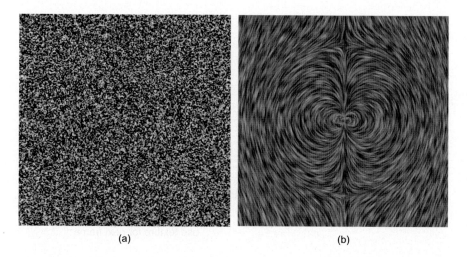

(a)   (b)

Figure 6.21. Line integral convolution visualization. (a) Input noise. (b) The resulting LIC texture.

neighboring flow lines. This basic principle set aside, the specific algorithms differ in many respects, such as the type of vector field they can depict (stationary or time-dependent), the dimension of the depicted domain (planar, curved surface embedded in 3D, or volumetric), whether they generate a still or an animated texture, and the actual implementation used to create the texture. We point the interested reader to a survey article on this topic [Laramee et al. 04].

A particularly attractive algorithm for texture-based vector visualization is the Image Based Flow Visualization method, or IBFV [van Wijk 02a]. IBFV and its variants [van Wijk 03, Telea and van Wijk 03] produce not just static, but animated, flow textures in real time, can handle both stationary and instationary fields defined on domains ranging from planar 2D to volumetric ones, and are quite simple to implement.

6.6.1 IBFV Method

In this section, we detail the IBFV method that operates on 2D planar domains, which is also the simplest to implement in its class. The principle of the method is sketched in Figure 6.22. To understand IBFV, consider a time-dependent scalar property $I : D \times \mathbb{R}_+ \to \mathbb{R}_+$ such as the

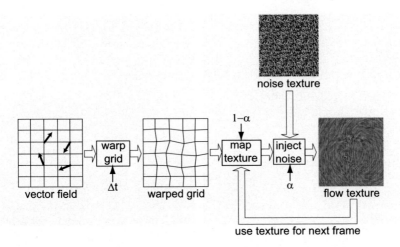

noise texture

vector field   Δt   warped grid

warp grid

map texture

inject noise

flow texture

1−α

α

use texture for next frame

Figure 6.22. Principle of image-based flow visualization (IBFV).

image intensity, defined on a 2D domain D. The value $I(x,t) \to [0,1]$ describes our property at a given point $x \in D$ of the flow domain D at a time moment t. The advection in time of the property I in a vector field $\mathbf{v} : D \times \mathbb{R}_+ \to \mathbb{R}^2$ is given by

$$I(x + \mathbf{v}(x,t)\Delta t, t + \Delta t) = I(x,t). \tag{6.11}$$

This process is sometimes called *forward advection*, as it states that the property I at a location $x + \mathbf{v}(x,t)\Delta t$ downstream and at a future moment $t + \Delta t$ is equal to the current property $I(x,t)$ at the current moment t. In contrast, the *backward advection* expresses the property I at a location x at the current moment t as a function of the property at an upstream location $x' = x - \mathbf{v}(x',t - \Delta t)\Delta t$ at a previous moment $t - \Delta t$. The time step Δt discretizes the time and allows us to solve Equation (6.11) iteratively. As stated earlier, we would like to advect a noise texture so that we obtain an image with low contrasts along a pathline and high contrasts across neighboring streamlines. However, if we simply advect an initial image $I(x,0) = N(x)$, where $N : D \to [0,1]$ is a noise texture like the one shown in Figure 6.22, different points in the flow domain placed on the same pathline will "overwrite" each other's property values I in different ways, depending on the order in which we solve Equation (6.11) for the different points. Moreover, we would also like to solve the question of how to create an animated flow texture.

These goals can be met if we add a so-called *injection term* to Equation (6.11). Intuitively, this term can be seen as ink or dye that is injected into the flow domain at every point x in space and moment t in time. The combined advection and injection process is described by

$$I(x+\mathbf{v}(x,t)\Delta t, t+\Delta t) = (1-\alpha)I(x,t)+\alpha N(x+\mathbf{v}(x,t)\Delta t, t+\Delta t). \quad (6.12)$$

Here, $N(x,t)$ describes the injected property, which is also a function of space and time. The parameter $\alpha \in [0,1]$ controls the ratio of advection to injection. A value of $\alpha = 1$ states that there is no advection, so our property I simply equals the injected signal N. A value of $\alpha = 0$ states that there is no injection, i.e., yields the pure advection Equation (6.11). Setting α to a value between 0 and 1 yields an image that exhibits both local variation (due to the injected noise) and also coherence along pathlines (due to the advection). Good values in practice are $\alpha \in [0, 0.2]$.

There remains the question of which noise texture $N(x,t)$ to inject. Let us first consider a time-independent signal $N(x)$. To achieve a high spatial contrast, neighboring pixels should have different colors. We can achieve this by setting N to a random signal consisting of black and white dots, as shown in Figure 6.22. The size d of the dots should be correlated with the velocity magnitude. In practice, using a dot size $d \in [2, 10]$ pixels gives good results.

Applying Equation (6.12) for a few steps results in flow textures such as the one shown at the right in Figure 6.22. However, we can do better than producing static flow images. For this, let us take a time-dependent noise texture $N'(x,t)$ that is obtained from our original stationary noise texture $N(x)$ as

$$N'(x,t) = f((t + N(x)) \bmod 1). \quad (6.13)$$

Here, $f : \mathbb{R}_+ \rightarrow [0,1]$ is a periodic function with period 1. Intuitively, Equation (6.13) says that the intensity of every pixel x of the time-dependent texture $N(x,t)$ oscillates in time controlled by the periodic function f, but all pixels have different (random) initial phases controlled by the static noise $N(x)$. This is illustrated in Figure 6.23 for a one-dimensional time-dependent noise signal $N(x,t)$ for a sinusoidal function f. Using N' instead of N in Equation (6.12) produces an animated texture that seems to

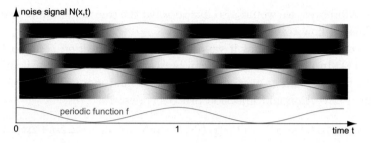

Figure 6.23. Time-dependent noise signal design. The red curves show the periodic function f shifted by random phase values. A vertical cross-section of the grayscale stripes gives the noise texture $N(x,t)$ at a given moment t.

move with the flow, an effect that is especially suited for visualizing time-dependent vector fields $\mathbf{x}, \mathbf{t}$. The implementation of both the stationary and time-dependent IBFV methods is described later in this section.

6.6.2 Implementation

We have described a method to produce dense flow textures by advecting and injecting noise textures. We shall now sketch a simple and effective way to implement this process using OpenGL. For a detailed discussion, we refer to the original IBFV publication [van Wijk 02a]. All notations here and in the implementation code (see Listing 6.2) refer to the advection-injection Equation (6.11), which is at the core of the IBFV method.

The implementation uses in total NOISE + 1 textures called tex[0], tex[1],...,tex[NOISE]. The first NOISE textures encode the time sampling of one period of the noise signal $N(x,t)$. We use here NOISE = 32 samples, which is typically enough to capture the periodic behavior of the function f in Equation (6.13). In the following example, we set f to a simple step function. Other functions can be used, such as an exponential decay, a sawtooth, or a sine wave. The last texture tex[NOISE] is a work buffer into which the image $I(x)$ is constructed. The complete process consists of an initialization step (function init() in Listing 6.2) followed by an endless loop consisting of three steps: advection, noise injection, and construction of the work texture (function run()).

The advection itself (see Equation (6.11)) is implemented using an OpenGL polygon mesh (function advect()). We consider the 2D flow domain D to be covered by a set of polygons $\{P_i\}_{i=1..N}$ that have the 2D vertex coordinates $\{x_{ij}\}_{j=1..n(i)}$ and $\{y_{ij}\}_{j=1..n(i)}$. If D has a rectangular shape, we can use a uniform grid of quadrilaterals P_i with equally spaced vertices. Generally, we can use an unstructured grid, as discussed in Section 3.5.4. The advection is done by drawing a polygon mesh whose vertices are slightly warped by the vector field $\mathbf{v}$, textured with the work texture. This deforms, or warps, the work texture in the vector field direction and saves the result into the frame buffer.

After advection, noise injection is implemented by cyclically blending one of the textures `tex[0]`,...,`tex[NOISE-1]`, which encode the time-dependent noise signal $N(x, y)$, on top of the warped texture (function `inject()`). This is done by drawing one large quad with corners $(0, 0); (1, 1)$ that covers the complete frame buffer, textured with the selected noise frame. The convex combination controlled by the factor α in Equation (6.12) is implemented by enabling OpenGL's alpha-blending mechanism (line 28). The α value is encoded in the textures' alpha channel (line 63) alongside the luminance channel that encodes the noise signal N (line 62).

After noise injection, the frame buffer contains the image $I(x, t + \Delta t)$ for the next time step, i.e., the left side of Equation (6.12). Since we use this image in the right side of the equation in the next step, we copy it into the work texture `tex[NOISE]` (line 80). Next, the animation loop repeats.

Finally, let us discuss the various parameters involved. The work texture and frame buffer are both of size ISIZE × ISIZE pixels. The noise textures are typically smaller, taking NSIZE × NSIZE pixels where NSIZE < ISIZE, thereby saving considerable memory. Given this, OpenGL both stretches and replicates the noise texture to cover the entire frame buffer area. The stretch factor NSPOT controls the actual size of the noise spots in the visualization. As explained before, good values are in the range of a few pixels. Similarly, the warping $\mathbf{v}\Delta t$ of the grid vertices should be small enough so that the grid polygons are not too badly distorted. On the other hand, the warping should be large enough so that the advection is visible, i.e., it is least a few pixels. If we are not interested in visualizing differences in velocity magnitude across the flow domain, the simplest solution to the warping issue is to normalize $\mathbf{v}$. If, however, we allow varying values for $|\mathbf{v}|$ on the flow domain, we can clamp $\mathbf{v}\Delta t$ for every warped point separately. Finally, if we are interested in still flow textures similar to the ones produced by the LIC method [Cabral and Leedom 93] rather than animations, we can execute a few tens of iterations of the main loop using a single noise texture (NOISE = 1) and obtain the desired image in the work texture.

Listing 6.2 covers less than two pages or under 100 lines of code and provides an almost fully functional IBFV program. For brevity, we omit the actual OpenGL implementation of the polygonal mesh $\{P_i\}$ and various bits of data scaling and OpenGL initialization code. The implementation of the IBFV method is described in further detail in [van Wijk 02b].

```
1  const  int      ISIZE = 512;    //image size
2  const  int      NSIZE = 64;     //noise texture size
3  const  int      NOISE = 32;     //how many noise frames
4  const  float  NSPOT = 4;        //size of noise spots
5  const  float  T = ISIZE/(NSPOT*NSIZE);
6  GLuint          tex[NOISE+1];   //noise and work textures
7  int             frame = 0;      //frame counter
8
9  float  f(int  t)                //Periodic function
10 { return (t>127)? 1 : 0; }
11
12 void  advect()                  //Advect the work texture
13 {
14     for(int  i=0;i<N;i++)
15     {
16         glBegin(GL_POLYGON);
17         for(int  j=0;j<n(i);j++)
18         {
19             glTexCoord2f($x_{ij}$,$y_{ij}$);
20             glVertex2f($x_{ij} + \mathbf{v}(x_{ij})\Delta t$,$y_{ij} + \mathbf{v}(y_{ij})\Delta t$);
21         }
22         glEnd();
23     }
24 }
25
26 void  inject()                  //Inject noise
27 {
28     glEnable(GL_BLEND);
29     glBindTexture(tex[frame % NOISE]);
30     glBegin(GL_QUAD);
31         glTexCoord2f(0,0);  glVertex2f(0,0);
32         glTexCoord2f(T,0);  glVertex2f(1,0);
33         glTexCoord2f(T,T);  glVertex2f(1,1);
34         glTexCoord2f(0,T);  glVertex2f(0,1);
35     glEnd();
36     glDisable(GL_BLEND);
37 }
```

Listing 6.2. IBFV implementation in OpenGL.

```
38
39  void init(float alpha)
40  {
41      glViewport(0,0,ISIZE,ISIZE);  //Select a 1-to-1 mapping of
42      glMatrixMode(GL_PROJECTION);  //the texture to the frame buffer
43      glTranslatef(-1,-1,0);
44      glScalef(2,2,1);
45      glEnable(GL_TEXTURE_2D);
46      glBlendFunc(GL_SRC_ALPHA,GL_ONE_MINUS_SRC_ALPHA);
47      glGenTextures(NOISE+1,tex);
48
49      int     phase[NSIZE][NSIZE];
50      float   noise[NSIZE][NSIZE][2];
51
52      for(int i=0;i<NSIZE;i++)      //Make spatial noise
53        for(int j=0;j<NSIZE;j++)
54          phase[i][j] = rand() % 256;
55
56      for(int k=0;k<NOISE;k++)      //Make temporal noise
57      {
58        int t = k*256/NOISE;
59        for(int i=0;i<NSIZE;i++)
60          for(int j=0;j<NSIZE;j++)
61          {
62            noise[i][j][0] = f((t+phase[i][j]) % 256);
63            noise[i][j][1] = alpha;
64          }
65        glBindTexture(GL_TEXTURE_2D,tex[k]);
66        glTexImage2D(GL_TEXTURE_2D,0,GL_LUMINANCE_ALPHA,NSIZE,NSIZE,
67                     0,GL_LUMINANCE_ALPHA,GL_FLOAT,noise);
68      }
69  }
70
71  void run()
72  {
73      init(0.10);              //Initialize textures
74      for(;;frame++)
75      {
76        advect();              //Advect work texture to frame buffer
77        inject();              //Inject noise
78                               //Copy frame buffer to work texture
79        glBindTexture(GL_TEXTURE_2D,tex[NOISE]);
80        glCopyTexImage2D(GL_TEXTURE_2D,0,GL_RGB,0,0,SIZE,SIZE,0);
81      }
82  }
```

Listing 6.2. continued.

6.6.3   Examples

Figure 6.24 shows two examples of two 2D flow datasets visualized with
the IBFV method. In the left image, the generated flow texture is encoded
in the luminance channel, whereas the hue shows the vector magnitude
via a blue-to-red colormap. In the right image, the luminance of the flow
texture is directly modulated by the vector magnitude, so bright areas
indicate high-velocity regions. As we can see, these static snapshots of the
IBFV animation have a quite similar look to the results of the LIC method
(see Figure 6.21(b)).

This example also illustrates more of the possibilities of texture-based
visualizations. In addition to the gray noise texture itself, three red, green,
and blue disc-shaped "ink sources" are advected in the flow field. If we implement the visualization using the IBFV method, the advection of the ink
sources is done by simply drawing them on top of every frame after drawing
the noise texture (step 77 in Listing 6.2). The position of the ink sources is
shown in the image by white circles. The trace left by the advected colored
ink is the texture-based equivalent of a dense set of streamlines seeded at
the ink sources. However, there are two differences. Streamline tracing
from a finite point seed set would produce a set of dense, yet distinct geometric primitives of constant opacity. In contrast, the texture-based ink
advection produces a continuous, gradually fading image.

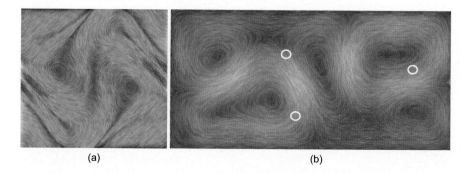

(a)   (b)

Figure 6.24. (a) Texture-based visualization with color-coded velocity magnitude.
(b) Texture-based visualization with luminance-coded velocity magnitude and
three ink sources.

Both methods have their specific strengths and focuses. Streamlines are often used in exact engineering applications where one wants to accurately determine the trajectory of a point starting from a precisely specified seed *location*. Ink advection is useful in getting insight into how the flow from a given seed *area* spreads out over a larger domain. Placing differently colored ink sources at the sources of a flow field, i.e., the points of high positive divergence (see Section 6.1) and letting them get advected until the process visually converges will produce an image showing the flow domain decomposed into several spatial components colored differently as a function of their corresponding source. The curves that separate these areas are called *separatrices* and are important advanced concept in the study of vector fields.

Texture-based visualizations are not limited to 2D planar domains. Figure 6.25(a) shows a texture-based visualization on a 3D surface. The actual surface is an isosurface of the vector magnitude of the 3D flow dataset presented earlier in this section (see, e.g., Figure 6.17). On this isosurface, we first project the vector field and next use the same type of texture-based vector visualization as in the 2D case. Shading is added to the texture on the surface in order to covey spatial cues about the object geometry. Since this is an isosurface of the velocity magnitude, it would be useless to color-code the vector magnitude as we did in the 2D case (see Figure 6.24). However, in practice, other available scalar attributes can be shown via colors, such as pressure, temperature, vorticity, or divergence.

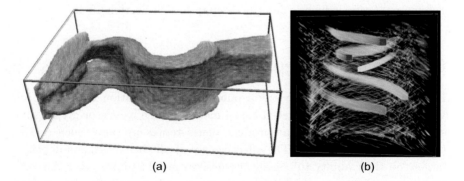

(a)   (b)

Figure 6.25. Image-based flow visualization for (a) 3D surface and (b) volumetric datasets.

Finally, we note that texture-based vector field visualizations can be also applied to volumetric datasets. Figure 6.25(b) visualizes a simple 3D helicoidal flow with the 3D equivalent of the IBFV texture-based method discussed previously for 2D images [Telea and van Wijk 03]. Similar to the 2D visualization shown in Figure 6.24(b), several colored ink sources are used to complement the grayscale noise. The 3D IBFV method follows a similar advection-injection principle to the method for 2D flat and 3D curved surfaces, with a few notable differences. First, producing a dense texture-based visualization requires using either 3D textures, which are still less widely supported by graphics cards than their 2D counterparts, or stacks of 2D textures. Second, the advection step, which is directly supported in OpenGL by drawing warped and textured polygons for the 2D cases, has no 3D counterpart. Indeed, there is, at the current moment, no 3D (volumetric) drawing primitive in OpenGL, and this situation will probably persist for a while. Implementing the advection step in 3D can be done by reducing it to a stack of 2D primitive renderings [Telea and van Wijk 03]. Finally, to be able to see through a 3D dense flow texture, the injection step is modified in the 3D case by adding *alpha*, or *transparency*, noise to the grayscale noise. The alpha noise plays the role of "erasers" injected in the flow volume, yielding a sparsely filled visualization that lets one see through the flow domain (see Figure 6.25(b)).

To visualize the result of the 3D IBFV method, we have to render the resulting texture volume, which contains both color and alpha (transparency) values. This can be done using a visualization technique called *texture-based volume rendering*, which is described separately in Section 10.4.

6.7   Simplified Representation of Vector Fields

In the previous section, we saw a number of visualization techniques for vector fields, ranging from seed-based methods such as vector glyphs and streamlines to methods that produce dense representations, such as the texture-based techniques. The effectiveness of all these methods depends largely on their ability to convey the desired insight into a given dataset. In many applications, this does not mean visualizing all the data points in the same way. Regions that exhibit important characteristics for an application area, such as vortices, speed extrema, or separation lines between regions of laminar flow, should be visualized in different ways as compared to the less-important regions, in order to help users detect their presence in a dataset. Such regions are also called *features* of the vector field.

One of the main reasons for this selective visualization of vector fields is the sheer size of the data. As we have seen in the case of 3D fields, dense visualizations can be quite hard to interpret due to occlusion. Designing visualizations that use a *simplified* version of the vector field is beneficial for large datasets if the simplification keeps (and emphasizes) the features of interest and removes a large amount of uninteresting data. Also, if we know in advance where such features are in a dataset, we can place visualization primitives at those locations, such as vector glyphs or stream objects, instead of doing a dense sampling of the whole domain. Several visualization methods exist which take this approach, as described in the following sections.

6.7.1 Feature Detection Methods

Feature detection methods reduce the vector field to a set of features of interest, described as a set of parameters, such as feature type, position, extent, and strength. Features can be defined either analytically by a feature energy-like function, in which case the detection method tries to find parameter combinations that maximize this function, or as a set of examples or patterns, in which case the detection method searches for best matches in the dataset of these examples. One of the features of interest in flow visualization is *vortices*. Although for most of us what a vortex looks like is quite intuitive, robustly quantifying and detecting one is surprisingly difficult in practice. Many methods for vortex detection have been designed over the last 15 years [Banks and Singer 95, Jankun-Kelly et al. 06]. For an overview of this topic, we point the reader to existing review papers [Post et al. 02, Post et al. 03b].

Although feature detection methods can give good results, they do not come without problems. First, it is hard to define precise numerical criteria to detect such features. For example, it is difficult to precisely quantify the presence and/or extent of a vortex. Second, features appear at different spatial scales in vector fields. In time-dependent fields, there exist also different temporal scales. Finally, there is often no clear spatial separation between a feature and a non-feature area or between several features of the same or different types.

6.7.2 Field Decomposition Methods

The second class of methods is formed by *field decomposition* methods. Such methods partition the vector dataset into regions of strong intra-region (internal) similarity and weak inter-region similarity. At the core of such methods is a similarity metric f that defines how similar two regions are. Different similarity metrics lead to different decompositions that model different end goals or questions. A frequently used similarity metric compares the direction and magnitude of the vector data. Two regions are considered highly similar if the vector field has the same orientation and magnitude on both regions, and dissimilar otherwise. After choosing the metric, decomposition methods usually perform a top-down partitioning or bottom-up agglomerative clustering of the dataset. In the top-down case, the dataset is recursively split in regions that have the least similarity. In the bottom-up case, we start with each sample point (or equivalent small area) being a different region and iteratively cluster the most-similar regions. Both methods produce a multiscale representation of the vector dataset that can be seen as a tree with the smallest regions, or data samples, as leaves and the whole dataset as root region. A desirable constraint for decomposition methods is to produce spatially compact regions, since these are easier to visualize and interpret, and also map well to the "natural" idea of what a vector field feature is. For top-down methods, this constraint can be added in the splitting step. For bottom-up methods, the constraint can be added either in the similarity metric (non-neighboring regions have minimal similarity) or the merging logic (non-neighboring regions are never merged).

An example of a top-down decomposition method is the technique by Heckel et al. [Heckel et al. 99]. Initially, all data points bearing vectors are placed in a single cluster. Next, this cluster is repeatedly subdivided using a weighted best-fit plane so that the variance of an error metric over its two children is minimized. For each cluster, a representative vector is computed as the average of the vector samples in that cluster. The error of a given split is defined as the difference between streamlines traced in the original field and the simplified one given by the representative vectors.

This method produces a vector field simplification that directly encodes elements of the visualization itself: a "good" simplification is that which produces streamlines close to the original field.

Many bottom-up clustering methods exist, and many are based on work on discrete and continuous data clustering performed outside of the visualization domain [Jain and Murty 99]. A simple bottom-up strategy is to use a greedy approach. We define a region as the triplet $R = (P(R), \mathbf{v}(R), O(R))$. Here, $P(R) = \{p_i\}_i$ is the set of sample points, or support, of the region, which is compact from the perspective of the point neighbor relationship. The simplest way we can represent the vector field over $P(R)$ is by a single vector $\mathbf{v}(R)$ located at an origin $O(R)$ inside the area covered by $P(R)$. We begin the clustering by defining, for every point p_j of the dataset, a region $R_j = (p_j, \mathbf{v}(p_j), p_j)$ containing the point and its vector attribute that has the origin at the point itself. The complete region set $\mathcal{R}$ is next simplified iteratively by clustering, at every step, the two most-similar regions $R_a \in \mathcal{R}$, $R_b \in \mathcal{R}$ to form a new region R_{ab}. This new region contains the union of all points in R_a and R_b and a vector $\mathbf{v}(R_{ab})$ that should best reflect the merging of R_a and R_b. A simple way to compute $\mathbf{v}(R_{ab})$ is as the average of $\mathbf{v}(R_a)$ and $\mathbf{v}(R_b)$ weighted by the number of points $|P(a)|$ and $|P(b)|$ in the merged regions. The origin $O(R_{ab})$ of this vector can be computed similarly to the origins of the

---

```
initialize the starting region set R⁰;

for(int  i=0;|Rⁱ| > N; i++)
{
    find  Ra ∈ Rⁱ,  Rb ∈ Rⁱ  so  that  f(Ra, Rb) = min;

    v(Rab) = (v(Ra)|P(Ra)| + v(Rb)|P(Rb)|)/(|P(Ra)| + |P(Rb)|);

    O(Rab) = (O(Ra)|P(Ra)| + O(Rb)|P(Rb)|)/(|P(Ra)| + |P(Rb)|);

    Rab = (P(Ra)∪P(Rb), v(Rab), O(Rab));

    Rⁱ⁺¹ = Rⁱ − {Ra∪Rb};  //eliminate  Ra  and  Rb  from  Rⁱ⁺¹

    Rⁱ⁺¹ = Rⁱ⁺¹∪{Rab};  //add  the  new  Rab  to  Rⁱ⁺¹

    set  Ra  and  Rb  as  children  of  Rab;
}
```

Listing 6.3. Bottom-up greedy clustering of vector data.

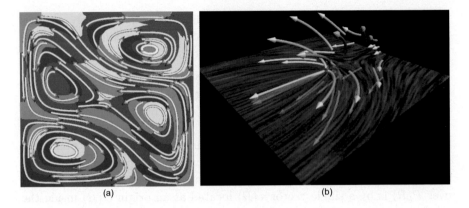

Figure 6.26. Simplified vector field visualization via bottom-up clustering of (a) a 2D field and (b) a 3D field.

merged regions. Finally, we set R_a and R_b as children of R_{ab}, so that a region tree gets constructed during the clustering. The complete algorithm is described in Listing 6.3. From the initial $\mathcal{R}'$, the clustering creates region sets $\mathcal{R}^1, \ldots, \mathcal{R}^F$ until reaching a final region set $\mathcal{R}^F$ that contains a user-specified number of N regions. These regions are the roots of several *region trees* that encode the clustering, as described previously. We can use these trees to obtain several types of simplified representations of our vector field. A *simplified representation*, or *s-rep*, is a region set $\mathcal{R} = \{R_1, \ldots, R_k\}$ of k disjoint regions that are nodes in one of the region trees described earlier and whose union $\bigcap_{i-1}^{k} R_i$ covers the complete dataset.

Having such a s-rep, a visualization of the vector field can be produced by displaying the representative vectors for all regions, streamlines seeded at the region origins and clipped by the region boundaries, or the regions themselves colored in different colors (the last option is effective mainly for 2D domains). By controlling N, one can answer the question "show a vector field with N curved arrows." Figure 6.26 shows such visualizations for 2D and 3D vector fields. The similarity metric used favors vectors with the same direction and magnitude, which explains the elongated shapes of the regions shown in Figure 6.26(a). In Figure 6.26(b), arrow-capped stream tubes are drawn for every region and an additional horizontal slice plane, textured with a spot noise visualization of the vector field, is used to provide an extra visual cue.

Several s-reps can be created from the region trees. The easiest is to use any of the region sets $\mathcal{R}^i$ constructed during the clustering. However, choosing the level i to look at is not very intuitive, as we do not know how many regions it has. Other options for constructing the s-rep are to take regions at a user-given depth from the root in the region trees or an s-rep containing a user-specified number n of regions. Since the decomposition is saved in the region trees, dynamically changing the decomposition level-of-detail and associated visualization can be done in real time, which encourages interactive exploration.

From a reconstruction perspective, the bottom-up clustering method using one representative vector per region is roughly equivalent to a piecewise constant interpolation. Every region support $P(R_i)$ can be thought as the support of a vector basis function $\phi_i = \mathbf{v}(R_i)$ equal to the region's representative vector over $P(R_i)$ and zero outside $P(R_i)$. The hierarchy of simplified representations $\mathcal{R}^i$, $i \in [0, F]$ can be thought as generating a hierarchy of constant bases $\Phi^i = \{\phi_i^j\}_j$ that approximate our vector dataset at various levels of detail. From this perspective, visualizing the regions with streamlines (instead of displaying the representative vector) is slightly misleading from the clustering's approximation perspective. However, our approach is still logical if we regard the clustering strictly as a smart technique for seeding streamlines as a function of the data variation.

The idea of producing a hierarchy of bases that approximates a given vector field at several levels of detail can be taken further by using more sophisticated clustering techniques. One such technique employs a state-of-the-art mathematical tool called the *algebraic multigrid (AMG)* [Griebel et al. 04]. In brief, this method works as follows. Given a vector dataset that has an underlying grid with n sample points $p_1, \ldots, p_n$, we define a so-called coupling matrix $M = \{m_{ij}\}_{1<i,j<n}$. Given two points p_i and p_j, the entry m_{ij} essentially encodes the similarity metric f between the vector values $\mathbf{v}(p_i)$ and $\mathbf{v}(p_j)$ as follows:

$$m_{ij} = \begin{cases} f(p_i, p_j), & i, j \text{ are grid neighbors,} \\ 1 - \sum_{k \in \text{neighbors}(i)} m_{ik}, & i = j, \\ 0, & \text{otherwise.} \end{cases} \qquad (6.14)$$

Intuitively, the entries m_{ij} of the symmetric square matrix M can be thought of as couplings of the grid points in the vector field. Neighboring points that have similar vectors are strongly coupled; neighbors that have dissimilar vectors are weakly coupled. Points that are not neighbors are not coupled at all. The diagonal entries m_{ii} describe the so-called self coupling, which is set so that the sum of couplings of a point with all other points is 1.

For the more formally and mathematically oriented readers, the preceding matrix M describes the finite element discretization of an anisotropic diffusion operator using piecewise linear basis functions. Let us detail this. Given some domain $D \in \mathbb{R}^n$, the equation

$$\partial_t u - \mathrm{div}(A\nabla u) = 0. \tag{6.15}$$

describes the diffusion in time of a scalar function $u : \mathbb{D} \times [0, \infty) \rightarrow \mathbb{R}$ starting from an initial value $u(t = 0)$. In Equation (6.15), div denotes the divergence operator defined by Equation (6.1). The speed of diffusion, or diffusivity, can have different values in different directions in the domain D, a property which is called *anisotropy*, and which is described by the tensor A. The discretization of the operator $\mathrm{div}(A\nabla u)$ produces our matrix M. In finite element terminology, M is called a *stiffness matrix*, a term that suggests the metaphor of coupling of the grid points.

The matrix M encodes the vector field structure on the finest level given by the dataset grid. Our aim is to simplify this structure in order to visualize the field at various levels of detail. This can be done using the AMG technique, as detailed in [Griebel et al. 04]. Given a matrix M, AMG constructs a sequence of matrices $M^0 = M, M^1, \ldots, M^k$. The size (number of rows or columns) of each matrix M^i is a fraction s of the size of the previous matrix M^{i-1}, starting with the size S of the matrix M^0 until the final matrix M^k, which has size 1, i.e., is a scalar value. Hence, the sequence has $k = \log_s S$ levels. This reduction in size is done by eliminating matrix entries involved in weak couplings and merging neighboring entries involved in similar strong couplings. This process is similar to the bottom-up agglomerative clustering described in Listing 6.3. However, actual implementations of the AMG technique are relatively complex, as these are capable of producing high-quality clusterings of huge matrices of tens of millions of entries in minutes on a normal PC. Designing an effective and efficient AMG algorithm is difficult, both from the mathematical and implementation points of view, and this topic is treated extensively by a separate field of research [Trottenberg et al. 01, Griebel and Schweitzer 06]. Luckily, for our vector field simplification perspective, we can use an existing AMG implementation as a black box.

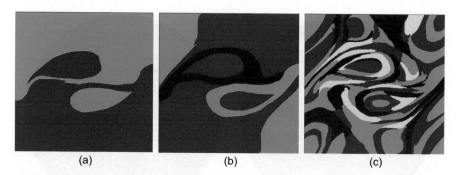

Figure 6.27. Vector field decomposition using the AMG technique. Three decomposition levels are visualized.

Following the finite element paradigm, for every matrix M^i produced by the AMG we can construct a basis Φ^i containing as many basis functions ϕ^i_j as the matrix size. At the finest level, the basis functions ϕ^0_j are exactly the linear basis functions implied by the grid cell types (see Section 3.4). Since the simplified matrices contain couplings that follow the field structure, it can be shown that the shapes of the basis functions ϕ^i_j on the higher simplification levels follow the vector field, too. Figure 6.29(a) shows several basis functions on several levels of the AMG clustering. The function range of $[0, 1]$ is mapped via a blue-to-red colormap. The vector field decomposition is shown in Figure 6.29(b) with regions and stream tubes.

We can use these basis functions to visualize the vector field in several ways, as described next. Given a simplification level $1 < l < k$, we can use the basis $\Phi^l = \{\phi^l_i\}_i$ to construct several regions R^l_i. Every region R^l_i corresponds to the points of the grid G where its basis function ϕ^l_i is maximal over Φ^l:

$$R^l_i = \{p \in G | \phi^l_i(p) > \phi^l_j, \forall j \neq i\}. \qquad (6.16)$$

Since ϕ^l_i is maximal over R^l_i, we can say that R^l_i best approximates the extent of that vector field feature which is captured by ϕ^l_i. Next, we can visualize these regions either as colored areas or by using arrow-capped stream tubes, similar to the discrete clustering visualization in Figure 6.26. Figure 6.27 shows the regions on three different decomposition levels, ranging from coarse to fine from left to right, for the already-familiar MHD flow

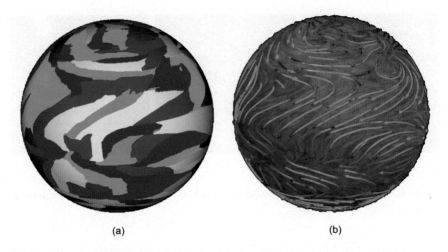

(a)   (b)

Figure 6.28. AMG-based simplified visualization of wind vector field on the surface of the Earth.

field used by other visualization methods earlier in this chapter. Comparing these images to the vector glyph visualizations shown in Figure 6.5 and 6.7, we see that the regions clearly reflect the symmetric structure of the flow, the presence of two large drop-shaped vortices, and the existence of two thin layers surrounding and flowing in opposite direction to the vortices. The AMG decomposition technique works also for curved surfaces or volumetric domains. Figure 6.28(a) shows the region decomposition of a flow field encoding the wind direction and force over the surface of the Earth. Figure 6.28(b) depicts the same flow field visualized with arrow-capped stream tubes overlaid on top of an IBFV texture visualization. The stream tubes, colored by the velocity magnitude, show a simplified view of the flow field while the texture shows a detailed, fine-scale visualization of the same field.

A second way to use the AMG simplification results for our aim is to visualize the basis ϕ_j^l functions themselves. Here, we turn again to the image-based flow visualization (IBFV) visualization technique presented in Section 6.6. As we recall, IBFV advects a spatial noise signal whose luminance changes periodically in time in a given vector field, creating the effect of thin, contrasting animated stream lines that move with the flow. A limitation of the original IBFV method was the size, or graininess, of the

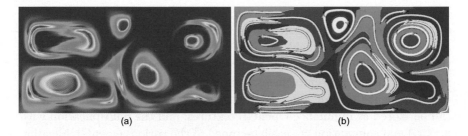

(a) (b)

Figure 6.29. AMG flow-field decomposition. (a) Basis functions. (b) Regions and streamline-based visualization.

noise signal. Fine noise elements produce high-quality flow animations but are limited in conveying the coarse structure of the vector field. Increasing the size of the noise elements does not solve this issue, and actually creates strong visible artifacts, since the noise signal is sampled on a regular image-like grid. What we actually need is a noise signal on a coarse spatial scale that is coherent with the flow. This is the point where the AMG basis functions come in.

Consider again the original fine-scale IBFV noise $N(x, y, t)$ that was sampled on a $n \times n$ image. Every pixel of this image can be seen as being represented by a constant basis function ψ_i which is 1 over that pixel and zero elsewhere. Hence, the noise term from Equation (6.12) can be rewritten as

$$N(x, y, t) = \sum_{i=1}^{n^2} \psi_i(x, y) f((t + N_i) \mod 1). \qquad (6.17)$$

Here, $f(t)$ is exactly the same periodical function as in Equation (6.13), whereas N_i is the noise phase of the ith region corresponding to ψ_i, which is equivalent to the per-pixel noise phase $N(x)$ in Equation (6.13). An interesting observation is that now the basis functions ψ_i are similar to the AMG basis functions ϕ_i^0 on the first level that corresponds to the input coupling matrix M^0. We can generalize this observation and define a multiscale noise signal:

$$N^j(x, y, t) = \sum_{i=1}^{s_j} \psi_i^j(x, y) p(t + r_i). \qquad (6.18)$$

Here, we use the basis functions on any level $1 < j < k$ of the AMG decomposition. As we see in Figure 6.29(a), these functions have shapes that follow the vector field, so advecting them in the field, as done by the IBFV method, considerably reduces the appearance of noise-like visual artifacts. In terms of implementation, Equation (6.18) can be efficiently coded in terms of OpenGL imaging operations. The basis functions ψ_i^j can be stored as luminance OpenGL textures, and the multiplication with $p(t+r_i)$ and summation are easily mapped to the various OpenGL blending modes. Since $N^j(x, y, t)$ is a periodic function, we can precompute several tens of samples of one period, save them into textures, and then use these during the IBFV animation to obtain maximum performance.

By replacing the initial fine-scale noise $N(x, y, t)$ with any of the multiscale noise signals $N^j(x, y, t)$ defined by Equation (6.18), we obtain a multiscale image-based flow visualization, or MIBFV method. MIBFV keeps all the strong points of its predecessor (dense field representation, real-time animation, intuitive representation, simple implementation) and adds a spatial multiscale aspect that emphasizes the vector field features at a user-chosen scale k. Figure 6.30 shows the difference between the fine-scale IBFV (Figure 6.30(a)) and MIBFV on three coarse scales (Figures 6.30(b–d)). MIBFV can be used also to combine several scales in a single visualization. The coarse-scale MIBFV images show less detail but exhibit a higher contrast than the IBFV visualization, an element which helps users discern the global coarse scale features of the depicted vector field. Figure 6.30(c) shows an MIBFV coarse-scale context visualization in the background blended with four IBFV fine-scale detail visualizations centered and covering the extents of the four main vortices of the considered flow field. The centers of the IBFV visualizations are marked by red dots, which indicate points of interest chosen by the user. This image is a typical example of the use of focus-and-context techniques in data visualization: high detail is shown over a focus region, typically specified by the user, surrounded by a context region showing a low amount of detail.

MIBFV is less suited to visualize time-dependent vector fields than IBFV. If the vector field changes, we must re-run the AMG decomposition and noise texture computation (see Equation (6.18)) after every time step. Even a very efficient AMG implementation still needs seconds to tens of seconds to produce the multiscale basis functions, so MIBFV cannot provide interactive frame rates on time-dependent vector fields.

Figure 6.30. (a) IBFV visualization and (b, c, d) multiscale IBFV visualization on three different scales of the same field.

Using the AMG technique to produce simplified representations and visualizations of vector field is an advanced subject that requires an implementation effort way beyond that of computing streamlines or vector glyphs. However, this topic provides good insight into the recent possibilities of vector field visualization and illustrates once again the mix of different techniques such as mathematical analysis, imaging, and graphics that are needed to tackle this great challenge of getting insight in complex, time-dependent vector datasets.

The use of the AMG method for decomposing vector fields for visualization purposes is a typical example of a number of recent techniques that can be used to simplify the massive amount of data present in large vector datasets in order to create visualizations that emphasize the most salient elements of a given vector field. Several other techniques take a similar path in clustering, or merging, similar sample points in a vector field in order to reduce the data complexity and simplify its visual interpretation. A set of techniques closely related to the AMG method presented here employs diffusion-based clustering of vector fields [Preusser and Rumpf 99, Bürkle et al. 01]. These methods solve the diffusion problem encoded by Equation (6.15) starting with an initial noise scalar value $u(t = 0)$ similar to the advected noise $N(x, t)$ of the IBFV method. After a certain time t, small-scale noise patterns get clustered in the direction of the vector field, while still exhibiting high noise-like contrast in the orthogonal direction. These methods create vector field visualizations that are very similar to the MIBFV method (Figure 6.30(b–d)).

6.8   Conclusion

In this chapter, we have presented a number of visualization methods for vector fields. Given the large variety of techniques, but also the difference in focus and goal of the many application domains where vector field visualizations are used, it is hard to provide a simple and uniform classification of these visualization methods. In terms of both visual and implementation complexity, these methods range from simple visual representations supported by a straightforward implementation, such as the vector glyphs, up to multiscale textures animated in real time, supported by complex implementations that combine advanced mathematics and graphics, such as the MIBFV method. In the recent years, the increase in computing and graphics processing power have stimulated the creation of whole new families of vector field visualization techniques that exploit animation and dense visual representations, such as textures, as opposed to the "classical" vector field visualizations that use sparse geometric primitives, such as glyphs, streamlines, and stream surfaces.

Another classification of vector field visualization methods is based on the dimensionality of the data domain. Two-dimensional surfaces, whether planar or curved ones, permit a straightforward mapping to the 2D graphics viewport, which simplifies the visualization problem. Three-dimensional volumetric vector fields pose, in contrast, a much more challenging problem, due to the inherent occlusion of the visualization primitives, especially in the case of dense visualizations. When one adds the time dimension, the problem becomes even more challenging. Animation is an intuitive means of representing the time-dependent aspect.

Being able to visually follow complex 3D flow animations and discern all events of interest that take place in such processes is a difficult problem. Multiscale methods for simplified visual representations of vector fields, which have become increasingly interesting in the last years, are an effective answer to the problem of data size and complexity. However, the challenge of creating insightful visualizations of three-dimensional time-dependent vector fields describing complex phenomena, far from being exhausted, is still an active area of research.

Chapter 7

Tensor Visualization

A s explained in Section 3.6.4, tensor data encode some spatial property that varies as a function of position and direction, such as the curvature of a 3D surface at a given point and direction. Most visualization applications deal with rank 2 symmetric tensors, so in this chapter we shall treat only the visualization of such tensors. When represented in a global coordinate system, such tensors are 3×3 matrices. Every point in a tensor dataset carries such a matrix as its attribute data.

Tensor datasets are common in different application domains. Properties of 3D surfaces, such as curvature, can be described by curvature tensors. Material properties in mechanical engineering, such as stress and strain in 3D volumes, are described by stress tensors [Reddy 93]. Diffusion of water in tissues can takes place either isotropically, that is, with equal speed in every direction, or anisotropically, that is, with different speeds in different directions. For example, in human brain tissue, diffusion is stronger in the direction of the neural fibers and weaker across the fibers. These fibers, consisting of bundles of axons, are also known as *white matter*, given the characteristic color of the myelin layer covering them. At a given point in the tissue volume, diffusion can be described by a 3×3 diffusion tensor matrix. As diffusion is stronger in the direction of the fibers, by measuring the diffusion tensor and visualizing, for example, the direction of strongest diffusion, we can get insight into the complex structure of neural fibers in the human brain. The measurement of the diffusion of water in living tissues is done by a set of techniques known as *diffusion tensor magnetic resonance imaging (DT-MRI)*. The overall process that constructs visualizations of the anatomical structures of interest starting from the measured diffusion data is known as *diffusion tensor imaging (DTI)* and is an active area of research in scientific visualization and medical imaging. DTI techniques have been used in the diagnosis and analysis of various types of brain diseases, and in the study of the connection between the brain structure and functions (functional brain anatomy).

As we saw in the previous chapter, visualizing 3D vector fields is a difficult problem, since we have to map three independent values to a graphical representation for every data point. In the case of a tensor field, the problem only becomes more difficult. Now we have to visualize a complete 3×3 matrix for every data point. We could try to visualize the entries of these matrices as separate scalar fields using scalar visualization methods such as isosurfaces or color-coded slice planes. However, this would not help us much in understanding the way the data encoded by our tensor actually varies as a function of direction. Luckily, tensor data has an intrinsic structure that we can exploit to produce more useful visualizations. Computing this structure is done by a technique called *principal component analysis*, as explained in the next section.

The structure of this chapter is as follows. We begin by providing in Section 7.1 a short overview of principal component analysis. This technique is used to process a tensor matrix and extract from it information that can directly be used in its visualization, and forms a fundamental ingredient of many tensor data processing and visualization algorithms. In Section 7.4, we show how the results of the principal component analysis can be visualized using the simple color-mapping techniques introduced in Chapter 5. Next, we show in Section 7.5 how the same data can be visualized using tensor glyphs, following the vector visualization techniques introduced in Chapter 6. A further elaboration of the similarities between tensors and vectors is shown in Section 7.6 and 7.7, which introduce streamline-like visualization techniques for tensor fields. Finally, Section 7.8 concludes this chapter.

7.1   Principal Component Analysis

Let us consider again, for illustration purposes, the curvature tensor of a 3D surface, which we introduced in Section 3.6.4. Consider a local coordinate system xyz centered at a point x_0 on our surface, where the z-axis coincides with $\mathbf{n}$, the surface normal at x_0. In this coordinate system, our surface can be described as some function $z = f(x, y)$, with $f(x_0) = 0$. We have shown that we can compute the normal curvature at some point x_0 in some direction $\mathbf{s}$ in the tangent plane as the second derivative $\partial^2 f / \partial s^2$ of f using the two-by-two Hessian matrix of partial derivatives of f (see Equation (3.25)). For smooth surfaces, the normal curvature varies smoothly as the direction vector $\mathbf{s}$ rotates around the current point in the tangent plane. In many applications, we are actually interested only in the extremal (minimal and maximal) values of the curvature as a function of the direction $\mathbf{s}$. Since these directions depend only on the surface shape at a given point, they are invariant to the choice of the local coordinate system.

How can we compute these directions? Since $\mathbf{s}$ is a unit direction vector, we can write it as $\mathbf{s}^T = (\cos\alpha, \sin\alpha)$, where α is the angle between $\mathbf{s}$ and the x-axis of our local coordinate system, and the superscript T denotes a transposed column vector. Plugging this into Equation (3.25), we get

$$\frac{\partial^2 f}{\partial s^2} = s^T H s = h_{11} \cos^2\alpha + (h_{12} + h_{21}) \sin\alpha \cos\alpha + h_{22} \cos^2\alpha, \quad (7.1)$$

where h_{ij} are the entries of the symmetric Hessian matrix H. This expression is maximal when its derivative with respect to α is zero. This means

$$-h_{11} \cos\alpha \sin\alpha - \frac{h_{12} + h_{21}}{2} (\sin^2\alpha - \cos^2\alpha) + h_{22} \sin\alpha \cos\alpha = 0. \quad (7.2)$$

It is easy to show that Equation (7.2) is equivalent to the system of equations

$$\begin{cases} h_{11} \cos\alpha + h_{12} \sin\alpha &= \lambda \cos\alpha, \\ h_{21} \cos\alpha + h_{22} \sin\alpha &= \lambda \sin\alpha, \end{cases} \quad (7.3)$$

where λ is any real value. And Equation (7.3) can be rewritten as

$$H\mathbf{s} = \lambda\mathbf{s}. \quad (7.4)$$

Summarizing, the directions $\mathbf{s}$ in the tangent plane for which the normal curvature has extremal values are the solutions of Equation (7.4). For 2×2

matrices, we can solve Equation (7.4) analytically, obtaining two solutions λ_1 and s_1 and λ_2 and s_2 respectively. For this, we rewrite $Hs = \lambda s$ as $(H - \lambda I)s = 0$ where I is the 2×2 identity matrix. From linear algebra, we know this is equivalent to the determinant of $H - \lambda I$ being equal to zero, as we are looking for nontrivial solutions $s \neq 0$. Hence, we get

$$\det(H - \lambda I) = 0. \tag{7.5}$$

For a 2×2 matrix, Equation (7.5) can be solved analytically and yields our two solutions λ_1 and λ_2, as follows. For the matrix

$$H = \begin{pmatrix} h_{11} & h_{12} \\ h_{21} & h_{22} \end{pmatrix}, \tag{7.6}$$

the determinant is $\det(H) = h_{11}h_{22} - h_{12}h_{21}$. Hence, Equation (7.5) becomes

$$\det(H - \lambda I) = (h_{11} - \lambda)(h_{22} - \lambda) - h_{12}h_{21} = 0. \tag{7.7}$$

Equation (7.7) is nothing but a second-order equation in λ, whose solutions are our eigenvalues λ_1 and λ_2. Plugging these into Equation (7.4) immediately yields the corresponding s_1 and s_2.

Figure 7.1 shows the principal directions of the curvature tensor for a 3D surface. The surface (shown in green) has minimal curvature in the direction s_1 (shown in yellow) and maximal curvature in the direction s_2 (shown in red). A number of other directions in the tangent plane orthogonal to the surface normal n at the considered point are shown in black. Along these directions, the surface curvature takes values between the minimal and maximal ones.

The solutions s_i of Equation (7.4) are called the *principal directions*, or *eigenvectors*, of the tensor H. The quantity encoded in the tensor has extremal values in these directions, equal to λ_i. These values are called also *eigenvalues* of the tensor. Computing the eigenvalues and eigenvectors of a tensor by this technique is called *principal component analysis*. One can show that, for an $n \times n$ symmetric matrix, the principal directions are perpendicular to each other. Hence, these directions form a local coordinate system whose axes are directions in which the quantity encoded by the tensor, such as curvature in our example, reaches extremal values.

This reasoning can also be applied identically for a 3×3 tensor. For example, in the case of a 3D surface given by an implicit function $f(x, y, z) =$

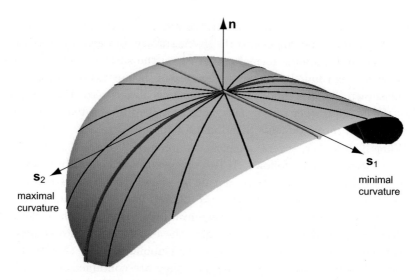

Figure 7.1. Principal directions of curvature for a surface.

0 in global coordinates, we have a 3×3 Hessian matrix of partial derivatives, as explained in Section 3.6.4 (see Equation (3.27)). This matrix
has three eigenvalues and three eigenvectors that we compute by solving
Equation (7.4). These can be computed as follows. Given a 3×3 matrix
$H = (h_{ij})$, it can be shown that the determinant $\det(H - \lambda I)$ is given by

$$\det(H - \lambda I) = \lambda^3 - J_1 \lambda^2 + J_2 \lambda - J_3, \tag{7.8}$$

where the quantities J_1, J_2, and J_3 are given by

$$
\begin{aligned}
J_1 &= h_{11} + h_{22} + h_{33}, \\
J_2 &= h_{11}h_{22} + h_{11}h_{33} + h_{22}h_{33} - h_{12}^2 - h_{23}^2 - h_{31}^2, \\
J_3 &= 2h_{12}h_{23}h_{31} + h_{11}h_{22} + h_{33} - h_{11}h_{23}^2 - h_{22}h_{31}^2 - h_{33}h_{12}^2.
\end{aligned}
\tag{7.9}
$$

Equation (7.8) is a third-order equation in λ whose solutions are the three
eigenvalues λ_1, λ_2, and λ_3 of the tensor H. These can be computed using
analytic formulas for solving Equation (7.8). A better method to use in
practice is the Jacobi iteration method, which solves Equation (7.5) numerically for arbitrary-size $n \times n$ real symmetric matrices [Press et al. 02].

If we order the eigenvalues in decreasing order $\lambda_1 > \lambda_2 > \lambda_3$, the
corresponding eigenvectors $\mathbf{e}_1$, $\mathbf{e}_2$, and $\mathbf{e}_3$, also called the major, medium,

and minor eigenvectors, have geometric meaning: in the case of a curvature tensor, e_1 and e_2 are tangent to the given surface and give the directions of maximal and minimal normal curvature on the surface, and e_3 is equal to the surface normal. In the particular case of the curvature tensor, it can also be shown that the smallest eigenvalue λ_3 is always zero. However, this is not the case for other tensor data, such as a 3D diffusion tensor obtained from DT-MRI measurements [Kindlmann 04b].

What if, however, several eigenvalues are equal? For a 3×3 matrix, there are two cases, as follows. If two eigenvalues are equal but different from the third $\lambda_1 = \lambda_2 \neq \lambda_3$, it can be shown that this is equivalent to the columns of the matrix $H - \lambda I$ being identical and equal to the eigenvector e_3 corresponding to the eigenvalue λ_3. However, the other two eigenvectors e_1 and e_2 corresponding to the equal eigenvalues cannot be determined uniquely. All that can be said about them is that they are orthogonal to each other and to e_3, i.e., they are contained in the plane orthogonal to e_3. The second case is the situation when all eigenvalues are equal $\lambda_1 = \lambda_2 = \lambda_3$. In this case, any three orthogonal vectors satisfy Equation (7.4) and are valid eigenvectors of H.

Intuitively, when several eigenvalues are equal, one cannot determine preferential directions of maximal or minimal variations of the quantity encoded by the tensor. Consider again a 2×2 matrix describing a curvature tensor for several surfaces (see Figure 7.2). The ellipsoid surface in Figure 7.2(a) clearly admits two orthogonal principal directions (eigenvectors) of maximal and minimal curvature, respectively. In both these directions, the curvature is nonzero. A cylinder surface also admits two such unique directions (see Figure 7.2(b)). However, the minimal curvature (eigenvalue) is, in this case, zero. Indeed, the cross section along this direction is a line. On a spherical surface, however, the curvature has equal (nonzero) values in all directions, so the eigenvectors can be any two orthogonal vectors that are tangent to the surface. The same situation happens for a plane, where, in addition, the curvature (eigenvalues) is also zero in all directions. The same type of situation is encountered for 3×3 tensors, too.

In the following sections, we describe several visualization methods for tensor datasets. We begin with the simplest method, which visualizes the individual components of the tensor matrix (Section 7.2) and next detail more advanced visualization techniques that use the results of principal component analysis.

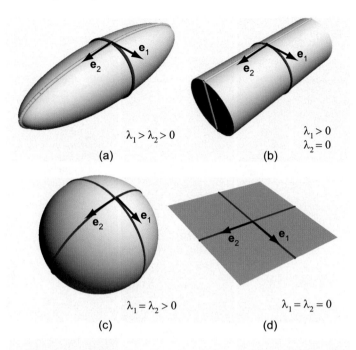

Figure 7.2. Principal directions of the curvature tensor for various shapes. Cross sections tangent to the eigenvectors are colored to denote the eigenvalue type. Red denotes the major eigenvector direction; yellow denotes the minor eigenvector direction. Blue denotes cases when the eigenvector directions are arbitrary, as eigenvalues are equal.

7.2 Visualizing Components

The simplest way to visualize a tensor dataset is to treat it as a set of scalar datasets. Given a 3×3 tensor matrix H, we can consider each of its nine components h_{ij} as a separate scalar field. Figure 7.3 shows these components for a single 2D slice taken from a brain diffusion tensor volumetric dataset.[1]

Each component of the tensor matrix is visualized using a grayscale colormap that maps scalar value to luminance. Note that, for the ease of

---

[1] Brain dataset courtesy of Gordon Kindlmann, Scientific Computing and Imaging Institute, University of Utah, and Andrew Alexander, W. M. Keck Laboratory for Functional Brain Imaging and Behavior, University of Wisconsin-Madison.

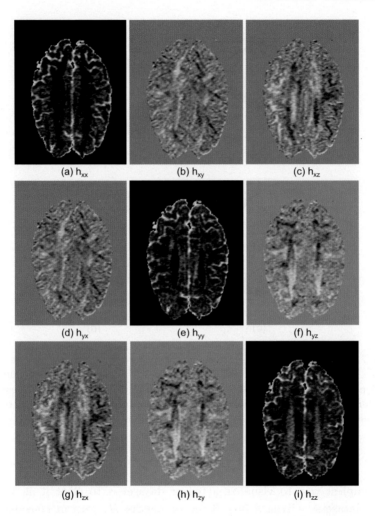

Figure 7.3. Visualization of the nine components h_{ij} of a 3×3 diffusion tensor from a DT-MRI scan.

interpretation of the images, the points that fall outside the actual tissue, i.e., correspond to air and therefore contain noisy tensor values, have been set to a neutral uniform gray background color. Also, note that due to the symmetry of the tensor matrix, there are only six different images in the visualization (i.e., $h_{12} = h_{21}$, $h_{13} = h_{31}$, and $h_{23} = h_{32}$).

In general, the tensor matrix components encode the second-order partial derivatives of our tensor-encoded quantity with respect to the *global* coordinate system. Often, the orientation of this system has absolutely no deep relation with the data variation, so these partial derivatives, taken *separately*, are quite meaningless. For example, in the case of a DT-MRI dataset, the measured tensor describes the diffusion strength of water in the brain tissue with respect to the coordinate frame that describes the position of the patient in the scanner device. Clearly, this coordinate frame has little to do with the actual orientation of the anatomical structures of interest that are to be visualized. In contrast, visualizing the eigenvectors and eigenvalues gives the directions and sizes of extremal variations of our tensor-encoded quantity, which are *independent* of any coordinate system. If extremal variations are meaningful for our problem then visualizing these eigen-quantities can help. Visualizing the results of the PCA analysis is discussed in the following section.

7.3 Visualizing Scalar PCA Information

A better alternative to visualizing the tensor matrix components is to focus on data derived from these components that has a more intuitive physical significance. As a first example, we shall use the average of the diagonal entries $\frac{1}{3}(h_{11} + h_{22} + h_{33})$. It can be shown that this quantity is equal at each point to the mean diffusivity measured in the tissue, i.e., the average of the measured diffusion over all directions at that point.[2] Figure 7.4 visualizes this scalar quantity over three axis-aligned slice planes using a grayscale colormap. Apart from the particular scalar value visualized here, using three orthogonal slice planes to get a quick insight in a volumetric dataset is a popular technique. In medical imaging, these planes bear special names, i.e., the sagittal, axial, and coronal sections respectively.

Further insight can be gained by visualizing the results of principal component analysis. Recall that the eigenvectors of a tensor give the directions of extremal variations of the quantity encoded by the tensor in a given point, and the corresponding eigenvalues given the values of those extremal variations. In case of diffusion data, the eigenvalues can be used to describe the degree of *anisotropy* of the tissue at a point. In an isotropic

---

[2]This quantity is also equal to the mean of the eigenvalues $1/3(\lambda_1 + \lambda_2 + \lambda_3)$.

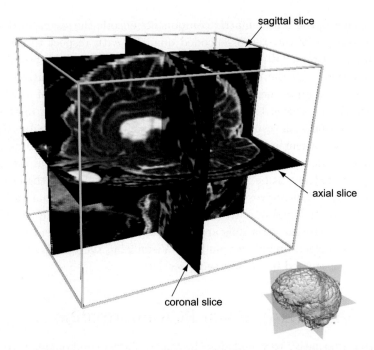

Figure 7.4. Visualization of the mean diffusivity over sagittal, axial, and coronal slices. The small image in the lower-right corner displays the brain surface together with the three slices for orientation purposes.

medium, all directions are identical. In our particular case, this means the diffusivity has the same value in all directions around a point. Anisotropic media exhibit different properties in different directions. In our case, this means different diffusivities in different directions around a point. Visualizing the anisotropy of a tensor dataset can give valuable insight into separating the neural fibers, which are highly anisotropic, from the rest of the tissue.

Several techniques have been proposed to estimate the anisotropy of a diffusion tensor in medical imaging. All use, in one way or another, the results of PCA on the tensor data. We will now describe a few of the best-known and simplest-to-compute anisotropy measures.

A first set of metrics proposed by Westin [Westin et al. 97] estimates the certainties c_l, c_p, and c_s that a tensor has a linear, planar, or spherical

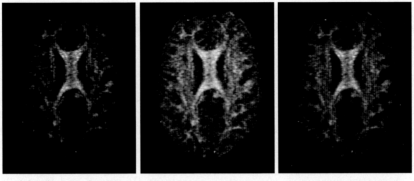

(a) c_l linear estimator   (b) fractional anisotropy   (c) relative anisotropy

Figure 7.5. Different anisotropy measures for diffusion tensor data.

shape, respectively. If the tensor's eigenvalues are $\lambda_1 \geq \lambda_2 \geq \lambda_3$, the respective certainties are

$$
\begin{aligned}
c_l &= \frac{\lambda_1 - \lambda_2}{\lambda_1 + \lambda_2 + \lambda_3}, \\
c_p &= \frac{2(\lambda_2 - \lambda_3)}{\lambda_1 + \lambda_2 + \lambda_3}, \\
c_s &= \frac{3\lambda_3}{\lambda_1 + \lambda_2 + \lambda_3}.
\end{aligned}
\tag{7.10}
$$

The expressions of the tensor shape certainties in Equation (7.10) describe how "far off" one eigenvalue is from the smaller ones. The division by the mean diffusivity $\lambda_1 + \lambda_2 + \lambda_3$ is used to normalize the estimations and obtain dimensionless numbers. Intuitively, the confidence values suggest how diffusion acts in the tissue. Imagine a spherical drop of water placed at the current point and left to diffuse for a while. Its shape will grow faster in the directions of high anisotropy and slower in the other directions. A visualization method that directly uses such shapes to show the tensor eigenvalues and eigenvectors is described in Section 7.5. For the time being, a simple way to use the anisotropy metrics proposed previously is to directly visualize the linear certainty c_l scalar signal. High values of this metric indicate regions where the fibers are clearly delineated. Figure 7.5(a) shows the c_l certainty plotted on a 2D axial slice. The white area in the middle outlines a highly anisotropic region, anatomically known under the name of *corpus callosum*. The gray values indicate regions of low anisotropy that correspond to the *gray matter* tissue in the brain.

Another frequently used measure for the anisotropy is the *fractional anisotropy* [Pierpaoli and Basser 96], which is defined as

$$FA = \sqrt{\frac{3}{2}} \frac{\sqrt{\sum_{i=1}^{3} (\lambda_i - \mu)^2}}{\lambda_1^2 + \lambda_2^2 + \lambda_3^2}, \tag{7.11}$$

where $\mu = \frac{1}{3}(\lambda_1 + \lambda_2 + \lambda_3)$ is the mean diffusivity. Figure 7.5(b) shows the fractional anisotropy for the same dataset and slice as for the c_l certainty discussed before. Again, the corpus callosum area is clearly visible in this image.

A related measure is the *relative anisotropy* [Pierpaoli and Basser 96], defined as

$$RA = \sqrt{\frac{3}{2}} \frac{\sqrt{\sum_{i=1}^{3} (\lambda_i - \mu)^2}}{\lambda_1 + \lambda_2 + \lambda_3}. \tag{7.12}$$

Figure 7.5(c) shows the relative anisotropy for the previous dataset.

Overall, the methods presented in this section reduce the visualization of a tensor field to that of one or more scalar quantities, such as the anisotropy, computed from the PCA analysis performed on the tensor data. These can be examined using any of the scalar visualization methods presented in Chapter 5, such as color plots, slice planes, and isosurfaces.

7.4   Visualizing Vector PCA Information

In the previous section, we saw how to visualize various anisotropy metrics computed from the PCA analysis of a tensor field using standard scalar visualization methods such as color mapping. However, in many cases, we are interested in visualizing not just the amount of anisotropy, but also the directions in which this anisotropy takes place.

Let us start with the simpler case when we are interested only in the direction of maximal variation of our tensor-encoded quantity. For this, we can visualize the major eigenvector field using any of the vector visualization methods presented in Chapter 6. Figure 7.6 illustrates an application of this idea. Here, we show a hedgehog plot of the major eigenvector over a coronal slice in the same DT-MRI dataset used in Figure 7.3. Vectors are uniformly seeded at all points where the accuracy of the diffusion measurements is above a certain confidence level (similar to Figure 7.3). The

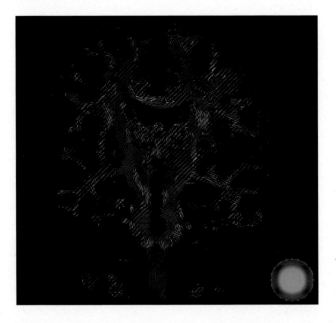

Figure 7.6. Major eigenvector visualized with line glyphs colored by direction.

hue of the vector coloring indicates their direction. For this, we use the following simple color-mapping function:

$$\begin{aligned} R &= |\mathbf{e}_1 \cdot \mathbf{x}|, \\ G &= |\mathbf{e}_1 \cdot \mathbf{y}|, \\ B &= |\mathbf{e}_1 \cdot \mathbf{z}|. \end{aligned} \qquad (7.13)$$

Using this function, horizontal vectors are colored in red, vertical ones in green, and vectors aligned with the depth (z) axis of the dataset coordinate frame are colored in blue, respectively. The icon in the bottom-right corner of Figure 7.6 illustrates the direction of color mapping. This icon has to be interpreted as a shaded sphere, where the color of each point maps the direction of the radial vector at that point. The luminance indicates the measurement confidence level. Bright vectors indicate high confidence measurement areas, whereas dark vectors indicate low confidence (noisy) measurements.

In addition to a hedgehog plot, other vector visualization techniques described in Chapter 6 can be used. A relatively popular technique in this

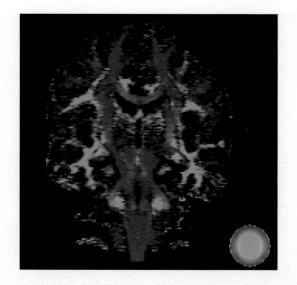

Figure 7.7. Major eigenvector direction visualized on a slice plane colored by eigenvector direction.

class is to simply color-map the major eigenvector direction. For this, we use Equation (7.13) to color a slice plane. Figure 7.7 shows the result on a coronal slice of the same brain dataset discussed previously. As discussed in Chapter 5, the advantage of this technique is that it produces a relatively more densely sampled visualization than when using hedgehogs. However, tensor datasets still have at the current moment a relatively low resolution, typically less than 512^3 voxels, which will be visible in the color-coded slice planes, too. For example, the slice plane in Figure 7.7 has only 148×160 distinct pixels.

However insightful, visualizing a *single* eigen-quantity at a time, whether vector or scalar, may be not enough. In many cases, the ratios of eigenvalues, rather than their absolute values, are of interest. Consider the surface curvature example. For a plane, both major and medium eigenvalues are zero. For a cylinder, the major eigenvalue gives the cylinder curvature, as computed along one of the circular surface cross-sections normal to its axis, whereas the medium eigenvalue is zero, denoting that the cylinder is flat in the direction of its axis. For a sphere, both major and medium eigenvalues are equal, but not zero, since a sphere has a non-null curvature. How can we visualize all eigenvalues and eigenvectors of some tensor dataset together? Several techniques try to answer this question, by building upon various elements from the scalar and vector visualization techniques presented in the previous chapters. These techniques are presented next.

7.5 Tensor Glyphs

The method for visualizing tensor data presented next is a generalization of the glyph concept used for visualizing vectors (see Section 6.2). We sample the dataset domain with a number of representative sample points. For each sample point, we construct a *tensor glyph* that encodes the eigenvalues and eigenvectors of the tensor at that point. For a 2 × 2 tensor dataset, this means encoding two eigenvalues and two eigenvectors per sample point. To do this, we construct a 2D ellipse whose half axes are oriented in the directions of the two eigenvectors and scaled by the absolute values of the eigenvalues. For a 3 × 3 tensor dataset, we construct a 3D ellipsoid that encodes the three eigenvectors and eigenvalues in a similar manner. In both cases, the overall tensor glyph visualization algorithm is quite simple. After performing the principal component analysis at a given sample point, we scale the ellipsoid glyph with the eigenvalues, rotate it using a matrix that has the eigenvectors as columns, and translate it at that point. We repeat the process for all sample points where we want to draw tensor ellipsoids.

Figure 7.8(a) illustrates the shapes that the ellipsoid glyph can assume.[3] At the triangle corners, the extremal situations are shown, when each of the linear, planar, and spherical certainties c_l, c_p, and c_s (see Equation (7.10)) has maximal value of one, and the other two are zero. These situations correspond to line, disc, and sphere glyph shapes, respectively. The in-between glyph shapes correspond to different certainty values. Note that the triangular "glyph space" can be parameterized by c_l, c_p, and c_s, using the fact that $c_l + c_p + c_s = 1$, so we can see the different glyph shapes as reflecting different values of the certainties and the corresponding eigenvalue ratios.

Besides ellipsoids, several other shapes can be used to encode the tensor information, each offering a different trade-off between visual clarity

---

[3]All figures in this section are generated by the freely available Teem software by Gordon Kindlmann [Kindlmann 06].

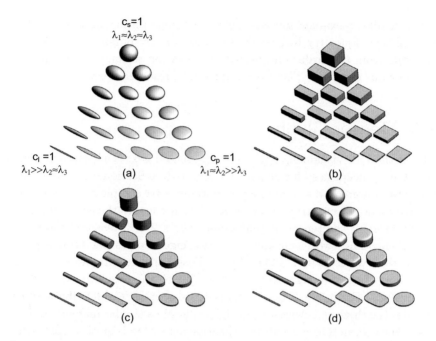

Figure 7.8. Different types of tensor glyphs. (a) Ellipsoids. (b) Cuboids. (c) Cylinders. (d) Superquadrics.

and power of expressing information. For example, we can use parallelepipeds (also called sometimes cuboids) or cylinders instead of ellipsoids. Figure 7.8(b) and (c) show the shapes such glyphs can assume for different certainties or eigenvalue ratios.

Figure 7.9 demonstrates the use of various shapes to visualize a DT-MRI diffusion tensor dataset. The figure shows a zoomed-in detail of the corpus callosum structure (red glyphs). The glyphs are colored by direction, similar to the hedgehog visualization used in Figure 7.7. The color saturation is modulated using the fractional anisotropy. Saturated glyphs indicate regions of high anisotropy, whereas gray ones indicate low-anisotropy regions. In contrast to the hedgehog visualization in the previous section, where seeds were distributed over a 2D slice, the tensor glyphs are here seeded over a 3D region. As we can see from this figure, smooth glyph shapes like those provided by the ellipsoids provide a less-distracting picture than shapes with sharp edges, such as the cuboids and cylinders.

Figure 7.9. Zoomed-in view of a DT-MRI dataset visualized with (a) ellipsoid, (b) cuboid, (c) cylinder, (d) and superquadric glyphs.

The cuboid, ellipsoid, and cylinder glyphs each have their own advantages and disadvantages. Cuboids are very good at clearly indicating the eigenvector directions with their facets, but thereby also fail to convey the directional ambiguity for eigenvectors corresponding to equal eigenvalues. Cylinders clearly convey the major eigenvector by their axis, but will brusquely rotate their shape by 90 degrees upon small eigenvalue changes that cause another eigenvector to become major (see Figure 7.8(c) middle). This causes confusing discontinuities in the visualization. Ellipsoids do not have any of these problems, but their two-dimensional projection does not always convey a non-ambiguous 3D orientation when viewed from certain angles. To solve this problem, superquadric glyphs have been introduced by Kindlmann [Kindlmann 04a]. These are defined as superquadric shapes parameterized as functions of the planar and linear certainty metrics c_l and c_p, respectively [Kindlmann 04b]. If we express the superquadric shape as an implicit function $q(x, y, z) = 0$, the actual superquadric glyph formulations become

$$q(x, y, z) = \begin{cases} \left(y^{2/\alpha} + z^{2/\alpha}\right)^{\alpha/\beta} + x^{2/\beta} - 1 = 0, & \text{if } c_l \geq c_p, \\ \text{where } \begin{cases} \alpha &= (1 - c_p)^\gamma, \\ \beta &= (1 - c_l)^\gamma, \end{cases} \\ \left(x^{2/\alpha} + y^{2/\alpha}\right)^{\alpha/\beta} + z^{2/\beta} - 1 = 0, & \text{if } c_l < c_p, \\ \text{where } \begin{cases} \alpha &= (1 - c_l)^\gamma, \\ \beta &= (1 - c_p)^\gamma. \end{cases} \end{cases} \quad (7.14)$$

Figure 7.8(b) shows the shapes the superquadric glyphs can assume for different values of the certainties. Figure 7.9(d) shows the use of superquadric glyphs in visualizing the same tensor dataset that was targeted by cuboids, cylinders, and ellipsoids in the same image.

Yet another tensor glyph used in practice is an *axes system*, formed by three vector glyphs that separately encode the three eigenvectors scaled by their corresponding eigenvalues. This is essentially nothing but visualizing three superimposed vector fields with vector glyphs, as described in Chapter 6. This method may be easier to interpret for 2D datasets, where the glyph overlap is controllable by limiting the glyph size to the distance between sample points. However, for 3D datasets, ellipsoid glyphs tend to work better than axes glyphs. The latter simply create too much confusion due to the 3D spatial overlap, whereas the rounded, convex ellipsoid shapes tend to be more distinguishable even when a small amount of overlap is present. Just as for vector glyphs, scaling the tensor ellipsoids must be done with care. Eigenvalues can have a large range, so directly scaling the tensor ellipsoids by their values can easily lead to overlapping or even self-intersecting glyphs. We can solve this problem as we did for the vector glyphs by imposing a minimal and maximal glyph size, either by clamping or by using a nonlinear value-to-size mapping function.

Overall, tensor glyphs are a probably one of the simplest ways to visualize tensor datasets. However, since they produce a sampled, discontinuous image, tensor glyph visualizations suffer from the same problems as vector glyphs. That is, they are prone to cluttering and have a limited spatial resolution. Moreover, in some datasets such as DT-MRI tensor fields, one is interested in specifically emphasizing certain structures, such as neural fibers, a task that glyphs cannot do. In the next section, we describe a method that is better suited for the visualization of such structures.

7.6   Fiber Tracking

The use of tensor glyphs for visualizing tensor fields is analogous to that of vector glyphs, presented in Section 6.2 for visualizing vector fields. It is therefore natural to wonder whether one can construct counterparts to other vector field visualization techniques for visualizing tensor data.

Streamlines are one of the most effective and popular techniques for visualizing vector fields (see Section 6.5). The question arises whether (and how) we can use streamlines to get insight into a tensor field. Let us consider, for illustration purposes, the particular case of a DT-MRI tensor dataset. As explained earlier in this chapter, regions of high anisotropy in general, and of high values of the c_l linear certainty metric in particular, correspond to neural fibers aligned with the major eigenvector e_1. If we want to visualize the location and direction of such fibers, it is natural to think of tracking the direction of this eigenvector over regions of high anisotropy. In order to do this, we can readily use the streamline technique previously introduced in the context of vector fields.

A typical method for tracking fibers proceeds as follows. First, a seed region is identified. This is a region where the fibers should intersect, so it can be detected, e.g., by thresholding one of the anisotropy metrics presented in Section 7.3. Second, streamlines are densely seeded in this region and traced (integrated) both forward and backward in the major eigenvector field e_1 until a desired stop criterion is reached. The stop criterion is, in practice, a combination of various conditions, each of which describes one desired feature of the resulting visualization. These can contain, but are not limited to, a minimal value of the anisotropy metric considered (beyond which the fiber structure becomes less apparent), the maximal fiber length (just as for vector streamlines), exiting or entering a predefined region of interest specified by the user (which can describe a previously segmented anatomical structure), and a maximal distance from other tracked fibers (beyond which the current fiber "strays" from a potential bundle structure that is the target of the visualization).

After the fibers are tracked, they can be visualized using the stream tubes technique (see Section 6.5.2), to further emphasize their geometry. Just as with vector visualization, the constructed tubes can be colored to show the value of a relevant scalar field, e.g., the major eigenvalue, anisotropy metric, or some other quantity scanned along with the tensor data.

The process of tracking fibers in DT-MRI datasets is quite delicate and typically requires a fair amount of user intervention, mainly during the step of defining the seed region. In order to assist users in this process, various integrated tools have been designed that allow the interactive visualization of scalar quantities on slices in the tensor dataset, the computation of anisotropy metrics, and the definition of regions of interest to be used to seed the fiber tracking process. Figure 7.10 shows a snapshot from such a tool, called Slicer.[4] In the lower part of the tool snapshot, we see three axial, sagittal, and coronal slices displaying the fractional anisotropy metric, similar to Figure 7.5(b). The middle slice shows, in light blue, a region of interest that has been selected by the user based on the high anisotropy values. This region corresponds to a sagittal cross-section through the corpus callosum structure in the brain. The top image in Figure 7.10 shows again the sagittal slice together with fibers tracked from seed points densely distributed in the region of interest. The fibers are colored by the fractional anisotropy metric, using a blue-to-red rainbow colormap, and visualized using stream tubes. The fibers end when the c_l planar certainty metric falls below a value of 0.15.

By removing the slice plane from the fiber visualization, we can analyze the resulting fiber structure in more detail (see Figure 7.11(a)). We notice here the symmetric fanning out of the fibers that emerge from the corpus callosum and "radiate" into the two hemispheres of the brain. Besides these fibers, we also notice a number of fibers whose directions are close to horizontal, which correspond to the structure of the corpus callosum itself. However useful, this visualization shows a large number of disjoint fibers. In the actual anatomy, fibers are grouped into bundles containing quasi-

---

[4]The images in this section have been produced using the open source Slicer 2.6 visualization software available from NA-MIC [Slicer 06] and the sample datasets provided with the software itself.

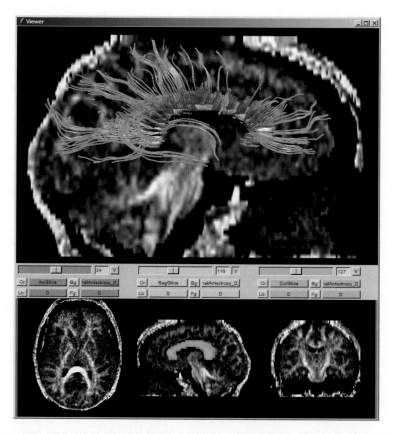

Figure 7.10. Fiber tracking from a user-selected region in the corpus callosum constructed with the Slicer 3D medical visualization tool.

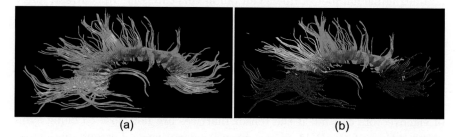

Figure 7.11. (a) Fiber tracking detail of Figure 7.10. (b) Fiber clustering based on the mean closest-point distance.

parallel structures. It can be interesting to construct a visualization that
mimics this behavior, as described by O'Donnel and Westin in [O'Donnel
and Westin 05]. To do this, we first define the directional similarity of
two fibers as follows. Given two fibers a and b that are described as two
3D parametric curves $a = a(t)$ and $b = b(t)$ with $t \in [0,1]$, we define the
distance

$$d(a,b) = \frac{1}{2N} \sum_{i=1}^{N} (|a(i/N), b| + |b(i/N), a|), \qquad (7.15)$$

i.e., as the symmetric mean distance of a number N of sample points on
a fiber to the (closest points on) other fiber. In Equation (7.15), the ex-
pression $|p(t), q|$ denotes the smallest distance between a point $p(t)$ on a
fiber and all points on the fiber q, i.e., $\min_{\tau \in [0,1]} |p(t), q(\tau)|$. Fibers that are
parallel and closely located will yield a low distance value. The similarity
is defined as the inverse of the distance. Using this distance, the tracked
fibers are next clustered in order of increasing distance, i.e., from the most
to the least similar, until the desired number of clusters is reached. Figure 7.11(b) shows this technique of the same set of tracked fibers as in
Figure 7.11(a). Here, five clusters are shown, using a different color for
the fibers in each cluster. We notice several structures in this visualization that correspond to fibers emerging from distinct regions of the corpus
callosum.

Although similar to streamline tracing, fiber tracking poses a number
of specific problems. First, tensor data acquired via the current DT-MRI
scanning technology contains in practice considerable noise and has a sampling frequency that misses several fine-scale details. Given their size, a
non-negligible number of fibers can fall in this category. In contrast, many
vector fields in the visualization practice come from numerical simulations
of physical processes, where there is no acquisition noise involved. Moreover, tensors are not directly produced by the scanning device, but obtained
via several preprocessing steps, of which principal component analysis is
the last one. All these steps introduce extra inaccuracies in the data, which
have to be accounted for. To give just an example, the PCA estimation
of eigenvectors can fail if the tensor matrices are not close to being symmetric. Even if the PCA works, fiber tracking needs a strong distinction
between the largest eigenvalue and the other two ones, in order to robustly
determine the fiber directions.

Fiber tracking in DT-MRI datasets is an active area of research. New techniques are being designed for better and easier definition of the seed regions, as well as more robust criteria for stopping the streamlines. New rendering techniques, such as volume rendering with data-driven opacity transfer functions, are also being developed to better convey the complex structures emerging from the tracking process. Although fiber tracking, as a term, is mainly encountered in the medical visualization arena, the techniques presented here can be used for any tensor dataset, once suitable seeding and stopping criteria have been defined.

7.7   Hyperstreamlines

In the previous section, we saw how fiber tracking can be used to visualize tensor data. Essentially, the principle of fiber tracking is based on integrating streamlines along the major eigenvector component of the tensor field, using various stop criteria determined by other derived quantities from the tensor data such as, for example, the anisotropy measure in case of DT-MRI datasets. However, fibers do not visualize directional information from the tensor field beyond the major eigenvector. As discussed in Section 7.1, this information is important, as it gives directional insight in how the tensor anisotropy varies in space. In contrast, tensor glyphs did visualize this information, but lacked, just as their vector counterparts, the spatial continuity of streamlines. The question arises whether we can enhance the streamline metaphor to visualize this additional information, i.e., combine the advantages of streamlines and tensor glyphs.

Hyperstreamlines provide an answer to this question. Their principle is quite simple. First, we perform principal component analysis as explained in Section 7.1 to decompose the tensor field into three eigenvector fields $\mathbf{e}_i$ and three corresponding scalar eigenvalue fields $\lambda_1 \geq \lambda_2 \geq \lambda_3$. Next, we construct stream tubes in the major eigenvector field $\mathbf{e}_1$, just as done for the fiber tracking method described in Section 7.6. At each point along such a stream tube, we now wish to visualize the medium and minor eigenvectors $\mathbf{e}_2$ and $\mathbf{e}_3$. For this, instead of using a circular cross section of constant size and shape, as we did for the fiber tracking, we now use an elliptic cross section, whose axes are oriented along the directions of the medium and minor eigenvectors $\mathbf{e}_2$ and $\mathbf{e}_3$ and scaled by λ_2 and λ_3 respectively.

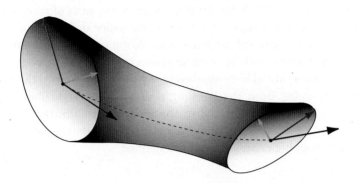

Figure 7.12. Hyperstreamline construction. The major, medium, and minor eigenvectors at the hyperstreamline's start and end points A and B are depicted in blue, red, and green, respectively. The streamline of the major eigenvector field $\mathbf{e}_1$ is drawn dashed.

Figure 7.12 illustrates this process for a hyperstreamline traced between two points A and B in a tensor field. The local thickness of the hyper-streamlines gives the absolute values of the tensor eigenvalues, whereas the ellipse shape indicates their relative values as well as the orientation of the eigenvector frame along a streamline. Circular cross sections indicate that the medium and minor eigenvalues are equal. If we want to show the value of the major eigenvalue, we can encode it as color.

Figure 7.13 shows the usage of hyperstreamlines in a diffusion tensor imaging (DT-MRI) brain dataset. Several hyperstreamlines are seeded at a number of locations in the dataset, following the techniques described for fiber tracking in Section 7.6. However, instead of tracing stream tubes of circular cross section, we now use hyperstreamlines. Color indicates the local direction of the hyperstreamlines, following the technique discussed in Section 7.4. Tracing the hyperstreamlines is stopped when the local anisotropy falls below a certain threshold. This is visible in the fact that some hyperstreamlines end in large, funnel-like, structures. At these points, the eigenvalues corresponding to the medium and minor eigenvectors are relatively large, so the anisotropy is low, denoting a less pronounced fiber structure.

Several variations of this construction are possible. Any of the three eigenvectors can be used for the hyperstreamline direction. Besides ellipses,

Figure 7.13. DT-MRI brain dataset visualized with hyperstreamlines colored by direction. (Image courtesy of A. Vilanova, Eindhoven University, the Netherlands.)

other shapes can be used for the cross section. For example, we can use a cross whose arms are scaled and rotated to represent the medium and minor eigenvectors. In general, hyperstreamlines provide better visualizations than tensor glyphs. However, just as for the standard streamlines, appropriate seed points and hyperstreamline lengths must be chosen to appropriately cover the domain, which can be a delicate process. Moreover, scaling the cross sections must be done with care, in order to avoid overly thick hyperstreamlines that cause occlusion or even self intersection. For this, we can use the same size scaling techniques as for vector and tensor glyphs (see Section 6.2).

7.8 Conclusion

In this section, we have presented a number of methods for visualizing tensor data. Starting from a 2D or 3D dataset containing 2×2 or 3×3

tensor matrices at each sample point that typically contains second-order partial derivatives of some quantity, we use principal component analysis (PCA) to extract the eigenvectors and eigenvalues of the tensor data. These describe the directions of extremal variation of the quantity encoded by the tensor. These directions are independent of the coordinate frame in which the partial derivatives contained in the tensor matrix have been computed. In many applications, these directions have a particular meaning, so they are a prime input for the visualization.

Tensor data van be visualized by reducing it to one scalar or vector field, which is then depicted by specific scalar or vector visualization techniques. These scalar or vector fields can be the direct outputs of the PCA analysis (eigenvalues and eigenvectors) or derived quantities, such as various anisotropy metrics. Alternatively, tensors can be visualized by displaying several of the PCA results combined in the same view, such as done by the tensor glyphs or hyperstreamlines.

Tensor visualization is an active, growing research area. Many visualization methods have emerged that target particular application areas that have specific questions, such as clinical investigations of DT-MRI medical datasets. These visualization methods often integrate more datasets in one single view, apart from the tensor information, and also provide sophisticated user interaction mechanisms for exploring the datasets, such as selecting regions of interest, adjusting color transfer functions, and controlling the various parameters of the visualization process. For more detailed information on these tools and techniques, we refer to the documentation of the tools themselves [Kindlmann 06, Slicer 06, Schroeder et al. 04, NLM 06].

Chapter 8

Domain-Modeling Techniques

DOMAIN-MODELING techniques form the last class of visualization techniques. By domain-modeling techniques, we mean those operations on datasets that modify the sampling domain representation (e.g., the grid) but not the sampled data. As we shall see, domain modeling techniques *can* modify the actual values of the data attributes stored on a given grid, for example in the case of resampling the data on a different grid. However, this modification does not change the reconstructed function, so the *meaning* of the data attributes stays the same, even though their internal representation may change. In this chapter, we shall present a number of different modeling techniques: cutting (Section 8.1), selection (Section 8.2), constructing grids from scattered points (Section 8.3), and grid processing techniques (Section 8.4).

8.1 Cutting

Cutting methods are domain-modeling techniques that map the data from a given source domain to a target subdomain. Consider some function f defined on a domain D. Given a domain $D' \in \mathbb{D}$, how can we compute the restriction of f to D'? Let us now consider that f on D is represented by a sampled "source" dataset $\mathcal{D}_s = (\{p_i\}, \{c_i\}, \{f_i\}, \{\Phi_i\})$, as described in Section 3.3. Cutting the domain D with the domain D' means, essentially, resampling f from D to D'. This implies creating a new "target" dataset $\mathcal{D}'_s = (\{p'_i\}, \{c'_i\}, \{f'_i\}, \{\Phi'_i\})$, as described in Section 3.9.1. The grid points $\{p'_i\}$, cells $\{c'_i\}$, and interpolation functions $\{\Phi'_i\}$ of the target dataset are all user specified, since it is up to the user to say where to resample the source dataset. The attribute values $\{f'_i\}$ are computed by sampling the reconstructed function $\tilde{f}$ of the source dataset at the locations p'_i of the target dataset, using Equation (3.2). The cutting operation has several properties. First, the target domain is assumed to be a subset of the source domain. More exactly, we assume the points $\{p'_i\}$ of the target dataset to be contained in the cells $\{c_i\}$ of the source dataset. Since we use convex cells in our datasets (see Section 3.4), this means that all cells $\{c'_i\}$ in the target dataset are also contained in the cells $\{c_i\}$ of the source dataset. We never attempt to evaluate the source dataset outside its sampling domain, hence the name "cutting." A second property of cutting is that the dimensionality of the source and target datasets, and hence the interpolation functions Φ_i and Φ'_i of the two, need not be the same. The only restriction is that the target dataset is of equal or lower dimensionality than the source dataset, so that the latter can be a subset of the former. For example, this means that we can cut a 3D volume with another 3D volume, a 2D curved surface, or a 1D curve.

The implementation complexity and efficiency of the cutting operation, however, depends strongly on the way we wish to define the cutting dataset. We will now present some of the most widely used variants of the cutting operation: extracting a brick, slicing, cutting with an implicit function, and generalized cutting.

8.1.1   Extracting a Brick

Extracting a brick, also called *bricking* or extracting a *volume of interest (VOI)*, is a cutting operation that produces a target dataset with the same dimensionality as the source dataset. Moreover, the target grid points are a subset of the source grid points, $\{p'_i\} \in \{p_i\}$. Bricking takes advantage of the regular structure of sample points in uniform, structured, and rectilinear grids to efficiently implement the cutting operation. Recall from Section 3.5 that uniform, structured, and rectilinear grids arrange

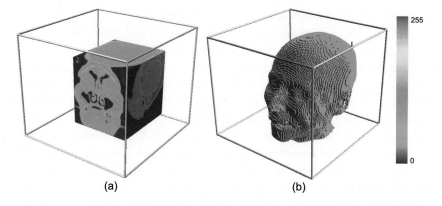

Figure 8.1. (a) Brick extraction. (b) Selection of cells with scalar value above 50.

their sample points in a regular axis-aligned lattice. For a d-dimensional dataset, we can identify every sample point by d integers $n_1, \cdots, n_d$, called *structured coordinates*. Hence, we can easily specify the target domain as an axis-aligned "brick" contained in the source dataset, defined by its minimum and maximum integer coordinates $(m_1, M_1), \cdots, (m_d, M_d)$, where $1 < m_i < M_i < n_i$ for all $i \in [1, d]$. This set of structured coordinates is called the *brick extent*. Implementing bricking is now very simple: given a dataset that has a uniform, structured, or rectilinear grid, we produce a new dataset that has the same grid type. In the target dataset, we copy all points, cells, and corresponding data attributes that fall within the specified brick extent. Note that when we use this definition of bricking, the extracted object extent is parallel with the dataset extent and not the coordinate axes, and the extracted brick contains only whole cells. Consider, for example, the case of the structured grids shown in Figure 3.9.

Figure 8.1(a) shows a brick extracted from a volumetric MRI scan of a human head. The dataset extent is shown by the wireframe and the brick surface is color-mapped with the scalar values at the respective points of the extracted brick.

8.1.2 Slicing in Structured Datasets

Slicing is a cutting operation that is very similar to bricking. Given a uniform, rectilinear, or structured grid, we define a *slice* as all grid points that have one of the structured integer coordinates $n_1, \cdots, n_d$ equal. Extracting a slice can be seen as a bricking operation where the brick extent $(m_1, M_1), \cdots, (m_d, M_d)$ is equal to the grid extent for $d - 1$ of the dimensions, except for the slicing axis s, where $m_s = M_s$. Slicing a d-dimensional dataset generates a $d - 1$ dimensional dataset. As explained in Chapter 3 where we introduced the geometrical and topological dimensions of a dataset, this means that slicing creates cells of a lower dimension, but whose vertices are points in the same three-dimensional space as the source dataset. The most common type of slicing is extracting a set of planar cells, or a slice, from a volumetric dataset, hence the name "slicing." Just as bricking, slicing is simple to implement: we iterate over all the sample points in the slice, in order of the structured coordinates $n_i, i \neq s$ that span the slice. Since our source dataset has a uniform, rectilinear, or structured grid, these integer coordinates directly correspond to $d - 1$-dimensional cells on the slice itself. In the target dataset, we save the sample points and the $d - 1$-dimensional cells on the slice plane, as well as their data attributes. In case of cell attributes, we must create these, since we also created the cells. We can do this easily by using the method of converting from point to cell attributes presented in Section 3.9.1.

The most common use of slicing is to extract 2D datasets from 3D volumes, and then visualize the extracted slices by one of the 2D visualization methods, such as color mapping or isolines for scalar data or streamlines for vector data. Figure 8.2 shows this technique applied to three slices perpendicular to the x-, y-, and z-axes of the same MRI scan uniform dataset as the one used in Figure 8.1. All three slices are taken at the middle of

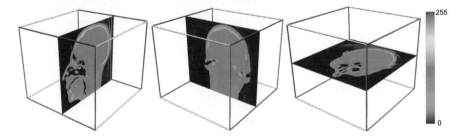

Figure 8.2. Slicing with planes perpendicular to the x-axis (left), y-axis (middle), and z-axis (right).

the respective axes of the dataset. In medical imaging, slices with these orientations are also called *sagittal, axial,* and *coronal* slices.

If desired, slicing can reduce the dimensionality of the dataset by more than one dimension at a time. For example, by extracting all points that share two integer coordinates from a structured dataset, we obtain a curve parallel to one of the integer coordinate axes. Slicing works also in higher dimensions. For example, extracting a time step from a 4D time-dependent volumetric dataset is equivalent to slicing the dataset with respect to the time axis.

8.1.3 Implicit Function Cutting

Slicing is a powerful and widely used visualization technique, especially when one wants to quickly browse through a large, high-dimensional dataset, without having to resort to slower, more complex visualization methods. However, slicing, as described previously, is limited to structured topology datasets. Moreover, even for such datasets, slicing limits the extraction to subsets spanned by the dataset's integer coordinate axes.

We can generalize the slicing concept that reduces the topological dimensionality of a dataset to different subspaces than those spanned by integer coordinates in structured datasets. One way to do this is to cut an arbitrary dataset with a given lower-dimensional domain. A simple, yet powerful way to specify the cutting domain is to use *implicit functions.* Given some function $\phi : D \rightarrow \mathbb{R}$, where D is the domain of the source dataset, we define the target, or cutting, domain as all points $p \in D$ for which $\phi(p) = 0$. To cut the source dataset, we now proceed as follows. First, we compute a scalar dataset $\mathcal{D}_{\text{cut}}$ that has the same grid as the source dataset and that evaluates ϕ. Second, we compute a contour of $\mathcal{D}_{\text{cut}}$ for the value zero. As explained in Section 5.3, this yields an unstructured grid. This grid is our sampled representation of the cutting domain. Finally, we resample the source dataset attributes on this unstructured grid, using one of the available forms of interpolation (e.g., constant or linear), and we obtain the desired result.

Cutting with implicit functions generalizes the axis-aligned slicing presented in Section 8.1.2. Indeed, if we consider the implicit equation of a plane $Ax + By + Cz + D = 0$ with appropriate coefficients A, B, C, and D, we immediately obtain axis-aligned slice planes, at least for uniform and rectilinear grids. By changing the coefficients, we can obtain slice planes oriented at arbitrary angles with no added difficulty. Cutting through 3D volumes using more complex surfaces, such as spheres, cylinders, quadrics, or ellipsoids, is also trivial. Finally, we can now cut through all types of datasets, including unstructured ones. The added cost of implicit function slicing resides in the computation of the implicit function isosurface, which we did not need for the simpler case of slicing uniform datasets.

8.1.4   Generalized Cutting

We can generalize the cutting technique presented in the previous sections by allowing a target dataset of arbitrary definition. Instead of using a target dataset defined by structured coordinates or an implicit function, we can use an arbitrary grid, as long as its cells are contained in the source dataset. In this case, the cutting operation is identical to the last part of the implicit function cutting procedure described previously. The source attributes are interpolated at the locations of the target grid vertices (if the target dataset uses linear interpolation) or target grid cell centers (if the target dataset uses constant interpolation).

8.2   Selection

In contrast to cutting, which projects the values of a source dataset to a target domain, *selection* methods extract the data from a source dataset based on data properties. Cutting enforces various geometrical and/or topological properties on the target domain, since the target grid is speci-fied by the user, but cannot explicitly enforce any properties on the data values, as these are fully specified by the source dataset. In contrast, selec-tion explicitly specifies which data values we are interested in, but cannot enforce, in general, a certain topology and/or geometry of the shape or connectivity of the extracted dataset domain.

In the most general case, selection produces just a set of sample points and/or cells from the source dataset for which the data-based selection criterion holds. The simplest variant of selection produces a domain D' that contains just the sample points whose data values meet the selection criterion

$$D' = \{p \in D | s(p) = \text{true}\}. \tag{8.1}$$

Here, $s : D \rightarrow \mathbb{B}$ is a boolean function representing the user-specified selection operation based on the attributes of the point p.

If we wish to extract cells, there are several ways to apply the selection criterion on a cell. A cell can meet the selection criterion if one of its vertices, all vertices, or its center point meet the selection criterion as defined for a point. The one-vertex criterion produces more cells, essentially selecting cells that are neighbors of the ones produced by the all-vertex selection criterion. The center point criterion is equivalent to applying the one-point selection criterion on a slightly different sampling grid. If cells are selected in the output dataset, we assume these to have the same interpolation functions as in the input dataset, since we just copied them from the input dataset. If only points are selected in the output dataset, we actually create a scattered dataset (see Section 3.9.2). Finally, the output dataset is assumed to have the same interpolation functions as the input dataset, since it is essentially just a subset of the input points and/or cells.

Since selection generally yields an arbitrary subset of points and cells from the input dataset, its output is an unstructured grid. Implementing selection is relatively simple: depending on what we want to select (points or cells), we iterate over all the input dataset's points or cells, apply the selection criterion, and copy the elements that pass the criterion to the output dataset, including their data attributes as well.

Many types of selection criteria are used in visualization applications. Selection based on the scalar value matching a given target value s_0 produces results related to the contouring operation, as explained later. Selection based on the scalar value being larger (or smaller) than a given threshold s_0 produces one or more compact subsets of the input dataset, depending on the data monotonicity. Such an operation is also known as *thresholding* or *segmentation*. A variant of segmentation tests the scalar value against a given value range $[s_{\min}, s_{\max}]$. Segmentation is discussed in more detail in Chapter 9 in the context of image-processing algorithms. In addition to using the scalar values themselves, one can use their derivatives, too. In the case of scalar values that represent the luminance, or intensity, of an image, selecting data points based on the derivative values is related to edge-detection methods (see Section 9.3). Similar selection methods can be designed that use vector, color, and tensor data attributes, depending on the data at hand and application type.

Finally, let us mention that selection can also involve other properties than the data attributes of the current point. Selection methods that implement Equation (8.1) are essentially *local* methods, in the sense that they treat each point or cell of the dataset separately. On one hand, this is advantageous, as it lets us implement such methods simply by designing different types of local selection functions $s : D \to \mathbb{B}$. Moreover, such selection methods can be easily parallelized, as they treat all data points independently. However, in some cases, we are interested in selection criteria that have a quasiglobal or global nature. This means, on one hand, that the selection criterion needs to check more points together to determine whether they pass or fail the test. On the other hand, the selection will output all these points as a set instead of separately.

Such a nonlocal selection function can be described as a function $s : \mathbb{D} \to \mathbb{D}$, where $s(D) = D' \in D$ is the result of the selection applied on the domain D. Nonlocal selection operations occur when we must enforce the connectivity of the resulting domain D'. For example, consider the operation "select all *connected components* $D'_i \in D$ from an input domain D where the scalar values exceed some threshold $s_{\min}$ and whose size $|D'_i|$ exceeds some minimal size $\tau_{\min}$." This operation essentially enhances basic thresholding with a connectivity and minimal size condition on the resulting subsets. Implementing the minimal-size connected components operation is described later in Section 9.4.

Figure 8.1(b) shows a selection of all cells from our sample MRI dataset whose scalar values are greater than or equal to 50. Data values in such an MRI scan correspond to different types of tissue. In our case, a value of 50 roughly corresponds to skin tissue, while greater values correspond to denser tissues, such as muscles or bone, hence the result of the selection shown in the image.

Selection is related to the contouring operation (see Section 5.3). Indeed, selecting all cells in a dataset whose data values are equal to a given target value τ is conceptually equivalent to producing a piecewise constant approximation of the contour at value τ. In other words, the contour is approximated by a set of cells, which gives it the blocky appearance visible in Figure 8.1(b). The marching squares and marching cubes algorithms discussed in Section 5.3 will compute the same isosurface, but use a piecewise linear approximation. In other words, the contour is approximated by a set of planes (in 3D) or lines (in 2D). Comparing Figures 8.1(b) and 5.17(d), the difference in quality of the two approximations is obvious.

8.3 Grid Construction from Scattered Points

In Section 3.9.2, we described the use of scattered point interpolation as an alternative to grids for reconstructing a piecewise continuous function from sampled data. Gridless methods are attractive when one has to manipulate datasets that contain very large numbers of unstructured point samples, which have a rather high point density. One of the uses of gridless interpolation is to render surfaces represented as 3D dense point clouds. However attractive, gridless methods have also several drawbacks: they trade the grid storage and management for storing and managing some type of spatial search structure for neighboring sample points, and they use radial basis functions that are computationally more expensive compared to piecewise linear basis functions. Moreover, most visualization software packages would require the data to be in a grid-based representation of one of the standard dataset types (see Section 3.3) before it can be processed by the available algorithms. Direct support for processing and visualizing data in gridless representations is not frequent. In such cases, constructing a grid from the scattered point set is a better alternative.

There are several methods that construct grids from scattered points. These differ in the assumptions they make about the original signal the sample points are coming from, the dimension they work in, and the type of cells they produce. We will now present several such methods.

8.3.1 Triangulation Methods

Triangulation methods are probably the most-used class of methods for constructing grids from scattered points. Given a set of points p_i (sometimes also called *sites*), a triangulation method produces a grid (p_i, c_i) by generating a set of cells c_i that have the sample points p_i as vertices. The cells c_i form a tiling of the *convex hull* of the point set $\{p_i\}$. In other words, triangulation methods produce a grid that samples a domain D identical to the convex hull of the triangulated point set.

Delaunay triangulations. The best-known triangulation method is the *Delaunay* algorithm [de Berg et al. 00]. This method generates triangular cells c_i for a set of 2D points $p_i \in \mathbb{R}^2$ and tetrahedra for a set of 3D points $p_i \in \mathbb{R}^3$. A Delaunay triangulation of a point set consists of a set of triangles that covers the convex hull of the point set. An important property of a Delaunay triangulation is that no point from the input point set $\{p_i\}$ lies in the circumscribed circle of any triangle in the triangulation. Triangulations that obey this property are called conforming Delaunay triangulations. Given a set of scattered points with data values recorded at the point locations, using the Delaunay triangulation is the most "natural" way to create a C^1, piecewise linear, interpolation of the data values over the convex hull of the points. To do this, we define piecewise linear basis functions over the triangles contained in the unstructured grid generated by the Delaunay triangulation, and use these functions to interpolate the vertex data values, as explained in Section 3.3. Figure 8.3(a) shows a Delaunay triangulation of a random point set containing 600 points. The point density is higher in the center, which causes the creation of smaller triangles in that area. Another example of Delauney triangulation is shown in Figure 3.11 (middle).

Voronoi diagrams. With every Delaunay triangulation, there exists an associated geometric structure called a *Voronoi diagram*. A Voronoi diagram consists of a set of convex polygonal cells in 2D and polyhedral cells in 3D, respectively. The vertices of the Voronoi cells are the centers of the circumscribed circles of the triangles present in the associated Delaunay triangulation. The edges of the Voronoi cells are line segments perpendicular to and passing through the midpoint of the edges of the triangles present in the associated Delaunay triangulation. The centers of the Voronoi cells are the vertices of the Delaunay triangulation, i.e., the given scattered points. Figure 8.3(b) shows the Voronoi diagram of the same point set whose Delaunay triangulation is given in Figure 8.3(a).

Every location x in a Voronoi diagram is included in the Voronoi cell that has as center the closest point p in the input point set $\{p_i\}$. Hence, Voronoi diagrams can be used to quickly find the closest point p from a given scattered point set to a given test location x. Note that the Voronoi cells corresponding to vertices on the convex hull of the input point set are unbounded, as they contain all points in the 2D plane that are closest to

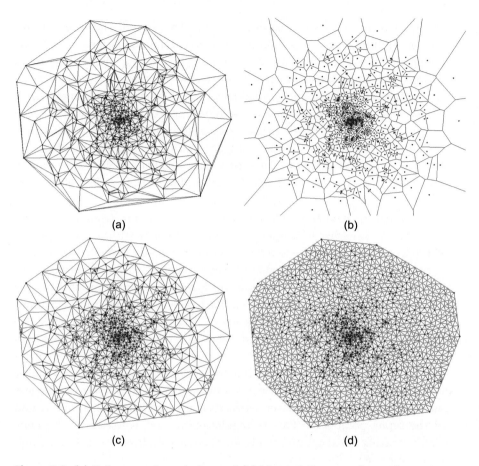

(a)   (b)

(c)   (d)

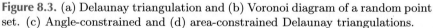

Figure 8.3. (a) Delaunay triangulation and (b) Voronoi diagram of a random point set. (c) Angle-constrained and (d) area-constrained Delaunay triangulations.

every point on the input's convex hull. Voronoi diagrams are a natural way to create a $\mathcal{C}^0$, piecewise constant, interpolation of data values sampled at the scattered points, where the supports of the piecewise constant basis functions are the Voronoi cells themselves. However, Voronoi diagrams are not frequently used in practice to produce piecewise constant data approximations, since the Voronoi cells can be n-sided polygons in general, as compared to the simpler triangles of a Delaunay triangulation.

Variation of the basic techniques. Several variations of the basic Delaunay triangulation idea exist. Angle-constrained triangulations enforce the triangle angles to lie within a given range $[\alpha_{min}, \alpha_{max}]$. For many applications, the approximation quality of a triangle grid is directly related to the triangle shapes and, consequently, to their angles. Triangles with angles close to 60 degrees provide a higher approximation quality, hence the use of angle-constrained triangles. Figure 8.3(c) shows a triangulation of the same point set as in Figure 8.3(a), where all angles lie between 20 and 140 degrees. To satisfy this constraint, 361 extra points, the *Steiner points* (drawn in yellow), are added to the original 600 points (drawn in red).

Area-constrained triangulations enforce a maximum triangle area and are useful in creating a sampling of a given domain with a user-specified density, which is in turn useful for representing signals with nonuniform variation with a minimal number of sample points, as explained in Chapter 3. Figure 8.3(d) shows the area-constrained triangulation of the same point set as discussed previously. Similar to the angle constraint, the minimal area constraint forces the creation of 1272 extra (Steiner) points. The original point set is colored in red, while the extra points are colored in yellow. In addition to angle and area constraints, geometric constraints can be used too. For example, the triangulation can be forced to cover the inside area of a specified convex or concave polygon whose vertices are part of the input point set, instead of covering the entire convex hull of the input point set. This triangulation variant is useful in automatically creating unstructured grids for domains with complex shapes and boundaries.

In the previous examples, we have used only the Euclidean metric to define the closest-point notion that underlies the construction of Voronoi diagrams and corresponding Delaunay triangulations. Variants of these diagrams can be obtained if we use other metrics. The additively weighted Euclidean metric, where the distance to every site p_i is biased by some constant value w_i, yields the Johnson-Mehl diagrams whose cell edges are hyperbolic arcs, describing the growth of crystal cells from a set of given seed sites [Okabe et al. 92]. The multiplicatively weighted Euclidean metric, where the distance to every site p_i is multiplied by some constant value w_i, yields the Apollonius diagrams whose cell edges are circle arcs, which are used to model plant cell growth, the tree coverage of areas in forests, and areas of best reception for radio transmitters [Sakamoto and Takagi 88]. Voronoi diagrams based on the Manhattan distance $d(p, q) = |p_x - q_x| + |p_y - q_y|$ are used to model coverage areas of sites such as fire or police stations in cities where the distances are measured on a Cartesian grid.

Delaunay triangulation and Voronoi diagram generation are involved topics, whose details are beyond the scope of this book. For definitions of and results involving Delaunay triangulations, constrained and conforming versions thereof, and other aspects of triangular mesh generation, see the excellent survey by Bern and Eppstein [Bern and Eppstein 92].

Implementing robust, efficient, and scalable algorithms for these mesh generation methods is a complex task. Fortunately, several high-quality software implementations for Delaunay triangulation and Voronoi diagram computation are available in the open-source arena, such as the Triangle mesh generator [Shewchuk 06, Shewchuk 02]. Triangle provides a rich set of Delaunay triangulation algorithms, including the conforming and area, angle, and geometry constrained variants, as well as the computation of Voronoi diagrams, and is capable of triangulating hundreds of thousands of input points in a few seconds and with high precision on a modern PC. All examples presented in this section are computed with the Triangle software. Another high-quality open-source library providing Delaunay triangulation and Voronoi diagram operations is the Gnu Triangulated Surface Library (GTS) [GTS 06]. The interface of the GTS library is relatively more complex than that of the Triangle library. However, the GTS library offers many extra features, such as set operations on surfaces, multiresolution surface representation capabilities, and kd-trees for fast point location.

8.3.2 Surface Reconstruction and Rendering

A particular use of scattered-point interpolation is to render a 3D surface that is stored as a point cloud. This task consists of two steps. First, we must specify which is the actual surface that the given point cloud approximates. Second, we must render this surface. We next discuss both steps briefly.

For every point in the point cloud, we assume we have three pieces of information: the point's location p_i, the surface normal $\mathbf{n}_i$ at that location, and the average distance R_i to the neighboring points on the surface at that location. The question is: how to construct a surface that sufficiently approximates the point cloud? In the following sections, we describe several approaches for this.

Using radial basis functions. We approach this goal by first using 3D radial basis functions (RBFs) to construct a function $\tilde{f} : \mathbb{R}^3 \to \mathbb{R}$

$$\tilde{f}(x) = \sum_i \Phi(T_i^{-1}(x)), \forall x \in \mathbb{R}^3, \tag{8.2}$$

where Φ is the reference RBF in 3D and T_i^{-1} is the world-to-reference system coordinate transform for sample point p_i. Both Φ and T^{-1}, as well as the concept of RBFs, are detailed in Section 3.9.2.

If our basis functions $\phi_i = \Phi(T_i^{-1}(x)$ satisfy the partition of unity property (see Equation (3.5)) then the actual surface $\mathcal{S}$ is an isosurface $\tilde{f}(x) = 1$ of the function $\tilde{f}$.

We can reconstruct the surface $\mathcal{S}$ by first computing a 3D volumetric dataset that samples the function $\tilde{f}$ and then extracting and rendering the isosurface $\tilde{f} = 1$, using the marching cubes algorithm (see Section 5.3). However, this has several disadvantages. First, we must explicitly compute, and possibly store, the 3D dataset that samples $\tilde{f}$. Second, we must extract the isosurface, using, e.g., the marching cubes algorithm (see Section 5.3), and store it as a separate 3D unstructured mesh. This is expensive from both computational and memory viewpoints. Third, the basis functions we use must satisfy the partition of unity property. As discussed in Section 3.9.2, this is not the case unless the sample points in the point set are equally spaced or special normalization measures are taken. The last problem can be alleviated by using different ways to define the function $\tilde{f}$ whose isosurface determines our surface. A final problem is that the extracted isosurface will actually give a *double* surface representation, since our function f in Equation (8.2) is symmetric, i.e., does not distinguish between the inside and outside of the surface.

Using signed distance functions. A refinement of the previous method is to use a *signed* distance function. One of the first methods to do this was proposed by Hoppe et al. [Hoppe et al. 92] and works as follows. For every point p_i in the point cloud, we compute a *tangent plane* $\mathcal{T}_i$ that approximates our surface $\mathcal{S}$ in the neighborhood of p_i. The plane $\mathcal{T}_i$ is defined by its center c_i and normal $\mathbf{n}_i$. Computing $\mathcal{T}_i$ can be done as

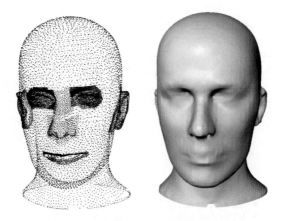

Figure 8.4. Scattered point cloud (left) and surface reconstruction with isosurface (right). (Data courtesy of H. Hoppe [Hoppe et al. 92].)

follows. For every point p_i in the point set, we determine a neighbor set $N_i = \{p_j \| p_j - p_i | \leq R_i\}$ that contains all neighbors of p_i closer than a fraction k of the support radius R_i of p_i. Next, we compute T_i as the plane that minimizes the sum of the squared distances $\sum_{p \in N_i} d(p, T_i)^2$ to the points in N_i. It can be shown that the center c_i is the centroid of the points in N_i:

$$c_i = \frac{\sum_{p \in N_i} p}{|N_i|}, \tag{8.3}$$

where $|N_i|$ denotes the number of points in the neighbor set N_i, and the plane normal $\mathbf{n}_i$ is the eigenvector corresponding to the smallest eigenvalue of the 3×3 *covariance matrix* of the points $p \in N_i$:

$$A = (a_{jk}) = \begin{pmatrix} a_{11} & a_{12} & a_{13} \\ a_{21} & a_{22} & a_{23} \\ a_{31} & a_{32} & a_{33} \end{pmatrix} = \sum_{p \in N_i} (p^j - c_i^j)(p^k - c_i^k). \tag{8.4}$$

Here, p^j denotes the jth component, or coordinate, of point p. Computing eigenvalues and eigenvectors of matrices was discussed in Chapter 7.

Once we have the tangent planes T_i, we define a function $f : \mathbb{R}^3 \to \mathbb{R}_+$ such that $f(x)$ is the signed distance between a given point $x \in \mathbb{R}^3$ and the tangent plane T_i at the point p_i closest to x:

$$f(x) = (x - c_i)\mathbf{n}_i. \tag{8.5}$$

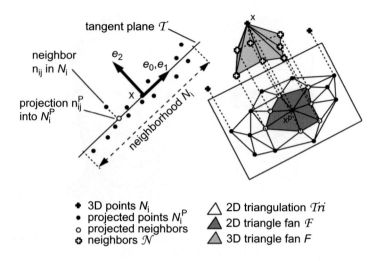

Figure 8.5. Mesh reconstruction from scattered points with local triangulations.

Finally, our desired surface S is simply the isosurface $f = 0$ of the preceding function. Figure 8.4 illustrates the reconstruction process for a point cloud of 12,772 points representing a mannequin head.

Using local triangulations. Another class of methods constructs an unstructured triangle mesh from a scattered point set by performing local 2D Delaunay triangulations [Linsen and Prautzch 01, Clarenz et al. 04]. These methods work as follows (see also Figure 8.5). First, we compute a tangent plane T_i for every point p_i, using its neighbor set N_i, as described previously. Next, we project the points in N_i on T_i and compute the 2D Delaunay triangulation Tri of these projections, as described earlier in this section. Next, we add to our mesh those triangles that have p_i as a vertex, i.e., the triangle fan around p_i. Although this method is not guaranteed to produce a consistent triangle mesh, since it treats every point p_i separately, it usually produces meshes with no defects such as holes or intersecting triangles. Also, this method is more memory efficient and computationally faster than the isosurface-based method first described, as it does not need to compute a volumetric distance field first. For a point cloud of P points in total and N points in an average neighbor set N_i, we need to perform P 2D Delaunay triangulations of N points each. For most point clouds, values of

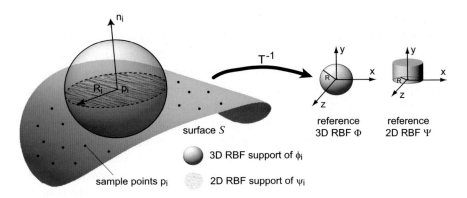

Figure 8.6. Radial basis functions for surface reconstruction.

N ranging between 10 and 50 points give a good compromise between tangent plane stability and geometric noise elimination (which requires larger neighborhoods) and surface feature preservation (which requires smaller neighborhoods).

Surface splatting.   The surface reconstruction methods presented so far produce a surface represented as a triangular mesh, whether via the marching cubes algorithm or directly by triangulating the point set. However, sometimes we would like a simple-to-implement and fast, albeit not always very accurate method to directly render the surface S from the scattered points, without having to perform any explicit surface reconstruction. To explain how to do this, imagine the restrictions $\psi_i : \mathbb{R}^2 \to \mathbb{R}$ of the 3D radial functions ϕ_i on our surface S (see Figure 8.6). The 3D RBFs ϕ_i have compact supports on the spheres of radii R_i, so the restrictions ψ_i also have compact supports, which are the intersections of these spheres with the surface S. If we assume the surface to be almost flat in a neighborhood of radius R_i around every p_i then the restrictions ψ_i are actually 2D radial basis functions defined on the surface.

To display the surface S described by our point set, we can render the 2D radial basis functions ψ_i. Just as for the 3D RBFs, the 2D RBFs ψ_i are transformed versions of a reference 2D radial basis function that we shall call Ψ. If Φ is a 3D Gaussian then Ψ is a 2D Gaussian, whose graph is the familiar shape shown in our elevation plot in Chapter 2 (see Figure 2.1, for example). If Φ is a 3D constant RBF, whose graph would be a sphere of radius R_i, then Ψ is a 2D constant RBF, whose graph is a disc of radius R_i. To draw our surface $\mathcal{S}$, we have to draw the radial domains of ψ_i, which are nothing but discs of radius R_i, centered at every sample point p_i and oriented in the local tangent plane to $\mathcal{S}$, which is perpendicular to the surface normal $\mathbf{n}_i$ at p_i. We can do this efficiently by taking advantage of the rendering primitives offered by modern graphics hardware. First, we regularly sample the 2D radial basis function Φ on a pixel grid and store it as a 2D transparency texture T, where the value $\Phi = 1$ maps to a totally opaque pixel $T = 1$ and a value $\Phi = 0$ maps to a totally transparent pixel $T = 0$. The size of the texture T is taken so that T encloses the compact support of radius R of Φ.

Next, we implement the two-dimensional equivalent of Equation (8.2) by drawing the texture T mapped onto square supports centered at the sample points p_i, rotated to be orthogonal to the surface normals $\mathbf{n}_i$ and scaled to the radius R_i. For constant RBFs, this actually means drawing an opaque disc of radius R_i at every point p_i. For Gaussian RBFs, this draws a set of textures of variable opacity. To sum these up as described in Equation (8.2), we turn on additive alpha blending before rendering the textures. In both cases, we can use any desired lighting model, such as the Phong model described in Chapter 2, to compute the actual color to be used on the rendered elements. We compute the surface lighting at the sample point locations p_i only, using the available surface normals $\mathbf{n}_i$ at those locations. The texture T that encodes a 2D RBF is sometimes called a *splat* or *surfel*. Hence, the previous surface reconstruction is also called *splatting*. We shall encounter splatting in Section 11.5.2 in a different setting when visualizing graph data.

Splats can encode other surface-information data necessary for the rendering besides the normal, color, and radius. All in all, a splat is a rendering element for a 3D surface that is analogous to the pixel, which is the rendering element for a 2D image. If we use constant RBFs, the splats are fully opaque discs stored as 2D textures. The splatting process is simple to implement and actually requires no blending support, but can easily create rendering artifacts. If we use Gaussian RBFs, the splats are variable-transparency 2D textures. However, we must ensure that the sum of the splats' transparencies at every rendered pixel is exactly one. In case of nonuniform point distributions, this condition does not hold by

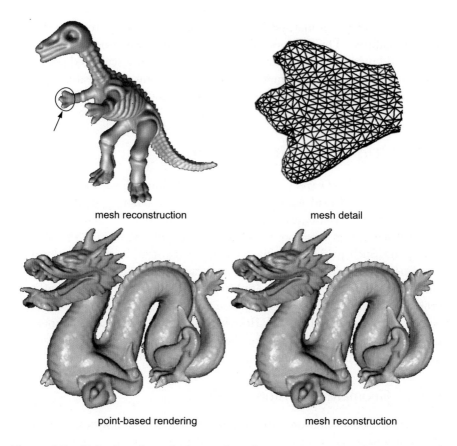

mesh reconstruction · mesh detail

point-based rendering · mesh reconstruction

Figure 8.7. Point-based rendering and surface reconstruction from scattered points.

default. If this condition is not enforced, this leads to pixels on the rendered surface that have transparencies below one, an artifact that is visible as half-transparent "spots" on the surface. More sophisticated definitions of RBFs and blending mechanisms that guarantee the partition of unity property are possible [Ohtake et al. 03].

Figure 8.7 shows two examples that illustrate point-based rendering and surface reconstruction from scattered points. The dragon 3D model, shown in the lower part of the image, is rendered using both disc splats (left) and a triangular mesh that has the same points as vertices (right) constructed by the tangent plane method [Clarenz et al. 04]. Clearly, the two images are very similar. The dinosaur 3D model shown in Figure 8.7 (upper-left) is rendered using a reconstructed triangle mesh from a scattered point set. The quality of the triangle mesh, as well as the point set density, is visible in the detail image (Figure 8.7 (upper-right)).

8.4   Grid-Processing Techniques

Grid-processing techniques are methods that change both the grid geometry (locations of grid sample points) and its topology (grid cells). By "grid-processing techniques," we mean those techniques that manipulate the grid itself, and have no knowledge about data attributes sampled on that grid. Such grid-processing techniques are used in many application domains besides data visualization, such as numerical methods and simulations or computer-graphics applications. There exist a wealth of grid-processing methods. Studying all these methods in depth would be a standalone subject matter by itself. However, since grid processing is important for visualization applications, we shall present a selection of some of the most-used grid-processing methods in data visualization.

8.4.1   Geometric Transformations

Geometric transformations are domain-modeling techniques that change the position of the sample points, or grid points, but do not modify the underlying basis functions, cells, or data attributes. These are probably the simplest grid-processing techniques. Transformations in this class include affine operations such as translation, rotation, and scaling, but also nonaffine operations, such as tapering, twisting, and bending. These transformations are relatively straightforward, so we are not going to detail them further.

A second type of geometric transformation changes the position of the sample points based on the data attributes. We have encountered such techniques in the form of warping, height plots, and displacement plots, for the visualization of scalars (see Section 5.4) and vectors (see Section 6.4).

A third type of geometric transformation changes the position of the sample points based on the characteristics of the grid itself. Grid-smoothing techniques fall in this class. Given the relative importance and complexity of such techniques, we describe them separately in Section 8.4.4.

8.4.2   Grid Simplification

Many visualization applications produce large datasets that take considerable time to manipulate and store. Often, one wants to reduce the size of these datasets, yet keep the data features that are important for the task at hand. In this section, we discuss several methods that allow us to simplify the underlying grid of a dataset. By "grid simplification," we mean situations involving grids that describe two-dimensional surfaces embedded in 3D, such as isosurfaces or polygonal models. The more general case of simplifying n-dimensional datasets by means of reducing the number of sample points (resampling) was discussed in Section 3.9.1.

We make a second assumption. The simplification criteria we shall look at here are mainly geometric, i.e., based on the shape of the grid. However, such criteria can be adapted to include information about the data attributes stored on the grid itself. An example of this technique is the progressive meshes method [Hoppe 97, Hoppe 98], which is also described later in this section.

Let us first state the generic problem. Consider a surface S that is sampled on a geometric grid S. As we saw in Chapters 2 and 3, the quality of the approximation is dependent on the sampling rate, in case we use uniform sampling. However, uniform sampling uses too many grid points in areas of low surface curvature that can be approximated well by larger cells, i.e., fewer sample points. Given a densely sampled grid S, the aim of geometric grid simplification is to produce a surface S' that contains fewer points than S but still provides a good approximation of S. Usually, the points of S' are a subset of the points of S obtained by eliminating points from areas that are oversampled with respect to the desired approximation quality. However, depending on the simplification method, the points of the simplified model do not have to be a subset of the original points.

Several grid-simplification algorithms exist. The field is huge, given the applicability in computer graphics, data compression, mesh storage and transmission, shape matching, terrain visualization and rendering, and data visualization. It is, hence, impractical to aim for a comprehensive overview of grid-simplification methods in the current context. For the interested

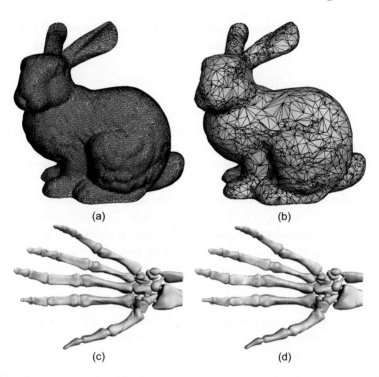

(a)   (b)

(c)   (d)

Figure 8.8. Decimation of a surface grid. (a) Original grid with 36,000 points and (b) decimated grid with 3510 points. (c) Original isosurface with 373,000 points and (b) decimated version with 6536 points.

reader, we point to a number of survey papers [Luebke 01, Garland 99, Heckbert and Garland 97]. We next briefly describe a number of the main techniques used in this field, following the classification given by Luebke: triangle mesh decimation, vertex clustering, simplification envelopes, and progressive meshes [Luebke 01].

Triangle mesh decimation. Decimation algorithms [Schroeder et al. 92] were originally designed to reduce the huge number of triangles produced by the marching-cubes method (see Section 5.3). Given a triangle mesh, the algorithm does multiple passes over the mesh vertices, checking each vertex for removal. A vertex (and its triangle fan) are removed if the removal does not change the mesh topology and if the resulting surface

lies within a user-specified distance from the unsimplified surface. The
hole left in the mesh is then retriangulated. Decimation continues until
a user-specified reduction factor and/or some maximal error criterion are
met. The decimated model contains a subset of the original mesh vertices,
which is convenient for reusing the vertex information (position, normals,
color, and eventual data attributes). However, this constraint can limit
the decimation accuracy. A variant of the decimation algorithm can also
handle topological changes [Schroeder 97].

Figure 8.8 shows two grid decimation examples produced by the latter
algorithm. The bunny geometric model (see Figure 8.8(a)) is simplified
to under 10% of the initial 36,000 grid points, yielding the result in Figure 8.8(b). As visible from the grid rendering, the simplification works
adaptively. More triangles are kept in the high-curvature area around the
bunny's ear, marked red in Figure 8.8(b) in order to preserve the surface
shape. In low-curvature areas, such as the bunny's back, the simplification
reaches its maximum. Figure 8.8(c) shows an isosurface of the skeleton
of a human hand from a CT scan. The input data is a 3D uniform grid,
so the marching-cubes algorithm produces an unstructured triangle mesh
with almost constant point density, since the isosurface points are always
located on the edges of the input grid (see Section 5.3). The isosurface is
simplified to 6536 points, i.e., to less than 2% of the original isosurface. After the simplification, surface vertex normals are computed by cell normal
averaging (see Chapter 2), which lets us create a rendering of the isosurface
(see Figure 8.8(d)) of comparable quality to the original.

Vertex clustering. Several algorithms simplify meshes by clustering (collapsing) vertices. One such algorithm [Rossignac and Borrel 93] works
as follows. Every vertex gets an importance value. Vertices attached to
large polygons and vertices of high curvature are more important than vertices attached to small polygons and vertices of low curvature. Next, a
3D grid is overlaid onto the mesh to be simplified. All vertices within a
grid cell are collapsed to the most important vertex within that cell. The
polygons whose vertices are collapsed together become degenerate and are
removed.

A different clustering algorithm, called *floating-cell clustering*, works as
follows [Low and Tan 97]. Vertices are sorted in importance order, similar
to Rossignac and Borrel [Rossignac and Borrel 93]. A cell of user-specified

size is centered on the most-important vertex. All vertices within the cell are collapsed to the most-important vertex, which becomes the center of the next cell, and the process repeats. Different error metrics can be used to reposition this most-important vertex in order to ensure a simplified mesh close to the original [Garland and Heckbert 97].

Simplification envelopes. Given a surface, we construct its *simplification envelopes* [Cohen et al. 96]. These are two copies of the surface offset at some small distance ϵ from the original surface. Conceptually, the simplification envelopes are identical to the two components of the distance-function isosurface described in Section 8.3.2. However, we compute the envelopes here by displacing each surface vertex in the normal direction with a distance of 0.5ϵ for the outer envelope and -0.5ϵ for the inner envelope, respectively. After building the envelopes, vertices and triangles are iteratively removed from the original surface, and the holes are retriangulated, similar to the decimation method discussed previously. The simplification only occurs if the simplified surface stays between the envelopes, which guarantees that the result never deviates from the original by more than ϵ. Yet, these restrictions can sometimes limit the simplification. The implementation is quite involved, but is fortunately available to the public [Cohen et al. 07].

Progressive meshes. A *progressive mesh* consists of a base mesh, created by a sequence of edge *collapse* operations on a polygonal mesh, and a sequence of vertex *split* operations [Hoppe 97]. A split is the dual of a collapse, and it replaces a vertex with two edge-connected vertices, creating an extra vertex and two extra triangles. The base mesh can be exactly transformed into the original model via splits, and the model is transformed into the base mesh via collapses. Intermediate versions correspond to progressive simplifications.

The collapses (simplification) are driven by an energy function. Different types of energies can model simplifications driven by mesh geometry, normals, and color, but also additional data attributes [Hoppe 98]. Attributes are classified as discrete, e.g., material and texture IDs, and scalar, e.g., color, normal, and texture coordinates. All edges are put into a priority queue in decreasing order of effect on the energy. The mesh is simplified by collapsing edges in this order, until topological constraints prevent further simplification. The remaining edges and triangles form the base mesh, and the (reversed) sequence of collapse operations become the split operations.

As its name suggests, this method is able to produce a hierarchy of progressively simplified meshes of high quality. Also, from a data visualization perspective, this method is additionally attractive, as it is able to drive the simplification effort as a function of scalar and vector data attributes, not just geometric grid characteristics [Hoppe 99].

8.4.3 Grid Refinement

Grid refinement is the opposite of grid simplification. Given a coarse grid G that approximates some dataset D, refinement produces a grid G' that also approximates D but has more sample points than the original grid G. In terms of sampling, the refined grid G' can be seen as a supersampling of D as compared to the original grid G. Grid refinement has several uses. First, rendering a refined grid can produce a higher-quality image than rendering a coarse grid, for example by decreasing the banding artifacts caused by the linear Gouraud shading. A second use of refinement is as a preprocessing step before applying other grid manipulation operations. For example, smoothing, deforming, or free-editing a refined grid gives better results as compared to performing the same operations on a coarse grid, as the refined grid has more degrees of freedom to accommodate the changes. Also, deformations such as strong stretching change an uniformly sampled grid into a nonuniformly sampled one that exhibits coarsely sampled areas. Grid refinement can be used to bring such grids back to a densely sampled version. Finally, grid refinement can be used to (partially) reverse previous grid simplification operations.

Following this sampling perspective, several grid-refinement methods exist. In case the dataset D represents a surface, we can first reconstruct the surface from the original grid G, using radial basis functions, for example, as explained earlier in this chapter, and then sample the reconstructed surface to a denser level than G to obtain the refined grid G'. Another approach goes directly from G to the refined grid G', avoiding the cost of explicitly reconstructing the dataset D. In this latter class of methods, several variants exist. For one variant, the points of the original grid G can be a subset of the points of the refined grid G'. In the second variant, the

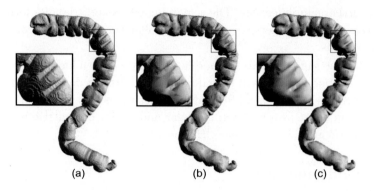

Figure 8.9. Refining an isosurface. (a) Original grid. (b) Simplified grid. (c) Refined grid. The zoomed-in insets show the grid quality.

points of G' are obtained from those of G but do not necessarily need to be a superset of them.

Refining a grid by adding extra sample points to the existing ones is a simple but effective strategy. To explain the procedure, consider an unstructured triangle grid that approximates some surface.

Figure 8.9 shows a grid-refinement scenario. The process starts with an isosurface of a human colon (Figure 8.9(a)) containing 315,600 points. As visible in the image, the isosurface exhibits strong staircasing artifacts due to some type of nearest-neighbor approximation used at some earlier point on the input data. We can render this isosurface using fewer data points and yet achieve a better visual quality. First, we simplify the surface using the decimation method discussed earlier in this chapter. The simplification yields about 13,000 points but also decreases the visual quality of the surface (see Figure 8.9(b)). If we refine the simplified surface by subdividing every triangle into four other triangles, we obtain a surface with around 52,200 points and also a visibly better quality (see Figure 8.9(c)). The final result has a sixth of the points of the initial isosurface and also arguably a better quality and smoother appearance.

Just like grid simplification, refinement can also proceed adaptively by inserting more points where the surface varies more rapidly. As a measure of surface variation, we can use curvature or a similar quantity. Finally, if data attributes are defined on the original surface, these can be transferred to the refined surface by interpolation.

8.4.4   Grid Smoothing

Grid-smoothing methods are a separate class of geometric transformations. Grid-smoothing methods are typically used for grids that represent 2D curved surfaces embedded in $\mathbb{R}^3$, although they can be used also for 3D volumetric grids or 1D curve grids. Recall that, for such grids, we can reconstruct a piecewise continuous surface $\tilde{x}$ from the grid sample points x_i by using the reconstruction formula (see Equation (3.2)) on the grid point coordinates themselves. The aim of a grid-smoothing algorithm is to modify the positions of the grid sample points such that the surface $\tilde{f}$ reconstructed by the grid becomes smoother. Intuitively, a smooth surface is a surface that contains mostly blunt creases instead of sharp ones. Mathematically, this can be described by a surface with a low curvature (see Section 3.6.4 for a discussion on surface curvature). Grid-smoothing methods are useful in case the available grids contain *geometric noise*. This can be due either to the way the surface was acquired or to some other grid-processing operations that have been previously applied on the sampled surface.

A simple-to-implement grid smoothing method is the *Laplacian smoothing*. At the core of this technique is the *diffusion equation*

$$\partial_t u - \mathrm{div}(k\nabla u) = 0. \tag{8.6}$$

If k is constant, this equation can be written as $\partial_t u = k\Delta u$. Here, Δu is called the *Laplacian* of u, hence the name of the diffusion process. If $u(x, y, z)$ is a 3D scalar field, the Laplacian of u is defined as the sum of the second partial derivatives of the field with respect to the variables x, y, and z, which is in turn equal to the divergence of the gradient of the field u:

$$\Delta u = \mathrm{div}\ \nabla u = \frac{\partial^2 u}{\partial x^2} + \frac{\partial^2 u}{\partial y^2} + \frac{\partial^2 u}{\partial z^2}. \tag{8.7}$$

The simplest way to think about diffusion is as smoothing. Given some signal $u_0 : D$, the solution $u : D \times [0, \infty) \rightarrow \mathbb{R}$ of the diffusion equation (Equation (8.6)) describes the smoothing of our signal u_0. The time t plays the role of smoothing strength: higher t values correspond to more smoothing. The constant k describes the diffusivity, or diffusion strength, of the process: higher k values yield faster smoothing. The smoothing properties of the diffusion equation are used in many filtering applications

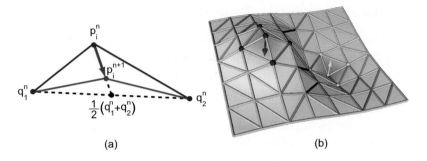

Figure 8.10. Laplacian smoothing principle for (a) 2D and (b) 3D geometries.

for scalar, vector, and tensor datasets. Putting it simply, smoothing re-moves the high-frequency, small-scale variations in the data, such as small sharp spikes in a mesh or noise grains in an image. Smoothing is useful as a preprocessing operation for data manipulations that are noise sensitive, such as computing derivatives (see Section 3.7).

In particular, we can apply smoothing to the signal that represents the geometric coordinates of the grid. The diffusion process moves the grid vertices in the direction that smooths out the sharp features of the grid. The diffusion time t controls the amount of smoothing: the initial value $u(t = 0)$ is equal to the input grid to be smoothed, whereas high t values produce strongly smoothed grids.

Using the definitions of the derivatives on a discrete grid presented in Chapter 3, it can be shown that the discrete form of Equation (8.6) on a grid containing the sample points $\{p_i\}$ is

$$p_i^{n+1} = p_i^n + k \sum_{j=1}^{N} (q_j^n - p_i^n). \qquad (8.8)$$

Here, $(q_j)_{j=1..N}$ denote the neighbors of p_i, i.e., those grid points connected to p_i by edges. Equation (8.8) is solved iteratively, the superscript n de-noting the iteration number. We start with the initial grid points p_i^0, apply Equation (8.8) n times, and obtain the smoothed grid points p_i^n. Intuitively, this process shifts every grid point toward the barycenter $b = \frac{1}{N} \sum_{j=1}^{N} q_j^n$ of its neighboring point set. Figure 8.10(a) illustrates this for the simple case of 2D polyline geometry. The smoothing process has the effect of

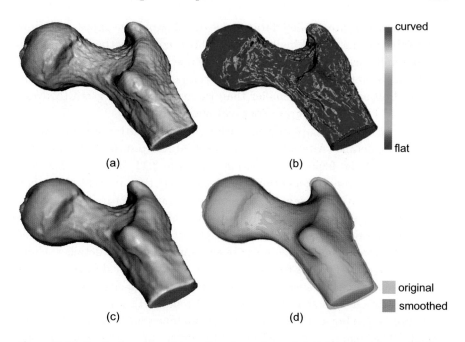

Figure 8.11. Laplacian smoothing of an isosurface. (a) Original surface. (b) Surface curvature. (c) Smoothed surface. (d) Comparison of original and smoothed surfaces.

flattening both convex and concave point neighborhoods, as illustrated in Figure 8.10(b) for a 3D triangle mesh. Both the convex area (marked by red points) and the yellow area (marked by yellow points) get flattened out as the indicated points are moved toward the barycenter of their neighbors. This process has the effect of decreasing the object volume, so using too many smoothing steps must be avoided, as this can excessively shrink the object. Also, choosing a diffusivity k that is too high can lead to self-intersecting or other ill-conditioned meshes due to too large displacements of the grid points.

Figure 8.11 shows the Laplacian smoothing in action on an isosurface showing a femur. The number of iterations combined with the diffusivity k can be used to control the scale of details one wants to remove from a given dataset. In Figure 8.11(c), small-scale irregularities of the original surface (Figure 8.11(a)) are smoothed out in approximately 100 iterations.

If more iterations are applied, larger-scale details would disappear, which is undesirable in this case. Finally, Figure 8.11(d) compares the initial object (green, semitransparent) with the smoothed one (gray, opaque) after 10,000 iterations, by rendering both objects overlapped in the same image. The smoothed object is visibly smaller than the original in the green (convex) regions and larger in the gray (concave) ones.

Like any filtering, Laplacian smoothing removes both noise and small-scale surface details. An undesired effect is that sharp surface creases, such as the edge of the femur cross-section in Figure 8.11, also get smoothed out. Several advanced smoothing methods exist that prevent this. For example, one can use weighted diffusion in Equation (8.6). The diffusion coefficient k is set to be inversely proportional to the surface curvature instead of a using constant value. Weighted diffusion has the effect of strongly flattening small-scale noise but maintaining sharp details such as edges and creases. For this to work, we must use a smoothed (e.g., low-pass filtered) version of the surface curvature so that small-scale noise details are not visible in this signal. Figure 8.11(b) shows the smoothed surface curvature for the bone model color-coded from blue (flat) to red (maximally curved). The edge-preserving effect can be further improved by forcing the diffusion process to be strong in the direction of the surface edges and weak across the edges. Anisotropic techniques that perform this type of smoothing are an advanced subject and are described further in specialized literature [Perona and Malik 90, Weickert 98, Bajaj and Xu 03].

Grid-smoothing and grid-refinement methods can be effectively combined to produce high-quality grids. A simple way to do this is to first refine the grid, in order to create enough sample points so that the smoothing can act on a small spatial scale, and next perform a number of smoothing steps until the desired surface quality is reached. More efficient implementations can alternate smoothing and refinement steps and also introduce grid-decimation steps, all in order to redistribute the points to the optimal locations on the surface in order to achieve the desired quality.

8.5 Conclusion

Grids are a fundamental element of visualization datasets. They provide a discrete representation of a compact spatial domain on which the signals to be visualized are sampled. Grids can vary in several respects: the type of cells, the regularity of the discretization, and the types of basis functions used to perform interpolation on the grid.

In this chapter, we have presented a number of fundamental methods for grid manipulation and processing. Since grids are used in visualization as a representation of the underlying domain of a signal, these methods are referred to as domain-modeling techniques. Cutting techniques extract a lower-dimensional domain from a higher-dimensional one, such as when slicing a volume with a surface, or a subdomain with the same dimensionality, such as in the case of bricking. Selection techniques extract a set of cells or points from a dataset, based on data properties. These techniques are useful when we are interested in extracting a specific subset of interest from a larger dataset.

Grids can be constructed from scattered points using triangulation techniques. An alternative is to use gridless techniques, e.g., using radial basis functions. Triangulation has the advantage of producing a cell-based grid, which can be further used by all grid-based visualization methods. Gridless methods do not require the usually complex triangulation step, require less memory because they do not explicitly store cells, offer fast surface interpolation (rendering) using splatting, but bear additional computational costs. Either of these techniques can be used when we need a continuous domain representation, such as a surface, and all we have is a set of scattered points.

Grids can be processed by a variety of operations, such as simplification, refinement, and smoothing. These operations are especially useful when the grid itself is the visualization target, such as when it represents a surface of interest, e.g., produced by contouring techniques. All in all, domain modeling techniques are an indispensable element of the visualization process, as grids are an indispensable ingredient of datasets.

Chapter 9

Image Visualization

I N this chapter, we give an overview of a number of image-processing techniques. The term *image processing* refers to methods that input and output an image. Image-processing methods belong to the earliest developments in computer graphics. In the last decade, a large number of such methods have been researched and put into practice. Such methods range from simple filtering operations that remove noise from digital photographs up to complex techniques that extract and manipulate two-dimensional shapes from video sequences. Given the sheer size of the field, we shall limit ourselves here to presenting only mainstream methods that are encountered in a large class of applications, and in particular those image-processing methods that are frequently encountered in visualization applications.

We start our overview of image processing by describing how images are represented in terms of datasets (Section 9.1). Next, we describe the place and role image processing has in the visualization pipeline (Section 9.2). The main part of this chapter details a number of image-processing algorithms that are frequently used in data visualization (Section 9.3). Next, we describe how image data can be refined by extracting higher-level representations from it, such as shapes (Section 9.4). We conclude the chapter with a discussion in Section 9.5.

9.1   Image Data Representation

What is an image? If we start from an implementation perspective, we shall quickly notice that virtually all computer graphics applications and graphics toolkits offer one or several data representations of images under several names, such as bitmaps, pixmaps, textures, or RGB or grayscale images. If we factor out the various differences related to implementation constraints, we can say an image is a two-dimensional array, or matrix, of pixels. In the large majority of cases, pixels have square shapes, i.e., an aspect ratio of 1 to 1. Every image pixel contains one or several scalar values. Grayscale, or monochrome, images contain one scalar value per pixel, whereas color images usually contain three such scalar values, corresponding to a RGB or HSV encoding of the pixel color.

In terms of the data representation concepts described in Chapter 2, an image is thus nothing more than a uniform two-dimensional dataset (see Section 3.5.1). Monochrome images contain one scalar attribute per pixel, indicating the luminance, or intensity, of each pixel. Color images contain one color attribute per pixel. In practice, color is represented as a triplet of scalar attributes, which correspond to a RGB or HSV color encoding (see Section 3.6.3). Given that the value of a pixel is typically considered constant over the entire pixel surface, we can say, following Section 3.2, that images use a piecewise constant interpolation of luminance or color samples evaluated at the pixel centers.

In practice, however, there are some important differences between representing an image by a uniform 2D dataset as described in Section 3.5.1 and the various image implementations provided by different software toolkits or image file formats. The main difference concerns the attribute *resolution*. The dataset attributes, as described in Section 3.6, are essentially floating-point values, which take four bytes on typical 32-bit computer architectures. Hence, a luminance or gray value would take four bytes, whereas a RGB color represented as three floats takes 12 bytes or 96 bits. Most imaging toolkits and image formats encode image attributes with less precision than a full float. Usually, image formats allocate one byte per luminance attribute, using fixed point-encoding, or three bytes (24 bits) for a color attribute in full-color images. The reason for allocating less than a full float per attribute is practical. Given a typical photograph, humans would not perceive the small luminance or color discretization errors caused by the limited attribute resolution. When the attribute resolution, or number of bits per pixel, decreases, however, color quantization errors become apparent to the human eye.

In addition to full-color images, there exists also a separate class of image formats called *indexed* or *palette-based* image formats. These formats do not encode the value of the color or luminance attribute of each pixel independently. Instead, each pixel contains an integer index into a fixed-size color palette. If we think of this index as a scalar data attribute of each pixel, this mechanism is identical to the scalar-to-color mapping technique detailed in Section 5.1, where the color palette plays the role of a colormap. Indexed image formats trade storage cost for accuracy. Typical implementations would store an eight-bit index per pixel into a 256-color palette. This requires three times less memory than when storing the same image in a full-color RGB format, but provides only 256 different colors instead of 2^{24} different colors.

From a data visualization perspective, we would like to treat images as any other scientific dataset. This has two implications. First, we use a full float resolution to encode each image data attribute, instead of the less-precise 24-bit or palette-based formats. Having this precision is essential, as we would like to perform several operations on images without losing accuracy. Secondly, we allow images to store any number (and type) of data attributes. Besides luminance or color, image datasets can store vector or tensor data attributes. This flexibility is important in order to allow a wide range of processing operations to take place on image data (see Section 9.3). Finally, representing images as uniform datasets with floating-point attributes allows us to directly use many visualization algorithms on images without any modification.

Finally, let us mention that image datasets and image-processing operations are not restricted to two dimensions. While 2D images are still the most common, the vast majority of image data representations and imaging algorithms have been extended to 3D as well. 3D imaging has become an indispensable tool in medical sciences, especially in the visualization and analysis of CT and MRI datasets, so that 3D imaging and data visualization have become tightly interconnected disciplines. The visualization of 3D images, or volumes, is discussed separately in Chapter 10.

9.2   Image Processing and Visualization

Now that we have seen that images can be represented as 2D scalar-attributed datasets, a further question to answer is: what is the place of image processing in the visualization pipeline?

Recall the visualization pipeline, i.e., the set of operations performed on data in order to produce meaningful pictures (see Figure 4.1). The output of the complete pipeline is an image, which is typically displayed and analyzed to obtain the desired insight into the visualized data. However, in some cases, we would like to further enhance this image in order to better understand the encoded information. Examples of operations that are applied at this stage involve contrast enhancement and color adjustment, which are typical image-processing techniques. Such generic operations can be applied to *any* type of image, regardless of the visualization pipeline that has been executed to produce it. In this scenario, the imaging operations, or imaging pipeline, follow the visualization pipeline.

However, image-processing operations can be applied also at earlier stages of the visualization pipeline. Consider, for example, an application that produces a 2D uniform, scalar-attributed dataset at some stage of the filtering process (see Figure 4.1). This can be, for example, a slice extracted from a medical dataset (see Figure 5.3), a color-coded height field, or a two-dimensional flow texture representing a vector dataset (see Figures 6.24 and 6.30). The straightforward way to visualize such results is to map and render them using a suitable scalar-to-color mapping. However, imaging operations can be applied at this stage to enhance the data, e.g., by performing image segmentation (see Section 9.4.1) followed by shape analysis (see Section 9.4). In this scenario, the imaging pipeline is integrated as part of the visualization pipeline.

Finally, consider the case when the input data of the visualization pipeline is an image, such as a 2D slice from a medical dataset. In this case, the visualization and imaging pipelines become virtually the same.

9.3   Basic Imaging Algorithms

In this section, we present a number of the basic algorithms for image processing. Although there are many other image-processing algorithms that are applied in several areas of data visualization, we have chosen the ones included here based on their widespread applicability and generality. As stated in the title, the focus of this section is on *basic* imaging algorithms. By this, we mean those algorithms which manipulate discretizations of two-dimensional scalar functions $f : \mathbb{R}^2 \to \mathbb{R}$ that are sampled on images or, in visualization terminology, uniform scalar-valued, two-dimensional datasets. Consequently, the algorithms presented here will have a strong signal processing flavor. Data is manipulated at the level of its individual samples or *pixels*. In the next section, algorithms that manipulate image data at the higher level of *shapes* are presented.

We start by presenting the elementary operations that allow enhancing of the image contrast and brightness by applying simple transfer functions (Section 9.3.1). Histogram equalization, a simple but useful technique in the same class, follows (Section 9.3.2). Next, we present the technique of smoothing images by applying a Gaussian filtering operation (Section 9.3.3). We conclude this section with another basic image-processing operation, the detection of edges (Section 9.3.4).

9.3.1 Basic Image Processing

In Section 5.1, we presented the color mapping technique. As illustrated by the example shown in Figure 5.3, color mapping creates gray values or colors from a set of scalar values. The design of the transfer function $f : \mathbb{R} \to [0, 1]^n$, which maps scalars to gray values ($n = 1$) or RGB colors ($n = 3$), is essential to producing a good visualization.

However, there are cases when we cannot perform all the desired information extraction and enhancing within such a transfer function. One such case is in situations when we do not have access to the visualization application that has produced the datasets to be examined, nor to the datasets themselves. The only data to work with is an image produced, e.g., by color mapping some scalar dataset. A second case is when the image itself is the dataset, e.g., in the case of landscape information acquired by aerial photography, video information acquired by measurement or surveillance cameras, or X-ray photography. In all these cases, the dataset to work with is the image itself. We shall present several basic image-processing operations that are widely used in the visualization practice. We confine ourselves here to operations that process each image pixel individually and only affect its gray value or color. Such operations can be described by functions $f : [0,1]^n \to [0,1]^n$ both for grayscale images ($n = 1$) and colors ($n = 3$). These image-processing operations have similar expressions to the transfer functions. Hence, there exists an overlap between the purposes and effects that can be achieved with scalar-to-color transfer functions and color-to-color image-processing functions. All operations presented in this section can be used either as standalone image-processing tools or as part of the color-mapping process.

The simplest and probably also most used image-enhancement operation consists in applying a *transfer function* on the pixel luminance values. By using different function profiles, one can emphasize certain gray value ranges or value transitions. Figure 9.1 illustrates this. In the first image (Figure 9.1(a)), a slice from a CT scan is shown using a one-to-one mapping of the scanned value, which reflects tissue density, to a linear grayscale ranging from black to white. The graph under the image (Figure 9.1(a) middle) shows the transfer function applied to the image luminance. Together with the graph, the *image histogram* is shown in gray. The histogram of an image shows, for every luminance value, the number of image pixels that have that value. In this histogram, we see two peaks. The leftmost one corresponds to the large number of near-black pixels showing low intensity. The right one corresponds to the large number of gray values showing soft tissue. The small-scale histogram variations are too small to be visible on this graph in comparison with its maxima. Using a logarithmic scaling of the histogram y-axis, the smaller histogram variations become more visible (see Figure 9.1(a) bottom).[1]

For the original image, the transfer function is the identity function $f(x) = x$. In this image, bright pixels denote hard tissues, e.g., bone, whereas dark pixels denote soft tissues, e.g., fat. The darkest pixels denote air, which has the lowest density. Suppose now that we are interested in emphasizing the hard tissues and we are not interested in seeing the differences between the various types of soft tissues. We can achieve this by using a transfer function as shown in the graph in Figure 9.1(b). This function has near-zero values for the soft tissue range, followed by a rapid transition to high values close to the maximal intensity of 1 for input pixel

---

[1] All image processing examples shown in this chapter, except distance transforms and skeletons, are computed and visualized using the freely available GIMP image-processing tool [GIMP 06].

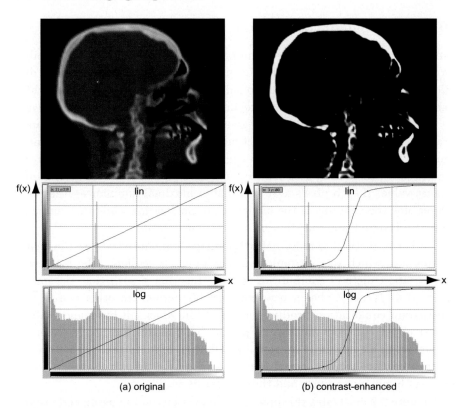

Figure 9.1. Image contrast enhancement. Images (top), linear histograms (middle), and logarithmic histograms (bottom). (a) Original image. (b) Contrast-enhanced image using nonlinear transfer function.

intensities corresponding to the hard tissues. The result (Figure 9.1(b) top) is an image with clearly increased contrast on which bone tissue are clearly visible.

Different types of transfer functions can be used to address different questions. High-slope functions enhance the image contrast, while low-slope functions attenuate it. Step functions essentially perform a selection of pixels with luminances in a given range, as detailed later in Section 9.4.1. For color images, transfer functions can be applied separately on each image component, both for the RGB or HSV systems (see Section 3.6.3).

9.3.2   Histogram Equalization

Images acquired by means of scanning or video technologies often exhibit
low contrast, which makes distinguishing individual shapes and details difficult. Several methods allow us to enhance the contrast of an image while
keeping the relative ordering of pixel luminances. The simplest way is to use
a linear luminance normalization: given an image with effective luminance
range $[I_{min}, I_{max}]$, the transfer function $f(x) = (x - I_{min})/(I_{max} - I_{min})$ normalizes the luminance in order to use the entire $[0, 1]$ range. However, in
many cases, there are just a few pixels in an image that have a given luminance value. If such pixels have minimal or maximal luminances, they will
determine the outcome of the luminance normalization while they actually
have an insignificant contribution to the image itself.

A better method to renormalize the image luminance is to use the image
histogram, which was introduced in the previous section. The *histogram
equalization* method computes a transfer function f such that the image
$I'(x, y) = f(I(x, y))$ has a near-constant histogram. In other words, the
histogram equalization produces an image in which all luminance values
cover about the same number of pixels. This makes the image easier to
visualize, as we now have an equal distribution of luminances to look at as
compared, for example, to an image where just a few pixels would share
certain luminance values, and thus be hardly visible.

Figure 9.2 illustrates this process for an actual data imaging and visualization application. In this application, scientists are interested in studying
the growth of the rice plant roots. The roots, grown in a half-transparent
jelly, are photographed with a high-resolution digital camera. The results
(see Figure 9.2(a)) need to be analyzed in order to assess various root characteristics, such as number of branches, length of the main branches, and
average length of the small branches. In Section 9.4.6, we shall present a
method that extracts a simplified representation of the plant's roots from
the image. For this type of analysis, one often requires the input images to
have a high contrast. Histogram equalization lets us perform this type of
enhancement (see Figure 9.2). Comparing the logarithmic scale histograms
of the two images (see Figure 9.2(a–b) bottom), we see that the image luminances, which were confined to a narrow area in the original image (see
Figure 9.2(a)), get spread almost evenly over the complete luminance range
$[0, 1]$ after the equalization (see Figure 9.2(b)). Looking carefully at the

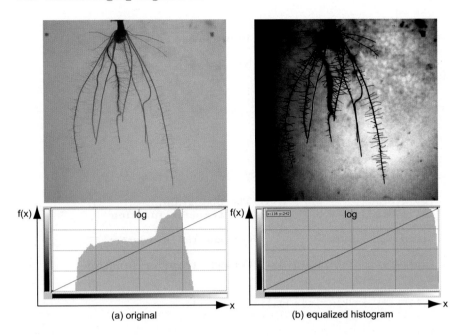

Figure 9.2. Histogram equalization showing images (top) and their logarithmic histograms (bottom). (a) Original image. (b) Image after histogram equalization.

histogram, we notice that the result is not a perfect horizontal line. This is a hard-to-avoid effect that is due to the fact we are computing histograms of discrete image.

Listing 9.1 sketches the code for computing an image histogram and using it for histogram equalization. Here, images are represented, for simplicity, as two-dimensional integer arrays of size $NX \times NY$ pixels, where each pixel can have $0 \dots \text{SIZE} - 1$ different gray values. The histogram of some input image is computed and stored in an integer array int h[SIZE]. Next, we use this histogram to construct the transfer function

$$f(x) = (\text{SIZE} - 1) \sum_{i=0}^{x} h[i] \tag{9.1}$$

that will perform the histogram equalization [Myler and Weeks 93]. Finally, we apply this function to all pixels of the input image.

```
int     image[NX][NY];    //The input image

void histogram(int image[NX][NY],int h[SIZE])
{
   for(int i=0;i<SIZE;i++) h[i]=0;

   for(int i=0;i<NX;i++)
     for(int j=0;i<NY;j++)
       h[image[i][j]]++;
}

void equalize(int input[NX][NY],int output[NX][NY])
{
   int h[SIZE];             //The histogram
   int f[SIZE];             //The transfer function

   histogram(input,h);      //Compute the histogram

   for(int i=0;i<SIZE;i++)  //Compute transfer function
   {
     f[i]=0;
     for(int j=0;j<=i;j++) f[i] += h[j];
     f[i] *= SIZE-1;
   }

   for(int i=0;i<NX;i++)    //Apply transfer function
     for(int j=0;j<NY;j++)
       output[i][j] = f[input[i][j]];
}
```

Listing 9.1. Histogram computation and equalization.

Another use of histogram equalization is in applications where we need to compare similar images taken under slightly different illuminations or with different exposure settings. By equalizing the images, direct luminance comparison is much easier to do.

9.3.3 Gaussian Smoothing

Many applications use images that are acquired by scanning, photography, or video sources. In all these cases, the image data inevitably contains a small amount of *noise*. There are several ways to characterize noise. Consider, for example, a function $f : \mathbb{R} \to \mathbb{R}$. Noise can be described as rapid variations of high amplitude, or regions where higher-order derivatives of f have large values. In signal theory, noise is characterized by its frequency. Every continuous periodic function $f(x)$ with period T can be written as the sum or superposition of a potentially infinite set of sine and cosine waves of increasingly higher frequencies and decreasing amplitudes, or strengths:

$$f(x) = a_0 + \sum_{n=1}^{\infty} a_n \sin(\omega_n x) + \sum_{n=1}^{\infty} b_n \cos(\omega_n x), \qquad (9.2)$$

where the coefficients a_n, b_n and the frequencies ω_n of the individual wave components $(n \in \mathbb{N})$ are defined by

$$\omega_n = n\frac{2\pi}{T}, \qquad (9.3)$$

$$a_n = \frac{2}{T} \int_0^T f(t) \sin(\omega_n t) dt, \qquad (9.4)$$

$$b_n = \frac{2}{T} \int_0^T f(t) \cos(\omega_n t) dt. \qquad (9.5)$$

Equation (9.2) is also called the *Fourier series* expansion of the function f. For smooth functions, it can be shown that, as n increases, the amplitudes a_n and b_n of the waves decrease. Moreover, the more terms (higher n) we use in the Fourier series, the better we approximate the original function f. This is illustrated in Figure 9.3. Here, we approximate a square wave $f(x)$ consisting of increasing, followed by decreasing, blocks by a Fourier series with a finite number of terms. Clearly, the approximation with $n - 24$ terms (drawn in red) gets closer to the original signal (drawn in black) than an approximation using fewer ($n = 10$) terms. In both cases, however, the approximation cannot follow exactly the block-like shape of the original signals. The approximation error is apparent in the form of small-scale wavy patterns, which are known in signal processing as *ringing artifacts*.

Looking at the graphs at the right of Figure 9.3, we notice that the higher coefficients a_n and b_n have quite small values compared to the first coefficients.

What if the signal is not periodic? Such a signal can be thought of as having an infinite period $T \rightarrow \infty$. This will yield a Fourier representation with wave components of extremely densely spaced frequencies ω_n (see Equation (9.3)). In practice, this means that a_n and b_n are no longer

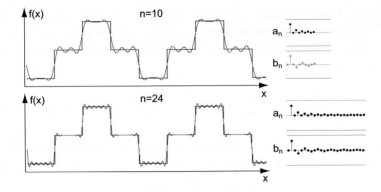

Figure 9.3. Fourier approximation (drawn in red) of a square signal (drawn in black). Approximation with $n = 10$ terms (top) and $n = 24$ terms (bottom). The values of the coefficients a_n and b_n are shown in the right images.

discrete sequences of amplitudes, but will become continuous functions of ω, e.g., $A(\omega)$ and $B(\Omega)$. This representation, which associates two continuous real-valued functions $A(\omega), B(\omega)$ to a given spatial function $f(x)$, is called the *Fourier transform* of $f(x)$, and can be denoted compactly as a single two-valued function $F(\omega) = (A(\omega), B(\omega))$. In practice, we usually have nonperiodic signals, so the Fourier transform is used instead of the Fourier series. The Fourier transform is invertible, i.e., we can use $F(\omega)$ to compute $f(x)$. Finally, discrete versions of both the direct and inverse Fourier transform exist for sampled signals [Ambardar 06]. For efficient, freely available software implementations of these, we refer the reader to the FFTW website [Frigo 07].

The Fourier transform is an extremely useful instrument for understanding, as well as processing, signals. Generalizing from the previous example, it can be shown that small-scale, rapidly changing noise corresponds in the frequency space to nonzero coefficients a_n or b_n for high values of n (for periodic signals), or equivalently high $A(\omega)$ or $B(\omega)$ for high ω values (for nonperiodic signals). Intuitively, this can be explained as small-scale noise corresponding to signals that have short periods T, which means signals with high frequencies ω.

Now that we understand this, we get an idea of how we can filter, or remove, noise. Given a signal, removing noise of a frequency within a given frequency band $[\omega_{\min}, \omega_{\max}]$ means removing, or reducing the amplitude of, the Fourier transform for $\omega \in [\omega_{\min}, \omega_{\max}]$. This can be done by multiplying the Fourier transform components A, B with a suitable transfer function $\Phi(\omega) \to \mathbb{R}$, which keeps the values outside the frequency band to filter but damps those in the band. Given such a frequency transfer function Φ, filtering a function f can be done by the following algorithm:

1. Compute the Fourier transform $F = (A(\omega), B(\omega))$ of f.

2. Multiply F by the transfer function Φ to obtain a new $G = F \cdot \Phi$.

3. Compute the inverse Fourier transform G^{-1} to get the filtered version of f.

This method, called *frequency filtering*, is effective when we have a simple and compact representation of the desired filtering in the frequency domain in terms of our frequency transfer function $\Phi(\omega)$. However, in practice, it is quite expensive (and complex) to implement filtering in this way, as this involves one direct and one inverse Fourier transform, which each have a complexity of $N^2 \log N$ for a discrete dataset with N samples. In many cases, there is, luckily, a simpler way to perform filtering. This different method is based on a fundamental signal processing result called the *convolution theorem*. We define the convolution of two continuous signals $f(x)$ and $g(x)$ as a new function

$$(f * g)(x) = \int_{-\infty}^{\infty} f(t)g(x-t)dt. \tag{9.6}$$

For discrete datasets $\{f_i\}$ and $\{g_i\}$, where $\leq i \leq N$, the discrete convolution is defined similarly as

$$(f * g)_i = \sum_{k=0}^{N} f_k g_{N+i-k}. \tag{9.7}$$

Now if we denote the Fourier transforms of f and g by F and G, the convolution theorem says that the Fourier transform of the convolution $f * g$ equals the product $F \cdot G$ of the corresponding Fourier transforms F and G. Having this result, we immediately see that the filtering operation can now be implemented much more easily by simply computing the convolution

$f * \phi$ of the desired input signal $f(x)$ with the filter function $\phi(x)$, which is the inverse Fourier transform of the frequency transfer function $\Phi(\omega)$. Using convolutions to filter signals has the main advantage of computing the filter function ϕ from the frequency transfer function Φ only once. After we have ϕ, we simply convolve the input signal f with ϕ to filter it.

In practice, one can classify such filter functions Φ by the type of frequency band they damp as:

- low-pass filters: increasingly damp frequencies above some maximal ω_{max}.

- high-pass filters: increasingly damp frequencies below some maximal ω_{min}.

- band-pass filters: damp frequencies within some band $[\omega_{\text{min}}, \omega_{\text{max}}]$.

To remove noise, which is of high frequencies, we must use the first type of filter. One of the most-used low-pass filters has, as a frequency transfer function, a Gaussian function Φ centered at the origin. It can be shown that its inverse Fourier transform $\phi(x) = F^{-1}(\Phi(\omega))$ is also a Gaussian function, or

$$F(e^{-ax^2}) = \sqrt{\frac{\pi}{a}} \, e^{-\pi^2 \omega^2 / a}. \tag{9.8}$$

Hence, we can implement low-pass filtering in order to remove high-frequency noise artifacts simply by convolving the input signal, e.g., the image, with a Gaussian function. The width a of the Gaussian filter, in function space, controls the amount of smoothing. Using a high a value yields a slowly decaying Gaussian $\Phi(\omega)$, i.e., performs little or no filtering. Using a low a value yields a sharply decaying Gaussian $\Phi(\omega)$, i.e., performs strong filtering. As a practical rule of thumb, the value $1/a$ is a good estimate of the size of the noise features that this filtering removes. In practice, the Gaussian $\phi(x)$ will reach very low values beyond a certain distance x. For efficiency, we simply threshold it to zero at that distance, hence we limit the number of samples N used to discretize it (see Equation (9.7)). The more smoothing we want, the slower ϕ will decay, hence the larger the filter size N will be. Figure 9.4 illustrates filtering an image using a Gaussian filter. The left image was corrupted artificially by adding random noise to it. The size of the noise features is around two pixels. The

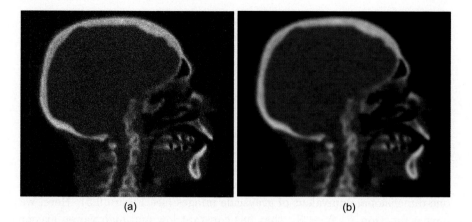

(a)   (b)

Figure 9.4. (a) Noisy image. (b) Result after filtering with a Gaussian filter.

right image shows the result after smoothing the image with a Gaussian
filter with a width $1/a$ equal to 10 pixels. Clearly, the added noise is removed successfully, as its size is smaller than the filter width. However, if
we compare the filtered image with the original image before the addition
of noise (see Figure 9.1 (left)), we notice that small-scale details, such as
sharp image edges, have also been smoothed out together with the noise.

In order to preserve image details but still remove undesired noise, more
advanced filters can be used. A first enhancement to the Gaussian filters
described previously is to modulate the strength of the filtering, i.e., the
width a of the Gaussian function in Equation (9.8), with an estimation of
the number of image details at the current point. In this way, image areas
containing significant details will be filtered less, while areas containing
fewer details, thus potentially more noise, will be filtered more. Different ways to estimate the presence of details in the image exist. A widely
used method defines details as the presence of luminance edges, which can
be detected as described next in Section 9.3.4. A second enhancement
of the preceding selective filtering is to bias not only the filter strength,
but also its *shape*, such that the smoothing is stronger in the direction
of the image edges, and weak across the edges. This technique strength-
ens the image edges while, in the same time, removing small-scale noise
in relatively smooth parts of the image. These techniques are known as
anisotropic image-filtering techniques [Perona and Malik 90]. For details

on their implementation, we refer to the specialized literature on image processing [Perona and Malik 90, Weickert 98].

9.3.4 Edge Detection

Edges are important visual elements in images. Informally speaking, edges in 2D images can be defined as 1D curves that separate image regions of different luminance, for grayscale images, or hues, for color images. Detecting edges in images is an important step in the process of extracting shapes from unstructured image data (see Section 9.4).

To better understand the issues involved in detecting edges, consider the one-dimensional equivalent of grayscale images (see Figure 9.5). Here, we have a function $f : \mathbb{R} \to \mathbb{R}_+$ that has constant low and high values except for a narrow band of width δ, which corresponds, in grayscale images, to

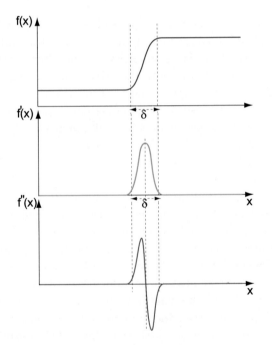

Figure 9.5. Edge detection using image derivatives. Image (top), first derivative (middle), and second derivative (bottom). Edges correspond to maxima of the first derivative or, alternatively, zero-crossings of the second derivative.

the region where edges are localized. This region corresponds to an area where the first derivative f' of the function is maximal. This leads us to the first method of computing edges in images: given an image I, compute the image gradient ∇I, which is equivalent to the first derivative, and select the points where the gradient magnitude is maximal. In practice, this is implemented by selecting the points where $|\nabla I|$ exceeds a certain lower threshold:

$$|\nabla I(x, y)| = \sqrt{\left(\frac{\partial I}{\partial x}\right)^2 + \left(\frac{\partial I}{\partial y}\right)^2}. \tag{9.9}$$

Gradient-based edge detection. Given a discrete image I_{ij}, where (i, j) denote the integer coordinates of a given pixel, we must be able to estimate the gradient magnitude. Naturally, this involves a discrete estimation of the image derivatives. Given that image datasets use piecewise constant interpolation, as explained earlier in this chapter, the partial derivatives at some pixel center (i, j) can be estimated as follows (see Section 3.7):

$$\frac{\partial I}{\partial x}(i, j) = I_{i+1j} - I_{ij},$$
$$\frac{\partial I}{\partial y}(i, j) = I_{ij+1} - I_{ij}. \tag{9.10}$$

Using the expressions of the partial derivatives from Equation (9.10) and Equation (9.9), we can directly compute an estimation of the gradient magnitude to find edges. Figure 9.6(b) demonstrates the gradient-based edge detector for the rice roots image used to demonstrate the histogram equalization technique in Section 9.3.2. The strength of the edges is mapped to the image luminance: white denotes strong edges, while black denotes no edges.

In practice, many variations exist of edge detectors that use the first derivative of the image intensity. Several of the most popular first-order derivative image detectors, sometimes also called edge detection *operators*, are briefly outlined next. The *Roberts operator* computes edges by lower thresholding a variant of the gradient magnitude given by

$$R(i, j) = \sqrt{(I_{i+1j+1} - I_{ij})^2 + (I_{i+1j} - I_{ij+1})^2}. \tag{9.11}$$

Essentially, the Roberts operator computes the gradient magnitude estimated for a coordinate system rotated at 45 degrees with respect to the

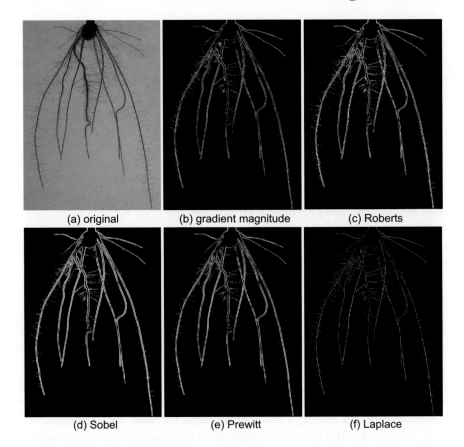

Figure 9.6. Edge detection. (a) Original image and (b–f) several edge detectors. Edge strength is mapped to image luminance.

standard (i, j) system. Figure 9.6(c) illustrates the Roberts edge detector. Several variations of the Roberts operator consider the sums of the absolute values of the partial derivatives [Schalkoff 89] or the maximum of these absolute values.

However simple to implement and efficient to compute, the various versions of the Roberts operator can be quite sensitive to small-scale image noise, since they essentially consider only three or four pixels, i.e., two-by-two neighborhoods, when estimating the value of the edge detector for one given pixel. In practice, the effects of small-scale image noise manifest themselves in the edge detection process by having several disconnected, spurious false positives, i.e., pixels that are erroneously detected as being part of edges, or false negatives, i.e., pixels that are part of edges but are not found as such. A general-purpose method for improving the robustness of edge detection, or for that matter of any other image processing operation involving derivatives, is to remove small-scale noise. This corresponds to removing sharp image variations, i.e., high-frequency image components. This can be done by filtering, or smoothing, the image with a Gaussian filter of limited size, as explained in Section 9.3.3, prior to the derivative computation. However, as is usually the case, Gaussian smoothing also removes small-scale details, which means thin objects with spatially close edges, such as the thin roots in Figure 9.6, may be discarded.

A complementary technique for stabilizing edge detection in the presence of noise is to use larger neighborhoods when estimating first-order derivatives. One such technique is known as the *Sobel operator* [Sobel and Feldman 73]. This involves estimating the image partial derivatives as

$$\frac{\partial I}{\partial x}(i,j) = I_{i+1j-1} + 2I_{i+1j} + I_{i+1j+1} - I_{i-1j-1} - 2I_{i-1j} - I_{i-1j+1},$$

$$\frac{\partial I}{\partial y}(i,j) = I_{i+1j+1} + 2I_{ij+1} + I_{i-1j+1} - I_{i+1j-1} - 2I_{ij-1} - I_{i-1j-1}.$$

$$(9.12)$$

Just as for the gradient magnitude detectors, the Sobel edge detector can use either the square root of the partial derivatives estimated using Equations (9.12) or the maximum of their absolute values. The Sobel operator is illustrated in Figure 9.6(d).

An alternative detector is the *Prewitt operator* [Prewitt and Mendelsohn 66], which estimates the image partial derivatives as

$$\frac{\partial I}{\partial x}(i,j) = I_{i+1j-1} + I_{i+1j} + I_{i+1j+1} - I_{i-1j-1} - I_{i-1j} - I_{i-1j+1},$$

$$(9.13)$$

$$\frac{\partial I}{\partial y}(i,j) = I_{i+1j+1} + I_{ij+1} + I_{i-1j+1} - I_{i+1j-1} - I_{ij-1} - I_{i-1j-1}.$$

The Prewitt operator is illustrated in Figure 9.6(e).

However, a problem with most of the edge detectors that use first-order derivatives is the setting of the threshold against which the image gradient magnitude is checked. In most images, edges do not separate regions of equally high luminance differences, or contrasts. Hence, choosing the threshold to use can be quite delicate. If we do set the threshold too high, lower maxima corresponding to weaker edges pass undetected. If we set it too low, we obtain "thick edges" instead of pixel-thin ones. To help choose such thresholds, histogram techniques can be used on the gradient magnitude. Another approach in computing image edges is using higher-order image derivatives, as presented next.

Laplacian-based edge detection. Using higher-order derivatives to detect edges in images has several advantages as compared to finding the maxima of the image gradient magnitude. To illustrate this, consider again Figure 9.5. The bottom image depicts the second derivative f'' of the given function. The point of highest variation speed of the function, i.e., maximum of its first derivative, coincides with the point where $f'' = 0$, or the *zero crossing* of the second derivative. Searching for these zero crossings corresponds to finding the center points of the original image edges. In the case of two-dimensional images $I(x, y)$, this corresponds to finding the points where the absolute value of the image Laplacian $|\Delta I(x, y)| = |\frac{\partial^2 I}{\partial x^2} + \frac{\partial^2 I}{\partial y^2}|$ is equal to zero. Notice that, in contrast to the image gradient, which is a vector indicating the direction in which the image luminance has maximal change, the image Laplacian is a scalar value. In practice, finding edges using the image Laplacian is implemented by selecting the points where $|\Delta I(x, y)|$ exceeds a certain lower threshold.

Just as for the gradient estimation, we must compute the image Laplacian given a discrete image. For a one-dimensional signal $f(x)$, the second-order derivative can be discretely approximated by $\frac{\partial^2 f}{\partial x^2} = f_{i+1} - 2f_i + f_{i-1}$. It can be shown that the Laplacian of a discrete image can be approximated by

$$\Delta I(i, j) = 4I_{ij} - I_{i+1j} - I_{i-1j} - I_{ij+1} - I_{ij-1}. \tag{9.14}$$

Estimating the image Laplacian involves computing second-order derivatives, which is a more sensitive operation with respect to image noise than computing first-order derivatives. Indeed, the higher the order of the derivative that we estimate, the stronger the exacerbation of high frequencies present in the image. However, if a robust Laplacian estimation is available, finding edges is easier, since we can now look for its zero crossings. While thresholding the gradient magnitude may skip edge pixels or deliver thick edges, looking for the zero crossings of the Laplacian yields pixel-thin edges. The Laplacian edge detection is illustrated in Figure 9.6(f). If we compare this image to the various first-order derivative edge detectors discussed so far (see Figures 9.6(b–e)), we see that the former yields thin edges.

A last remark concerns the size of the neighborhoods involved in the various edge estimators discussed so far. The Sobel and Prewitt operators use 3×3 pixel neighborhoods to estimate first-order image derivatives, which are more stable compared to the 2×2 neighborhoods used by the Roberts operator. In terms of signal processing, it can be shown that the Sobel and Prewitt operators correspond to estimating derivatives on smoothed versions of the original image [Jain et al. 95]. In contrast, the Laplace operator uses a 3×3 neighborhood too, but this does imply signal smoothing: estimating second-order derivatives requires larger neighborhoods by definition. If we want to perform additional smoothing when using Laplacian edge estimators, this involves using neighborhoods of a size exceeding 3×3. An example is the Marr-Hildreth operator, which is equivalent to computing the Laplacian of an image presmoothed with a Gaussian filter [Jain et al. 95], which uses a 5×5 pixel neighborhood. Since Gaussian smoothing eliminates high-frequency information, this type of operator yields more stable edge detection than directly applying the Laplacian.

9.4   Shape Representation and Analysis

So far, we have treated images as uniform 2D datasets with scalar, color, and vector data attributes. As we saw in the previous section, this representation suitably supports a wide range of image-processing operations, such as image denoising, filtering, edge detection, and contrast manipulation. However, in many applications, we want to manipulate the information present in images at a higher level than the pixel level. We can explain this best by means of an example. Consider an image that contains a 2D slice from a 3D volumetric medical dataset, such as the one shown in Figure 5.3. On such images, we can describe and identify areas of interest in terms of their scalar value. For example, certain anatomical structures share the same scalar value, or values located within a specific scalar range. In the first instance, we can try to extract such structures or *shapes* from image data using algorithms such as contouring and thresholding (see Sections 5.3 and 8.2). However, this scenario is of limited flexibility in two respects. First, local algorithms such as contouring and thresholding cannot detect and extract shapes that are based on complex, nonlocal definitions. Second, some applications require shape descriptions that are richer than just the set of cells contained in an unstructured grid created by a selection operation.

Shape representation and analysis is a research field concerned with models and methods for representing, extracting, and analyzing shapes. This field is situated at the crossroads of digital imaging, perception, computer vision, and computer graphics. In our discussion, a *shape* is defined to be a usually compact subset of a given 2D image that exhibits some properties. Typical properties include the shape geometry (form, aspect ratio, roundness, or squareness), the shape topology (genus, number, and ramification of the boundary protuberances), and the shape texture (color, luminance, shading). Shapes are usually characterized by a boundary and an interior. Although shapes can be extracted directly from grayscale or color images, one usually first reduces such images to a *binary* image. A binary image consists of foreground (or object) and background pixels. In dataset terms, a binary image is described by a boolean attribute data type. For such images, we can define *boundary* pixels as being those foreground pixels that have at least one neighboring background pixel.

The pipeline of a typical application using shape analysis is shown in Figure 9.7. First, images are acquired, e.g., using scanning technology. Next, low-level imaging operations such as the ones described in Section 9.3 are applied to remove noise and prepare the image for shape extraction. In the shape extraction step, various properties of the shape (geometry, topology, texture) are used to detect and separate one or several shapes from the unstructured 2D image. Finally, these shapes are further analyzed to extract high-level, application-specific information. Figure 9.7 illustrates this for a computer-vision application used to analyze human silhouettes. Images acquired from a video camera are processed with an edge-detector operation to separate sharp luminance transitions that correspond to silhouettes projected on a dull background. Next, a segmentation algorithm uses these edges to extract the largest region in the image that corresponds to these edges (see Section 9.4.1). Finally, the extracted region is reduced to a 1D structure called a skeleton, which can be further ana-

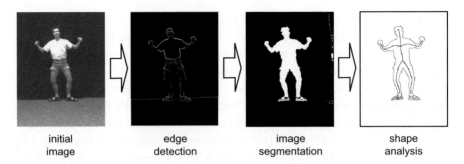

| initial | edge | image | shape |
| image | detection | segmentation | analysis |

Figure 9.7. Imaging and shape analysis pipeline.

lyzed to detect whether the silhouette corresponds to a human figure (see Section 9.4.5).

Shape representation and analysis is an increasingly important research area of data visualization. Given the complexity of datasets and represented phenomena and the growing amounts of data, visualization applications are increasingly designed to be capable of filtering high-volume, low-level, unstructured datasets into low-volume datasets containing high amounts of information. In many cases, this filtering corresponds precisely to a process of detecting and analyzing patterns and shapes in the data. For example, in medical applications, vascular structures are segmented from MRI images, analyzed, and simplified to yield a tree-like representation. In other applications, anatomical shapes are automatically extracted from similar images. Further shape classification is used to detect, e.g., whether these shapes are healthy or not. In flow visualization, shape analysis can be used to detect and classify vortex structures.

In the following sections, we describe several frequently used techniques in the process of extracting and analyzing shapes from 2D images.

9.4.1   Segmentation

As explained at the beginning of Section 9.4, one of the first operations in shape analysis is the extraction of shapes from a given input image. The first step in extracting such shapes is to *segment* or *classify* the image pixels into those belonging to the shapes of interest, also called *foreground pixels*, and the remainder, also called *background pixels*.

Segmentation is strongly related to the operation of selection, which selects certain dataset points or cells based on their properties (see Section 8.2).[2] Segmentation can be thought of as a dataset operation that creates a new boolean data attribute that has the value *true* for foreground pixels and *false* for background ones. The segmentation criterion has to encode domain-specific knowledge. For example, if we know that our foreground shapes have a certain luminance, we segment the image using a luminance threshold or, for better robustness, a luminance range. Hue can be used if we know the shapes we are looking for have specific hues. Many other information types can be used for segmentation. Edge detection (see Section 9.3.4) can be used to find the foreground-background boundaries, followed by a flood-fill operation to identify pixels enclosed by these boundaries. In addition to hue and luminance, other attributes can be used to discriminate foreground from background pixels, such as type of texture, shading, or the values of additional datasets defined on the same domain.

In this section, we shall detail luminance-based segmentation, which is a widely used segmentation method used in practice. An important question is how to set the threshold parameters in order to obtain an accurate segmentation. This is a very difficult problem in practice, since shapes in acquired images often have soft, fuzzy borders and a nonuniform luminance and hue. A useful tool in setting the thresholds is the image histogram, introduced in Section 9.3.2. For a grayscale image, for example, the histogram shows the number of image pixels that have a certain luminance. Histogram peaks indicate high numbers of pixels with similar luminances, which can in turn indicate the presence of particular structures in the image. Figure 9.8 demonstrates this. The top row shows three grayscale images of an MRI scan slice having values between 0 and 255. The middle row shows the luminance histogram. The bottom row shows the same luminance histogram, this time normalized on a logarithmic scale to emphasize small values. The left image (Figure 9.8(a) top) shows the original image. We see here a large number of gray pixels of average luminance that correspond to soft tissues such as skin and muscles. In the histogram (Figure 9.8(a) bottom), these correspond to the pronounced peak in the middle of the image. Selecting pixels with grayscale values in the range [70, 90] produces the image in Figure 9.8(b) top, which shows the soft tis-

---

[2]In some sense, selection can be seen as a *tool* that helps in the segmentation *task*.

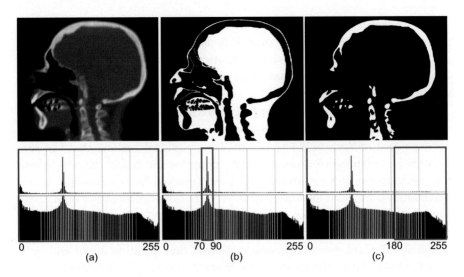

Figure 9.8. Histogram-based image thresholding. The red rectangles on the histograms indicate the selected value range.

sues. Selecting pixels with grayscale values above some higher threshold, e.g., 180, produces the image in Figure 9.8(c) top, which corresponds to the hard (bone) tissue.

In the previous example, we used the image histogram as a visual guide for setting the segmentation thresholds. This procedure still requires a fair amount of trial-and-error, being far from automated. Several more advanced methods analyze the histogram in order to automatically detect segmentation thresholds that are optimal from several points of view, e.g., entropy minimization [Jansing et al. 99]. For more information on thresholding images, see Fisher et al. [Fisher et al. 96]. Finally, let us mention that similar segmentation methods are used for extracting volumetric structures from three-dimensional datasets. For example, anatomical structures consisting of mainly one type of tissue can be extracted by analyzing the density values obtained from a CT or MRI scan.

9.4.2 Connected Components

In some applications, we must enforce several nonlocal properties on the pixels that constitute the result of a segmentation operation. If such pixels are to represent a shape, it is natural, in many applications, that they form a connected component. Moreover, it is desirable to enforce the additional constraint that the area of such a component be above a minimal threshold. This constraint eliminates small-scale spurious components that appear due to thresholding a noisy image.

Connected-component detection proceeds as follows. First, a segmentation operation separates the image into foreground and background pixels, as explained in Section 9.4.1. Let us, for simplicity, assume that the segmentation creates an integer attribute comp for the image dataset, where the background and foreground pixels are marked by the reserved values BACKGROUND and FOREGROUND respectively. To hold the identifier of the next component to be found, we use an integer variable C, which we initialize to zero. Next, we scan the image, e.g., row by row. When we find the first FOREGROUND pixel, we set its comp value and that of all its direct and indirect FOREGROUND neighbors to C, increment C, and repeat the scanning until all FOREGROUND pixels are exhausted. At the core of the algorithm is the process of finding all FOREGROUND pixels that are direct or indirect neighbors to a given pixel. This operation, also known as *flood fill* in computer graphics, can be easily implemented using a stack data structure holding pixel coordinates. The code of the connected components algorithm is sketched in Listing 9.2. The floodFill function assumes pixels are connected, i.e., part of the same component, if they have the FOREGROUND value and are vertical or horizontal neighbors of a pixel already in the considered component. This choice would not identify diagonally neighboring pixels as being connected, and would place them in different components. If we want components to be diagonally connected as well, we have to add four more push statements to the floodFill function, corresponding to the diagonal neighbors $i-1, j-1; i-1, j+1; i+1, j-1;$ and $i+1, j+1$ of the current pixel i, j. It is also noteworthy to add that several speed and space optimizations can be applied to Listing 9.2 that have been omitted here for conciseness. For example, the test image[i][j]!=FOREGROUND in floodFill can be more efficiently executed before pushing each new element on the stack than when popping it. This can significantly decrease the stack size.

After the function connectedComponents returns, the array comp contains every pixel marked by the nonnegative identifier of its connected component or the BACKGROUND value. Figure 9.9 shows the connected com-

```
const int FOREGROUND = -1;
const int BACKGROUND = -2;
const int NX,NY;                    //image sizes

void connectedComponents(int comp[NX][NY])
{
    int C=0;
    for(;;)                         //process all foreground pixels
    {
      bool cont = true;
      for(int i=0;i<NX && cont;i++)
        for(int j=0;j<NY && cont;j++)
        if (comp[i][j]==FOREGROUND)
        {
            floodFill(comp,i,j,C);
            C++; cont=false;
        }
      if (cont) break;              //all foreground pixels processed
    }
}

void floodFill(int comp[NX][NY],int i,int j,int C)
{
    stack<pair<int,int> > s;
    s.push(make_pair(i,j));

    while(s.size())                 //flood fill from (i,j)
    {
      int i = s.top().first;
      int j = s.top().second;
      s.pop();
      if (image[i][j]!=FOREGROUND) continue;
      image[i][j]=C;
      s.push(make_pair(i-1,j));
      s.push(make_pair(i+1,j));
      s.push(make_pair(i,j-1));
      s.push(make_pair(i,j+1));
    }
}
```

Listing 9.2. Connected components detection.

ponents for the segmented bone structures shown in Figure 9.8(c). Each component is color-coded by a different hue. We can now easily distinguish the largest component, marked in red, which corresponds to the cranial bone. If desired, we can now filter the components based on size. For this, we count the number of pixels in every connected component, e.g., using

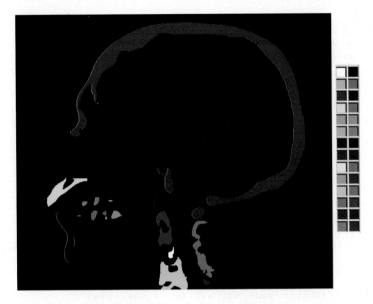

Figure 9.9. Connected components.

a scan-line traversal of the image or a flood fill from the first pixel belonging to that component, and next mark components whose size is below the desired threshold by the BACKGROUND value. Removing small connected components is also known as *island removal* [Schroeder et al. 04].

9.4.3 Morphological Operations

As we saw in the previous section, computing connected components and eventually removing the small ones that correspond to discretization noise is a powerful tool for extracting shape information from image data. However, noise can have another unpleasant effect that is not addressed by the small-size component removal. Figure 9.10 illustrates this. In this application, scientists are interested in studying the growth of the rice plant roots. The roots, grown in a half-transparent jelly, are photographed. The results (Figure 9.10(a)) needs to be analyzed in order to assess various root characteristics, such as number of branches, length of the main branches, and average length of the small branches. To accomplish this, we must extract the shape of the root using image-processing methods.

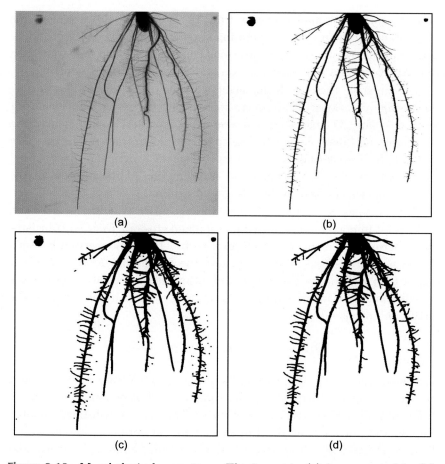

Figure 9.10. Morphological operators. The image in (a) is segmented in (b). (c) Dilation and erosion are used to close holes. (d) The largest connected component is selected. (Data courtesy of R. Peikert, ETH Zürich.)

The first extraction step is a histogram-based segmentation using the image luminance (see Section 9.4.1). The result (see Figure 9.10(b)) shows many small disconnected components, corresponding to the fine branches, as well as two large round components in the upper part of the image, corresponding to impurities in the jelly. Directly applying connected-component analysis to extract the root structure is tempting, but problematic. The segmentation has created numerous small holes in the root structure that both separate the small branches from the stem but also fragment the main branches themselves. Extracting size-thresholded connected components will remove many important small components, yield a disconnected root structure, and also leave the two undesired large round structures.

We can solve these problems using a number of *morphological* image-processing operations. These operations involve a structuring element, or footprint. For 2D images, this is also a 2D image. Given a structuring element e and binary image I, a morphological operation produces a new image I' by translating the structuring element e over the pixels of I.[3] The resulting image I' is generated as a function of the position of the structuring element with respect to the foreground pixels of I, as follows.

Several types of morphological operations exist. We describe here two of the most important ones, called dilation and erosion. *Dilation* translates the structuring element over each pixel p of I. If the intersection between the element translated at p, $T_p(e)$, and the foreground $F(I)$ of I is not empty then p is marked as foreground; otherwise p becomes background. The dilation of an image I using a structuring element e thus contains the foreground pixels given by

$$D_e(I) = \{p \in I | T_p(e) \cap F(I) \neq \oslash\}. \qquad (9.15)$$

Of course, the result depends on the structuring element e. If we want to dilate an image isotropically, i.e., equally in all direction, we can use a disc with radius R as structuring element. The dilation will then "inflate" the boundary of I's foreground at every point in normal direction with a distance R. As a net effect, dilation thickens thin foreground regions, and also fills holes and closes background gaps that have a size smaller than the element size R.

Erosion is the opposite of dilation, and can also be thought as translating a structuring element e over each pixel p of an image I. If the translated element at p, $T_p(e)$ is completely contained in the image foreground $F(I)$ then p is marked as foreground; otherwise p becomes background. The erosion of an image I using a structuring element e yields thus the foreground pixels given by

$$E_e(I) = \{p \in I | T_p(e) \in F(I)\}. \qquad (9.16)$$

---

[3]This process is closely related to the convolution operation (see Section 9.3.3).

Just as for dilation, a frequently used erosion element is a disc of radius R. The erosion of an image with such an element has the net effect of thinning the image foreground, removing small connected components that have a diameter smaller than R, and also potentially breaking connected components into several parts at points where these are thinner than R.

Figure 9.10(c) shows the effect of dilation and erosion applied on the segmented binary image in Figure 9.10(b). First, a dilation with a disc structuring element of radius $R = 15$ pixels is done, followed by an erosion with a disc element of radius $R = 5$ pixels. Next, we remove all connected components except the largest one. The dilation has the desirable effect of inflating the thin root branches and also closing the small gaps between various branch components, yielding a far less-fragmented shape than after segmentation. The erosion has the effect of thinning branches that were excessively thickened by dilation. After these operations, the root structure is essentially a single connected component, which also has the largest area. Hence, the size-based connected component filtering removes all remaining spurious small-scale elements that have not been connected to the main structure by the inflation because of being too far away from it, and also removes the two large undesired round structures. At the end, we are left with a single connected component that captures well the shape of the plant roots (see Figure 9.10(d)). We shall discuss later in Section 9.4.6 how this shape can be processed further to obtain more information.

The combination of a dilation followed by an erosion operation is called morphological *closing*, and is used in practice to remove small background holes in binary images. The converse combination of an erosion followed by a dilation operation is called morphological *opening*, and is used in practice to remove small islands, or foreground components, from binary images. As in our example, both operations are usually part of more complex imaging pipelines in real-world applications.

9.4.4 Distance Transforms

As explained in the previous section, the dilation and erosion operations using a disc structuring element have the net effect of "shifting" the boundary of a binary image with a distance R outward or inward in a direction normal to the boundary itself. The concept of deforming a shape by shifting its boundary in normal direction is closely related to another fundamental operation in image processing: distance transforms.

The distance transform DT of a binary image I is a scalar field that contains, at every pixel p of I, the minimal distance to the boundary of the foreground of I:

$$DT(p) = \min_{q \in F(I)} |p - q|. \qquad (9.17)$$

Different distance metrics can be used in Equation (9.17), such as the Euclidean or Manhattan, or farthest-point distance, leading to different types of distance transforms.

The distance transform can be thought of in a broader context than discrete binary images. Given any shape $\Omega \in \mathbb{R}^n$ that has a boundary $\partial \Omega$, the distance transform DT of Ω associates to every point $p \in \mathbb{R}^n$ the minimal distance to $\partial \Omega$. Hence, DT of Ω is a scalar field defined over a domain embedded in $\mathbb{R}^n$:

$$DT(p) = \min_{q \in \partial \Omega} |p - q|. \qquad (9.18)$$

Distance transforms can also be computed in the signed variant. The signed distance transform is identical to the unsigned one defined by Equation (9.18), but has positive values outside the object Ω and negative values inside. To compute the signed distance transform, the surface $\partial \Omega$ must be closed and orientable.

A related quantity is the *feature transform* [Cuisenaire and Macq 97]. Given a shape Ω, the feature transform FT associates to every point $p \in \mathbb{R}^n$ the set of closest boundary points $q \in \partial \Omega$ to p:

$$FT(p) = \{q \in \partial \Omega \,|\, |p - q| = DT(p)\}. \qquad (9.19)$$

Figure 9.11 illustrates the distance transform. Consider the binary image of a leaf. The shape Ω is shown in gray, its boundary $\partial \Omega$ is marked in black, and the background points are white (Figure 9.11(a)). Consider two points a and b, respectively outside and inside the leaf shape. The feature transform $FT(a)$ of a is the point $b \in \partial \Omega$ that is the closest boundary point to a. The feature transform $FT(b)$ is the set of two points $\{q_1, q_2\}$ that are the closest boundary points to b. The distance transforms of a and b are the lengths of the segments ab and pq_1 or pq_2 respectively. The vectors connecting a skeleton point with its feature points, e.g., $p - q_1$ and $p - q_2$

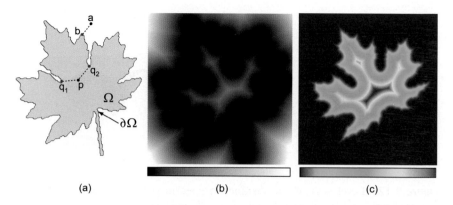

Figure 9.11. Distance and feature transforms.

for p, are also called feature vectors. Figure 9.11(b) shows the (unsigned) distance transform of the leaf shape with a luminance colormap, where black indicates the minimal (zero) distance and white the maximal distance to the leaf. Figure 9.11(c) shows the same distance transform, this time color-coded with a rainbow colormap, and only for the foreground image points.

Distance and feature transforms have a multitude of applications in graphics and visualization. The feature transform can be used to find the closest points, or closest objects, to a given spatial point, which is useful when placing shapes in a space populated with several given objects, such as in path-planning applications. Distance transforms are closely related to the morphological operations of dilation and erosion. Consider the contour $C(\delta)$ of a signed distance transform for some value δ, i.e., the set of points

$$C(\delta) = \{p \in \mathbb{R}^n | DT(p) = \delta\}. \tag{9.20}$$

The contours C for positive values $\delta > 0$ correspond to inflations of the shape Ω with a disc structuring element of radius δ. Similarly, the contours C for negative values $\delta < 0$ correspond to erosions of the shape Ω with a disc structuring element of radius $-\delta$. These contours are also known in many applications as *level sets* [Sethian 96].

Figure 9.12 illustrates the concept of level sets. Given the binary shape in Figure 9.12(a), we compute its distance transform. Figure 9.12(b) shows several isolines $C_k = \{p | DT(p) = k\delta, k \in \mathbb{N}\}$ of the distance transform for

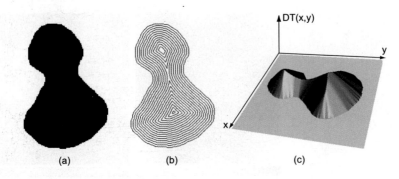

Figure 9.12. Level sets of the distance transform of a 2D shape. (a) Shape, (b) level sets, and (c) elevation plot of the distance transform.

equally spaced values $0, \delta, k\delta, \ldots$. Figure 9.12(c) shows an elevation plot of the distance transform. Note that the isolines in Figure 9.12(b) are also equally spaced in the (x, y) plane. This is an important property that will be exploited later when designing efficient computation methods for distance transforms.

Computing contours of the distance transform is useful when we want to inflate or shrink a geometric shape by a certain distance δ while keeping its overall appearance and aspect ratio (see for example Figure 9.12(b)). An important property of the level sets of distance transforms is that they naturally allow the inflated or shrunk shape to change topology without having to consider any special precautions. In contrast, if we were to perform the same inflation or shrinking operations, e.g., by translating the vertices of a sampled version of the shape boundary $\partial\Omega$ in normal direction, many problems appear. First, the surface can easily self-intersect for too large translations. Second, an evenly sampled surface quickly becomes nonuniformly sampled as points spread in convex surface areas and get closer in concave areas, an effect that adversely affects the representation quality. Finally, topological changes must be tracked and handled explicitly, which is a complex operation.

Distance and feature transforms can be computed by many algorithms. In practice, however, there are several, often subtle trade-offs between the various algorithms. These trade-offs involve the type of computed information, grid type, result accuracy, computation speed, and memory consumption. We shall describe three such algorithms. These algorithms take as input a binary image, obtained, e.g., by segmenting a grayscale or color image. As output, they produce a floating-point image containing the values of $DT(q)$, such as those visualized in Figures 9.11(b) and (c).

Brute-force implementation. The simplest way to compute an exact distance transform is to iterate through all image pixels and compute, for each one, the minimal distance to all the boundary pixels. The code for this algorithm is shown in Listing 9.3. First, we identify all boundary pixels, as explained at the beginning of Section 9.4, and store them in a separate Boundary data structure for quick access. Next, we iterate over all image pixels and compute the minimal distance to the Boundary pixels.

```
const int NX,NY;                        //image sizes

void dt(bool image[NX][NY], float dt[NX][NY])
{
    typedef set<pair<int,int> > Boundary;
    Boundary b;                         //stores the image boundary
    const int MAX_DIST = NX+NY;

    for(int i=0;i<NX;i++)               //extract the image boundary
      for(int j=0;i<NY;j++)
      {
        if (boundary(image,i,j))
            b.insert(make_pair(i,j));
        dt[i][j] = MAX_DIST;
      }
    for(Boundary::iterator i=b.begin(); i!=b.end(); i++)
      for(int i=0;i<NX; i++)            //compute DT of boundary
        for(int j=0;i<NY;j++)
        {
            int bi = (*it).first;
            int bj = (*it).second;
            float dist=sqrt((bi-i)*(bi-i)+(bj-j)*(bj-j));
            if (dist<dt[i][j]) dt[i][j]=dist;
        }
}

bool boundary(int i,int j,bool image[NX][NY])
//Returns true if (i,j) is a boundary pixel
{
    return image[i][j] && (!image[i-1][j] ||
    !image[i+1][j] || !image[i][j-1] || !image[i][j+1]);
}
```

Listing 9.3. Brute-force distance transform.

For an image of N pixels having a foreground with B pixels on its boundary, the brute-force method takes $O(NB)$ steps. In practice, this method is, however, too slow to be used in interactive applications that need to compute distance transforms of large images in subsecond time.

Distance transforms using OpenGL programming. An interesting approach is to use the high parallelism of graphics processing units (GPUs) to implement an efficient version of the simple distance-transform algorithm sketched previously. We shall next sketch an implementation of a GPU-based distance-transform algorithm using OpenGL. We proceed by constructing a distance *splat* or *footprint*. This is a 2D square luminance texture of size S^2 pixels, where S is an odd number. The luminance value at pixel (i, j) in this texture is equal to the distance between that pixel and the texture's center (see Figure 9.13(a)).

Having this texture, we iterate in the outer loop in Listing 9.3 over all the boundary points. At every point, we draw the texture centered at that point, using a special OpenGL blending operation called GL_MIN. Blending in OpenGL was discussed in Section 2.5. A first application of blending in visualization was presented in Section 6.6 for the texture-based visualization of vector fields. In these previous examples, we used the

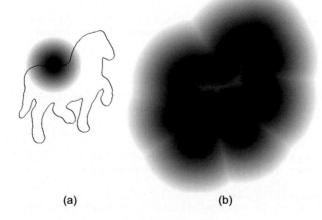

(a)   (b)

Figure 9.13. Computing distance transforms by texture splatting. (a) Contour and overlaid distance splat and (b) resulting distance transform.

standard OpenGL blending described by Equation (2.9), which adds the drawn primitive, or source, to the frame buffer, or destination, weighted by optional blending factors. To achieve our distance transform computation, we now use a different blending equation:

$$\text{dst}' = \min(\text{dst}, \text{src}). \tag{9.21}$$

We enable this blending equation using the OpenGL call

```
glBlendEquation (GL_MIN);
```

In contrast, the default OpenGL blending, as described by Equation (2.9), also called *additive blending*, is specified by

```
glBlendEquation (GL_ADD);
```

When blending is enabled using the GL_MIN operation, the graphics engine will retain the minimal value at every pixel between the drawn splat and the current frame-buffer value. This essentially implements the double for loop over the image pixels from Listing 9.3 with a single OpenGL function call that draws a texture. Figure 9.13(b) shows the result of splatting the shape contour shown in Figure 9.13(a) with a distance texture. We obtain the shape's distance transform encoded as luminance values in the frame buffer.

The code for the GPU-based distance-transform algorithm is sketched in Listing 9.4. The entry point is the function compute_dt, which receives the object boundary stored as an STL set of pixels. The algorithm proceeds as follows. First, we construct the splat in the make_splat function and store it as an OpenGL luminance texture called splat. Next, we enable the appropriate blending mode and draw the splat centered at every boundary pixel. The resulting distance transform is available in the frame buffer.

Several observations are to be made for this technique. First, the size S of the splat texture must be large enough so that it reaches the "deepest" pixel inside the object. In the worst case, for an object boundary whose bounding box has M by N pixels, this means setting S to $\frac{1}{2}\min(M, N)$. Second, the frame buffer used must have a bits-per-pixel resolution high enough to accommodate the complete distance range. Related to this, we must use a texture and frame-buffer pixel format that allows us to exactly encode all possible real-valued distances $0, 1, \sqrt{2}, 2, \sqrt{5}, \cdots, S$ that can oc-

```
struct Pixel { int x,y; };
const int S   = 256;                   //Splat diameter
const int R   = S/2;                   //Splat radius
GLuint splat;                          //Splat texture name

void make_splat()                      //Constructs splat texture
{
  float dt[S][S];                      //Stores splat before passing
  for(int i=0;i<S;i++)                 //it to OpenGL
    for(int j=0;j<S;j++)
    {
      float dst = sqrt((i-R)*(i-R)+(j-R)*(j-R));
      if (dst>R) dst=R;
      dt[i][j] = dst/R;                //dt must be in range [0..1]
    }

  glEnable(GL_TEXTURE_2D);
  glGenTextures(1,&splat);             //We need one texture
  glBindTexture(GL_TEXTURE_2D,splat);
  glTexEnvf(GL_TEXTURE_ENV,GL_TEXTURE_ENV_MODE,GL_REPLACE);
  glTexImage2D(GL_TEXTURE_2D,0,GL_LUMINANCE,DIM,DIM,0,
               GL_LUMINANCE,GL_FLOAT,dt);
}

void draw_splat(const Point& p) //Draws splat centered at p
{
  glBegin(GL_QUADS);
  glTexCoord2f(0,0); glVertex2i(x-R,y-R);
  glTexCoord2f(0,1); glVertex2i(x-R,y+R);
  glTexCoord2f(1,1); glVertex2i(x+R,y+R);
  glTexCoord2f(1,0); glVertex2i(x+R,y-R);
  glEnd();
}

void compute_dt(set<Pixel>& boundary) //Computes DT of boundary
{
  make_splat();                        //First, make the splat texture

  glEnable(GL_BLEND);                  //Enable the desired blend mode
  glBlendEquation(GL_MIN);
  glBlendFunc(GL_ONE,GL_ONE);

  for(set<Pixel>::iterator i=boundary.begin();
      i!=boundary.end();i++)
  {
    const Pixel& p = *i;               //Draw splat centered at every
    draw_splat(p);                     //boundary pixel p
  }
}
```

Listing 9.4. Computing distance transforms using hardware splatting.

cur on a pixel grid up to distance S. This can be done using fixed-point techniques and classic 32-bit RGBA textures. An easier and also more elegant way is to use the newer floating-point texture formats supported by OpenGL, combined with a minimization operation written as a fragment program or pixel shader [GPGPU 06]. For complete implementation details, we refer to Strzodka and Telea [Strzodka and Telea 04].

Fast marching method. As explained earlier in this section, the contours or level sets of the distance transform correspond to progressively inflated or shrunken versions of the shape boundary $\partial\Omega$. Consider two consecutive contours $C(d)$ and $C(d + \epsilon)$ of the DT for some small value $\epsilon > 0$. The gradient ∇DT at point p on contour $C(d)$ is, by definition, normal to $C(d)$, and has the length $(DT(q) - DT(p))/|q - p|$. However, the difference $DT(q) - DT(p)$ is by definition equal to the distance $|q - p|$, so the gradient ∇DT has unit magnitude. It can be shown that the distance transform DT of the boundary $\partial\Omega$ is the solution of the equation

$$|\nabla DT| = 1 \tag{9.22}$$

with initial condition $DT = 0$ on $\partial\Omega$. Equation (9.22) is also known as the *Eikonal equation*.

An efficient method to solve Equation (9.22) is the *fast marching method* introduced by Sethian [Sethian 96]. The fast marching method is based on the following observation. Imagine that we have computed the distances of all points up to some value DT_0. The distances $DT > DT_0$ of the remaining points can be computed considering only the points on the contour DT_0. In more general terms, the DT value of a pixel can be affected only by pixels that have strictly lower DT values. The fast marching methods use this observation by maintaining a *narrowband* containing the pixels being updated, i.e., the direct neighbors of the known pixels. The method initializes the narrowband to the boundary $\partial\Omega$ and next visits all image points and updates their DT values in strictly increasing distance order. During this process, pixels are in one of the following three states:

- known: $DT(p)$ is already computed (p is outside the narrowband);

- band: the DT of p is being updated (p is in the narrowband);

- unknown: p is inside the narrowband.

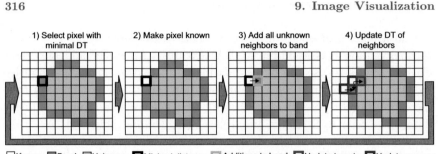

□Known ■Band □Unknown ■Minimal distance ▨Additions to band □Update targets ■Update sources

Figure 9.14. Fast-marching-method algorithm.

The algorithm maintains three data structures: the distance transform array DT; the **narrowband** containing pixels under update, sorted in increasing distance order; and an array **state** holding the state of all pixels. With these structures, the algorithm proceeds as sketched in Listing 9.5 (see also Figure 9.14). First, the **narrowband**, **state**, and DT data structures are initialized. The distance transform DT gets initialized to 0 on the boundary and background, and to some value MAX_VALUE larger than any possible distance on the considered grid on the foreground. After that, the DT of the narrowband pixel p that has the lowest distance gets fixed, and the pixel is marked as Known. Since this pixel has changed state, we must update all its still updateable, i.e., non-Known, neighbors, which we gather in a set nbs. We now update each such neighbor n using the DT values of its own Known neighbors. This action is described by the function **update** and deserves special attention.

How do we update the distance of a pixel n to some boundary if we know the distances of (some) of its neighbors? First, note that n may have Known, Band, and Unknown neighbors. Due to the way the narrowband advances from the outside toward the interior of the foreground object and the fact that pixels are updated in strictly increasing distance-to-boundary order, the Unknown neighbors will always have a larger distance value than the point n itself, so they cannot influence the distance of n. The Band neighbors also have larger distances than the Known ones, so the distance of n is determined first by the Known neighbors. We use only these values in **update**. The point n can have between one and four Known neighbors. We split these into four quadrants, compute the distance of n determined by each quadrant, and retain the minimal value of these possibilities as

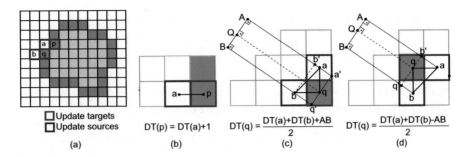

Figure 9.15. Distance computation in the fast marching method.

the value of DT of n. By using a quadrant at a time, we in fact compute the distance of n to a *piecewise linear* interpolation of the boundary of the discrete foreground object, i.e., the distance to the line set that connects the centers of all consecutive, neighboring pixels on this boundary. This is, for many applications, a more accurate estimation of the distance transform of the original shape captured by the binary image than if we computed the distance to the set of boundary pixel centers.

The distance computation performed by the function **update** is illustrated in Figure 9.15. As explained previously, the red pixels p and q will get their distances updated from the **Known** pixels marked in blue, i.e., a and a, b, respectively (Figure 9.15(a)). The distance value of p is clearly nothing more than the distance value of a plus 1, since p is one pixel "deeper" inside the shape than a (Figure 9.15(b)), i.e.,

$$DT(p) = DT(a) + 1. \qquad (9.23)$$

Consider now the point q (see Figure 9.15(c)). Imagine two circles of radii $DT(a)$ and $DT(b)$ centered at the pixels a and b. A line tangent to these circles in points A and B respectively would be a good local approximation of the boundary. There are two such tangent lines corresponding to the configurations in Figures 9.15(c) and (d). Let us consider the configuration in Figure 9.15(c) first. The distance of q to the boundary is approximated by the distance of q to AB, realized in a point called Q. Now construct a rectangle $R = ABq'a'$ so that $q \in q'a'$ and a segment bb' parallel to AB with $q \in R$. From the triangle $bb'a'$, we get that $bb' = \sqrt{2 - (DT(a) - DT(b))^2} = AB$, since $ab = \sqrt{2}$. The area of R is the sum of the area of the trapezoids $bBAa$ and $aa'q'b$, i.e.,

$$AB * DT(q) = AB\left(\frac{DT(a) + DT(b)}{2}\right) + AB\left(\frac{aa' + bq'}{2}\right). \qquad (9.24)$$

Since triangles $qa'a$ and $bq'q$ are equal, it follows that $aa' + bq' = a'q + qq' = a'q' = AB$. Replacing this in Equation (9.24), we get that

$$DT(q) = \frac{DT(a) + DT(b) + \sqrt{2 - (DT(a) - DT(b))^2}}{2}. \qquad (9.25)$$

If we consider the second possible tangent line to the two circles described earlier, we obtain the configuration in Figure 9.15(d). By following a similar reasoning to the one used earlier, we obtain

$$DT(q) = \frac{DT(a) + DT(b) - \sqrt{2 - (DT(a) - DT(b))^2}}{2}. \qquad (9.26)$$

In practice, we compute the distances given by both Equations (9.25) and (9.26) and use the smallest value of the two that exceeds $DT(a)$ and $DT(b)$ as result for $DT(q)$. Combining all the preceding elements, we obtain the function **update** in Listing 9.5.

```
enum      State            { Known, Band, Unknown};
struct    Pixel            { int i,j; };
State                      state [NX][NY];
bool                       image [NX][NY];
float                      DT[NX][NY];
Narrowband                 narrowband;
const  float               MAX_VALUE=NX+NY;

for(int  i=0;i<NX; i++)            //1. Initialization
  for(int  j=0;i<NY; j++)
    if  (boundary(image,i,j))
      {
        state [i][j]=Band;  DT[i][j]=0;
        narrowband.insert (DT[i][j],Pixel(i,j));
      }
    else  if  (image[i][j]==FOREGROUND)
      {
        state [i][j]=Unknown;  DT[i][j]=MAX_VALUE;
      }
```

Listing 9.5. Fast marching method algorithm.

```
    else // (image[i][j]==BACKGROUND)
    {
       state[i][j]=Known; DT[i][j]=0;
    }

while (!narrowband.empty())    //2. March the narrowband
{
   Pixel p = narrowband.getSmallest();
   state[p.i][p.j] = Known;

   set<Pixel> nbs;                //3. Get non-Known neighbors of p
   for(all Pixels n neighbors of p)
   {
      if (state[n.i][n.j]==Known) continue;
      nbs.insert(n);
      if (state[n.i][n.j]!=Band)
      {
         state[n.i][n.j]=Band;
         narrowband.insert(DT[n.i][n.j],n);
      }
   }

   for(all Pixels n in nbs)
   {                             //4. Compute DT of neighbors of p
      float d=DT[n.i][n.j];
      d = min(d,update(n.i-1,n.i,n.j,n.j-1));
      d = min(d,update(n.i+1,n.i,n.j,n.j-1));
      d = min(d,update(n.i-1,n.i,n.j,n.j+1));
      d = min(d,update(n.i+1,n.i,n.j,n.j+1));
      if (d!=DT[n.i][n.j])
      {
         reinsert n in narrowband in order of d;
         DT[n.i][n.j] = d;
      }
   }
}

float update(int lr,int i,int j,int tb)
//3. Find distance of (i,j) to its neighbors (lr,j) and (i,tb)
{
   Pixel a=(lr,j), b=(i,tb), q=(i,j);
   if (state[lr][j]==Known)
      if (state[i][tb]==Known)
      {
         float D1 = distance from Equation (9.25);
         float D2 = distance from Equation (9.26);
```

Listing 9.5. continued.

```
      if (D2>DT[lr][j] && D2>DT[i][tb]) return D2;
      if (D1>DT[lr][j] && D1>DT[i][tb]) return D1;
      return DT[i][j];
   }
   else
      return 1+DT[lr][j]; //Equation (9.23)
   else
    if (state[i][tb]==Known)
      return 1+DT[i][tb]; //Equation (9.23)
   return DT[i][j];
}
```

Listing 9.5. continued.

After computing the DT of a point n, the final step of the fast marching method is to reinsert n in order of the new value $DT(n)$ in the narrowband. Strictly speaking, this is not necessary if we design the narrowband's getSmallest method to search the point of minimal distance every time. However, this repeated search is costly, so it is more efficient to maintain the narrowband sorted ascendingly on distance, i.e., reinsert points in it whenever they get their distances updated.

We can implement the fast marching algorithm easily as follows. For the narrowband, we use a multimap<float,Pixel> STL container that keeps pixels sorted in increasing order of their DT. The method getSmallest will thus simply remove the first element, an operation of $O(1)$ cost. Reinserting a point into the narrowband upon distance update is a bit more delicate. For this, we need to quickly locate the point's position in the narrowband. We can do this efficiently by maintaining an additional data structure multimap<float,Pixel>::iterator pos[NX][NY], i.e., an array of iterators to the narrowband positions of every pixel. When pixels are inserted in the narrowband, we also insert the corresponding position iterator in the pos location of that pixel. To reinsert a pixel p in the narrowband, we simply erase the iterator pos[p.i][p.j] from the narrowband and next reinsert p with its new distance value.

The complexity of the preceding implementation is $O(N \log B)$ for an image of N foreground pixels having a boundary of B pixels. The log factor is the cost of (re)inserting an element in the sorted narrowband, which would typically be done internally using a hash or tree structure. Clearly, this cost can be more than one order of magnitude lower than for the brute-force method described in the previous section. Using this implementation,

2D distance transforms of large images can be computed in subsecond time on current PC computers [Telea and van Wijk 02, Telea 04, Telea and Vilanova 03]. To compute 3D distance transforms, a similar implementation can be designed. The main difference is the design of the `update` function, which will have consider eight octants. 3D distance transforms are useful, among others, in computing simplified representations of 3D shapes, such as centerlines, a subject discussed later in this chapter in Section 9.4.5.

Finally, let us mention that the fast marching method presented here is not limited to computing distance transforms. In the general case, this method can solve in n dimensions equations of the form

$$|\nabla T| = f, \tag{9.27}$$

where $f : \mathbb{R}^n \to \mathbb{R}_+$ is a speed function, with the boundary condition $T(\partial\Omega) = 0$. This equation describes the deformation, or evolution in time, of the shape boundary $\partial\Omega$ under normal speed. The *Eikonal equation*, whose solution is the distance transform of $\partial\Omega$, is a particular case of Equation (9.27) for unit speed. By setting the speed function f to depend on the position in space or other data attributes such as, e.g., the surface curvature, a large class of problems can be solved with applications in shape modeling, smoothing, filtering, and computer vision. For more insight into this topic as well as a more detailed mathematical treatment thereof, we point the reader to the reference book by Sethian [Sethian 96].

Other distance transform algorithms. The brute-force, GPU-based, and fast marching methods are not the only methods to compute distance transforms on binary images. Many other methods have been developed. The main differences between these methods concern the following aspects:

- precision: is the method exact? If not, what is its error?

- metric: are other distance metrics than Euclidean supported?

- dimension: does the method work in 2D, 3D, or nD?

- speed: what is the complexity of the method?

- simplicity: how easy is to implement the method?

Chamfer-based methods were among the first methods used to compute distance transforms [Thiel and Montanevert 92]. They are quite easy to implement and relatively fast, but compute only approximative distance transforms. Given the existence of several modern methods that are both exact and efficient, this class of methods has become less interesting in recent years. *Graph-search-based* methods consider the pixel neighboring graph and implement distance computation as search operations on this graph [Lotufo et al. 00]. *Raster-scanning* methods traverse the image pixels in row and column order and compute the distance transform [Danielsson 80, Mullikin 92]. Efficient implementations decompose the distance computation in one component per spatial dimension and implement the distance transform as several passes, one per dimension [Meijster et al. 00]. Such methods are very efficient, being able to compute exact distance transforms in $O(N)$ steps for an image with N pixels.

Overall, all these methods are relatively simpler to implement than the fast marching method presented in the previous section. However, as already explained, the fast marching method has the important advantage that it allows one to specify the speed function, i.e., the gradient of the distance metric, differently at each point of the domain. This allows one to easily implement complex space-dependent and anisotropic distance metrics, a feature that is not supported in general by the other methods listed in this section. A second advantage of the fast marching method is that it processes the image pixels in increasing distance order. This allows one to stop the distance computation when, e.g., a certain maximal distance has been reached. This feature is not supported by other methods such as the raster scanning class.

9.4.5 Skeletonization

As explained earlier in this chapter, many imaging applications have as a goal the analysis of the properties exhibited by certain shapes present in image data. We have seen that the first step in this process is segmentation, which separates the pixels contained by the shapes of interest from the remaining ones, called the background. However, the question remains: how should we analyze the shape formed by these pixels?

In the shape analysis field, there are many classes of methods used to characterize digital shapes. These methods address different goals:

- geometric analysis: the analysis of the geometric properties of the shape, such as aspect ratio, eccentricity, boundary curvature, and elongation.

- topological analysis: the analysis of the topological properties of the shape, such as genus and part-whole structure.

- retrieval: given a source shape and a set of target shapes, find the target shape most resembling to the source.

- classification: given several shapes and/or several shape classes, partition the shapes into self-similar classes or distribute the shapes in the given classes.

- matching: given two shapes, find geometrical and/or topological correspondences between the two.

To be able to process the shape data, most methods in the preceding classes first reduce a given shape to a set of (numerical) attributes, or a *shape vector*. This vector holds shape properties relevant for a given application area, which are extracted from the pixel representation. For example, among such simple properties are the shape area, aspect ratio, diameter, and average boundary curvature. However, such aggregated properties are clearly not enough to characterize a complex shape.

Skeletons, also known as medial axes, are a well-known, long-standing shape-representation instrument. In this section, we shall describe skeletons and their properties; present an efficient, robust, and simple to implement algorithm to compute skeletons; and give several examples of their usefulness in data visualization.

Skeletons were first introduced by Blum [Blum 67]. Given a 2D shape Ω, the original definition of the skeleton $S(\Omega)$ was the set of points $p \in \Omega$ that are centers of maximally inscribed discs in Ω, i.e., discs fully contained in Ω that are not included by larger discs in the same set. An equivalent definition defines skeletons as the sets of points situated at equal distance from at least two boundary points of the given shape, i.e.,

$$S(\Omega) = \{p \in \Omega | \exists q, r \in \partial\Omega, q \neq r, |p - q| = |p - r|\}. \qquad (9.28)$$

Note that this definition holds for shapes of $\Omega \in \mathbb{R}^n$ embedded in any spatial dimension.

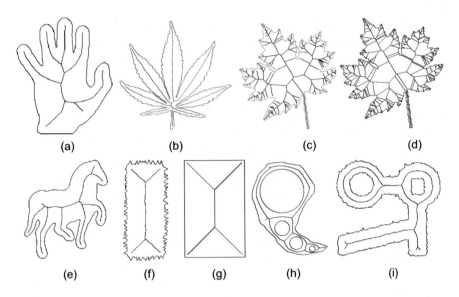

(a)   (b)   (c)   (d)

(e)   (f)   (g)   (h)   (i)

Figure 9.16. Examples of skeletons of 2D shapes. The skeleton is the one-dimensional structure located inside the shape's closed boundary.

Figure 9.16 shows examples of skeletons for several 2D shapes. These examples reveal several of the useful properties of skeletons. These properties are discussed next.

Centeredness. The main property of skeletons is that they are *centered* with respect to the shape boundary. In 2D, the skeleton consists of a set of curves, in the generic case. The nongeneric case is the skeleton of a circle, which consists of a single point, being its center. The centeredness of the skeleton is important. Several studies have shown that humans visually perceive symmetry as one of the most important shape attributes. Symmetry-related properties of a shape can be tested on the shape skeleton, which makes the latter an useful characterization instrument. For example, long, low-twisting, uninterrupted skeleton branches indicate symmetric shape components, e.g., the lobes of the leaf in Figure 9.16(b).

Structural and topological encoding. Skeletons have a strong ability to describe the *structure* of shapes. Intuitively, every skeleton branch corresponds to a shape component, and every skeleton junction, or intersection

of several branches, corresponds to one part where several shape components are joined with each other. By analyzing the graph structure of a
2D skeleton, we can make several high-level statements about the shape's
structure. For example, by analyzing a combination of elements including
the number of branch endpoints, branch intersections, and disposition of
branches in the skeletal graph, we can infer that the shape in Figure 9.16(b)
has eight lobes distributed radially around a center, where they all meet. A
similar analysis on the hand and horse shapes reveals information character-
izing the number of fingers of the hand and limbs of the horse respectively.

The skeleton also encodes the topological genus of its shape. Indeed,
every hole in the shape corresponds to a loop in the skeleton graph. A
skeleton of a shape without holes, i.e., of genus 0, is a tree. The skeleton of
the shape with five holes in Figure 9.16(h) is a graph with five loops. Note
also that the skeleton of a compact shape is compact, i.e., connected.

Geometrical encoding. Together with structure and symmetry, skeletons
also encode the shape geometry. Equation (9.28) states that for each skeleton point p, we have at least two different boundary points at equal distance from p. In the terminology introduced in Section 9.4.4, these are
the feature points of p. The distance between any of these points and the
skeleton point p is equal to the value of the distance transform DT of the
shape Ω evaluated at p. This distance gives a good estimation of the "local thickness" of the shape at p. A small distance indicates a locally thin
shape, such as if we consider any of the points on the twigs of the leafs
in Figure 9.16(b–d). High values indicate points deep inside the object,
such as any of the points on the central branch of the double-Y skeleton of
the rectangles in Figure 9.16(f–g). A large number of feature points of a
skeleton point p, or in the terminology introduced in Section 9.4.4 a high
cardinality of the shape's feature transform FT evaluated at p, indicates
the existence of circle arc segments on the boundary. For example, every
branch endpoint for the five skeleton branches of the fingers of the hand
shape in Figure 9.16(a) has a multitude of feature points located on the
corresponding round fingertip. Note that this property usually holds for
branch endpoints.

The combination $\{S(\Omega), DT_S(\Omega)\}$, that is, the skeleton of a shape plus
the shape's distance transform restricted to the skeleton points, is called
the *medial axis transform* or MAT. An MAT uniquely and fully encodes a

shape. Indeed, given the MAT we can reconstruct the shape's boundary as the hull of the boundaries of discs with radii $DT_S(p)$ centered at all points p of the skeleton S. In a discrete setting, a suboptimal but easy-to-implement reconstruction method can be implemented by drawing full discs having the respective radii using a given color on a background of a different color.

Multiscale shape encoding. The skeleton provides a multiscale representation of the boundary of a shape. In essence, every skeleton branch containing a free endpoint corresponds to a convex "bump" on the boundary, or a positive local maximum of the boundary curvature. If we remove such a terminal skeleton branch, that is, a branch that would not disconnect the skeleton tree, and reconstruct the object using the MAT, we obtain a shape similar to the original one, but where the bump corresponding to the removed branch has been replaced with a circle arc. This is a very important property of skeletons, as it lets one simplify complex boundaries in a controlled way. This mechanism can be used in many applications, such as hierarchical shape matching [Cornea et al. 05], shape compression, and shape denoising. For example, consider the two identical leafs in Figure 9.16(c) and (d). The left image shows a simplified skeleton, whereas the right image shows the "full" skeleton, where every small boundary bump produces a separate skeleton branch. Similarly, Figure 9.16(f) and (g) show a noisy and exact rectangle, respectively . If we simplify the skeleton of the noisy rectangle, as shown in the left image, we obtain a smooth structure that is very similar to the skeleton of the "clean" rectangle. Hence, we can use such simplified skeletons to describe the essence of a shape ignoring its small-scale details, or to compare or match shapes modulo small-scale noise.

This multiscale representation power of skeletons is related to one of their much-discussed weaknesses. Namely, consider a perfect rectangle that includes a very small bump or dent on the boundary. This deformation causes the apparition of a full skeleton branch connecting it with the main skeleton structure. No matter how small the bump size ϵ is, the length of this branch will never drop under a sizeable value δ. Hence, the skeleton function $S(\Omega)$ is continuous in the Cauchy sense (see Section 3.1). Such long branches caused by relatively short boundary details are also called *ligature* branches [Costa and Cesar 01]. We shall present in Section 9.4.6

a simple and effective way to make skeletons robust and continuous under small boundary perturbations.

9.4.6 Skeleton Computation in 2D

Recall the definition of a skeleton as the set of shape points situated at equal distance from at least two boundary points (Equation (9.28)). If we have a feature transform of our shape (see Equation (9.19)), we can compute the skeleton by simply selecting those points whose feature transform contains more than two boundary points. However, there is a practical problem with this idea. The definitions of the feature transform and skeleton (Equations (9.19) and (9.28)) hold, strictly speaking, in the continuous space only. Simply using the same definitions in the discrete space of image pixels does not lead to the expected results. The reason for this is that distances on a discrete grid do not take all possible values as they do in the continuous space, as explained earlier.

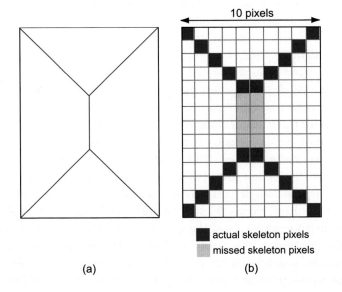

(a)   (b)

Figure 9.17. Skeleton sampling issues. (a) Continuous skeleton and (b) its counterpart as computed on a discrete grid of even pixel width. The discrete skeleton misses the central branch.

Figure 9.17 illustrates the problem. The left image shows the skeleton of a rectangular shape in the continuous $\mathbb{R}^2$ space. The right image shows a sampling of the rectangle on a discrete pixel grid of an even pixel width. Using the definitions from Equations (9.19) and (9.28) will miss the central skeleton axis, as there are no pixels in this area that are situated at *equal* distances from the vertical rectangle edges. Relaxing the distance equality criterion in the skeleton definition is also not a good solution. This makes the definition too permissive, which generates a large number of spurious, false skeleton points or thickens the correct skeleton branches unnecessarily.

We next present two classes of methods for computing skeletons of binary shapes.

Using distance field singularities. By definition, the skeleton points are situated at equal distance from several boundary points. Consider the distance transform of a binary shape, such as shown by the elevation plot in Figure 9.12. Points at equal distance from more than one boundary point are by definition *local maxima* of the distance transform. These correspond visually to the "ridges" of the distance transform graph. Detecting such ridges is equivalent to finding the skeleton of the shape. In a luminance plot of the distance transform, such as the one shown in Figure 9.13, these ridges correspond to local luminance maxima.

One class of skeletonization methods uses image- or signal-processing methods to detect such points. Remember that the distance transform is the solution of the Eikonal equation $|\nabla DT| = 1$ (Equation (9.22)). Hence, the gradient of the luminance of all pixels in Figure 9.13(b) should be one, except for the skeleton ones. To find these, we can compute the gradient magnitude of the DT image and then upper threshold it to find low gradient magnitude points. Figure 9.18 shows the application of a Sobel filter on the DT image from Figure 9.13(b) (masked with the shape itself), which produces an approximation of the gradient magnitude in the input image. The interpretation of the result is simple: White pixels in Figure 9.18 correspond to nonskeleton areas, where $|\nabla DT|$ equals one. Black pixels inside the white area correspond to skeleton points, where $|\nabla DT|$ has low values.

Although simple to implement, skeleton detection based on the distance field singularities has several problems. First, it relies on computing deriva-

Figure 9.18. Computing the skeleton using image-processing operations.

tives of discrete signals, an operation that is inherently noise-sensitive. Stabilizing such computations by, e.g., filtering the distance transform signal with Gaussian filters can be done, but this implicitly removes skeleton details. Secondly, singularity detection is a typically local operation, which cannot guarantee by itself a connected skeleton. Consider, for example, Figure 9.18. Look at those parts of the skeleton branches corresponding to the horse legs that are close to the main rump branch. We notice that these branch parts are less pronounced than the remainder of the leg branches. In general, we notice that those skeleton points with nearly opposite feature vectors are well detected, whereas the skeleton points whose feature vectors make a small angle are weakly detected. Indeed, the first kind of points are situated on a *constant-height* ridge of the distance transform, corresponding to shape areas of local constant diameter, hence they have a low *DT* gradient value. The second kind of points are situated on an *ascending* or *descending* ridge of the distance transform, corresponding to shape areas of varying local diameter, hence they have a larger *DT* gradient value. Several methods alleviate these skeleton detection problems, for example performing an explicit reconnection of the detected *DT* local maxima or combining maxima detection with morphological erosion algorithms. For a detailed review of skeleton detection methods using the distance transform singularities, see, for example, Ge and Fitzpatrick [Ge and Fitzpatrick 96].

Using boundary collapse metric. We present next a simple method that circumvents the preceding problems and is able to deliver connected and robust skeletons for any 2D binary shapes. The new method has three steps, as follows. In the first step, we augment the fast marching method for computing distance transforms presented in Section 9.4.4 with the capability of computing a *one-point* feature transform. This is a feature transform FT following the definition in Equation (9.18) with the simplification that it computes a single closest point, i.e., $|FT(p)| = 1, \forall p \in \Omega$. The one-point feature transform is stored in an additional array int FT[NX][NY]. Assuming that every boundary pixel has an unique integer id, the value FT[i][j] gives the id of the closest boundary pixel to a given pixel (i, j) in the shape. We make the convention that point IDs are consecutive positive integers starting from zero. Next to the one-point feature transform FT, we store also an array Pixel from[B] of B elements, where B is the boundary length. For every boundary point id, from gives the 2D location of that point.

```
    . . .
  narrowband.insert(DT[n.i][n.j],n);

  //Compute one—point feature transform
  float dmin = DIST_MAX*DIST_MAX;
  for(all Points q neighbors of n)
  {
    if (state[q.i][q.j]==Known) continue;
    Point c = from[FT[q.i][q.j]];
    int    d = (c.i−n.i)*(c.i−n.i)+(c.j−n.j)*(c.j−n.j);
    if (d>=dmin) continue;
    dmin=d; FT[n.i][n.j]=FT[c.i][c.j];
  }
    . . .
```

Listing 9.6. One-point feature transform.

We start computing the one-point **FT** by first initializing `from` and **FT** on the boundary. Next, we compute **FT** by adding the code in Listing 9.6 to the fast marching method in Listing 9.5, when a new point is added to the narrowband, i.e., right after the call to `narrowband.insert`. Basically, this code keeps propagating the id of the closest boundary point, found by minimizing the distance-to-boundary among the `Known` neighbors of the newly added point to the narrowband, while the narrowband advances inside the domain Ω.

Now that we have the one-point feature transform, in the second step we compute the skeleton by identifying points that have different features than their *neighbors*. Comparing the single feature of a point with its neighbors solves the pixel grid discretization problem explained previously (see Figure 9.17). Indeed, a pixel close to or on the skeleton will always have a different feature point than its neighbors. In order to prevent computing a two-pixel-thick skeleton, we only consider the right and lower neighbors n_R, n_L (or the upper and left ones) instead of all four.

The third and final step in the skeleton computation is to build in a multiscale representation of the shape. For a skeleton pixel p, we notice that the further apart two features $f_i, f_j \in \{FT(p), FT(n_R), FT(n_L)\}$ are, the more central to the skeleton the position of p is. Hence, we can define the importance $\rho(p)$ as

$$\rho(p) = \max \big[\max \big(\text{dist}(u(FT(n_R)) - u(FT(p)))$$
$$+ \text{dist}(u(FT(n_L)) - u(FT(p)))\big), \frac{|\partial \Omega|}{2} \big], \tag{9.29}$$

where $u : \partial \Omega \to \mathbb{R}_+$ is an arc-length boundary parameterization and $\text{dist}(a, b) = \max(|a - b|, \frac{|\partial \Omega|}{2})$ is the shortest distance along the boundary between two points. Implementing the complete skeletonization method starting from the fast marching code (see Listing 9.5), the one-point feature transform addition (see Listing 9.6) and the skeleton detector and importance measure ρ (Equation (9.29)) are left as an exercise for the reader.

The measure ρ in Equation (9.29) defines the importance of a skeleton point as being the maximal shortest distance along the boundary $\partial \Omega$ between two feature points of p. Note that this importance measure only holds for shapes of genus zero; that is, shapes without holes. For example, the importance of the skeleton point p in Figure 9.11(a) equals the length of the upper leaf lobe delimited by the boundary points q_1 and q_2. If we want to compare the importances of skeletons of different objects, we can normalize ρ in the range $[0, 1]$ by dividing it by half the boundary length $|\partial\Omega|/2$.

This measure also has an intuitive explanation. Imagine a level set evolution, such as the narrowband motion in the fast marching method, that carries along the initial boundary $\partial\Omega$, collapsing it gradually as the narrowband shrinks. At each skeleton point, the importance ρ will equal the length of the collapsed boundary, i.e., the piece of the original $\partial\Omega$ that has been shrunk to that point during the evolution. An important fact is that Equation (9.29) does *not* actually distinguish between skeleton and nonskeleton points. Indeed, nonskeleton points will always get an importance $\rho = 1$. Implementing the importance measure from Equation (9.29) is the second step of the skeletonization algorithm, and can be easily done in a single pass over all image pixels.

The preceding importance measure is known to have several desirable properties [Ogniewicz and Kubler 95, Costa and Cesar 01, Telea and van Wijk 02]:

- monotonicity: for genus 0 object whose skeleton is a tree, $\rho(p)$ increases as p moves from a branch endpoint to the skeleton root.

- geometry encoding: skeleton branches corresponding to short boundary pieces have a low importance, even if they are long (the ligatures).

All in all, the skeleton importance implemented via the fast marching method provides a skeletonization tool that fully satisfies all our earlier requirements: robustness against shape noise and discretization resolution, connected pixel-thin exact skeletons, and a simple and intuitive geometric scale parameter. Once we have the importance, defining a simplified skeleton $S(\Omega, \tau)$ means just thresholding the importance τ:

$$S(\Omega, \tau) = \{p \in \Omega | \rho(p) \geq \tau\}. \tag{9.30}$$

This thresholding is the third and last step of the skeletonization pipeline, and is also implemented as a pass over all image pixels. Further implementation details, e.g., for shapes with holes, are discussed in Costa and Cesar as well as Telea and van Wijk [Costa and Cesar 01, Telea and van Wijk 02].

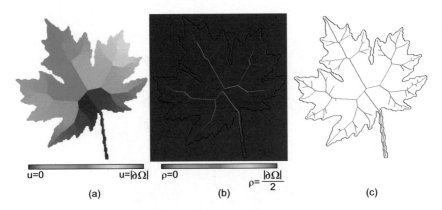

Figure 9.19. Skeletonization algorithm. (a) One-point feature transform. (b) Collapsed arc length. (c) Simplified skeleton.

Figure 9.19 illustrates the complete skeletonization pipeline for the leaf shape shown earlier. First, we compute the one-point feature transform of the boundary. Recall that this one-point feature transform assigns to the id of any interior point the id of the closest boundary point. Figure 9.19(a) shows this by color-coding the boundary point IDs, which run clockwise and in increasing order along the boundary starting from the tip of the leaf twig (bottom-most shape point). Figure 9.19(b) shows the importance field ρ. We see now how the skeleton branches corresponding to small boundary details are dark blue, i.e., unimportant, and how the importance gradually increases as we approach the skeleton center, or root (colored in red). The final image, Figure 9.19(c), shows the same skeleton as in Figure 9.16(c), which is the simplified version $S(\Omega, \tau = 10)$ of the full skeleton shown in Figure 9.16(d). Note that, in general, the lowest value τ can practically have is 2 pixels. Lower values essentially produce touching skeleton branches in the image, which are not very useful. The highest value, $\tau = |\partial\Omega|/2$, simplifies the skeleton to a single point, the root. Remark that this is *not* the same as the deepest point inside the object, at least not for concave shapes.

Let us examine Figure 9.19(a) in a bit more detail. This image shows how the fast marching process essentially transports the boundary IDs inside the object in distance order. Indeed, the isolines of this field, i.e., lines of constant id value (thus same color in the image) are identical to the

Figure 9.20. Isolines for the boundary id field (orthogonal to the boundary) and the distance transform field (parallel to the boundary), equally spaced at 5 units. Note how the two isoline sets are orthogonal to each other, except along the skeleton.

stream lines of the distance transform's gradient ∇DT, or the lines along which the IDs are transported from the boundary inward. These lines, as discussed in the previous section, are normal to the boundary. Figure 9.20 demonstrates this, showing a set of such isolines, equally spaced at 5 units, overlaid on the color-coded boundary id field. Hence, in this image there is a black isoline starting from every fifth boundary pixel. On top of this, we show also several isolines of the distance transform, equally spaced at 5 units in distance value. We see how the two sets of isolines are orthogonal to each other—except along the skeleton branches, shown as thick black lines. This is actually a problem of combining the assumptions of the marching squares algorithm used to extract the boundary id isolines with the data representation. As explained earlier and visible from Figure 9.19(a), the boundary id field has strong zero-order discontinuities along the skeleton, where IDs from different parts of the boundary meet. This is not a problem when we represent this data as a pixel image, which is identical to a piecewise constant interpolation based on samples taken at the pixel centers (see Section 3.5.1). However, we cannot actually contour such a dataset. As explained in Section 5.3, the marching square algorithm assumes *by definition* that the input field to contour is at least C^0 continuous over all its data cells. To contour the image, we must first convert it from the cell-based (C^0) to a vertex-based (C^1) representation, as explained in Section 3.9.1. However, besides changing the grid type, data resampling has the silent effect of also changing the interpolation type and continuity assumptions on the data! In our case, the boundary id field is not assumed to be piecewise linear. The net effect is that discontinuities are assimilated with rapid data variations. Hence, the result is that the boundary id isolines get gathered along the discontinuity (skeleton) lines, which is actually wrong. In practice, one should be aware of such aspects which, if ignored, can easily lead to misinterpreting the visualization. Besides this technical aspect, however, this image is a typical example of how classical visualization methods, such as colormaps and isolines, can help us understand mathematical datasets such as the gradient and distance fields computed by the fast marching method.

Applications. Two-dimensional skeletons have many applications in imaging and data visualization. Figure 9.21(a–b) shows an application of 2D skeletons for the problem of visualization of rice roots introduced earlier in Section 9.4.3. From the segmented root image (Figure 9.21(a)), we obtain the skeleton shown in Figure 9.21(b). Since from this structure it is quite easy to extract a 1D graph of pixel lines, we can directly perform topological and geometrical measurements and analyses on this dataset. A similar example is shown in Figure 9.21(c–d). Here, we visualize the skeleton of a neural cell, which has been segmented in a similar manner to the rice root from a grayscale photograph. Analysis of the cell skeleton graph is useful to reveal several properties of the cell, such as number and length of dendrites, or to compare this cell with a given reference cell stored in a database. Both skeletons in this image have been produced with the algorithm described in this section.

9.4.7 Skeleton Computation in 3D

As explained earlier, skeletons are not restricted to two dimensions. Three-dimensional skeletons are also a useful instrument for shape representation

in data visualization. Whereas the skeleton of a 2D shape Ω is a set of
1D curves, or a point in the degenerate case of a disc, the skeleton of
a 3D shape following the definition given by Equation (9.28) is a set of
intersecting manifolds, or surface sheets. Figure 9.22 shows the skeletons
of several 3D shapes. We easily see that the skeletal structure of these
shapes is much more complex than in the case of two-dimensional objects
of relatively comparable complexity. When the 3D shape has local circular
symmetry, such as a tubular structure, for example, the 3D skeleton is the
one-dimensional curve locally centered in the middle of the shape. Finally,
there is also the degenerate case of a ball having a point as a skeleton. In
general, the dimension of the skeleton is one lower than the space in which
the original shape is embedded.

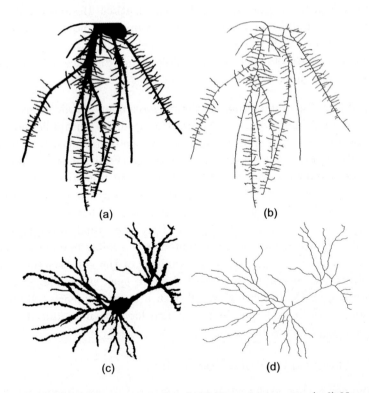

Figure 9.21. Skeletonization examples. (a,b) Rice plant roots. (c,d) Neural cell.

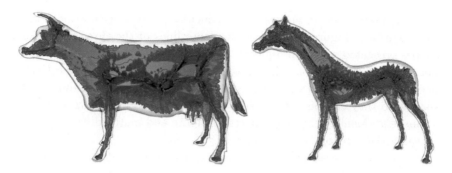

Figure 9.22. Skeletons of three-dimensional shapes. The shape is rendered transparent. The skeletal surface is rendered in blue.

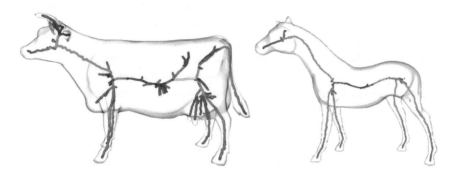

Figure 9.23. Centerlines of the 3D shapes shown in Figure 9.22.

Computing robust 3D skeletons for volumetric shapes is, however, much more complicated than in 2D. Moreover, although 3D skeletons can be used to perform various operations on 3D shapes, such as compression, matching, and analysis, they may not reduce the complexity of the original shape. For example, if we look at the skeletons of the shapes shown in Figure 9.22, we can even argue that they have a more complex structure than the shape itself. A more interesting route to take is to reduce 3D shapes to *one-dimensional* skeletal structures. This direction turns out to be very useful in practice. One-dimensional skeletons of 3D shapes, also called *centerlines* or *curve skeletons*, can be directly computed from a volumetric, voxel-based, shape description, directly bypassing the more complex surface skeleton. Intuitively, centerlines of 3D shapes can be described as

one-dimensional sets of curves that are locally centered with respect to the
shape surface. Figure 9.23 shows the centerlines of the three-dimensional
shapes presented earlier in Figure 9.22. Clearly, the structure of the centerlines is much simpler than that of the corresponding 3D skeletons. Centerlines have a topological structure similar to the skeletons of two-dimensional
shapes, so they can be easily used to perform various shape analysis operations, e.g., identify the shape parts, compare and match different shapes,
or study the topology of the shape.

Centerlines are especially useful in the visualization of shapes that have
an elongated, tubular structure. Such shapes are frequently encountered in
medical datasets such as CT and MRI scans. An application of centerlines
in visualization is the extraction and analysis of the coronary arterial tree
from multiple two-dimensional images of arteries [Chen and Carroll 00].
Centerlines have also been used in *virtual colonoscopy* [Wan et al. 01].
Colonoscopy is used in medical practice to examine the interior of the human colon using a miniature video camera, in search of potential lesions or
polyps that have the potential to develop into malignant structures leading
to colon cancer. Detecting and diagnosing such structures in an early stage
can lead to surgical interventions in an early phase, which is beneficial for
the patients. However effective, in-vivo colonoscopy is an invasive intervention that can be quite unpleasant for the patients. Virtual colonoscopy is a
noninvasive alternative. Here, the colon structure is extracted from a CT
scan of the patient, e.g., using an isosurface technique (see Section 5.3).
After extraction, the centerline of this isosurface is computed. Given the
tubular structure of the colon, its centerline is essentially a single curve.
This curve can be used as the path of a virtual camera to help the special-
ist navigate inside the isosurface in order to visualize the colon walls and
detect potential lesions, polyps, or other structures.[4] Figure 9.24 shows the
centerlines of two such isosurfaces. The left image (Figure 9.24(a)) shows
the centerline of the colon isosurface corresponding to the original folded
geometry of this organ in the human body. Given the relatively complex
folding and twisting of the colon shape, the centerline is a helpful aid in
guiding a virtual navigation by, e.g., constraining the 3D position of the
camera close to the centerline and the camera orientation to the tangent direction to this centerline [Wan et al. 01]. The right image (Figure 9.24(b))

---

[4]We must note for completeness that the visual examination of the colon cannot be
used, only by itself, to diagnose the presence or absence of malignant structures.

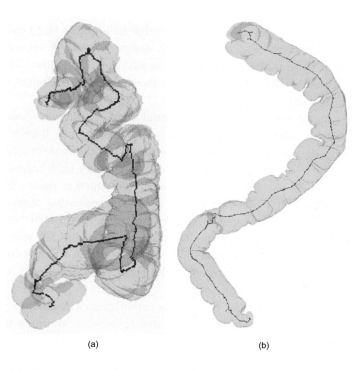

(a)   (b)

Figure 9.24. Centerlines of a human colon isosurface (a) in the original position and (b) in an unfolded position.

shows a similar colon isosurface and the corresponding centerline, this time computed from an unfolded colon after a dissection. Although the colon surface has a complex structure with many small-scale creases and folds, the centerline captures the main organ structure.

Besides providing simplified representations of anatomical structures, centerlines can be used to encode also other types of visualization datasets. For example, in flow visualization, regions of high vorticity correspond often to features of interest that need detailed study. Such regions can be segmented from the rest of the flow volume, e.g., using threshold-based criteria. In many cases, these regions consist of several elongated, tubular structures that split and/or merge at various points. This type of structure can be visualized using an isosurface, but also lends itself well to a centerline description. By reducing the segmented structures to their centerlines, one can perform several analyses, e.g., in order to identify the type of flow and the number and kind of split and merge points. A second use of centerlines is to construct a simplified visualization of the flow. Both types of applications are described in detail in Reinders et al. [Reinders et al. 99, Reinders et al. 00].

How can we compute one-dimensional centerlines from three-dimensional shapes? Similar to the 2D case, we would like to have a method that guarantees a number of requirements on the computed structure, such as connectivity, one-voxel thinness, and centeredness with respect to the original shape. A particular requirement is robustness to noise. We would like to obtain a simple one-dimensional centerline consisting of several connected, possibly smooth, curves that captures the main structure of the considered shape and ignores small-scale surface details. For example, for the virtual colonoscopy application, we want to obtain a single curve that is relatively smooth and centered in the same time, so we can use it to control the path of the virtual camera.

Several methods exist for computing centerlines. The most used methods in practice can be classified into three categories: thinning methods, distance field-based methods, and geodesic methods. We overview each class next.

Thinning methods. Thinning methods proceed as follows. First, a binary representation of the 3D shape is computed. Given a 3D volume, the shape is represented as a set of foreground voxels, whereas the voxels falling outside the shape are marked as background. This representation can be stored as a 3D uniform dataset having boolean attributes. Such representations can be computed from, e.g., CT or MRI scans using various value-based segmentation methods on the scanned density values, similar to the process described for grayscale images in Section 9.4.1. After the binary volume has been obtained, voxels are iteratively removed, or marked as background, from the foreground boundary, in a process known as *thinning*. Intuitively, this process can be thought of as peeling off those voxels from the boundary whose removal does not alter the object topology. Such voxels are also called *simple points*. Discriminating the simple points that can be removed from the points that must be kept, i.e., the centerline points, is done by checking against a set of precomputed *templates*.[5] These are usu-

---

[5]Templates are similar to the structuring elements described in Section 9.4.3.

ally small, 3×3 neighborhoods that capture all possible configurations in which foreground and background voxels can occur. By using different sets of templates in the iterative thinning, both surface skeletons and centerlines can be computed [Manzanera et al. 99, Palagyi and Kuba 99]. Moreover, voxels can be removed in increasing order of the distance-to-boundary, e.g., by first computing a distance transform of the foreground voxels, using one of the methods presented earlier in Section 9.4.4. However, in order to achieve higher speeds, several thinning algorithms do not compute an accurate distance transform to drive the removal order. For example, the *parallel* thinning algorithms achieve high speeds by deleting a whole set of such points at a time, e.g., by iteratively scanning the 3D volume in a set of left-right, bottom-top, back-front passes [Manzanera et al. 99, Palagyi and Kuba 99, Vilanova et al. 99].

Thinning methods can produce one-dimensional centerlines of 3D shapes with guaranteed connectivity and one-voxel thickness, and can easily handle shapes of arbitrary genus, thereby delivering centerlines with correspondingly many loops and branching points. Also, parallel thinning methods trade off centeredness for speed. More importantly, thinning noisy shapes typically leads to noisy centerlines. Although subsequent pruning of the centerline voxel graph, e.g., by removing centerline voxels close to branch end points, can deliver less-noisy structures, centerlines produced by thinning methods are overall characterized by a fair amount of noise.

Distance field methods. In contrast to thinning methods, which take a local approach based on connectivity templates to define the centerline, *distance field* methods take a more global approach. These methods compute the boundary's distance transform (DT) and define the centerline based on the DT's local maxima or "ridges," similar to the computation of two-dimensional skeletons from the DT singularities discussed earlier in Section 9.4.5. However, detecting such maxima using a discrete 3D distance transform usually yields a set of disconnected points, just as in 2D. This process is also quite sensitive to small-scale noise or details present on the shape boundary. In order to produce a connected, noise-free centerline, several strategies can be further applied. First, the extracted (disconnected) DT maxima can be explicitly connected by one-dimensional curves that are forced by construction to locally follow the DT ridges and also have

the desired smoothness [Zhou et al. 98, Zhou and Toga 99]. Another class
of distance-based methods extracts single-curve centerlines, i.e., centerlines
without branches, by computing the distance transform gradient and finding voxels on and close to the centerline by analyzing the gradient's local
variations, followed by reconnection of these voxels [Bitter et al. 00]. The
final centerline is computed by applying various cost-based path-tracing
methods on the connected set of extracted voxels. Essentially, this class
of methods can be thought of as fitting a curve model of the centerline in
the three-dimensional space such that various cost functions encoding the
curve's centeredness with respect of the shape boundary and local curve
smoothness are globally minimized. Such centerlines have the desired properties for, e.g., virtual camera path planning in medical applications such
as virtual colonoscopy. However, such algorithms cannot produce the correct centerlines with multiple branches that appear in case of objects with
holes, i.e., with genus higher than zero.

Geodesic methods. The third and last class of centerline methods attempts
to give a more formal, geometrically based definition of the centerline.
Indeed, many thinning and distance field-based methods such as the ones

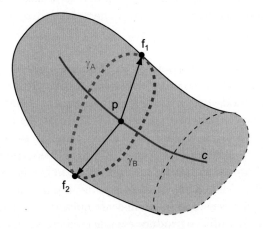

Figure 9.25. Defining centerlines using geodesics between feature points. Point
p has two equal-length shortest geodesics $|\gamma_A| = |\gamma_B|$ (the red and blue dotted
curves) between its feature points f_1 and f_2, so it is on the centerline C.

outlined previously do not explicitly reflect, in their definition, the local circular symmetry that centerlines are supposed to capture. This type of symmetry can be captured as follows. Consider a centerline point $p \in \Omega \subset \mathbb{R}^3$. Since p is a centerline point, it is also a skeleton point following the definition given by Equation (9.28). Hence, there exist at least two different feature points $f_1 \neq f_2 \in \partial\Omega$ that are at equal distance from p. We can use these points to express local symmetry by requiring that, if p is a centerline point, there exist two different shortest-path, or geodesic, curves $\gamma_A \neq \gamma_B \subset \partial\Omega$ that connect f_1 and f_2 and stay on the surface of the considered shape, and have the same length, i.e., $|\gamma_A| = |\gamma_B|$. As sketched in Figure 9.25, this geodesic-based criterion captures the local centeredness of a point with respect to the shape surface.

Geodesic-based centerlines have several advantages. They can be easily computed on voxel surfaces, e.g., using Dijkstra's shortest-path algorithm to find the shortest geodesics [Cormen et al. 01]. If needed, however, they can be computed also for polygonal surfaces using a piecewise-linear approximation of geodesics [Dey and Sun 06]. Being defined based on the existence of two different feature points, these centerlines are naturally part of the 3D skeleton. Yet, their computation involves tracing geodesics on the shape surface and comparing their lengths, an operation that is of integral nature, hence stable and robust with respect to the shape discretization, as compared, e.g., to finding local maxima of the distance transform. Finally, we can use the geodesics defining the centerline to compute an *importance* for its points. We proceed similarly to the collapsed boundary importance introduced in Section 9.4.6 for defining the importance of skeletal points of two-dimensional shapes. Specifically, if a point p belongs to a centerline as defined by the geodesic-based criterion explained previously, we notice that the two geodesics $\gamma_A \cup \gamma_B$ form a closed loop which, in case of genus zero shapes, divides the shape surface into two parts. We define the importance of p as the area of the smallest of these two parts. Note the analogy to the importance ρ used for two-dimensional skeletons given by Equation (9.29). Just as in 2D, we can now remove spurious centerline branches corresponding to small surface bumps by lower thresholding the importance measure. This area-based importance measure for centerlines is color-coded in Figure 9.23: blue points correspond to less-important centerline parts, while the red points indicate the most-important centerline points corresponding to the shape "core."

9.5   Conclusion

Image-processing techniques are an important and indispensable part of the visualization pipeline. First, such techniques can be used in visualization applications that work on image data to preprocess the input images in order to improve their suitability for further filtering operations, for example by removing noise. Imaging techniques are also useful for postprocessing the images output by visualization applications to help their clarity, e.g., by adjusting contrast and luminance. Finally, image processing can be used as part of the data-enrichment component of the visualization pipeline in order to extract higher-level information content from basic image data. Connected component detection and skeletonization operations fall within this class.

Image processing is a vast field with a long history. For a better overview and understanding of this domain, the reader is advised to study the specialized literature in this domain. A good starting point is provided by the book by Anil Jain [Jain 89], which offers a survey of many imaging techniques used in practice. A comprehensive overview of digital image processing illustrated with examples in MATLAB is provided by the two-book series by Gonzalez, Woods, and Eddins [Gonzalez and Woods 02, Gonzalez et al. 04]. The book by Kenneth Castleman [Castleman 96] offers an easily accessible introduction to image processing that requires a less-extensive mathematical background. For an introduction to image processing illustrated with pseudocode examples and with a particular focus on shape representation and classification, we recommend the book by Costa and Cesar [Costa and Cesar 01].

Finally, let us mention just a few of the many image-processing tools available. For the end user, the freely available GIMP program offers a large number of imaging operations that can be extended by user-written plug-ins [GIMP 06]. For the programmer, the Visualization Toolkit (VTK) [Schroeder et al. 04] and the Insight Registration and Segmentation Toolkit (ITK) [NLM 06] offer hundreds of imaging algorithms in terms of object-oriented libraries usable via several programming languages such as C++, Python, and Java. The OpenCV open-source library provides a rich set of both image-processing and low-level computational geometry algorithms geared toward computer-vision applications, but also easily usable in a general context [OpenCV 07]. In the commercial arena, MATLAB [Math-

Works, Inc. 07] and Mathematica [Wolfram Research, Inc. 07] provide sophisticated environments for both interactive manipulation and visualization of images as well as programming imaging algorithms.

Chapter 10

Volume Visualization

I N Chapter 5, we presented a number of techniques for visualizing scalar fields. Three-dimensional (volumetric) scalar fields are a particular case poses additional problems and difficulties for visualization. Such datasets are common in many application domains. In particular, in medical sciences, there are several types of data-acquisition processes that generate volumetric datasets, such as computed tomography (CT), magnetic resonance imaging (MRI), positron emission tomography (PET), single photon emission computed tomography (SPECT), and ultrasound scans. Such techniques can be used to record anatomical information, such as the shape and composition of various tissues in the human body, but also functional information, such as the concentration of various substances in living tissues (functional MRI). Moreover, these techniques can be used to record still, time-independent scans as well as scans that reveal the dynamic processes in the human body, such as the flow of blood or motion of muscles. As we have seen, such three-dimensional scalar fields can be visualized using techniques such as slice planes and isosurfaces. However, such techniques are limited in showing only a subset of the entire scalar volume.

In this chapter, we shall present a separate class of visualization techniques for volumetric scalar fields. Known in practice under several names, such as volume rendering and volume visualization, these techniques attempt to produce images of an entire three-dimensional scalar volume, as opposed to techniques such as slice planes and isosurfaces, which visualize only a subset of the data. Visualizing an entire volume brings additional insight and lets users discover aspects of the data that are not easily possible with the techniques presented so far. However, volume visualization techniques are confronted with additional difficulties, such as how to show an entire three-dimensional dataset on a two-dimensional image plane, and how to perform this operation efficiently for datasets containing millions of samples.

We begin our exposition by examining the need for volume visualization techniques (Section 10.1). Next, we present the fundamentals of volume visualization techniques (Section 10.2). The next two sections detail the two main classes of volume visualization techniques, called image-order techniques (Section 10.3) and object-order techniques (Section 10.4). Section 10.5 discusses volume visualization techniques, as opposed to their counterparts, which use polygonal geometries. Finally, Section 10.6 concludes the chapter.

10.1   Motivation

Let us consider again the task of visualizing a three-dimensional scalar dataset. For illustration, we consider the same dataset as was used to create the visualizations in Figures 8.1 and 8.2. This is a CT scan of a human head stored as a uniform grid of resolution 128^3 voxels. Each voxel contains a scalar value in the range 0..255. Low values indicate soft tissues, such as skin, whereas high values indicate hard tissues, such as bone. Figure 10.1 illustrates three of the scalar visualization methods discussed in Chapter 5 on this dataset. First, we visualize the boundary of the dataset as a color-mapped surface (see Figure 10.1(a)). Clearly, this visualization is not very useful, as it does not reveal any of the structures contained within the volume. A second option is to reduce the dataset dimensionality from 3 to 2 by slicing the volume with a color-mapped slice plane (see Figure 10.1(b)). This image shows detailed information on the considered 2D slice plane, but ignores all other points of the volume. Finally, we can extract an isosurface for some scalar value of interest (see Figure 10.1(c)). This reveals an interesting structure, in this case the skin surface, which corresponds to the selected isovalue, but again ignores all volume points that have other values.

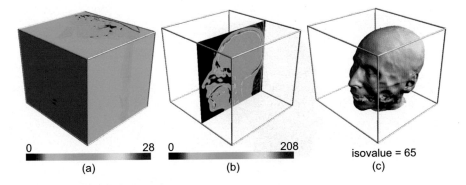

Figure 10.1. Visualizing a 3D scalar dataset. (a) Surface plot. (b) Slice plane. (c) Isosurface.

Essentially, all three methods illustrated in Figure 10.1 reduce the data dimensionality from 3D to 2D by displaying a particular 2D surface embedded in the 3D volume: the dataset boundary (Figure 10.1(a)), all points that have the same y-coordinate (Figure 10.1(b)), and all points that have the scalar value 65 (Figure 10.1(c)) respectively. Such visualizations are useful if we want to focus on a two-dimensional structure in the volume, we know in advance which that structure is, and we can map that structure to some particular condition on the sample point coordinates and/or values. However, in many cases we do not know which two-dimensional subset we would like to extract and examine, or the structures we are interested in are simply not to be reduced to two-dimensional surfaces. In such cases, volume-visualization techniques are a good candidate.

To introduce the concept of volume visualization, let us consider two examples based on techniques we have presented so far: isosurfaces and slice planes. Figure 10.2 shows two isosurfaces for the head CT scan dataset corresponding to the skin (isovalue = 65) and bone (isovalue = 127) materials, respectively. The isosurfaces are rendered using different colors. Also, the skin isosurface has a high transparency, and the bone isosurface has a low transparency. Compared to Figure 10.1(c), this visualization shows more information, i.e., the location in space of two structures (skin and bone) compared to a single structure (skin). We could generalize this idea by adding more isosurfaces for other scalar values corresponding to other anatomical structures, each with a different color and transparency.

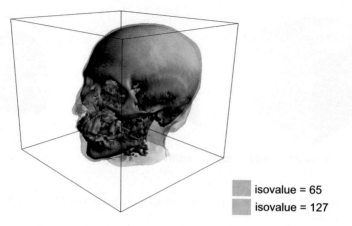

Figure 10.2. Visualization consisting of two isosurfaces.

As a second example, we could generalize the slice plane technique by visualizing several half-transparent slice planes in the same image. Figure 10.3 illustrates this idea. In Figure 10.3(a), 10 color-mapped slices are rendered that are orthogonal to, and at equal distances along, the y-axis.

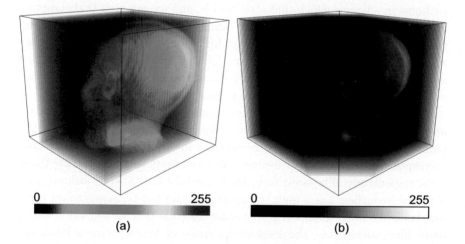

Figure 10.3. Visualization of scalar volume using (a) volume-aligned slices and (b) view direction-aligned slices

The transparency of each slice is 0.1, where 0 denotes full transparency and 1 full opacity. In the middle of the translucent structure created by the blending of the half-transparent slices, we see a structure emerging in the shape of the human head. Figure 10.3(b) illustrates a second variation on the half-transparent slices technique. Here, 10 slices are rendered, this time being orthogonal to, and at equal distances along, the viewing direction. Also, this visualization uses a grayscale colormap. We see a similar structure emerging from the slice blending, where the amount of white reflects the amount of material density at each pixel along the viewing direction.

The two examples shown in Figure 10.3 are coarse approximations of the volume-rendering technique. Although such visualizations are definitely of too low quality to be usable in practice, they illustrate the main ideas behind the volume-rendering technique. In the following section, we shall see how we can extend and perfect the idea of blending half-transparent colored structures to create insightful visualizations of 3D scalar datasets.

10.2   Volume Visualization Basics

The basic idea behind volume rendering is simple: create a two-dimensional image that reflects, at every pixel, the scalar data within a given 3D dataset along a ray parallel to the viewing direction passing through that pixel. The main power of volume visualization is in the choice of the function that maps an entire set of scalar values, corresponding to the voxels along such a ray, to a single pixel in the resulting 2D image. Appropriate choices for this function let us convey a wide range of insights into volumetric scalar datasets.

Figure 10.4 illustrates the conceptual idea. Consider a rectangular image area I in the viewing plane and a scalar signal $s : D \to \mathbb{R}$ defined on a volumetric domain D. For simplicity, let us first consider that D is a uniform dataset consisting of equally sized cubic voxels. For every pixel p of the image I, we trace a ray $\mathbf{r}$ perpendicular to the image plane, which will intersect the volume D in the points q_0 and q_1 respectively. The value $I(p)$ of the pixel p is going to be a function of the data values along the ray $\mathbf{r}$ between q_0 and q_1. We can express this easily by parameterizing the ray points q between q_0 and q_1 as $q(t) = (1 - t)q_0 + tq_1$ with $t \in [0, T]$. We denote the scalar values of these points by $s(t)$. Putting it all together, we

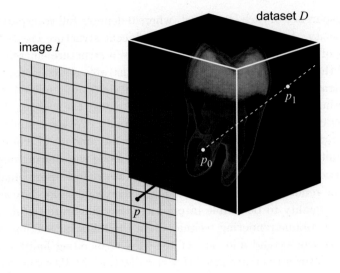

Figure 10.4. Conceptual principle of volume visualization.

can express the value of the image pixel p as

$$I(p) = F(s(t)), \quad t \in [0, 1]. \tag{10.1}$$

In the equation, $F : \mathbb{R} \to \mathbb{R}^3$ is the so-called *ray function*, which synthesizes the RGB color of the pixel p from the scalar values along the ray $\mathbf{r}$ corresponding to p. Different types of ray functions implement different visualization scenarios focusing on various aspects of a volume dataset. A number of ray functions frequently met in practice are discussed in the next sections.

10.2.1 Classification

At the core of every ray function, there is a common mechanism that maps the information from every point along the ray to a color and opacity (RGBA) value. This mechanism is called a *transfer function*, and is identical to the concept of the same name that we introduced in Chapter 5 when we discussed the scalar-to-color mapping technique. The most commonly used transfer functions map scalar values to colors and opacities. Hence, we can denote a transfer function by $f : \mathbb{R} \to [0, 1]^4$, or alternatively by its four components f_R, f_G, f_B, and f_A, each taking values in the $[0, 1]$ interval.

The transfer functions f are used in volume rendering to associate a color and opacity with desired scalar values or value ranges. The ray function F is used to combine the scalar values along a ray, together with the application of the transfer function f, and produce a single RGBA value per ray. Since such values typically correspond to different materials in the dataset, choosing suitable transfer functions enables us to create visualizations in which different materials will look different. Note that the same ray function F can be (and typically is) used with different transfer functions f. Indeed, while the transfer function specifies how a single scalar value is mapped to a single color, the ray function specifies how all the information along a given ray is mapped to a single pixel color. The process of designing and applying transfer functions to visually separate different types of materials based on their scalar values is known as *classification*. Choosing the right transfer functions, ray function, and additional visualization parameters to create a good classification is a difficult process that is crucial to obtaining effective visualizations.

Although the most common volumetric transfer functions map material density, or scalar value, to color and opacity, many other possibilities for classifying volume data exist. For example, one can use the gradient of the recorded scalar field to distinguish between different types of tissues [Levoy 88]. Using the gradient is essentially equivalent to an edge-detection operation performed on the volume data. This is useful when we want to focus on the sharp transitions of the data, i.e., borders between different materials, and ignore (large) homogeneous regions of near-constant values. For datasets where several scalar fields have been recorded over the same volume, combinations of the values of different fields, or their gradients, can be used. For example, some applications use an opacity transfer function that is the product of a scalar opacity function and a scalar gradient opacity function.

Classification can also be done as a separate preprocessing step prior to volume visualization. In this case, the output of the classification stage is a scalar volume dataset $c : \mathbb{D} \rightarrow \mathbb{R}$ that encodes the type of tissue at every voxel in a scalar value c. The selection technique discussed in Section 8.2 that produces a binary signal encoding selected voxels is a simple example of classification. Many additional sources of information, besides the scalar values, can be used to perform classification, such as distinguishing between tissues based on position information. When available, the transfer functions can use such a preclassified volume to map the classification information to visual appearance.

In the following sections, we shall present some of the most-used transfer functions in volume visualization. At the same time, we shall detail the construction of transfer functions used for classification of materials based on their scalar values.

10.2.2   Maximum Intensity Projection Function

One of the simplest transfer functions used in volume rendering is the *maximum intensity projection (MIP)*. For a pixel p, the MIP function first computes the maximum scalar value along the ray $\mathbf{r}$ of p, and then maps this value via the chosen transfer function f to the color of pixel p. Using the parameterized ray notation we can express the MIP ray function as

$$I(p) = f(\max_{t \in [0,T]} s(t)). \tag{10.2}$$

A second variant of the MIP function computes the maximum opacity along the ray instead of the maximum scalar value. For this, opacities for all points along the ray are computed using the opacity transfer function f_A. The ray pixel will finally take the color of the ray point that has the maximum opacity. In other words,

$$I(p) = f(s_m), \qquad f_A(s_m) = \max_{t \in [0,T]} f_A(s(t)). \tag{10.3}$$

This variant of the MIP function is useful if we want to emphasize in the rendering the presence of a given material. To do this, we can design an opacity function f_A that is maximal for that material, together with corresponding color transfer functions f_R, f_G, f_B. With this design, the material of interest will show up in the rendering with the chosen colors, even if its scalar value is not necessarily maximal. A third variant of the MIP function assigns to the current pixel the maximum of the intensities (colors) of all pixels computed along the viewing ray. This function emphasizes the "brightest" pixels.

As we see in Equation (10.2), the MIP function first reduces the scalars along the entire ray to a single (maximum) value, and then applies the

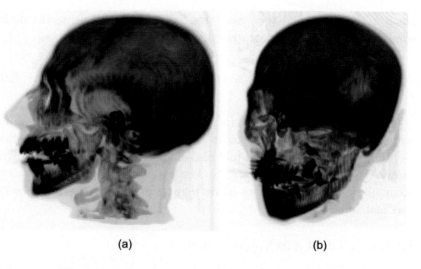

(a)   (b)

Figure 10.5. Maximum intensity projection rendering.

transfer function f to this value. The MIP ray function is useful to extract high-intensity structures from volumetric data. One typical usage of MIP is to extract vascular structures from medical MRI datasets, e.g., in angiography applications. However, MIP-rendered volumes fail to convey depth information. In other words, we see what the maximum intensity along a ray is, but not at what position (depth) along the ray that value occurs. Figure 10.5 shows two volume-rendered images of a human head CT dataset. Here, the transfer function used associates a gray value proportional to the scalar value, where white corresponds to the lowest scalar value (air) and black to the highest value (hard bone). The left image is easier to interpret than the right image, since it is taken from an angle where the lack of depth information is not so disturbing. One solution used in practice to compensate for the lack of depth information in MIP images is to animate the viewpoint and visualize the entire sequence of MIP renderings taken from several angles with close values.

10.2.3 Average Intensity Function

A second simple ray function is the *average intensity*. Similar to the maximal intensity projection, we compute the average intensity, or scalar value, along a given ray, and then map this value to a color using the desired transfer function. We can express this function as

$$I(p) = f\left(\frac{\int_{t=0}^{T} s(t)dt}{T}\right). \tag{10.4}$$

Intuitively speaking, the average intensity ray function produces volume renderings that are analogous to an X-ray image of the considered dataset, i.e., they emphasize the total material amount along each viewing ray. In contrast to the MIP function, the average intensity function shows the accumulation of scalar values along a ray rather than the presence of a maximal value.

10.2.4   Distance to Value Function

The third considered ray function is the *distance to value*. Given a fixed scalar value σ, this function computes for each pixel the distance along the viewing ray to the first point where the scalar value is at least σ and maps this distance via the transfer function

$$I(p) = f\left(\min_{t \in [0,T], s(t) \geq \sigma} t\right). \tag{10.5}$$

This function is useful in revealing the minimal depth, within the volumetric dataset, where a certain value σ is exceeded. Note that, in contrast to the previous ray functions, the focus is now on the *position* (depth) where a certain scalar value is met, not on the scalar *value* itself.

10.2.5   Isosurface Function

Ray functions can also be used to construct familiar isosurface structures. In order to construct the isosurface for a given scalar value σ, we must detect the presence, along a ray, of at least one point with the value σ. If such a point is found, the ray's pixel gets the color corresponding to the isovalue σ. If not, the pixel is assigned a "background" color I_0. This is expressed by the ray function

$$I(p) = \begin{cases} f(\sigma), & \exists t \in [0, T], s(t) = \sigma, \\ I_0, & \text{otherwise.} \end{cases} \tag{10.6}$$

If we directly apply this ray function, we only obtain a "binary" image consisting of two colors, i.e., $f(\sigma)$ and I_0, which is identical to rendering the desired isosurface with ambient color $f(\sigma)$ but without any shading. Of course, such a visualization is not directly useful. In practice, the isosurface ray function becomes useful when combined with volumetric shading, a topic which is further described in Section 10.2.7.

Figure 10.6 shows an isosurface of the tooth volume dataset computed using several methods. In particular, we see that the isosurface computed with the marching cubes method (Figure 10.6(a)) and the isosurface ray function (Figure 10.6(b)) are very similar.

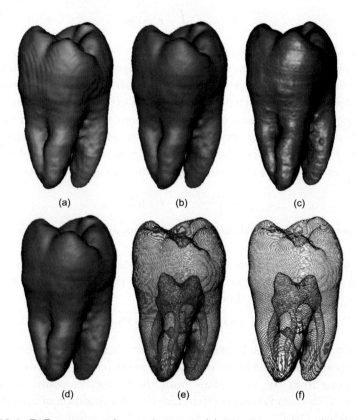

Figure 10.6. Different isosurface techniques. (a) Marching cubes. (b) Isosurface ray function, software ray casting. (c) Graphics hardware ray casting. (d–f) Compositing with box opacity function, different integration step sizes.

10.2.6 Compositing Function

The previous ray functions can be seen as particular instances of a more general ray function called the *compositing function*. To explain the compositing function, we shall consider a simple volumetric illumination model. In this model, we assume that the color $C(p)$ of a given pixel p is a superposition of the contributions of the colors $c(t)$ of all voxels $q(t)$ along the ray $\mathbf{r}(p)$ corresponding to the pixel p. Let us denote by $C(t)$ the contribution to C of a given voxel $q(t)$ that has the color $c(t)$. Then $C(p)$ can be expressed as an integral of the contributions of all points along the viewing ray:

$$C(p) = \int_{t=0}^{T} C(t)dt. \qquad (10.7)$$

Now we must compute the contribution $C(t)$ of $q(t)$ to the pixel p. In our illumination model, we assume that every pixel $q(t)$ along the ray emits light having the color (and intensity) given by $c(t)$, and also absorbs, or attenuates, the light emitted by other pixels $q(t'), t' > t$ that are further from the image plane than $q(t)$. If we denote the attenuation factor at position x by $\tau x \in [0,1]$, we can express the decrease of the cumulative intensity $C(t)$, as we look along the ray from position x toward the pixel at $x = 0$, or more usefully the increase of intensity dC/dx at position x, as

$$\frac{dC(t,x)}{dx} = -\tau(x)c(x). \qquad (10.8)$$

In this setup, the attenuation can also be thought of in terms of material opacity.

By integrating Equation (10.8) along the viewing ray from $x = 0$ to the position of the current point $x = t$, we obtain the contribution $C(t)$ of the point at position t to the final pixel color:

$$C(t) = c(t)e^{-\int_0^t \tau(x)dx}. \qquad (10.9)$$

Intuitively, Equation (10.9) states that a point's contribution on the view plane exponentially decreases with the integral (cumulative value) of the attenuations from the view plane until the respective point. If we now substitute $C(t)$ from Equation (10.9) into the superposition of contributions (see Equation (10.7)), we obtain an integral illumination model:

$$C(p) = \int_{t=0}^{T} c(t)e^{-\int_0^t \tau(x)dx}dt. \qquad (10.10)$$

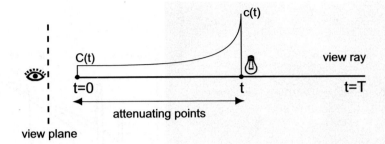

Figure 10.7. Volumetric illumination model: color $c(t)$ emitted at position t along a view ray gets attenuated by the values $\tau(x)$ of the points x situated between t and the view plane to yield the contribution $C(t)$ of $c(t)$ to the view plane.

The illumination model implemented by Equation (10.10) neglects several effects such as scattering or shadows. Nevertheless, this model is capable of producing high-quality images of volumetric datasets. The ray function implementing the previous illumination model is called a *compositing* function, as it superimposes, or composes, the intensities of all voxels along a given ray. Just as for the ray functions presented previously, the color c and attenuation τ for the composite ray function are computed using transfer functions based on the scalar value $s(t)$ along the ray.

Several choices are available when evaluating the composite ray function. Just as for the other ray functions, the color and opacity (attenuation) transfer functions control the material classification process. In contrast to the other ray functions, the composite ray function applies the transfer functions at every point along the ray and then combines their color and opacity results. Using appropriate transfer functions, this allows several materials along a ray to become visible in the final rendered image.

Figure 10.8 shows a first example of a composite ray function used to volume render the head dataset.[1] Here, we designed the transfer functions in such a way as to emphasize three types of tissues. In order of material density, or scalar value, these are skin, soft bone (present in the skull tissue), and hard bone (present in the teeth). We emphasize these three tissues using high-opacity values for their corresponding density ranges, as shown by the transfer function f_A (see Figure 10.8(b)). For the remaining

---

[1]The images in Figures 10.8 and 10.10 are produced by the freely available volume rendering software of Klaus Engel [Engel 02].

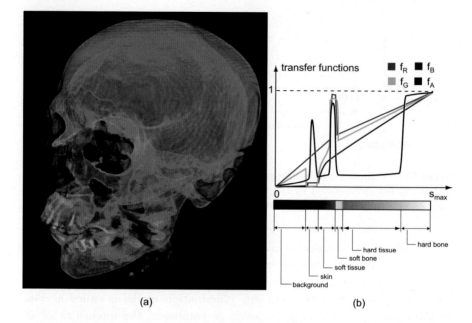

(a)   (b)

Figure 10.8. (a) Volume rendering of head dataset. (b) The transfer function used emphasizes soft tissue, soft bone, and hard bone.

density ranges, i.e., soft tissue such as muscles, and hard tissue ranging between the soft bone and hard bone values, we use low-opacity values. Next to this, we design the color transfer functions f_R, f_G, and f_B so that skin is rendered in dark brown, soft bone in light yellow, and hard bone in bright white, respectively, as shown by the color bar in Figure 10.8(b).

The design of appropriate color and opacity transfer functions is crucial for an effective material classification based on the scalar value. Several observations can be made here. First, in most cases, there is no hard border that separates different tissues in volumetric scanned datasets, but rather a (narrow) transition area where one type of tissue smoothly changes into another. Hence, the transfer and opacity functions used to visually separate different tissues should also have smooth variations across the transition area rather than abrupt, step-like jumps (see Figure 10.8(b)). This design also helps reduce the number of visual artifacts in case of noisy, coarsely sampled datasets.

A second choice regards the evaluation of the rendering integral given by Equation (10.10). An accurate, but slower, method is to evaluate the integral by taking samples along the ray in front-to-back order (see Section 10.3). A different approach approximates the rendering integral using back-to-front blending of textured polygons in graphics hardware (see Section 10.4). In both cases, the choice of the volume-sampling strategy is essential to obtaining high-quality renderings. Finally, let us note that several of the previously described ray functions can be seen as particular cases of the composite ray function, although this does not mean they are implemented in practice using the composite function. For example, the isosurface ray function would use a zero attenuation $\tau = 0$ everywhere and a zero emission $c(t) = 0$ except for the isovalue t_0. This is how the isosurface in Figures 10.6(d–f) are computed. The result is clearly very similar to the geometric isosurface computed by marching cubes (see Figure 10.6(a)) and the one computed using the isosurface ray function (see Figure 10.6(b)).

Let us note that volume rendering can also be applied to other datasets than scanned datasets containing material density values. Figure 10.9 illustrates this. Here, we visualize the velocity magnitude scalar field of the

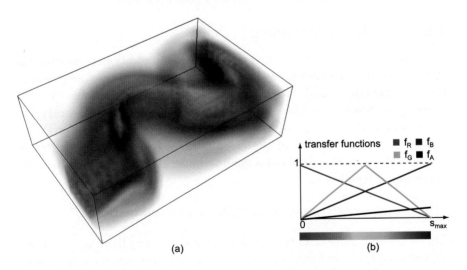

(a)   (b)

Figure 10.9. (a) Volume rendering of flow field velocity magnitude and (b) corresponding transfer functions.

3D flow field used in several of the visualization examples from Chapter 6 (e.g., Figure 6.8). The transfer functions f_R, f_G, f_B, and f_A that are used to map the scalar range $[0, s_{max}]$ to color and opacity respectively are shown in Figure 10.9(b). The opacity function has quite low values, thereby creating a half-transparent visualization that allows us to distinguish the deeper-nested, high-velocity flow structures. Using these functions, transparent, red areas indicate low-velocity points, whereas opaque, cold-colored (green and blue) areas indicate the high-velocity flow core. Compare this result with the visualization shown in Figure 6.9, where the flow core is displayed using an isosurface.

Although volume renderings of any scalar fields are possible, such as shown in Figure 10.9, the results can sometimes be harder to interpret than when volume rendering anatomical structures encoded in density fields. There are two reasons for this. First, CT and MRI datasets show structures that often are, by their own nature, easier to interpret than arbitrary volumetric scalar fields, when using the appropriate color and/or opacity transfer functions. Second, some volume datasets, such as the velocity magnitude field in Figure 10.9, exhibit no natural boundaries between regions with different scalar values. In contrast, in MRI and CT datasets, different tissues having different densities create such separations.

10.2.7   Volumetric Shading

As mentioned previously, shading is an important additional cue that can significantly increase the quality of volume renderings. In the case of isosurfaces (see Section 10.2.5), for example, shading is an indispensable element. Shading can be easily combined with the volume illumination integral given by Equation (10.10). Instead of directly using the colors $c(t) = f(s(t))$ delivered by the application of the color transfer function f on the scalar values $s(t)$ along the ray in the volume integral, we can use instead an illumination function

$$I(t) = c_{amb} + c_{diff}(t) \max(-\mathbf{L} \cdot \mathbf{n}(t), 0) + c_{spec}(t) \max(-\mathbf{r} \cdot \mathbf{v}, 0)^\alpha. \quad (10.11)$$

This is nothing more than the application of the Phong lighting model (see Equation (2.1)) to an imaginary surface located at the current point t along the ray, having the normal $\mathbf{n}$. Here, c_{amb} is the ambient lighting factor, which is constant for the entire volume. $c_{diff}(t)$ and $c_{spec}(t)$ are the diffuse and specular lighting factors, respectively, which are typically functions of position t. In a simple approximation, we can set $c_{\text{diff}}(t) = c_{\text{spec}}(t) = c(t)$. The vectors $\mathbf{L}$, $\mathbf{r}$, and $\mathbf{v}$ have the same meaning as in the original Phong lighting model (Equation (2.1)).

To apply the preceding lighting model, we need to estimate a surface normal $\mathbf{n}(t)$. For most locations in a volume dataset, we cannot actually speak about the existence of a physical surface. However, we can define such a surface as being the isosurface for the isovalue $s(t)$, which exists for every point. As explained in Section 5.3, the gradient of a function is normal to the function's contours. Hence, we can estimate the normal $\mathbf{n}(t)$ by computing the gradient vector of the scalar signal s

$$\nabla s(t) = \frac{\partial s(t)}{\partial x} + \frac{\partial s(t)}{\partial y} + \frac{\partial s(t)}{\partial z} \tag{10.12}$$

and normalizing the result to unit length. The partial derivatives of s with respect to the coordinate axes x, y, z can be computed as described in Section 3.7 by interpolating the discrete partial derivatives evaluated at the voxel corners.

Although this solution is possible, it can deliver noisy results in practice, as the gradient is quite sensitive to small-scale noise in the sampled dataset. This translates into small-scale wavy artifacts in the final shading, which are quite disturbing, especially if specular lighting is used. To enhance the robustness of the gradient estimation, we can apply several of the filtering techniques discussed for image processing in Chapter 9, such as the Sobel or Prewitt operators, or prefilter the scalar dataset prior to the gradient estimation.

Figure 10.10 illustrates the effects of volumetric lighting on a dataset rendered with a composite ray function. The transfer functions emphasize the hard tooth enamel (white, opaque) and the softer dentine material (brown, semi-transparent). The first image (Figure 10.10(a)) does not use volumetric lighting. Although we can observe the internal structure of the tooth, due to the low opacity, the actual material separation surfaces are hard to grasp from this static image. The middle image, which uses volumetric diffuse lighting, is significantly easier to understand due to the shading cues. The right image, which uses specular lighting, is similar to the middle image. The added value of volumetric shading is also visible

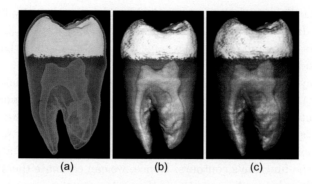

(a)   (b)   (c)

Figure 10.10. Volumetric lighting. (a) No lighting. (b) Diffuse lighting. (c) Specular lighting.

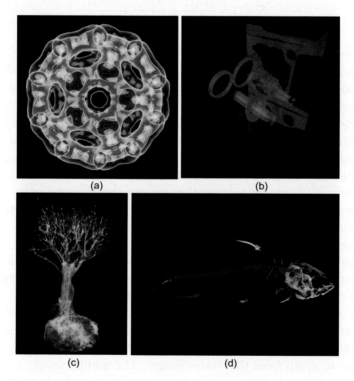

(a)   (b)

(c)   (d)

Figure 10.11. Examples of volume rendering. (a) Electron density. (b) Engine block. (c) Bonsai tree. (d) Carp fish.

if we compare Figure 10.8, produced without lighting, with Figure 10.12, which uses a combination of diffuse and specular lighting.

All in all, volume visualization techniques offer a rich set of possibilities in terms of the transfer functions, shading model, and material properties used. These allow us to create insightful, but also aesthetically pleasing renderings of volumetric datasets. Figure 10.11 shows a collection of visualizations of a variety of datasets created using different volume-rendering techniques and settings.[2] In the first example (Figure 10.11(a)), the electron density distribution in a complex molecule is visualized. The second example (Figure 10.11(b)) shows an engine block. Using an appropriate opacity map exposes the inner details of the engine structure to the viewer. The third example (Figure 10.11(c)) shows a bonsai tree. The fourth example (Figure 10.11(d)) shows a carp fish with the opacity transfer function set to emphasize the skeletal structure.

10.3   Image Order Techniques

The most straightforward way to implement Equation (10.10) is to evaluate the rendering integral by taking samples along the viewing rays. Given the way it works, this algorithm is also known as *volumetric ray casting*. The entire volume-rendering algorithm reduces to a sequence of nested for loops as illustrated in the following pseudocode:

```
for(all pixels p in the image plane I)
{
    v = ray perpendicular to I passing through p;
    q0,q1 = intersections of v with the volume;
    C(p) = 0; //color of pixel p
    for(float t=0;t<1;t+=Δt)
    {
        q = (1 − t)q0 + tq1 ;
        C(p)+ = c(t)e^{−∫_0^t τ(x)dx} Δt ;
    }
}
```

---

[2]The datasets in Figure 10.11 are from the public Volume Library [Roettger 06b]. The volume visualization software is the freely available Versatile Volume Viewer by Stefan Roettger [Roettger 06a].

Since the algorithm processes the image pixels one by one, it falls into a more general class of methods called *image-order* or *image-based* techniques. Another image-based technique discussed in Chapter 6 was the image-based flow visualization (IBFV) method, which generates textured views of vector fields (see Section 6.6).

Several acceleration strategies can be applied to the basic algorithm presented here. The inner integral $\int_0^t \tau(x)dx$ can be evaluated incrementally during the evaluation of the outer integral, i.e., during the front-to-back ray traversal. The same can be done if we evaluate the ray integral back-to-front, i.e., summing up the voxels' contributions from the furthest to the closest one to the view plane. If we discretize the ray using uniform steps of length δ, the volume integral in Equation (10.10) can be written as

$$C(p) = \sum_{i=0}^{N} c(i\delta)e^{-\sum_{j=0}^{i-1}\tau(j\delta)\delta}\delta. \tag{10.13}$$

By replacing the inner exponential term with a product of exponents of each term of the inner sum, we obtain

$$C(p) = \sum_{i=0}^{N} c(i\delta)\left(\prod_{j=0}^{i-1} e^{-\tau(j\delta)\delta}\right)\delta. \tag{10.14}$$

Here, $N = D/\delta$ is the number of sample points taken along the ray. Now, for small step sizes δ, we can approximate the exponential terms of the inner sum using the first term of a Taylor expansion, i.e., $e^{-t} \approx 1 - t$ for small values of t. Substituting this in Equation (10.14), we obtain

$$C(p) = \sum_{i=0}^{N} c(i\delta)\left(\prod_{j=0}^{i-1} (1 - \tau(j\delta)\delta)\right)\delta. \tag{10.15}$$

Let us now denote $c_i = c(i\delta)\delta$ and $\tau_j = \tau(j\delta)\delta$. We obtain

$$C(p) = \sum_{i=0}^{N} c_i \left(\prod_{j=0}^{i-1} (1 - \tau_j)\right). \tag{10.16}$$

We can evaluate Equation (10.16) in back-to-front order, i.e., from higher to lower indices. If we denote by C_i the accumulated color at position i

due to the contributions of the sample points $i..N$, we notice that

$$
\begin{aligned}
C_N &= c_N, \\
C_{N-1} &= c_{N-1} + (1 - \tau_{N-1})C_N, \\
&\vdots \\
C(p) = C_0 &= c_0 + (1 - \tau_0)c_1 + (1 - \tau_0)(1 - \tau_1)c_2 + \ldots .
\end{aligned}
\tag{10.17}
$$

These equations state that we can evaluate the composite ray function of a pixel by the back-to-front evaluation of a simple expression at every sample point i along the ray

$$
C_i = c_i + (1 - \tau_i)C_{i+1}.
\tag{10.18}
$$

This is nothing more than the back-to-front blending of the colors c_i multiplied by the opacities τ_i. Indeed, it states that the color accumulated at sample point i equals the emission c_i of sample point i itself plus the contribution C_{i+1} of the points $i..N$ times the transparency $1 - \tau_i$ of point i. Hence, evaluating the composite ray function can be seen as a particular case of alpha blending. In Section 10.4, we shall show how Equation (10.18) can be efficiently evaluated using the alpha blending provided by graphics hardware.

A similar expression to Equation (10.18) can be deduced for the front-to-back ray traversal. In this case, together with the accumulated color C_i over the samples $0..i$, we can also compute the accumulated opacity. Once the accumulated opacity reaches a value close to the maximum of 1, e.g., 0.95, we can stop tracing the ray further on the volume, as deeper points will have practically no influence on the final pixel color $C(p)$. This strategy, called *early ray termination*, can save substantial computational time, e.g., for datasets containing numerous high-opacity voxels.

10.3.1 Sampling and Interpolation Issues

The quality of a volume-rendered image depends on the accuracy of evaluating the discretized integral in Equation (10.13). Two main issues are involved here:

- the choice of the step size δ;

- the interpolation of color c and opacity τ along the ray.

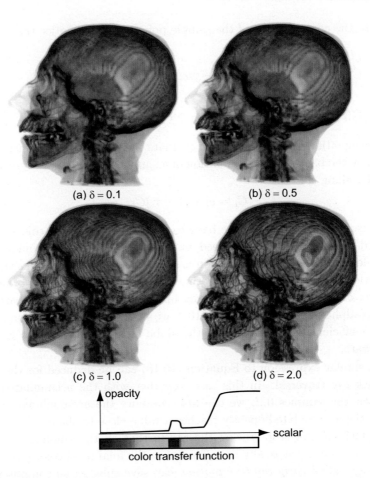

Figure 10.12. Volume rendering of head dataset for different values of the integration step size (in voxels). The color and opacity transfer functions used are shown at the bottom of the image.

As expected, smaller step sizes δ give better results, but increase the computation time. A better strategy is to correlate the step size with the data variation, i.e., take smaller steps where the data changes rapidly and larger steps over near-constant data regions. Since both c and τ are dependent on the choice of the transfer functions used, the choice of the step size should involve the characteristics of these functions as well. In practice, a good

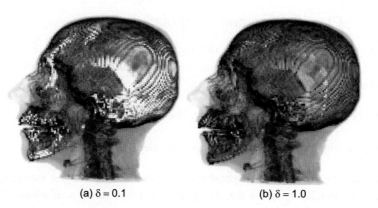

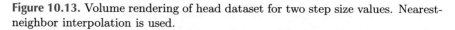

(a) $\delta = 0.1$ (b) $\delta = 1.0$

Figure 10.13. Volume rendering of head dataset for two step size values. Nearest-neighbor interpolation is used.

starting estimate is to set δ to values in the range of the voxel size, to ensure at least that every voxel contributes to the result.

Since the sample points i along a ray will, in general, not coincide with voxel centers, interpolation must be performed to evaluate c_i and τ_i. The simplest choice here is to use nearest-neighbor interpolation, i.e., use the color and opacity values respectively of the nearest voxel centers to every sample point i. This is also the computationally most efficient solution. As explained in Chapter 3, nearest-neighbor interpolation yields discontinuous signals, which translates into low-quality images.

A better solution is to use trilinear interpolation. This method produces smoother images for the same sampling resolution, albeit at a slightly higher computational cost. Figure 10.12 shows a volume rendering of the head dataset using a composite transfer function for several values of the step size δ, using trilinear interpolation. Strong color-banding artifacts alternating between dark yellow and red appear for step sizes larger than $\delta = 1$ voxel. In contrast, the image quality for the $\delta = 0.5$ and $\delta = 0.1$ step sizes looks almost identical.

Figure 10.13 shows the head dataset rendered with the same transfer functions for the step sizes $\delta = 0.1$ and $\delta = 1.0$, this time using the nearest-neighbor interpolation. The individual voxels become more apparent in these renderings as compared with the equivalent ones using linear interpolation (Figure 10.12(a–b)).

10.3.2   Classification and Interpolation Order

If trilinear interpolation along the ray is used, we have two choices with respect to the order of classification, i.e., evaluation of the color and opacity transfer functions, and interpolation. These are as follows:

- pre-classification: first classify, then interpolate;

- post-classification: first interpolate, then classify.

In general, pre-classification produces coarser-looking images, especially for color and opacity transfer functions that exhibit sharp variations. Moreover, color interpolation can sometimes produce wrong results. Interpolating between colors can create, for example, colors that never occur in the color transfer function codomain (colormap). In contrast, post-classification produces smoother images that only contain valid colors from the corresponding colormap. However, post-classification does interpolate the scalars, which uses the implicit assumption that the original signal is

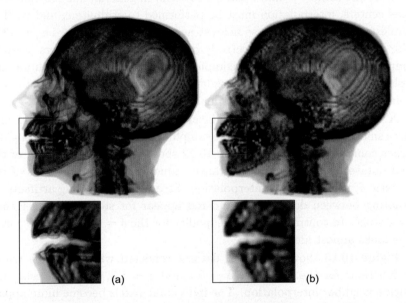

Figure 10.14. Comparison of (a) post-classification and (b) pre-classification techniques. The insets show a zoomed-in detail region from the large image.

piecewise continuous between the voxel centers. Hence, scalar interpolation may yield values that correspond to nonexistent materials at points where the sampled dataset exhibits inherent discontinuities. A similar phenomenon was discussed for image data in Section 9.4.6 (see Figure 9.20). Finally, let us note that the results of pre-classification and post-classification look very similar for smoothly varying datasets and transfer functions.

Figure 10.14 demonstrates the differences between pre- and post-classification. The left image shows the post-classification order, which is also the usual one in most applications. The image looks quite crisp. The right image shows the same dataset rendered with the pre-classification strategy. The result looks significantly more blurred.

10.4 Object-Order Techniques

A second class of volume rendering implementations is formed by *object-order* techniques. In contrast to image-order techniques, which traverse all pixels of the view plane once and evaluate the ray function for each pixel separately, object-order techniques traverse each object voxel once, and evaluate its contribution to the image pixel whose ray intersects that voxel. Hence, whereas image-order techniques visit every pixel once, object-order techniques visit the same image pixel multiple times, as a function of the number of voxels that contribute to its final color.

One of the most popular object-order methods is volume rendering using textures accelerated by graphics hardware. The main idea of this method is simple: evaluate the composite ray integral in back-to-front order, as described by Equations (10.17) and (10.18), using the high-speed texture-rendering capabilities of graphics hardware. Depending on the actual type of textures supported by the graphics hardware, two subclasses of methods exist, as follows. Two-dimensional texture methods assume only the support of 2D textures by the graphics hardware. To render a dataset, 2D texture methods slice the 3D volume with a set of planes orthogonal to the volume axis that is the most parallel to the viewing direction. This yields a set of parallel rectangles, typically equally spaced along the slicing axis. The rectangles are next textured with the corresponding voxels that they slice from the volume. Each rectangle gets an RGBA texture whose RGB and A values are given by the color and opacity transfer functions c and τ respectively, applied on the sliced voxel scalar values. Finally, the textured rectangles are rendered in back-to-front order with alpha blending enabled. To reproduce the compositing Equation (10.18), we would use in OpenGL additive blending with the blending function `glBlendFunc(GL_ONE,GL_ONE_MINUS_SRC_ALPHA)`. OpenGL additive blending was discussed in more detail in Section 6.6 in the implementation of the IBFV method. Also, let us note that the volume-rendering technique using 2D textures sketched here was used by the 3D IBFV method to create the dense visualizations of 3D flow fields discussed in Section 6.6 (see, e.g., Figure 6.25).

Volume rendering using 2D textures is quite simple to implement, as illustrated by the preceding pseudocode; is considerably faster than the front-to-back software-based ray casting discussed in the previous section; and requires only the support of 2D textures in graphics hardware, which should be available on most current graphics card. However, this method also has several limitations. The most visible is that the image quality is influenced by the viewing angle. Indeed, as we change the viewpoint, the distance between the viewing plane changes, from a minimal value δ reached when we look parallel to one of the volume axes, to a maximum of $\delta\sqrt{3}$ when we look along the volume diagonal. This distance is equivalent to the sampling step size used by the software ray-casting method described in Section 10.3. To prevent this distance from increasing further, which would cause a decrease in quality of the visualization, the volume is resliced anew once the axis most parallel with the view direction changes. This limits the quality decrease, but also creates a visible performance drop when the reslicing occurs, as a new set of 2D textures has to be re-created from the volume data and loaded into the graphics memory.

A better option for volume rendering is to use 3D textures, if these are supported by the available graphics hardware. In this case, the 3D texture is first loaded with the results of the color and opacity transfer functions applied on the entire dataset. Next, the 3D dataset is sliced with a set of planes perpendicular to the viewing direction. This delivers a set of polygons of various shapes, e.g., triangles, quads, pentagons, and hexagons. Finally, the polygons are rendered in back-to-front order, textured with the 3D texture, and blended using the same equation as described earlier for the 2D texture method. The result is functionally the same as for the 2D texture method, but of a higher quality. Indeed, the slice planes are now always parallel to the view plane, and data interpolation both across the view plane as well as along the viewing (slicing) direction is done by the texturing hardware. A second advantage of the 3D texture method is that it does not require regeneration of the texture during the interactive viewpoint manipulation, which can increase interactivity significantly.

However much faster than the software ray-casting method, the 2D and 3D texture methods described here also have some important limitations. First, the maximal dataset that can be rendered is limited by the texture memory available to the graphics card. For example, a graphics card with 256 MB of memory would be able to hold no more than a 3D RGBA texture of $512 \times 512 \times 256$ texels, or equivalently 256 2D textures of 512^2 texels, if we account for one byte per color or opacity component. Second, the straightforward implementation sketched here would only support pre-classification. Post-classification can also be achieved, but this requires the use of more-sophisticated pixel-shader techniques and loading the scalar data volume into a floating-point texture on the graphics card. Finally, if we use the frame buffer to accumulate the alpha blending of the textured slices, the accuracy of the result is limited by the frame buffer precision, which is typically eight bits per pixel per color component. This limits both the number of slice planes that can be drawn as well as the resolution of the color and alpha values that can be stored on each slice. In practice, this means that subtle opacity and/or color variations may be neglected. Again, higher precision can be achieved using modern techniques such as render-to-texture extensions and pixel shaders, at the expense of a relatively more complex implementation.

10.5 Volume Rendering versus Geometric Rendering

The volume-rendering techniques discussed in this chapter have many aspects in common with the geometric (polygonal) rendering techniques discussed in previous chapters. However, there are also a number of important differences between the two. In this section, we provide a brief comparison of the two types of techniques.

First, the *aim* of both types of techniques is often very similar: producing an image of a volumetric dataset that gives insight into the scalar values within. As we have seen, this leads in some cases to identical visualizations that are produced in different ways by volume rendering and geometric techniques. An example is isosurfaces, which can be computed using polygonal marching cubes or volumetric ray casting using an isosurface ray function (see Figure 10.6). Rendering several translucent isosurfaces also creates images that are similar to those produced by composite ray casting techniques using step-wise opacity transfer functions (compare, e.g., Figure 5.16 with Figure 10.10). However, as stated in Section 10.1, the main motivation and advantage of volumetric techniques is that they convey, at each pixel in the final image, insight into more than a few discrete data values. Moreover, whereas geometric rendering techniques always use sharp, clearly delineated primitives, volume rendering is capable of generating softer images, where the data values blend into each other without exhibiting sharp borders. This can better suit datasets where there is no clear-cut separation between different structures.

A second observation concerns the *complexity* of the two types of techniques. For this, let us consider a similar method, e.g., computing isosurfaces, implemented using ray casting versus a marching cubes implementation. Both implementations, in general, scale linearly with the number of dataset cells. However, marching cubes first computes the isosurface as an unstructured polygon mesh, which is then rendered from the desired viewpoint. In contrast, ray-casting techniques would typically need to traverse the volume anew when the viewpoint gets changed. Moreover, geometric techniques such as marching cubes typically compute and render a single geometry regardless of the screen resolution or number of pixels in the rendering window. Their performance is thus not influenced by the window size. In contrast, the performance of ray-casting techniques heavily depends on the number of rays, i.e., the rendering window size. The performance penalty incurred by ray casting tends to decrease in modern implementations that use pixel shaders to evaluate the ray function, yielding near–real-time performance even for large volumes and window sizes.

Volume-rendering techniques using (3D) texture-mapping hardware fall somewhere between purely geometric and ray casting methods. They render a stack of texture-mapped polygons, and their performance is less dependent on the rendering window size than in the case of software ray casting, due to the parallel execution of the pixel-rendering operations on the texture-mapped polygons in graphics hardware. Hence, 3D texture volume-rendering methods are in this respect similar to geometric methods. However, they must first compute a 3D texture volume, and also are viewpoint-dependent, as they must recompute the texture-mapped polygons whenever the viewpoint changes. These are typical attributes of ray-casting methods.

10.6 Conclusion

In this chapter, we have provided an introduction to the field of volume visualization. Volume visualization, also known as volume graphics and volumetric rendering, encompasses the set of techniques aimed at visualizing three-dimensional datasets stored as uniform (voxel) grids. Such techniques are mainly used to visualize scalar datasets. Such datasets occur frequently in medical practice and are acquired by various imaging technologies such as computed tomography and magnetic resonance. However, volume visualization has recently been used also to depict other types of data attributes, such as vectors and tensors, and also on different grid types beyond the uniform ones.

Volume graphics, just as image processing, is a field that has its own evolution. As such, this chapter cannot and does not claim to provide more than a brief overview of the advances, results, and problems encountered in the volume-visualization practice. From a data-visualization perspective, the key element of volume visualization, however, is simple: by rendering a three-dimensional dataset using appropriate per-voxel transfer functions that map data attributes to opacity and color, we can achieve a better, and quicker, understanding of complex volumetric structures than when using other techniques such as slicing and isosurfaces. However, as is often the case, volume visualization does not work best only itself, but in combination with other techniques. In practice, volume rendering is typically combined in applications with slicing, probing, glyphs, and isosurfaces.

Further information on volume visualization and its uses can be sought in the proceedings of the Volume Graphics workshop, published by IEEE Press. The book by Chen et al. on volume graphics provides a state-of-the-art overview of recent technological developments in the field [Chen and Carroll 00]. A different book, authored by Lichtenbelt et al., provides a practical presentation of volume rendering, from the perspective of the practitioner, and also includes software to support the material and datasets to start experimenting with. The book can be used as a hands-on guide to learn volume rendering by doing it, but provides also an extensive list of compiled references of this field. For an incursion into the field of medical visualization, with a focus on volumetric techniques, a highlight is the recent book of Preim and Bartz [Preim and Bartz 07].

Chapter 11

Information
Visualization

11.1   Introduction

IN the previous chapters of this book, we have concentrated our attention on the visualization of datasets that essentially contain the sampling of continuous quantities over compact domains of $\mathbb{R}^n$. We have seen that such datasets occur in many fields, ranging from engineering and computational fluid mechanics and mathematics to medical and Earth sciences. The field that studies the visualization of these data types and targets the aforementioned application domains is known as *scientific visualization (scivis)*. In this chapter, we shall discuss the visualization of a different, more abstract type of data. Examples of such data range from generic graphs and trees to database tables, text, and computer software. The nature of such data, as well as that of the application fields where it is used, generate additional, but also different, requirements and constraints to the visualization process.

The field that studies the visual representation of such data is known as *information visualization (infovis)*. This name is often used to distinguish it from the scivis field. In this chapter, we present a succinct overview of infovis methods and techniques. The ambition of this chapter is far from being a comprehensive presentation of the infovis field. For such a task, an entire book would be more appropriate. The aim of the current presentation is to make the reader aware of the existence of a wealth of visualization techniques and applications which do not directly fall within the focus of scientific visualization. On the other hand, many of the goals of infovis applications and its underlying techniques have interesting overlaps with the corresponding ones in the scivis field. Becoming aware of where the differences and similarities are is important for a deeper and more-nuanced understanding of the visualization discipline.

In Section 11.2, we give a brief characterization of the infovis field from the point of view of its goals, which serves as a starting point in our discussion. In Section 11.3, we discuss the similarities and differences between the scivis and infovis fields from a technical perspective. The following sections detail several of the data types and visualization methods that commonly occur in infovis applications. As illustration, several applications are used, mainly from the field of software engineering. We start in Section 11.4 with the visualization of database tables. Section 11.5 continues with the visualization of relational data, among which we look at trees, graphs, and diagrams. Section 11.6 overviews the visualization of multivariate data. Section 11.7 discusses the visualization of text documents. Section 11.7.3 discusses the visualization of the dynamics of software evolution. Finally, we conclude our incursion into the field of information visualization in Section 11.8.

11.2   What Is Infovis?

Information visualization is arguably the fastest-growing branch of the visualization discipline in the last decade. This rapid and sustained growth is visible both in the various industry branches that make use of infovis applications, ranging from banking, telecom, and the information technology (IT) field to the logistics and administrative departments of large companies. In all these cases, the challenge is the same: the various activities performed by the respective industry generate a huge amount of data. The question that infovis applications attempt to answer is

> *How can we assist users in understanding all that data?*

The dictionary definition of visualization, as quoted from Robert Spence's recent book on information visualization [Spence 07], says that to *visualize* is to "form a mental model or mental image of something." A broad definition of infovis is "visualization applied to abstract quantities and relations in order to get insight in the data" [Chi 02]. We see, thus, that the goals of scivis and infovis are quite similar.

However, infovis applications attempt to visualize a wider spectrum of data types than scivis applications, as we shall see in more detail in the next section. Scivis applications mainly focus on so-called *physical* data, which has an inherent spatial placement, such as the flow of water in a 3D recipient (see Chapter 6) or a medical scan of a patient limb (see Chapter 10). In such cases, the user already has a mental image of what the recipient or the limb looks like. Most importantly, the mental and the physical images overlap considerably—when we are asked to think of that the given limb or recipient looks like, our mental image will most probably bear a strong resemblance to an actual 3D rendering of the respective dataset. This considerably simplifies the visualization task.

In contrast, many infovis applications attempt to help users form a mental image about data that has no physical placement. Information has no "innate shape and color" [Koike 93], so its visualization has a purely abstract character. Information visualization covers areas such as visual reasoning, visual data modeling, visual programming, visual information retrieval and browsing, visualization of program execution, visual languages, visual interface design, and spatial reasoning [Morse et al. 02].

Examples of infovis data, also called *abstract* data, are everywhere in the information society: computer file systems, databases, documents from archives, and stock exchange courses. Clearly, such data have no physical representation.[1] Hence, infovis must cope with the added challenge of finding appropriate visual *representations* for such data. After these are found, they must be adequately *presented* to the user, possibly in an *interactive* setup. These three elements—representation, presentation, and interaction—form the fundamental ingredients of an infovis application [Spence 07].

As we have seen in the previous chapters, many of the users of scivis applications have a scientific or engineering background. These users can easily work with concepts such as data fields, resampling, isosurfaces, and streamlines. Exposing such elements in the user interfaces of scivis applica-

---

[1] One may argue that printed documents do have one. However, as we shall see in Section 11.3, it is the actual information in these documents that we want to understand.

tions, and using three-dimensional graphics for the visualization itself, are thus reasonable and natural options. In contrast, infovis applications target a larger audience, which often includes individuals who have limited mathematical or engineering training. As such, the design of the presentation and interaction components of many infovis applications should be tuned to make them usable for the targeted user group. This can have several consequences on the user-interaction design. For example, financial users are very familiar with data tables and bar and pie charts. Software developers often do most of their work within an Integrated Development Environment (IDE), where most graphics and interaction is two-dimensional. As a general rule, the design of infovis applications for any particular field should

- follow the conventions accepted by that field;

- integrate with other tools-of-the-trade of the field.

Following these two design principles maximizes the chance for the infovis application to be accepted by its users, and also speeds up the learning process.

Just as for scivis, different types of taxonomies, or classifications, have emerged for infovis applications. In his book, Spence classifies visualization applications into scivis applications, which address physical data; infovis applications, which address abstract data which lacks a spatial placement; and geovisualization (geovis) applications, which address a field between the two, where potentially abstract data is depicted in a spatial setting. A different taxonomy based on how the user derives a mental model from the data was proposed by Tory and Möller [Tory and Möller 04]. Yet another taxonomy, proposed by Chi [Chi 00], groups infovis techniques based on the data types and operations that are inherent to each visualization technique.

11.3   Infovis versus Scivis: A Technical Comparison

Since the rest of this book was about scivis, it is useful to see how infovis is similar to, and also how it differs from, scivis. In this section, we compare scivis and infovis from the technical perspective of data representation and manipulation.

First, let us briefly recall our discussion on the dataset concept that underlies the structure of the visualization pipeline (see Chapter 3). Datasets are containers that store application information which is to be processed and ultimately mapped to visual representations by the various algorithmic steps in the visualization pipeline (see Chapter 4). The dataset should, thus, accurately model the properties of the actual application-specific information, and, at the same time, lend itself to an efficient and scalable software implementation.

11.3.1 Dataset

The dataset model described in Chapter 3 was based on a number of assumptions, as follows:

- The *domain* is a compact subset of $\mathbb{R}^n$, discretized in a set of simple piecewise-linear primitives, such as lines in 1D, triangles in 2D, and tetrahedra in 3D. The discretization, consisting of the location of the primitives' vertices together with the connectivity information that describes the primitives themselves, is stored in a *grid*.

- The *data* consists of sample values of some numerical quantity of dimension m taken at the sample points. Scalar data has dimension $m = 1$, vector data has $m = 2$ or $m = 3$, and tensor data has $m = 4$ or $m = 9$. The sample points are typically either the primitive vertices or the primitive centers, depending on the type of interpolation used.

- The *interpolation functions* serve to reconstruct a piecewise continuous signal from the data samples, across the primitives' extents. Constant and linear interpolation are the most common forms in use.

The preceding is summarized in the sampling and reconstruction process sketched in Figure 3.4.

As explained in Chapter 3, the scivis dataset model is well suited to describe functions of the type $f : \mathbb{R}^n \to \mathbb{R}^m$. Data coming from numerical simulations and measurements of physical quantities over spatial regions fit

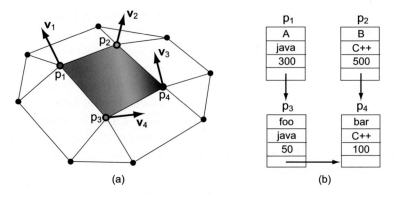

Figure 11.1. Examples of (a) scivis and (b) infovis datasets.

this model well. Figure 11.1(a) sketches a simple scivis dataset having an unstructured grid embedded in $\mathbb{R}^3$ that has a color and a vector attribute at each sample point p_i. The scientific visualization methods described in Chapters 5 up to Chapter 10 are designed to offer various ways to get insight in datasets that follow this model.

We can, however, find many examples of data that does not, or cannot be easily brought to, fit this model. Let us give two examples. Consider first the information stored in this book. This consists of an amount of text, which can be described, at the lowest level, as a sequence of characters from the ASCII character set. At a higher level of organization, the text is structured into words, sentences, paragraphs, subsections, sections, and chapters. Besides the textual information, there are also images, which can be described using the dataset model in Chapter 9. Apart from the previous, there are also cross-references in the text, such as the numbers that point to sections, figures, and bibliographic references.

The simplest form of visualizing text is by printing it in the actual form and layout this book has. Besides reading the physical book, the text can be visualized using interactive viewers for various electronic document formats such as Adobe's Portable Document Format (PDF) or PostScript. However effective for tasks such as reading the document and searching for the occurrence of certain text patterns, the visualization model provided by such viewers does not support the user in performing other tasks. Among these, the following are worth mentioning:

- Get an overview of the global document structure.

- Identify similar textual patterns at several levels of detail (word, sentence, paragraph, chapter).

- Compare two or several text documents and see the similarities and differences.

- Get insight into the global cross-reference structure.

- Understand how the usage of images is spread throughout the document.

- Observe how the structure and contents of a document have changed in time.

As a second example, consider the information stored during the development of a software project. This consists of the actual source code files, which contain program text usually structured, from high to low level, as a set of classes, functions, and individual statements. Besides the source code, other data items can be present, such as requirements, architectural and design diagrams, development log files, and bug traces. Figure 11.1(b) sketches an example of a simple dataset containing information about a software project. This dataset contains four data elements, or tuples. Tuples p_1 and p_2 describe two classes A and B, the first written in Java and the second in C++, and having 300 and 500 lines of code, respectively. Tuples p_3 and p_4 describe two functions foo and bar, the first having 50 and the second 100 lines of code respectively. The dataset additionally contains four relations, describing the fact that class A contains the function foo, class B contains the function bar, and that foo calls bar. These relations are indicated by the four arrows drawn in Figure 11.1(b).

Software developers and project managers want to accomplish a number of tasks on this kind of information, including the following:

- Get an overview of the structure of the software project.

- Understand the dependencies between the various software building blocks, such as functions, classes, and packages.

- Compare the structure of two software systems and/or two different releases of the same system.

- Get insight in the coding style of various developers.

- Get insight into how the bug reports and fixes correlate with the project structure.

The preceding tasks are targeted by a branch of information visualization called *software visualization*. A definition of software visualization is "the use of the crafts of typographic, graphic design, animation, and cinematography with modern human-computer interaction and computer graphics technology to facilitate both the human understanding and effective use of computer software" [Stasko et al. 98]. Depending on the type of targeted data, software visualization can be further subdivided into several domains: program structure visualization, behavior visualization, and program evolution visualization [Diehl 07]. We shall present several examples of software visualization methods and applications in the remainder of this chapter.

For the text and software data types given previously, two questions arise, just as for scivis:

- How can we design a dataset model that stores this information?

- How can we design visualization methods that allow us to get insight in this data?

This information cannot be naturally mapped to the scivis dataset model consisting of a grid of sample points, numerical sample values, and interpolation functions. Let us detail each of these elements in turn.

11.3.2 Data Domain

The domain of a scivis dataset typically describes a compact region of $\mathbb{R}^n$ sampled at several locations. The resulting grid structure consists of sample points and cells. Cells are used to reconstruct a piecewise continuous signal from its sampled values at the cell vertices using interpolation (see Section 3.2). In contrast, infovis datasets often do not contain spatial information (sample points), nor do they contain cells having the function of interpolation. Let us examine these two properties in turn.

A first observation we can make for the book contents and software project data examples is that these do not have an inherent spatial *location*. Of course, we could try to model a book as a set of 2D pages stacked on top of each other in 3D, i.e., regard it as a kind of tridimensional dataset. The sample points of such a grid would, probably, be taken at the locations of the graphical elements in the book such as text letters and illustrations. The sampled data could consist of the actual text characters and image pixels. Although it is technically possible to store a book in such a dataset format, this would create more problems than it solves. First and foremost, the spatial 3D layout of the actual book is, in many cases, of little relevance for the content and the questions targeting this content. Such a dataset would represent the *physical* book itself, and not the *information* that the book stores. In the case of the software project data, there is simply no "natural" spatial structure to describe the data over.

As we shall see in the next sections, some infovis attribute types do not support interpolation. Hence, we cannot use cells for signal reconstruction purposes such as in scivis. There is no direct equivalent in infovis to the notion and purpose of cells, such as defined in scivis datasets. As we shall see later in Section 11.5, there is a somewhat similar notion of cells in infovis datasets, which are relationships between sets of data tuples. For example, the call and containment relations shown in Figure 11.1(b) can be thought of as cells that connect the four data points $p_1, \cdots, p_4$. Although superficially similar to the scivis cell concept, this cell notion serves a different purpose.

11.3.3   Data Attributes

The sample values, or attribute values, stored at the grid points describe the actual data stored by the dataset. One important difference between scivis and infovis data that is easy to spot is that infovis data values are of more types than numerical values. In the previous examples, we can note elements such as text, syntactic entities (classes and functions), cross-references in a text and call relations in a software project, and bug information. All these data types go beyond the semantics of numerical values, and also exhibit different properties than numerical data.

As discussed in Chapter 3, scivis data types are classified by their dimension into scalar, vector, and tensor data. For infovis data, there exist several classifications. One way to classify attribute data types is based on the kind of scale within which the values of a parameter might be given [InfoWiki 06]. Following this classification, attributes can be classified into

Data type	Attribute domain	Operations	Examples
nominal	unordered set	comparison $(=, \neq)$	text, references, syntax elements
ordinal	ordered set	ordering $(=, \neq, <, >)$	ratings (e.g., bad, average, good)
discrete	integers $(\mathbb{Z}, \mathbb{N})$	integer arithmetic	lines of code
continuous	reals $(\mathbb{R})$	real arithmetic	code metrics

Table 11.1. Attribute data types in infovis.

nominal, ordinal, binary, discrete, and continuous. These data types, together with the domains the respective attributes take value in and their supported operations, are summarized in Table 11.1.

Another classification of attribute data types groups these into qualitative, quantitative, and categorical types. Nominal and ordinal attributes are said to be *qualitative*, as they do not allow arithmetic operations such as addition and multiplication. As we shall see next in Section 11.3.4, these operations are mandatory for performing attribute interpolation. In contrast, discrete and continuous data types are said to be *quantitative*, as they allow arithmetic operations and, therefore, also interpolation. Finally, nominal, ordinal, and discrete types are sometimes said to be *categorical*, when these attributes describe the fact that a data item belongs to a category rather than the value of a quantity.

Scivis attributes belong chiefly to the last category of continuous types. This is natural, when we recall that they describe physical measured or simulated quantities. Infovis attributes cover the whole spectrum of data types, and therefore cannot always support operations such as interpolation. A second important property of many infovis datasets is that they do not define attribute values for every data tuple. In the example in Figure 11.1, only the functions (p_3 and p_4) have the "calls" attribute, whereas the "contains method" attribute is present only in the class tuples (p_1 and p_2). Moreover, infovis attributes pose different requirements on dataset implementation. As described in Section 3.8.2, scivis attributes are implemented basically as several floating-point arrays with one value per grid point or cell. Infovis datasets may need to choose a different storage strategy, since the size of a single attribute is variable, e.g., in the case of text strings, and since one must cope with missing values.

Yet another classification of attribute data types proposes eight types: linear, planar, volumetric, temporal, multidimensional, tree, network, and workspace [Shneiderman 96, Card et al. 99]. This classification c both scivis and infovis attribute types and features, in the sense that both the spatiality of the attributes (e.g., linear, planar, volumetric, temporal, and multidimensional) and the relational aspect thereof (e.g., tree, network, and workspace) are present. Together with these eight data types, seven interaction functions an infovis application may provide are named: overview, zoom, filter, details-on-demand, relate, history, and extract. These functions can be related to the main steps of the visualization pipeline: filtering, mapping, and rendering. These two dimensions (data types and interaction types) create a matrix of possibilities within which a visualization application can locate its functionality.

The last classification of infovis data types we discuss here is into *values* and *relations*. All examples of data types listed previously, with the exception of references, fall in the value category. Value types contain their information within the data type itself. Relation types contain the information in the association, or relation, between two or more data values. As we shall see later in this chapter, relational data pose particular challenges to visualization.

11.3.4   Interpolation

As stated several times so far, continuous attributes such as used in scivis datasets admit interpolation. For example, we can interpolate the color attribute from the vertices $p_1, \cdots, p_4$ over the corresponding quad cell in Figure 11.1(a). However, it does not make sense to consider interpolating any of the attributes of the software dataset shown in Figure 11.1(b), i.e., the class and function names (text), programming language (nominal), call and containment relations (nominal), and lines of code (discrete). For the first three attributes, this statement is obvious. For the integer-valued lines of code attribute, one could, technically speaking, perform interpolation. However, this does not make much sense, as function and class data tuples are not part of a continuous space. For this reason, we can call the infovis data *inherently discrete*, in contrast to scivis data, which consists of samples of originally continuous quantities.

This distinction is very important. Together with the lack of inherent spatial placement, this influences the way the visualization methods for infovis data are designed.

	Scivis	**Infovis**
Data domain	spatial $\subset \mathbb{R}^n$	abstract, non-spatial
Attribute types	numeric $\subset \mathbb{R}^m$	any data types
Data points	samples of attributes over domain	tuples of attributes without spatial location
Cells	support interpolation	describe relations
Interpolation	piecewise continuous	can be inexistent

Table 11.2. Comparison of dataset notions in scivis and infovis.

Table 11.2 summarizes the differences between scivis and infovis datasets. These differences sketch an image of the generic infovis dataset that is quite similar to the data model used in relational databases or entity-relationship graphs: data consists of several tuples of variable length, each having a number of data elements. These data elements can be of virtually any type besides numeric ones. The tuples participate in various relations with each other. The "structure" of the dataset is precisely this graph-like network of tuples connected by relations. In scivis datasets, this structure was relatively fixed, i.e., consisted of uniform, rectilinear, structured, and unstructured grids (see Section 3.5), and encoded typically just spatial and sampling density information. In contrast, infovis datasets can have very complex network-like relational structures, which encode a wide range of domain-specific semantics. If we consider all the previous facts, we can conclude that infovis datasets pose considerable challenges to an effective and efficient implementation.

In practice, there exist many applications where scivis and infovis datasets are intimately mixed. For example, inherently spatial domains can carry both quantitative (real-valued) and qualitative (nominal) attributes, such as a map with height information and names of localities, road signs, and other annotations. Conversely, scivis attributes can be completely decoupled from their spatial context, such as in the case of a database containing tables with physical measurement values but no measurement locations. What is important to remember from the discussion in this section are which characteristics distinguish infovis from scivis datasets, as these influence the choice and design of visualization methods.

As discussed in Chapter 4, a visualization application is structured as a pipeline of data acquisition, data filtering and enrichment, mapping, and rendering algorithms that process datasets. This structure is common in infovis applications as well, as the main goals of getting insight into data, fact discovery, and hypothesis confirmation are common to both scivis and infovis applications. However, it is of interest to point out that the mapping stage of the infovis visualization pipeline has a relatively more difficult task to accomplish than the same step in scivis pipelines. As we recall, this step converts a generic dataset to a spatial, usually two- or three-dimensional, representation, which is next fed to the rendering step (see Section 4.1.3). As discussed previously, infovis data often has no spatial placement. Hence, the mapping step must cope with the added difficulty of creating a spatial representation for abstract high dimensional data. The effectiveness of many infovis visualization methods in conveying insight into such data is highly determined by the design choices made in this step, as we shall see next.

In the following sections, we present a number of visualization methods for several types of datasets that fall into the generic category described above: database tables, trees, graphs, and text.

11.4   Table Visualization

The first type of infovis data is the *table*. Most readers should be already familiar with data tables from different application areas. Consider, for example, a database. This consists usually of a set of tables, each being a two-dimensional array of rows and columns. Each column typically describes a separate attribute, which is instantiated on each row. The table cells can contain all the attribute types discussed in Section 11.3.3. Actual databases typically classify attributes into numerical, text, date and time, and references to other database cells. Databases are usually managed by means of interactive front-ends that allow users to perform query and editing operations on the tables as well as draw the contents of their tables in a two-dimensional grid of textual cell values. The actual data querying and modifications on the database contents are expressed in dedicated database languages. Of these, the Structured Query Language (SQL) is one of the most popular [Chamberlin and Boyce 74, SQL 06], and is implemented by a large number of database management systems (DBMSs) in use, both commercial, such as Oracle and Microsoft SQL Server, and open-source, such as PostgreSQL and MySQL.

id	category	name	date	time	open	high	low	close
636	sif	SIF1	2004-11-29	13:00	0.800000	0.800000	0.800000	0.800000
635	sif	SIF1	2004-11-29	14:00	0.800000	0.800000	0.800000	0.800000
633	sif	SIF1	2004-11-29	16:00	0.795000	0.795000	0.795000	0.795000
630	sif	SIF1	2004-11-30	14:00	0.795000	0.795000	0.795000	0.795000
632	sif	SIF1	2004-11-30	12:00	0.800000	0.800000	0.795000	0.795000
631	sif	SIF1	2004-11-30	13:00	0.795000	0.795000	0.795000	0.795000
628	sif	SIF1	2004-11-30	16:00	0.795000	0.795000	0.795000	0.795000
629	sif	SIF1	2004-11-30	15:00	0.795000	0.795000	0.795000	0.795000
627	sif	SIF1	2005-00-02	12:00	0.785000	0.790000	0.785000	0.790000
626	sif	SIF1	2005-00-02	13:00	0.790000	0.795000	0.790000	0.795000
625	sif	SIF1	2005-00-02	14:00	0.795000	0.795000	0.795000	0.795000
624	sif	SIF1	2005-00-02	15:00	0.800000	0.800000	0.800000	0.800000
620	sif	SIF1	2005-00-03	15:00	0.795000	0.795000	0.795000	0.795000
623	sif	SIF1	2005-00-03	12:00	0.795000	0.795000	0.795000	0.795000
622	sif	SIF1	2005-00-03	13:00	0.795000	0.795000	0.795000	0.795000
621	sif	SIF1	2005-00-03	14:00	0.795000	0.795000	0.795000	0.795000
619	sif	SIF1	2005-00-03	16:00	0.795000	0.795000	0.795000	0.795000
618	sif	SIF1	2005-00-06	11:00	0.790000	0.790000	0.790000	0.790000
614	sif	SIF1	2005-00-06	15:00	0.795000	0.795000	0.795000	0.795000
617	sif	SIF1	2005-00-06	12:00	0.795000	0.795000	0.795000	0.795000
616	sif	SIF1	2005-00-06	13:00	0.795000	0.795000	0.795000	0.795000
615	sif	SIF1	2005-00-06	14:00	0.795000	0.795000	0.795000	0.795000
613	sif	SIF1	2005-00-06	16:00	0.795000	0.795000	0.795000	0.795000
609	sif	SIF1	2005-00-07	14:00	0.790000	0.795000	0.790000	0.795000
612	sif	SIF1	2005-00-07	11:00	0.795000	0.795000	0.795000	0.795000
611	sif	SIF1	2005-00-07	12:00	0.795000	0.795000	0.795000	0.795000
610	sif	SIF1	2005-00-07	13:00	0.790000	0.790000	0.790000	0.790000
608	sif	SIF1	2005-00-07	15:00	0.790000	0.790000	0.790000	0.790000
606	sif	SIF1	2005-00-08	13:00	0.795000	0.795000	0.795000	0.795000
607	sif	SIF1	2005-00-08	12:00	0.790000	0.790000	0.790000	0.790000
605	sif	SIF1	2005-00-08	14:00	0.795000	0.795000	0.795000	0.795000

Figure 11.2. Textual visualization of a database table containing stock exchange data.

The simplest way to visualize a data table is to print its contents. While this allows detailed inspection of the actual table values, there are several limitations to this approach. First, printing cannot show more than a few tens of rows and columns simultaneously. Figure 11.2 shows a table containing stock exchange data.[2] Every table row contains information recorded about the trading of a share during a certain time interval. The information is saved for several time intervals during each trading day for a period of three years (2003 to 2005) for a few hundred traded stocks. Each table row contains, from left to right: the integer id of the respective row in the database, the industry category the stock is in and name of the stock, the date and time when the stock's value was recorded, the value at the beginning and end of the recording interval (open and close respectively), and the high and low values the stock reached during the respective interval. The table visualization can be scrolled to examine all the data rows, in this case over 45,000.

---

[2]Data originating from the Romanian Stock Exchange. Courtesy of C. Micu.

Stock brokers are interested in analyzing this data in order to find trends, outliers, and correlations between the various recorded items, such as share prices, periods, and companies. It is easy to see that the preceding visualization cannot assist such tasks to a great extent. One of the problems is that the data is not presented in a way that supports the considered tasks. For example, the table rows are not listed in an order that supports any task, but in the order they appear in the database.

Several simple improvements can be brought to this visualization to make it more effective. A first improvement is to sort the columns by their attribute value. This is useful to find out the range of the attribute, by examining the beginning and end of a sorted column. Simple queries can be answered in this way, such as "what is the monitored period?" or "what are the earliest and latest intraday trading moments monitored?" Sorting the names column also allows us to quickly locate the data rows corresponding to a given share of interest, by scrolling to that name. However useful, simple sorting does not directly support tasks such as "show the evolution in time of the price of a given share." We can accomplish this task using three sort operations. First, we sort the table rows by name, which groups together the records (rows) corresponding to the same share. Next, we sort the same-name row groups by date. Finally, we sort the same-date row groups created by the second sort operation by time. The three sort operations create a table visualization that lists the shares ordered by name and then by date and time. Following the price evolution in time of one share, e.g., *SNP*, is now much easier (see Figure 11.3).

Figure 11.3 shows three other enhancements besides the multiple sorting technique. The first enhancement helps us see how many intraday samples the dataset has. To do this, we draw the background of the table cells using alternating colors (light blue and white) that change between row groups belonging to different dates. We can now easily see that most trading days have four or five intraday samples. A second use of this visual cue is to facilitate focusing on the first and last intraday samples, which are important to assess a day's gains or losses, and also to compare the close of a day with the open of the next day.

The second enhancement helps us follow the evolutions of the cell values without having to read them. To do this, we blend each cell's background with a colored bar graph showing the actual cell value. The bar lengths are normalized over each entire column: short bars indicate small

rows of equal   first sort   then sort   and then   evolution
date value   on **name** on **date** on **time** icons

id	category	nam 1	date 2	time 3	open	high	low	close
1611	oil	SNP	2004-01-09	12:00	0.146200	▼0.146200	0.145200	0.145200
1610	oil	SNP	2004-01-09	13:00	0.145200	=0.146200	0.145200	0.145200
1609	oil	SNP	2004-01-09	14:00	0.145200	=0.145200	0.145200	0.145200
1608	oil	SNP	2004-01-09	15:00	0.145200	▼0.145200	0.144200	0.144200
1607	oil	SNP	2004-01-12	11:00	0.144200	▼0.144200	0.143200	0.143200
1606	oil	SNP	2004-01-12	12:00	0.143200	▼0.143200	0.142300	0.142300
1605	oil	SNP	2004-01-12	13:00	0.142300	▼0.142300	0.140300	0.141300
1604	oil	SNP	2004-01-12	14:00	0.140300	=0.140300	0.140300	0.140300
1603	oil	SNP	2004-01-12	15:00	0.140300	▲0.141300	0.140300	0.141300
1602	oil	SNP	2004-01-13	11:00	0.141300	=0.141300	0.140300	0.140300
1601	oil	SNP	2004-01-13	12:00	0.140300	▲0.142300	0.140300	0.141300
1600	oil	SNP	2004-01-13	13:00	0.141300	=0.142300	0.141300	0.141300
1599	oil	SNP	2004-01-13	14:00	0.141300	=0.142300	0.141300	0.142300
1598	oil	SNP	2004-01-13	15:00	0.141300	=0.142300	0.141300	0.141300
1597	oil	SNP	2004-01-14	11:00	0.141300	▼0.141300	0.140300	0.140300
1596	oil	SNP	2004-01-14	12:00	0.141300	=0.142300	0.141300	0.141300
1595	oil	SNP	2004-01-14	13:00	0.142300	=0.142300	0.141300	0.142300
1594	oil	SNP	2004-01-14	14:00	0.142300	▼0.142300	0.141300	0.141300
1593	oil	SNP	2004-01-15	11:00	0.141300	=0.142300	0.141300	0.141300
1592	oil	SNP	2004-01-15	12:00	0.141300	=0.141300	0.141300	0.141300
1591	oil	SNP	2004-01-15	13:00	0.141300	=0.142300	0.141300	0.141300
1590	oil	SNP	2004-01-15	14:00	0.141300	=0.141300	0.141300	0.141300
1589	oil	SNP	2004-01-15	15:00	0.141300	▲0.142300	0.141300	0.142300
1588	oil	SNP	2004-01-16	11:00	0.141300	▼0.141300	0.140300	0.140300
1587	oil	SNP	2004-01-16	12:00	0.140300	▲0.141300	0.140300	0.141300
1586	oil	SNP	2004-01-16	13:00	0.140300	=0.140300	0.140300	0.140300
1585	oil	SNP	2004-01-16	14:00	0.140300	=0.141300	0.140300	0.140300
1584	oil	SNP	2004-01-16	15:00	0.140300	▲0.141300	0.140300	0.141300
896	oil	SNP	2004-07-29	14:00	0.860000	=0.860000	0.860000	0.860000
895	oil	SNP	2004-07-29	15:00	0.855000	▲0.860000	0.855000	0.860000
894	oil	SNP	2004-07-30	12:00	0.860000	▲0.865000	0.860000	0.865000
893	oil	SNP	2004-07-30	13:00	0.860000	=0.860000	0.860000	0.860000
892	oil	SNP	2004-07-30	14:00	0.860000	=0.860000	0.860000	0.860000
891	oil	SNP	2004-07-30	15:00	0.860000	=0.860000	0.860000	0.860000
890	oil	SNP	2004-08-02	12:00	0.865000	=0.865000	0.865000	0.865000
889	oil	SNP	2004-08-02	13:00	0.870000	▼0.870000	0.865000	0.865000
888	oil	SNP	2004-08-02	14:00	0.870000	▲0.875000	0.870000	0.875000
887	oil	SNP	2004-08-02	15:00	0.875000	▲0.880000	0.875000	0.880000
886	oil	SNP	2004-08-03	11:00	0.875000	=0.875000	0.875000	0.875000
885	oil	SNP	2004-08-03	12:00	0.875000	=0.875000	0.875000	0.875000
884	oil	SNP	2004-08-03	13:00	0.875000	=0.875000	0.875000	0.875000

attribute bar graphs   zoom slider

Figure 11.3. Table visualization enhanced using multiple sorting, evolution icons, bar graphs, and same-value (date) row cues.

values, whereas a bar of the entire cell's length indicates the maximum value over the respective column. The date, time of day, and high course columns are rendered using bar graphs in Figure 11.3. The bar graphs help us discover several interesting facts. First, we notice a jump in the bar graph of the date column. Upon closer inspection of the text in the cells, we discover that there is a gap in the recorded data from the 16th of January 2004 until the 29th of July in the same year. The time column shows a different, sawtooth-like, evolution pattern. This pattern says that the intraday samples are relatively uniformly spaced between the same start time (11:00) and end time (15:00) for the considered data. However, we also discover an outlier: on the 29th of July 2004, the first day after the seven-month information gap, there are only two samples at 14:00 and 15:00. Finally, the high column bar graph shows two flat lines separated by an abrupt jump. This signals that the course of the respective share has not changed significantly in the monitored periods, but has exhibited a major increase during the gap period for which we lack information.

The third enhancement helps us follow the course variations during the monitored intervals. To do this, we display small icons, or glyphs, in the open column that indicate the difference between this column's value and the close column. A green upward-pointing arrow indicates a course increase, a red downward-pointing arrow shows a course decrease, and a blue equal-sign icon shows an unchanged course. These glyphs are essentially an indicator of the sign of the course derivative.

A different problem of the text-based table visualization discussed so far is its limited scalability. Although we can scroll the table both vertically and horizontally, this does not offer an overview of the entire data. Also, scrolling a table that has tens of thousands of rows or more is quite cumbersome. To solve this problem, we reduce the level of detail at which the table is shown, by zooming out the table visualization. This technique was originally introduced by Rao et al. as "table lens" [Rao and Card 94]. When the text size becomes too small to be readable, we drop displaying it and the same-value row cues and evolution icons, and only show the bar graphs. This allows us to "zoom out" the table visualization until each row is rendered by a single horizontal pixel line.

Figure 11.4 shows the entire stock dataset of over 45,000 rows visualized using the table lens technique, sorted by industry category, share name, and sampling time. In order to display this many rows on a display window of under 1000 pixels in height, the bar graphs in each column need to be undersampled by a factor of roughly 45 to 1. Note that this is not the same as undersampling the actual cell values. As explained in Section 11.3.4, interpolation (and, thus, undersampling too) of qualitative and categorical attributes can be problematic. However, the bar graphs map these attributes to a numerical value, which can be easily resampled.

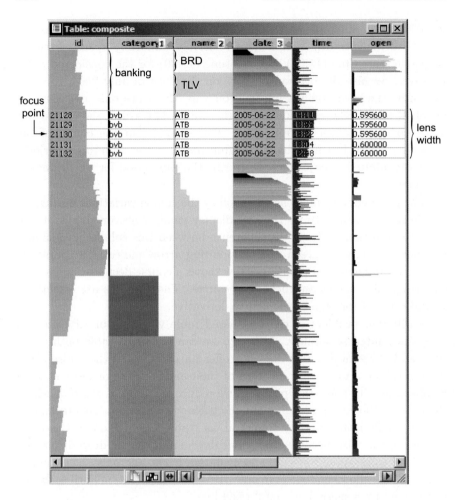

Figure 11.4. The table lens technique allows us to create overviews of large tables as well as show context information.

Different colormaps are used for the bar graphs in this image. The category column (nominal type) uses different brown hues to show the four industry categories present in the dataset, which are shown by the four different bar sizes (the first one, banking, has a zero width). The vertical bar sizes indicate the relative sizes of the industries in terms of monitored shares. The date column (discrete type) uses a luminance colormap, where dark indicates early dates and bright late dates in the monitored period. The open course column (continuous type) uses the by-now-familiar blue-to-red rainbow colormap. From Figure 11.4, we immediately see that the *BRD* stock has the highest, and increasing, open courses. In the same industry category of banking, there is a second share *TLV* that has a much lower, and rather constant, open course. A comparable course level to *BRD* is reached only for a very short period of time by another company in another industry category, as outlined by the narrow warm-colored spike halfway down the open column.

The previous visualization maximizes the information density. Every few pixels are used to convey a separate piece of data, so that overviews of large datasets are possible on a single screen without using navigation techniques such a zooming and panning. Such visualizations are known generically as *dense pixel displays*. We shall encounter dense pixel display techniques further in this chapter.

The table lens technique can combine the overview visualization with detailed textual context information similar to the one shown in Figure 11.3. For this, we display detailed information for a few rows centered at a given focus point placed somewhere in the row range. The effect is similar to placing a lens on top of the overview visualization. Moving the focus point interactively, e.g., with the mouse, allows us to get detailed information at any point of the overview picture. This is a good example of the widely used principle in visualization of *focus and context*.

The table-visualization techniques presented in this section are a useful instrument for getting insight into large tables containing tens of thousands of rows of various types. Their power resides in a combination of text and graphics displays and several interaction techniques that enable users to browse and display the data to support a variety of tasks.

11.5 Visualization of Relations

As discussed in Section 11.3.1, relational data are an important type of infovis data. Loosely defined, a relation is an association between two or more items. Relational data is fundamentally different from value data, as the information is located not in a data value, but in the fact that several such values are associated in some way.

Relational datasets are ubiquitous in many application domains. Examples are as diverse as computers communicating with each other in networks, web pages referring to each other in the World Wide Web, cities connected by roads on maps, suppliers and customers connected in a logistics network, and software components depending on each other in a software system architecture. Given this widespread presence of relation datasets, many methods have been designed for visualizing such datasets. In this section, we shall focus on the visualization of types of relational datasets that are frequently encountered in practice: trees, graphs, and Venn diagrams.

11.5.1   Tree Visualization

Trees are a particular type of relational data. Formally, a tree $T = (N, E)$ is defined as a set of nodes $N = \{n_i\}$ (also called vertices) and a set of edges $E = \{e_i\}$, where every edge $e_i = (n_j, n_k)$ is a pair of nodes $n_j \in N$ and $n_k \in N$. An essential property of a tree is that there is a unique path, defined as a set of nodes connected by edges, between any two nodes in the tree. Putting it simply, a tree is a network of connected nodes where there are no loops.

In practice, the node pair that defines an edge in a tree is ordered to encode application-specific semantics. In such cases, for an edge $e_i = (n_j, n_k)$, the first node (n_j) is called the *parent* of n_k and the second one (n_k) is called the *child* of n_j. Hence, a tree can be seen as a hierarchical structure of parent and child nodes. In this model, a parent node may have any number of children, but a child node can have only one parent. Given that all nodes in a tree are connected, we deduce that there is a single node in a tree that has no parents. This node is called the tree *root*, and represents the top level of the hierarchy encoded by the tree. Symmetrically, there are several nodes in a tree that have no children. These nodes are called *leaves*, and represent the bottom-most level of the hierarchy encoded by the tree. Finally, the depth of a tree is the length of the longest path (number of nodes) that connects a leaf to the root.

As already mentioned, trees encode different types of hierarchical relations. One such relation is *containment*, where parent nodes are seen as containers of child nodes. Examples of containment tree hierarchies are computer file systems (files in folders), the structure of software source code (statements in functions in classes in files), and the logical map of a store (products in boxes in shelves in storage rooms). Another hierarchical relation is *subordination*, where parent nodes are seen as controllers of their children. Examples of subordination tree hierarchies are the structures of organizations (employees, managers, executives), the control structure of mechanical assemblies (driven parts connected to controllers), or the electrical network in a house (devices, power sockets, central electricity meter).

How can we visualize tree datasets? Since a tree is a particular example of an entity-relationship structure (nodes connected by edges), the answer implies that we must visualize the nodes and the edges. Besides visualizing the structure, we should provide ways to visualize the additional data attributes that may be associated with both nodes and edges. In the following, we present two different methods for visualizing trees: ball-and-stick drawings and treemaps.

Ball-and-stick visualization. The *ball-and-stick* visualization, also known as *node-and-link* visualization, is probably the most widespread method of visualizing tree data structures. As its name suggests, this method maps the tree nodes to typically round glyphs,[3] and the edges to line or curve-like shapes that connect the related nodes. Ball-and-stick displays of trees are also known as node and link diagrams. This representation leaves two main degrees of freedom for both nodes and edges:

- the positions of the glyphs;

- the appearance (shape, color, texture, lighting, annotation) of the glyphs.

Many choices are possible for both degrees of freedom. However, a commonly used strategy is to assign position to the node glyphs only, draw edges as straight lines, and modulate the appearance of both nodes and edges to reflect the values of their various attributes. With this strategy, it is possible to decouple the tree-drawing problem into a geometric placement step that assigns coordinates to the nodes, followed by a mapping step that assigns appearance to the already-placed node glyphs.

---

[3]The concept of *glyph* was introduced for the visualization of vector data in Section 6.2.

The geometric placement step is commonly referred to as *layout*. There are many requirements that make a tree layout effective. These include, but are not limited, to the following:

- nodes and edges should ideally not overlap or the amount of overlap should be minimal;

- edges should not be unnecessarily long or, when curved edges are used, unnecessarily bent;

- the layout aspect ratio should be balanced, i.e., not too far off unity;

- the hierarchical root-to-leaves tree structure should be easily discernable from the visualization;

- the relative structures, sizes, and depths of the various subtrees of a given tree (or of different but related trees) should be easy to compare;

- the layout should be scalable, both in terms of clarity of the produced visualization and in terms of computational resources needed to compute it.

As there are many ways in which these and other related requirements can be satisfied, many tree-layout algorithms have been developed. For a comprehensive discussion of the problematics and implementation details of tree drawing, we refer to the book by Di Battista et al. [Di Battista et al. 99]. For a discussion on the aesthetics of tree layouts, see Bloesch [Bloesch 93].

To give a feeling of the different choices that can be made when computing the layout of a graph, we will illustrate these choices for the problem of understanding the structure of a file hierarchy. The example we consider is the distribution of the open-source FFmpeg software video codec [Bellard 06]. This distribution contains 785 files in 42 folders nested five levels deep. Several file types are included: source code, video, audio, binary (libraries and object code), images, hypertext, and plain-text documentation.

Figure 11.5 shows one of the most-frequently-used tree layouts, called the *rooted-tree* layout.[4] Here, all children nodes of the same parent have the same y-coordinate. Their position on the x-axis is used to reflect a

---

[4]The tree visualizations in Figures 11.5, 11.6, 11.7, and 11.8 are created using the Tulip open-source graph visualization software [Auber 07]

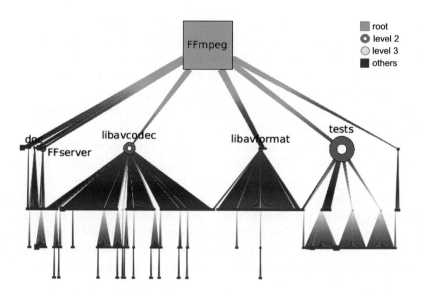

Figure 11.5. File hierarchy of the FFmpeg software distribution visualized using a rooted tree.

certain ordering. Here, the order in which files appear in a listing of their containing folder is used. Moreover, the placement of the children on the x-axis is done so that the horizontal extent of the entire subtree of a given parent node is centered with respect to the parent's x-coordinate. The appearance of the nodes reflects several attributes. The node glyphs and color show the file level in the hierarchy: a green square for the root, blue rings for the first-level folders, yellow balls for the second-level folders, and red squares for the remaining folders and files. The node glyph sizes reflect the size of the corresponding files or folders. However, these sizes range from a few tens of bytes for the smallest ones to over a hundred megabytes for the root folder. Making the glyph sizes directly proportional to the file sizes would render most files practically invisible when we scale the root glyph size to fit the image. To prevent this, we lower clamp the smallest glyph size to 1/20 of the largest (root) glyph size. This makes the smaller file glyphs visible, but their size does not exactly reflect their corresponding files' size any longer. Additionally, we display the folder names for some of the largest folders in the distribution. Finally, the edges are drawn as straight lines with a color that interpolates the colors of their two nodes, using the same technique described for Gouraud shading (see Chapter 2). This technique makes the color change smoothly from node to node, thereby creating a visualization with less-sharp transitions. Another advantage is that some very small nodes, which may not be visible at all, will convey their color to the relatively long edges, thereby making their presence visible in the final image.

The visualization in Figure 11.5 shows several aspects of the FFmpeg software distribution. We see that the FFmpeg root directory has seven subdirectories. Of these, tests has the largest size (largest glyph). One of the nicest features of this layout is that it maps the hierarchy levels to distinct parallel horizontal layers. This lets us easily see, for example, that the entire distribution is five levels deep. The horizontal width of the triangular "fans" consisting of a parent and its children shows the size, in number of files, of each folder. For example, we see that libavcodec has

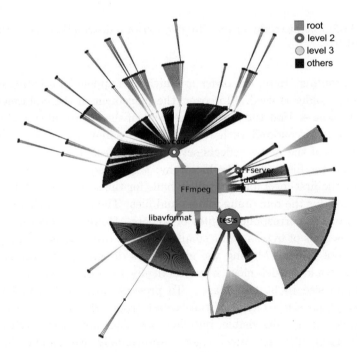

Figure 11.6. Radial-tree layout for the same file hierarchy as in Figure 11.5.

the largest number of files within (largest subtree drawing). Another useful property of this layout is that it reflects the "balancing" of the hierarchy, i.e., the distribution of number of files and subtree depths across the entire structure. Looking at Figure 11.5, we assert that this file hierarchy is well balanced. Indeed, there are no extreme depth or file count variations across the displayed subtrees.

The preceding layout works well for relatively well-balanced trees. However, "fat" trees that have parents with many children and few levels or very deep trees with few children per parent can yield layouts with poor aspect ratios. Tuning the distance between consecutive layers and the distance between consecutive children in the same layer can partially alleviate this problem.

A similar assessment of the file hierarchy structure can be obtained using the different tree layout shown in Figure 11.6. Here, the root is placed at the center of the image and its children are distributed in clockwise order along a circle centered at the root. Nodes on deeper levels are laid out on correspondingly wider circles. The (x, y) coordinate system used for the layout in Figure 11.5 is now replaced with a polar ρ, α coordinate system, hence the name *radial*. The advantage of the radial layout is that it always has a one-to-one aspect ratio, since the entire picture always fits in a circle. Moreover, more space is allocated, relatively speaking, to the deeper levels in the tree than in the previous layout. This is visible if we compare the space allocated to the leaves of the `tests` folder, drawn in red in Figures 11.5 and 11.6. In contrast, there is less space allocated to the upper levels of the tree. This can create problems when these nodes need more space to be drawn, as in the case of the first level of our example, whose nodes have large icons and also display textual annotations.

Figure 11.7 shows a different layout that uses the idea of circular node placement. In contrast to the radial layout, where a subtree occupies a pie sector of the entire layout, in this new layout a subtree always occupies an entire circle centered at the subtree's root. The entire layout can be seen as a placement of circles inside other larger circles, hence this layout is known as *bubble*, or balloon, layout [Boardman 00, Grivet et al. 04]. In contrast to the rooted and radial layout, the bubble layout offers a better visual separation of the subtrees. Additionally, this layout also keeps the tight aspect ratio of the radial layout. A difference between the two previous layouts is that edges have now considerably different lengths—subtrees with

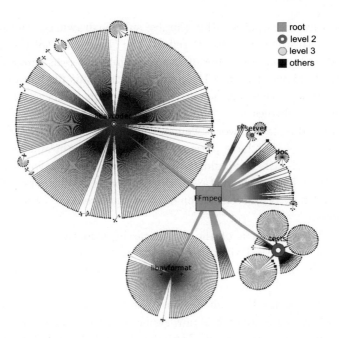

Figure 11.7. Bubble-tree layout for the same file hierarchy as in Figure 11.5.

fewer children will have shorter edges, since their bubbles will have smaller radii. This makes the visual size of the subtrees reflect their number of children more strongly than for the rooted and radial layouts.

A related tree layout to the bubble layout is the *cone* layout (see Figure 11.8). Here, the nodes are arranged in three dimensions, rather than two dimensions as in the three layouts discussed so far. Whereas a subtree was laid out in a circle in the bubble layout, it is now laid out as a cone with the subtree root placed at the apex [Robertson et al. 91]. The advantage of the cone layout is that its 2D rendering may be more compact than other layouts, when viewed from an optimal angle. Also, the visual separation of different subtrees may be easier when interactively rotating the viewpoint around the cone layout. Nevertheless, the cone layout inherits the typical problems of most 3D visualizations of discrete entities: occlusion, the chance of "getting lost" in the 3D space during interactive viewing, and the potential confusion created by the foreshortening of the perspective projection.

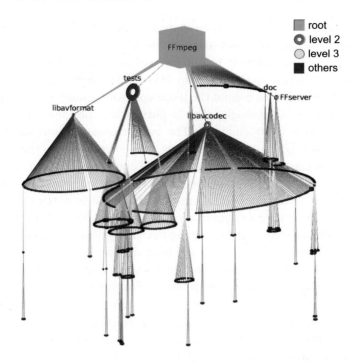

Figure 11.8. Cone-tree layout for the same file hierarchy as in Figure 11.5.

In conclusion, ball-and-stick visualizations of trees are a powerful instrument for getting insight into the structure and attributes of tree relational datasets. Their main attractions are being simple and efficient to compute and familiar and intuitive for the majority of users. The latter is an extremely important advantage that one should exploit, and that several other infovis techniques for visualizing abstract data do not have.

Treemaps. However intuitive, ball-and-stick visualizations of trees have a serious limitation: they take a considerable amount of space. This becomes critical when one wants to visualize trees that have tens of thousands of nodes. Although it is technically possible to compute and render such a layout, it simply takes too much screen or paper space to display it to be effective in practice. Visualization practitioners often say that such layouts "waste" the white space that resides between the node and edge glyphs. When the data amounts to be visualized increase and the screen space stays constant, one often hears of screen space as being a rendering "real estate," which has to be carefully and sparingly used.

Treemaps are a different layout for tree structures that use virtually every pixel of display space to convey information [Johnson and Shneiderman 91]. The basic idea behind the treemap layout is simple: every subtree is represented by a rectangle, that is partitioned into smaller rectangles which correspond to its children. The basic treemap layout algorithm is straightforward. Given a start rectangle that corresponds to the tree root, slice it into as many smaller rectangles as its number of children by drawing lines along the shortest rectangle edge (vertical or horizontal). The exact position of the slicing lines determines the relative sizes of the child rectangles, which can be used to convey a scalar node attribute. For every child, repeat the slicing recursively, swapping the slicing direction from vertical to horizontal or conversely as we go one level deeper. The complete result is a nested sequence of rectangles that depict the tree leaves. This algorithm is known as *slice-and-dice* treemap layout [Shneiderman 92].

The intermediate (nonleaf) nodes are not shown explicitly in this layout. If one wants to allocate screen space to these nodes, e.g., to show some attributes, this can be done by making every child slightly smaller. This will create a border between the child and its parent, which can be used to show parent information by means of color or annotations.

Figure 11.9 shows a treemap visualization for the same file hierarchy as discussed in the previous section.[5] Here, rectangle sizes map to file sizes, and rectangle colors indicate file types. The rectangles have black borders in order to allow the visual separation of same-color neighbors. This visualization is more compact than the ball-and-stick visualizations shown in the previous section for the same data. Also, the nesting of the rectangles carries the strong suggestion of containment, which is exactly the type of relation we want to encode. However, this visualization has two problems. First, the aspect ratios of the rectangles can become quite far from unity. Thin, skinny rectangles are not good, as they are hard to separate visually. More seriously, given the finite resolution of a pixel display and the wide range of file sizes, some thin rectangles will have

---

[5]Figures 11.9 and 11.10 have been produced using the freely available file system visualization tool SequoiaView [van Wijk 06]. Similar functionality is implemented by the WinDirStat visualization tool, for which the complete open-source code is available [Schneider and Seifert 06].

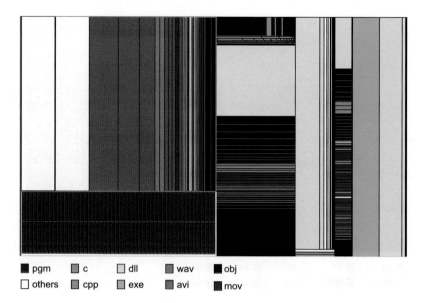

Figure 11.9. Treemap layout for the same file hierarchy as in Figure 11.5. Colors indicate file types; rectangle areas indicate file sizes.

a subpixel width or height, which will make them show up only as borders, i.e., appear fully black. This phenomenon is clearly visible in the large black rectangle in the lower middle of Figure 11.9, which actually denotes a folder containing subpixel-thin rectangles. The second problem is that the actual distribution of files, shown as rectangles in the visualization, within the folders is not easily visible. Although we can sometimes guess where a folder border occurs by looking at the vertical and horizontal black line pattern change, this is not easy. In some cases, such as a file hierarchy where all leaves (files) are of equal size, the treemap layout produces a uniform grid that makes detecting the actual folder structure impossible.

Both the aspect ratio and the nonleaf node visibility problems are addressed by a variant of the treemap layout shown in Figure 11.10. Let us first consider the layout. The principle of partitioning the rectangle of a subtree root into smaller rectangles corresponding to its children, sized to reflect the children sizes, stays the same. However, instead of using the simple horizontal-vertical alternating slicing, we use now a more involved

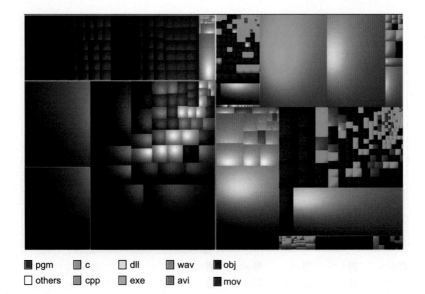

Figure 11.10. Improved treemap visualization using squarified layout and shaded cushion rendering.

technique that tries to create cells of near-unity aspect ratio. The implementation of this technique, called *squarified treemap layout*, is described in detail by Bruls et al. [Bruls et al. 00], and can be easily reimplemented by the interested reader. In order to obtain good aspect ratios, the squarified layout trades the order of the children rectangles, which now do not reflect the actual order of the children in the tree. Moreover, if we change the aspect ratio of the rendering target, the order of the rectangles in the squarified layout can change significantly. Several other treemap layouts exist, such as ordered and quantum treemaps [Bederson et al. 02] and cluster treemaps [Wattenberg 99], which offer several trade-offs concerning the ordering of the leaf nodes, aspect ratios of the leaf rectangles, and layout stability upon changing the target rendering area. Implementations of these algorithms, as well as an educative history of the evolution and use of treemaps, are available online [Shneiderman 06].

The second design element present in the tree visualization shown in Figure 11.10 is the use of shading to reflect the hierarchical structure.

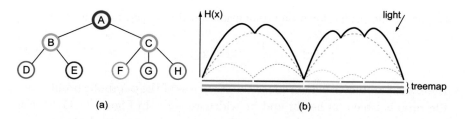

Figure 11.11. (a) The tree structure is visualized with (b) a cushion treemap. The actual cushion surface is indicated by the bold black line in (b). The same color is used to indicate the same node in the ball-and-stick tree drawing, the treemap, and the cushion profiles.

Since only the tree leaves are explicitly rendered, we shall use their surface to show structural information on their position in the tree. Figure 11.10 shows a set of convex "bumps." Given their appearance, these bumps are called *shaded cushions* in the literature [van Wijk and van de Wetering 99]. If we look carefully, we notice that these bumps occur at several levels: each treemap rectangle, which corresponds to a tree leaf, displays a small-scale bump. However, larger bumps are also visible in the shading signal or, to be more precise, in the luminance discontinuities of the shading. For example, if we look at the upper-left corner of the image, we see that the purple small-scale cushions appear to be grouped into two large cushions of roughly the same size. These large cushions actually correspond to the nonleaf nodes of the tree. Using the shaded cushions, several levels of the tree hierarchy can be displayed with no additional screen space by borrowing from the screen space already allocated to show the leaf nodes.

To understand the construction of the shaded cushions, consider the one-dimensional treemap visualization in Figure 11.11(b), which displays the tree shown in Figure 11.11(a). The tree, as well as its corresponding treemap, has three levels, whose nodes are colored in hues of blue, green, and red from top to bottom. For every treemap cell, whether it corresponds to a leaf or nonleaf node, we construct a profile whose shape is a convex parabolic function that passes through zero at the cell's borders and reaches maximum at the cell's center. Following the model proposed by van Wijk and van de Wetering [van Wijk and van de Wetering 99], the expression of the parabolic profile for a one-dimensional cell $C = [x_1, x_2]$ is given by

$$h(x) = \frac{4k}{x_2 - x_1}(x - x_1)(x_2 - x). \qquad (11.1)$$

Here, the parameter k determines the steepness of the parabolic profile, i.e., the ratio between its height and its width $x_2 - x_1$. In Figure 11.11(b), the profiles for each node of the considered tree are drawn with dotted lines.

After we have defined a cushion profile for each treemap cell, we sum up all profiles and obtain a surface $H(x)$, as indicated by the black bold profile in Figure 11.11(b), which is the sum of the dotted profiles. The one-dimensional equivalent of Figure 11.10 is obtained by rendering this surface illuminated from a direction as indicated in Figure 11.11(b). If we now use increasingly flatter cushions for deeper nodes in the tree, we obtain an image in which the magnitude of the illumination discontinuity, which is proportional to the depth of the "valleys" between neighbor bumps, reflects the depth of the corresponding node in the tree. To achieve this effect, we let the cushion shape parameter k decrease with the depth d in the tree of the considered node, e.g., by setting $k = f^d K$, where $f \in [0, 1]$ is a flattening factor and $K \in [0, 1]$ the steepness of the top-level, largest cushions.

The shaded cushion construction proceeds similarly for the two-dimensional case. The cushion profiles are now parabolic surfaces instead of curves. The complete, easy-to-replicate implementation of the shaded cushion treemap method is detailed by van Wijk and van de Wetering [van Wijk and van de Wetering 99]. The reader is encouraged to implement the algorithm following this reference.

Several considerations on the shaded cushion treemap visualization are of interest. First, we outline again the high scalability of the method. On a computer screen of n by n pixels, one can render a single-hue treemap with approximately $(\frac{n}{2})^2$ leaves. Here, we consider that a leaf cell needs at least 2×2 pixels to visibly display the parabolic shaded profile, which needs to show illumination variation in both directions. Rendering smaller treemap cells may be dangerous, as large clusters of adjacent minimal-size cells may appear as single large cells if the individual cell profiles are not visible. Yet, even with this restriction, the shaded cushion treemap is easily capable of displaying trees with over a hundred thousand leaves on a typical computer screen. Just as the table lens technique discussed in

Section 11.4, this visualization is also an instance of the dense pixel display, or space-filling, method. An evaluation of several space-filling techniques for displaying hierarchical structures is provided by Stasko et al. [Stasko et al. 00].

A second observation relates to the angle of the directional light source used. If we set the light to be exactly shining from above, i.e., orthogonal to the treemap supporting plane, the cushion surface get maximal illumination, which helps us distinguish small-scale details. However, this also creates a symmetric and zero-order continuous shading profile over all cells. This makes the identification of the importance of the cell-separating edges harder, as the luminance signal does not exhibit strong discontinuities. If the light vector is slightly tilted from the vertical direction, some parts of the cushion surface will be completely in the dark, whereas their neighboring cushions will have maximal illumination. Hence, the luminance signal will exhibit zero-order discontinuities at those cell borders, which makes them easier to grasp visually. However, a drawback is that detail on the surface parts left in the dark will not be visible.

As already explained, hue can be combined with shading to show tree node attributes together with the tree structure. However, care must be exercised when modulating the cushion shading with hues. Dark hues, such as the blue used in Figure 11.10 for the object files, decrease the luminance range that is used to show structure, which can make small-scale details hard to discern. This problem can be alleviated by using brighter hues. Specular lighting (see Section 2.2) can also add supplementary visual contrast, at the expense of using larger cushions in order to accommodate the size of the specular highlight.

From an implementation perspective, shaded cushions are similar to the texture-based visualization methods (see Section 6.6) in the sense that they do not generate polygonal primitives that undergo a rendering step, but directly create the final image. The original implementation of shaded cushions [van Wijk and van de Wetering 99] renders the cushion treemap in software by applying the Phong lighting (see Equation (2.1)) at every pixel of the treemap image, using an analytically computed normal from the summed profiles. This method works well for treemap images of moderate size, but cannot render full-screen images at interactive rates. When this is required, such as in applications where the user needs to change various visualization parameters and quickly regenerate the treemap ren-

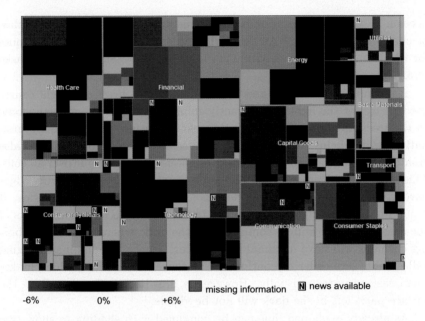

missing information   N news available

-6%   0%   +6%

Figure 11.12. The Map of the Market [SmartMoney 07] rendered using a treemap.

dering, pixel-shader techniques can be used to compute the shaded cushions in graphics hardware.

We conclude our discussion on treemaps with a different example. Figure 11.12 shows a snapshot from the very successful Map of the Market tool provided by SmartMoney [SmartMoney 07]. This image shows a treemap that describes the evolution of a stock exchange over a period of one year. The treemap has two levels: industry sectors and companies. The sizes of the leaf rectangles (companies) represent the market capitalization, i.e., the stock price times the number of outstanding shares. The colors show the stock price variation over a period of one year, as indicated by the colormap below the image. Gray rectangles indicate companies for which no data was available. Finally, an "N" glyph indicates companies for which news of financial interest are available. Strong market movers can be easily found by looking for large bright green or bright red rectangles.

In contrast to the file system visualization discussed previously, the Map of the Market treemap uses a layout with similar properties to the squarified layout [Wattenberg 99], but no shaded cushions to convey hier-

archy. Instead, borders are drawn to visually segregate the nodes, where
the border width conveys the node level. These design choices are backed
up by the fact that there are only two levels in the hierarchy, the full set of
leaf nodes (companies) does not exceed a few hundred, and the entire visualization is supposed to run as a lightweight Java plug-in in a web browser.
Several interaction mechanisms are provided to allow users to search for
companies of interest, display annotations, and control the color mapping
and selection of displayed data, all of which deliver a simple but effective
instrument for visually analyzing the stock market.

11.5.2   Graph Visualization

Graphs are the most general type of relational data. Formally, a graph
$G = (N, E)$ is defined as a set of nodes $N = \{n_i\}$ and a set of edges
$E = \{e_i\}$, where every edge $e_i = (n_j, n_k)$ is a pair of nodes $n_j \in N$ and
$n_k \in N$. In contrast to trees, graphs can contain loops. Similar to trees, the
node pair of an edge in a graph can be ordered or not. Graphs that contain
ordered edges are called *directed*, whereas graphs where the edge node pairs
are unordered are called *undirected*. An important notion in graph theory is
the number of connected components a graph has. Informally, a connected
component is defined as a set of nodes and corresponding edges such that
any two nodes in the set are connected by a path.

Depending on the type and size of graph, different visualization methods
are most applicable. In the following, we overview some of the most popular
methods for visualizing graphs.

Hierarchical graph visualization. The first class of methods for graph visualization is quite similar to the ball-and-stick visualizations of trees discussed in Section 11.5.1. The main structure of the algorithm is the same.
First, a layout is computed for the given graph, subject to the same type
of constraints described for trees. Second, the laid-out graph is drawn using appropriate glyphs for nodes and edges, which can optionally encode
additional data attributes.

The graph layout discussed in this section can be seen as a generalization
of the rooted-tree layout illustrated in Figure 11.5. The similarity resides
in the fact that both layouts exploit the notion of hierarchy. While for a
tree this notion is inherent, the situation is different for graphs. However,
there exist graphs that are naturally structured in a hierarchical manner by

means of their actual semantics. For these graphs, the nodes are grouped into layers, identified by integers, such that the directed graph edges always point from a node in a lower layer to a node in a higher layer. Essentially, such graphs are identical to trees but allow nodes with several parents and several root nodes, which are the nodes in the lowest layer. An example of such a hierarchical graph is a class inheritance diagram in object-oriented software. Whereas some languages, such as Java, admit only single inheritance, in which case the inheritance diagram is a tree, there exist languages such as C++ that allow a class to have multiple parents, also called *base classes*. The inheritance diagram is, in this case, a hierarchical graph.

Such hierarchical graphs can be laid out by a two-step algorithm [Sugiyama et al. 81]. In a nutshell, the algorithm works as follows. First, the nodes are assigned y-coordinates that are proportional to their layer numbers. This places nodes in the same layer at the same height (y-coordinate). Next, the nodes in each layer, from the root layer onward, are permuted to minimize the number of edge intersections, also called edge crossings, between layers. Since the crossing minimization problem is computationally expensive, several heuristics are used in practice to obtain a good result with a limited number of permutations [Gansner et al. 93].

Clearly, not all graphs have an intrinsic hierarchical semantics as described here. Still, the hierarchical graph layout algorithm described here can be used with any graph, as long as we are able to assign meaningful hierarchy layers to its nodes. Different methods can be applied when assigning layers to nodes, which creates different hierarchies with corresponding layout properties. Examples are the maximal layer width method, which computes a hierarchy whose layers are guaranteed to have a maximal number of nodes [Coffman and Graham 72] and hence guarantees a bounded layout width; the longest path ranking, which uses a minimal number of layers and hence guarantees a minimal layout height [AGD 06]; and the depth-first search method, which computes a hierarchy from a user-supplied set of root nodes. Such methods are beyond the scope of this book, so we refer the interested reader to the specialized literature [Di Battista et al. 99, Sugiyama et al. 81, Gansner et al. 93, AGD 06]. However, we should stress that, even though we can associate layer information with any graph and thereby use a hierarchical layout to visualize it, the resulting images may not be insightful or may even be misleading. Indeed, a hierarchical layout strongly conveys the sense of layering, which should reflect some application semantics. For graphs where such a layering is not natural, other layout methods may perform better (see Section 11.5.2).

An important difference between trees and hierarchical graphs from the layout perspective is that, for the latter, edges can connect nodes situated on nonconsecutive layers. In this case, it is impractical to draw edges as straight lines, as we did for trees, since this would create too many edge crossings. A better solution is to draw edges using smooth curves such as splines. This can be done as follows. For each edge $e = (m, n)$ that connects nodes situated on nonconsecutive layers L_i and L_j, one dummy node is inserted on each layer situated between L_i and L_j, and replaces the original edge with a set of edges (path) connecting the nodes m and n via the intermediate dummy nodes. Next, the edge crossings, between consecutive layers only, are minimized, as these are the only edges we have now. Finally, a spline or another smooth curve is constructed from node m to node n via the in-between dummy nodes. This curve is used as an edge glyph to map the original edge e. The dummy nodes are now discarded, and not visualized, as they were only used for construction of the splines.

Figure 11.13 shows a first example of the hierarchical graph layout. The depicted graph illustrates the evolution of the UNIX operating system.[6] The vertical axis roughly indicates the timeline, with the early versions of UNIX depicted at the top and the most-recent versions at the bottom respectively. The edge directions indicate the same evolution pattern. The twelve horizontal layers roughly correspond to the number of evolution steps, or phases, that the original "5th Edition" UNIX has evolved through. This picture, generated from the directed graph description using the dot tool from the open-source GraphViz graph-drawing software [GraphViz 06], gives intuitive insight into how the 47 versions of the UNIX system are related to each other from an evolution perspective. From a single initial version, no less than seven versions have emerged after two evolution steps. We see, however, that the version proliferation stays contained, as only four versions (FreeBSD, NetBSD, OpenBSD, and System V.4) are present on the latest evolution layer. We also notice how splines are used to map edges that connect nodes on nonconsecutive layers.

---

[6]The UNIX evolution data is part of the GraphViz graph visualization software [GraphViz 06].

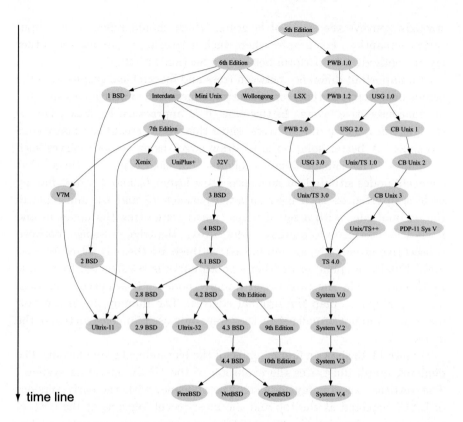

Figure 11.13. The evolution of the UNIX operating system, displayed as a hierarchical graph.

Figure 11.14 shows a more complex example. In the following, we describe the example and a possible investigation scenario based on this visualization. The nodes depict the functions of a C program that consists of two subsystems: a main program and an application library. The edge directions run from top to bottom and indicate relations between a caller function (top) and called function (bottom). Such graphs are known as *call graphs* in software engineering and are a useful tool for understanding the structure of large software source code bases. Let us examine this picture in more detail. The program entry point, i.e., the **main()** function, is colored in cyan, and is placed at the top, since it is the unique root node for this

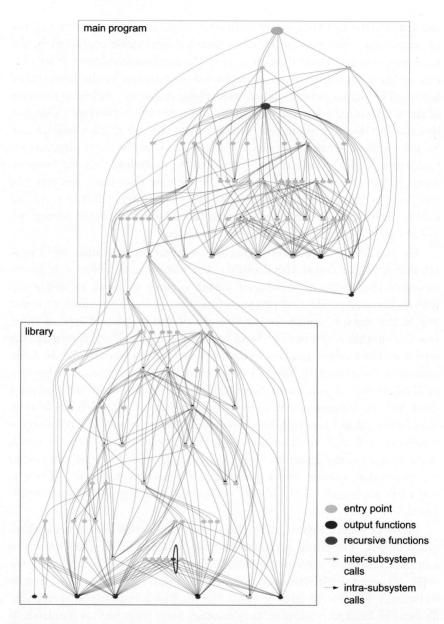

Figure 11.14. The call graph of a program visualized using a hierarchical graph layout. Note the separation between the main program and library subsystem.

call graph. One fact that we see right away is the two-layer structure of the program: the functions are clearly separated into those contained in the main program and those that are part of the application library. Note that this visual separation was not constructed on purpose by the hierarchical layout. The layout actually shows that there is, indeed, a clear separation of the software into a main subsystem and a library subsystem. This is a fact that we discover about our software using the call graph visualization. To gain further insight into which library functions the main program actually uses, and who calls them, we colored the call edges that run between nodes in the two subsystems in red. We see now that there are just five functions in the main subsystem that call the library. This is a second indication of good design. If we wanted to replace or drop the library, we would only need to modify these five functions.

We can learn more facts about the software by encoding additional attributes in the graph visualization. For instance, we color in blue the functions that perform text-based output operations, such as displaying text on the screen. We find two such functions in the main subsystem and five in the library (shown at the bottom of the graph). Three of these last five functions are heavily used by the library itself, as shown by the numerous black edges pointing to the respective nodes, and also by the main subsystem, as shown by the red edges running from the main subsystem to those nodes. Upon closer inspection of the source code, we find that these blue nodes correspond to text-printing functions, which are heavily used by the library for displaying warning and error messages. By following the edges back from the blue nodes to their callers, we can discover which parts of our library generate such messages, if desired. Finally, we color the nodes that contain edges pointing to themselves in purple. There is one single such node in the library subsystem, which indicates a recursive function.

However useful, Figure 11.14 also shows a limitation of the hierarchical graph layout. The edges, although carefully laid out using spline curves to minimize crossings, are still quite tangled and hard to tell apart from each other. In general, although the hierarchical graph layout described here is technically scalable to large graphs, the produced visualizations can easily become hard to read when they contain more than several hundreds of edges. Addressing this problem in general is quite difficult. In practice, two classes of approaches exist. First, one can modify the graph to eliminate

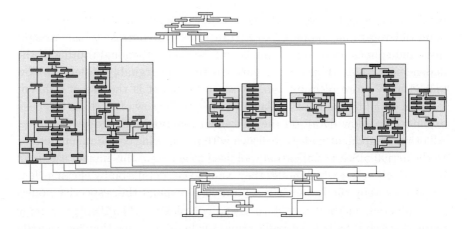

Figure 11.15. Containment and dependency relations in a software system, visualized using a hierarchical graph layout with orthogonal edge routing.

edges that are of little interest for the problem at hand, or group related edges together, until a reduced edge count is reached that can be satisfactorily handled by the available layout. This solution implies, however, that we know beforehand how to simplify our graph without losing important information.

A different type of variation of the hierarchical graph layout is shown in Figure 11.15.[7] The graph shown in this figure depicts the structure of a software system. Nodes represent software components, which are in this case modules (drawn in yellow) and functions (drawn in blue). The graph has two types of relations, or edges. Containment edges describe the nesting of subcomponents in parent components. Dependency edges describe functional dependencies between communicating components. Nodes are drawn as rectangular glyphs. The containment relation is shown by drawing the contained subcomponent glyphs inside the container (parent) component glyph. The dependency relation is shown by drawing the graph edges connecting the related components explicitly. Arrows on edges indicate the direction from a dependent component to the component(s) this depends on. The main organization of the layout follows the hierarchical layered principle used in Figures 11.13 and 11.14. The layout strives to put de-

---

[7]This figure has been generated using the aiSee software visualization tool [AbsInt 07].

pendent nodes at the top of the nodes they depend on. Yet, there are two main differences as compared to Figure 11.14. In contrast to the straight lines and splines used so far, this layout uses an orthogonal routing of the dependency edges. This creates patterns that are arguably easier to follow and visually more pleasant too. A second element is the use of different levels of detail throughout the layout. The middle row of modules has been expanded to show detail on the contained function nodes, drawn in blue. All other component nodes are drawn without showing containment details. In the actual aiSee visualization tool used to generate this image, users can interactively select which nodes they want to get details on by clicking their glyphs, whereby the layout is recomputed to expand the respective nodes.

A different method to reduce visual complexity when displaying large hierarchical graphs is to visually group, or bundle, edges that are visually close to each other, thereby reducing the visual clutter without throwing away information explicitly. Let us illustrate this method for the same problem of understanding complex call graphs. As shown in Figure 11.14, it is useful to visualize the relation in a software system of the function calls to the system layering. The layering describes how source code elements are contained within each other in a hierarchical fashion. A typical layering in object-oriented systems has three levels: methods (functions), classes, and files. We would like to extend the visualization from Figure 11.14 to show call relations between all layers.

Technically, we have now a graph with three types of nodes, i.e., methods, classes, and files, and two types of relations, i.e., call and containment. The proposed method, described by Holten [Holten 06], works as illustrated in Figure 11.16. First, we lay out all the graph nodes in three concentric rings. The inner ring shows the functions, the middle ring the classes, and the outer ring the files. Every node is shown as a ring sector. The relative positioning of the sectors along the three rings indicates containment. For example, in the lower-left area of Figure 11.16(a), the green-colored methods are all contained in a single light blue-colored class, which is in turn contained in the yellow-colored file. After the nodes are laid out, the layout of the call relations proceeds. Every call edge is laid out using a spline curve whose start and end points are the caller and called nodes on the inner ring. The spline's control points are constructed using a radial tree layout (not shown in Figure 11.16) of the method, class, and file nodes and the containment relations. The net effect of this method is that

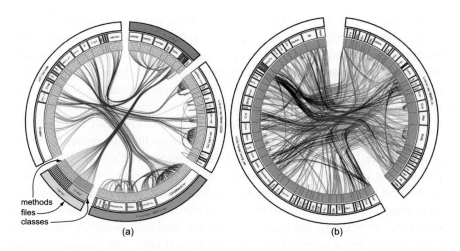

methods
files
classes
(a)   (b)

Figure 11.16. The call graphs of two programs visualized in relation to their hierarchical layering. The layout used suggests that the left system is more modular than the right system.

edges emerging from methods in the same class and which go to methods in another class are "bundled" together as they get farther from the circular sector corresponding to that class. The same bundling occurs at a higher level when call edges connect methods in two different files. Finally, the edges are drawn using a two-color scheme interpolated along the edge, where one color stands for caller and the other for called methods, respectively. For example, in Figure 11.16(a), blue indicates caller and red called methods. We encourage the reader to study the layout's design details from Holten [Holten 06] and implement this method as an exercise.

The visualization shown in Figure 11.16 allows us to discover several aspects about the structure of a software system. The first system (Figure 11.16(a)) has five files, which roughly correspond to different subsystems. If we look at the central area, we can easily identify four main call bundles between these files. These correspond to "strong" interactions between the respective subsystems. Consider, for example, the tight bundle going from the yellow subsystem (lower left) to the orange one (upper right). This bundle indicates that the yellow subsystem calls the orange one. To be more precise, most methods in the yellow subsystem call the purple class in the orange subsystem. In contrast, the large, dark green subsystem (lower right) exhibits many calls to itself, as indicated by the localized curved edges. Finally, both the yellow file and the large (uncolored) file in the upper-left part of the image have mostly blue edges, which indicates that these are calling subsystems, which probably contain application logic rather than library code. The orange subsystem is connected with the rest via red edges only, which suggest this is called (library) code. If we examine its label, we find, indeed, the name "Libraries/Database."

The second system visualized with the hierarchical edge bundle technique (Figure 11.16(b)) tells a quite different story. The system has a comparable hierarchy of methods, classes, and files, of roughly the same size as the first system. However, we see far less clearly delimited call bundles. This suggests that the software system has a considerably less modular structure, or what in software development parlance is called "spaghetti code."[8] A different edge coloring scheme is used here: blue denotes virtual function calls and green normal (statically resolved) function calls respectively. The edge direction is encoded by luminance: bright denotes caller, and dark called. Although the call structure is quite complex, we see that there are considerably fewer virtual method calls (blue curves) than ordinary calls (red). Also, we notice a high concentration of virtual calls going to the orange-colored class. This suggests an interface class that is heavily used throughout the system.

Force-directed layouts. In the previous sections, we have shown how to construct layouts for relational data that form a hierarchical structure, such as trees and hierarchical graphs. However, as already noted in Section 11.5.2, in many applications one is confronted with the problem of visualizing a general graph that does not form a natural hierarchy. For such graphs, a different class of layouts may produce better results. These layouts, known as *force-directed layouts* or *spring embedders*, are described in this section.

The main idea behind force-directed layouts can be formulated in terms of an optimization problem, as follows. Given a graph $G = (N, E)$, we define a so-called energy function $\mathcal{E}$ that measures the quality of a layout of G in terms of a positive number. The lower the energy value is, the higher the quality of the layout. The energy function should be designed to measure the various quality parameters we are interested in. On the other hand, the energy function should depend on the controllable parameters

---

[8]The visual metaphor strongly suggests the spaghetti code denomination.

of our layout, such as node and edge shapes and positions. Once we have an appropriate energy function, we minimize it using some optimization algorithm. The resulting parameters are our desired layout.

This generic framework can be particularized in several ways. Several decisions are to be made, including the following:

1. how we measure the quality of a layout;

2. what elements of the layout we parameterize;

3. how we efficiently and effectively minimize the energy function.

These decisions are interrelated in several ways. We should only measure those layout quality attributes that can be influenced by the parameterized layout elements. As described in Section 11.5.2, a good layout has few edge crossings and edge bends, few node overlaps, favors short edges, and has a balanced aspect ratio. More subtle, and thus harder to measure and constrain, quality considerations are that the layout should reflect the graph symmetry and structure. Finally, although we may be able to design an energy function that measures all our quality attributes, finding the parameter values for which this function is minimal can be very costly and difficult.

To illustrate the preceding technique, we shall use a simple energy function that, nevertheless, is able in practice to produce good graph layouts [Fruchterman and Reingold 91]. This energy function attempts to enforce two quality criteria:

- connected graph nodes should be close;

- no two different nodes should be too close.

A simple way to describe an energy function that models these quality criteria is to use a physical analogy. Imagine that every node in the graph is a charged electric particle and every edge is an elastic spring. Hence, nodes connected by edges will exert an attraction force upon each other. This models the quality constraint that edges should be short. Additionally, all nodes will exert a repelling force on each other, regardless of whether they are connected or not. This models the second quality criterion that nodes should not overlap. We know, from classical mechanics, that the force is equal to the gradient of the potential energy, $\mathbf{F} = -\nabla E$. Our attractive and repulsive forces are indeed induced by a potential energy, as they only depend on the position of the graph nodes. Hence, to minimize the energy $\mathcal{E}$, we should move every graph node in the direction of the resultant force acting on it.

We now have to choose explicit expressions for the attractive and repulsive forces. Many choices are possible, some based on physical motivations, and some others following heuristics that yield good results in practice. A popular model for obtaining good quality layouts is to use the following forces:

$$
\begin{aligned}
\mathbf{F}_a(n_i, n_j) &= \frac{|\mathbf{p}_i - \mathbf{p}_j|^2}{k}, \\
\mathbf{F}_r(n_i, n_j) &= -\frac{k^2}{|\mathbf{p}_i - \mathbf{p}_j|},
\end{aligned}
\tag{11.2}
$$

where $\mathbf{F}_a$ is the attraction force and $\mathbf{F}_r$ is the repulsion force between two graph nodes n_i and n_j, $\mathbf{p}_i$ and $\mathbf{p}_j$ are the positions of these nodes, and k is a constant. Following Fruchterman and Reingold, we set k to $\frac{\sqrt{A}}{|N|}$, where A is the area in which we want to do the layout, and $|N|$ is the number of graph nodes [Fruchterman and Reingold 91].

Another model for the forces is as follows [Eades 84]:

$$
\begin{aligned}
\mathbf{F}_a(n_i, n_j) &= k \log |\mathbf{p}_i - \mathbf{p}_j|, \\
\mathbf{F}_r(n_i, n_j) &= -\frac{k}{|\mathbf{p}_i - \mathbf{p}_j|^2}.
\end{aligned}
\tag{11.3}
$$

Yet another energy model is the following [Kamada and Kawai 89]:

$$
\mathcal{E} = \frac{1}{2} \sum_{i=1}^{N-1} \sum_{j=i+1}^{N} c_{ij} (|\mathbf{p}_i - \mathbf{p} - j| - d_{ij})^2.
\tag{11.4}
$$

where c_{ij} is one if nodes n_i and n_j are connected, otherwise it is zero, and d_{ij} is the length of the shortest path in the graph connecting n_i and n_j. Essentially, this energy model states that a good layout has the geometric distances between connected nodes proportional to the distances in the graph. If desired, forces equal to the energy gradient can be computed in order to minimize the energy, as described next.

In all the previous models, the attraction forces between node pairs can be multiplied with an edge weight factor, which models the strength of the respective relation. This is useful if some relations are to be visually emphasized more than others. In the elastic spring metaphor, this is equivalent to using springs of different stiffnesses.

```
for(int i=0;i<N;i++)           //Initialize layout to random positions
   p_i = random position;
float t = t_0;                  //Initial maximal allowed move

for (int i=1;i<ITER;i++) //Do the layout
{
   for(int i=0;i<N;i++)        //Apply repulsive forces F_r
   {
      p'_i = 0;
      for (int j=0;j<N;j++)
         if (j!=i)
            p'_i += (p_i-p_j)/|p_i-p_j| F_r(i,j);
   }

   for (int e=0;e<E;e++)       //Apply attractive forces F_a
   {
      int f = e.first;         //Get index of first node of e
      int t = e.second;        //Get index of second node of e
      e = p_f - p_t;
      p'_f -= e/|e| F_a(f,t);
      p'_e += e/|e| F_a(f,t);
   }

   for(int i=0;i<N;i++)        //Limit displacement of nodes
   {
      d = p'_i - p_i;
      p_i+ = d/|d| min (|δ|,t);
   }
   t -= Δt;                    //Reduce maximal allowed move t
}
```

Listing 11.1. Force-directed graph layout algorithm.

Given a force model, we now minimize the energy by moving each node in the direction of the resultant force acting on it, i.e., in the direction that decreases the energy the most. This direction coincides with the sum of the attraction forces corresponding to all edges connected to that node and the repulsive force between that node and all other nodes in the graph. The pseudocode of the complete force-directed layout algorithm is given in Listing 11.1. The algorithm receives as input a graph with N nodes and E edges, each edge e connecting two nodes denoted e.first and e.second. The output of the algorithm is the set of N nodes positions $\mathbf{p}_i$.

The force-directed layout algorithm has three phases. First, we compute the repulsive force $\mathbf{F}_r$ for every node, following either of the models given by Equations (11.2) or (11.3), and apply these forces to determine new positions $\mathbf{p}'_i$ of the nodes. Next, we compute the attractive forces $\mathbf{F}_a$ along each edge and use these to update the positions of the edge nodes accordingly. Finally, we set the actual node positions $\mathbf{p_i}$ to the computed ones $\mathbf{p}'_i$. After each complete position-update iteration, we decrease the maximal amount t that any node is allowed to move by a factor Δt. The parameter t is sometimes referred to as the *temperature* of the layout algorithm, since its decrease determines a reduction of the nodes' motion, which is analogous to the temperature-controlled Brownian motion of small-scale particles in physics. A good starting value t_0 for t is a small fraction, e.g., one-tenth of the size of the drawing space the layout should fit in. A good decrease factor for t is a small fraction Δt of the current maximal move, e.g., one-tenth of it. These heuristics gradually limit the motion of the nodes, which in turn favors the convergence of the layout. The entire node-moving process is repeated ITER iterations, after which the forces should be small and, hence, energy $\mathcal{E}$ should be close to its minimum. In practice, several tens up to several hundreds of iterations should deliver good results for most graphs [GraphViz 06].

Figure 11.17 shows a call graph of a C++ program of approximately 1000 lines of code, visualized using a force-directed layout.[9] The graph nodes, depicting functions, are drawn using spherical glyphs colored to indicate the function type, in a manner similar to Figure 11.14. Warm colors show methods of the five core application classes; green indicates methods of string handling classes; blue indicates methods of Standard Template Library (STL) container classes, e.g., trees, maps, and sets [Plaugher et al. 00]; and white indicates other functions, such as those from the standard C library. The program entry point (main() function) is shown by a slightly larger cyan spherical glyph. The edges are drawn using Gouraud-shaded lines, similar to Figure 11.5, from dark (caller) to white (called).

Several aspects are visible in this image. Probably the most salient elements we see are the three similar-color node clusters corresponding to the core functions (warm colors), containers (blue), and string functions (green). These indicate, in a rough way, a system decomposition into groups of functions strongly related to each other, by means of calls. A way to interpret the layout is that the system core uses string functions, which,

---

[9]The layout is computed by the neato program, which is part of the freely available GraphViz software [GraphViz 06].

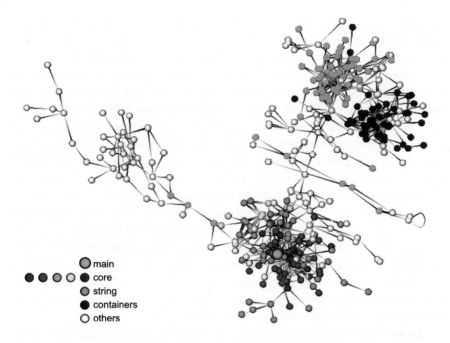

Figure 11.17. Call graph of a C++ program visualized using a force-directed layout. The node colors indicate the function types. The graph contains 314 nodes (functions) and 718 edges (calls).

in turn, use container functions. However, the core does not directly use container functions, as there is no edge between the warm-color cluster and the blue cluster. A fourth cluster containing gray nodes is visible in the left of the image. Since this cluster is connected with the rest of the system via a single green (string function) node, marked A in Figure 11.17, it is probable that functions in this cluster contain implementation features for the function A. The main function is, not surprisingly, laid out close to the center of the core subsystem. This indicates that this function calls, hence strongly depends on, many other core functions. Using this visualization, we can quickly isolate the system core from the remaining functions to analyze it in further detail, e.g., by selecting the respective nodes and zooming on them in a separate view.

However useful, this visualization also outlines some of the limitations of force-directed layouts. The force-directed layout attempts to realize several aesthetic criteria, such as a distance between nodes that reflects their connectivity, by numerically minimizing an energy function. The force-directed algorithm, based on the pseudocode in Listing 11.1, cannot guarantee that it always finds the global minimum of the energy function, since it works by seeking the steepest energy decrease at every step. The algorithm may stop at a local energy minimum that is far from the global one. Several heuristics are used in practice to solve this problem and also to accelerate the minimization process. A good example of such heuristics is given by the graph embedder algorithm (GEM) [Frick et al. 94]. GEM adds a supplementary force that pulls the nodes toward their barycenter, thereby accelerating the layout convergence. A second addition is a set of heuristics that detect whether the minimization oscillates or rotates parts of the graph, which indicates a potential blocking in a local minimum. To escape such situations, random shakes of the graph nodes are added. Such heuristics help the energy-minimization process, but have the drawback that they introduce nondeterminism in the layout: introducing a small change in a graph, or even running the same layout algorithm on the same graph, may lead to different visualizations.

From a computational viewpoint, force-directed layouts are more computationally demanding than the hierarchical layouts discussed in Section 11.5.2. In practice, many force-directed algorithms will not produce good layouts for dense graphs with more than a few thousands edges, or will take minutes or even longer to compute such layouts. Multiscale layout methods address this problem up to a certain extent by first laying out a simplified graph and then using this layout as a skeleton to construct the layout of the entire graph [Harel and Koren 00, Koren et al. 03]. Such methods can deliver a tremendous speed-up of the layout, but their quality is highly dependent on the heuristics used to simplify the graph, as well as on how the actual graph structure fits those heuristics. As explained in Section 11.3.4, relational attributes do not allow interpolation. Hence, one must find a different way to simplify, or subsample, a graph than, for example, a signal sampled on a spatial grid.

Speaking of the layout quality, one must note that even if a global minimum of the used energy function is found, this does not guarantee an easy-to-understand visualization. A typical problem with force-directed layouts is clusters of highly interconnected nodes, such as the ones discussed for Figure 11.17. The force-directed layout is able to separate the clusters

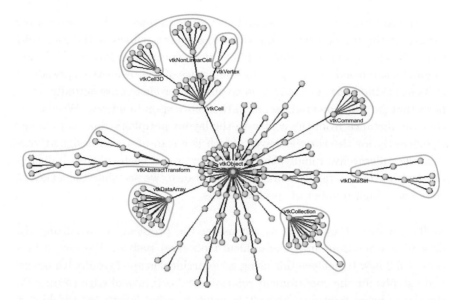

Figure 11.18. Inheritance relations in the VTK class library visualized using the GEM force-directed layout. Specialization subtrees are indicated by blue outlines and labeled by the respective subtree root class.

themselves, but does not offer a clear picture of how the nodes within a cluster are connected. As a rule of thumb, a good layout algorithm will most often produce a visually structured layout if the concerned graph does indeed have a clear structure, but will have a limited effectiveness on laying out densely connected graphs.

What if we use a force-directed algorithm to lay out a highly structured graph, such as a tree? Figure 11.18 shows the tree of inheritance relations in the Common subsystem of the popular Visualization Toolkit (VTK) library [Schroeder et al. 04]. VTK is a class library written in C++ using single inheritance almost exclusively, hence the inheritance relations between its classes form a tree structure. The force-directed layout shown in Figure 11.18, produced with the freely available GEM force-directed layout software [GEM 07], is strikingly similar to radial layouts such as the one in Figure 11.6. There is less regularity in the force-directed layout of a tree, e.g., nodes the same distance from the root are not exactly placed on a circle centered at the root, as in the case of the radial layout. Nevertheless, the resulting image is clear and easy to comprehend. We immediately locate, at the image center, the class vtkObject, which is the hierarchy root. Next, we discover that vtkObject is specialized into several sub-hierarchies, labeled in the figure by the names of the respective specialized classes (vtkDataSet, vtkCell, and so on). These classes are actually interfaces that get implemented deeper in their corresponding trees. We also see that the distance from the center to the layout periphery does not change significantly for the various leaves, which is a sign of a well-designed, mature class hierarchy. Finally, the fan-out, or size of each subtree, indicates the number of specialized classes. For instance, we see that the vtkCell class has a high number of specializations.

Multiple views. Finally, let us reconsider the problem of visualizing the dependency relations in a hierarchical (software) system. We saw in Section 11.5.2 how to achieve this using a hierarchical graph layout with nested node glyphs for the containment relations and orthogonal edge routing for the dependency relations, as well as using a radial layout for the hierarchy and bundled splines for the dependency relations. We can achieve a similar insight using force-directed layouts, too. Figure 11.19 demonstrates the method. In contrast to the previous visualizations, we have now three different views, depicted by the three corresponding subwindows.

The bottom view shows the hierarchical structure of a software system using a rooted-tree layout. For this system, we want to visualize the call relations between several subsystems. In this example, the user has selected, by means of direct mouse interaction, two subtrees in the bottom view, which correspond to two subsystems. The selected subtrees are rendered in red. For this selection, the top-left view displays the call and hierarchy relations. For every node (system), its contents (subsystems) are laid out using a force-directed layout in a bottom-up manner, i.e., from the leaf nodes upward, considering the call relations between the respective subsystems. The size of a node is set to the bounding box of its children's layout. Leaf nodes that have no dependency relations are laid out separately in a tightly packed gridlike pattern, to save space. The call relations are rendered as in Figure 11.17, i.e., using lines connecting the respective nodes. Whereas Figure 11.16 showed containment by means of correlated concentric rings, we now show the same by means of the nesting of the nodes. This layout is quite similar to the one depicted in Figure 11.15, with two main differences. Whereas the layout in Figure 11.15 uses a hierarchical node arrangement on the vertical axis and orthogonal edge routing, we use here a spring embedder to arrange nodes and straight lines to draw the edges, respectively.

It is interesting to compare the top-right view in Figure 11.19 with Figure 11.15. Although Figure 11.15 shows a larger graph, we can argue that this visualization is easier to follow than the one in Figure 11.19. An important reason for this is the highly structured ordering of both nodes and edges in orthogonally-aligned patterns in Figure 11.15, as compared to the less structured placement provided by the force-directed layout in Figure 11.19 (top-right). Moreover, the layout in Figure 11.15 has no overlaps

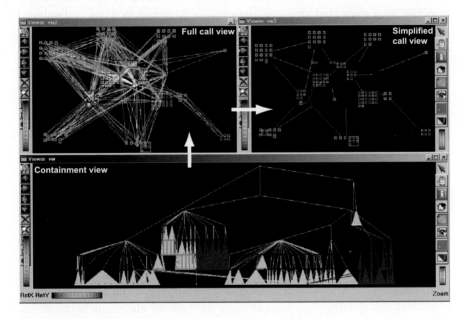

Figure 11.19. Hierarchical and call relations in a software system visualized with a combination of tree and force-directed layouts. The bottom view shows the entire system hierarchy, where two subsystems of interest have been selected (rendered in red). The top-left view shows the call and hierarchy relations in the selected subsystems using a force-directed layout. The top-right view shows a simplified view of the latter, where several call relations have been filtered out. The arrows between the images show the order of creating and examining the visualizations.

between edges and nodes, while the edge crossings always occur at right angles. In contrast, the force-directed layout in Figure 11.19 (top-right) poses no constraints on the intersections of edges with nodes or with other edges.

Since there are numerous call relations, the top-left image in Figure 11.19 is quite hard to understand. A second step that helps is to filter the relations and preserve only those that connect *sibling* nodes, i.e., nodes that are direct children of the same parent. This produces the visualization in the top-right of Figure 11.19, which is easier to follow.

The preceding visualization illustrates several common design decisions used in practice in showing relational datasets. First, several views are used to show several aspects. The views are *correlated*, in the sense that a selection in a view (bottom one) determines a change in what is displayed in the other views (top ones). The correlation is strengthened by using the same colors for the same node types in all three views. The views work at different levels of detail. The bottom view serves as an *overview* of the entire dataset, whereas the top views are successively simplified *detail* views. Finally, the two types of relations in the dataset are mapped using simple techniques: containment is shown as vertical tree layers (overview) or nested boxes (detail views), whereas association (calls) is shown as lines between nodes (detail views). This visualization is arguably less compact and requires extra interaction as compared to the one shown in Figure 11.16. On the other hand, the tree layout, box nesting, and lines-between-boxes are more familiar and accepted visual representations to a large class of users than the bundled splines and radial layout. As always in visualization design, there is no clear-cut answer, but the task of optimizing is a design problem.

Graph splatting. Although they use different layouts, the tree and graph visualizations described in the previous sections all share the same visual representation of node glyphs connected by one-dimensional curves that represent the edges. As we have seen, such visualizations often have a limited scalability. Indeed, it is hard for the eye to effectively interpret drawings with more than several hundreds of such elements, given a drawing surface of finite size.

Making a visualization scalable can be approached from two main directions. First, we can simplify the *data* to be visualized such that, given a certain mapping technique, it yields understandable images. Second, we can leave the input data unchanged, but design visual level-of-detail techniques such as zooming that simplify the *image* produced by the mapping process. In the first case, we need a way to simplify, or subsample, the application data itself. In the second case, we need a way to simplify, or subsample, the mapped image.

For many scivis applications, both data and the mapped images exhibit continuous properties, as they actually represent smooth signals defined over two- or three-dimensional spaces. This allows the use of a wide array of signal sampling strategies both before and after the mapping stage. For graph data displayed using ball-and-stick visualizations, the situation is different. First, the process of subsampling a relational dataset, such as a graph, is usually more complex and application-dependent than, for example, subsampling an image. Given this, we shall not discuss graph simplification methods here, but refer the reader to the specialized literature in this field [Tutte 01, Di Battista et al. 99]. Second, the ball-and-stick graph drawings discussed in the previous sections are inherently discrete. A point of the displayed image either belongs to a node or edge glyph or it does not. Simply zooming out the graph rendering works well only for relatively simple graphs and small zoom factors. When zooming out a large graph rendering, the clutter may actually increase rather than decrease, making the zoomed-out view harder to understand.

However, the *space* in which the layout takes place is one element of the graph-drawing process that does exhibit continuous properties. Since *distances* in such spaces are continuous quantities, zoom-out techniques should work well, provided that we are able to ensure the same continuity property for the mapped shapes for nodes and edges.

A solution to the problem of creating a visually continuous mapping of graph data is the *graph splatting* technique [van Liere and de Leeuw 03]. The easiest way to describe this technique is by means of an analogy to image processing. Consider a discrete two-dimensional line drawing consisting of lines (foreground) and empty space (background). If we apply a Gaussian filter on this drawing, we obtain a continuous, smooth image where the sharp transitions between foreground and background are blurred (see Section 9.3.3). The blurred edges become now two-dimensional shapes. Given a sufficient amount of blurring, we can now gradually zoom out the image and see both nodes and edges vanish progressively.

If we assume that we use a graph layout that places strongly related nodes close to each other, we can refine this idea further. We first compute the desired layout and obtain a 2D position $p_i \in \mathbb{R}^2$ for each node $i \in [1..n]$. Next, let us assume that every point i has a scalar *importance* value $f_i \in \mathbb{R}$. We can now compute a continuous signal $f(p)$ by summing up Gaussian radial basis functions (RBFs) $\Phi_i(p) = e^{-k|p-p_i|^2}$ centered at the node positions p_i and scaled by the node importances f_i:

$$f(p) = \sum_{i-1}^{n} f_i \Phi_i(p). \tag{11.5}$$

This yields a continuous 2D scalar signal $f(p)$ that reflects the density of graph nodes in the two-dimensional space, weighted by the node importances. The node importances can be chosen to reflect data of interest of the underlying graph, or set to 1, in case all nodes are equally important. Close to high densities of points or to highly important points, this signal will be high. The signal is low in areas far away from high point densities, or from important points. The graph-splatting technique is quite similar to the scattered point interpolation technique using Gaussian RBFs described in Section 3.9.2 and the reconstruction of surfaces from scattered point sets using radial basis functions of finite support (see Section 8.3.2). However, there are some differences. For large graphs, a good layout tries to pull clusters of highly interconnected nodes apart from each other, in order to emphasize the graph structure. Hence, the splatted signal $f(p)$ exhibits strong variations which, when visualized, let users detect the location and compactness of such clusters. In contrast, a good point distribution for surface reconstruction is close to a uniform density value which, when isosurfaced, delivers the surface itself. Indeed, note that the RBFs in Equation (11.5) are not normalized to obey the partition of unity property, as we did for the scattered point interpolation (see Equation (3.44)).

After computing the density signal from the graph layout, we can display it using any of the scalar visualization techniques discussed in Chapter 5.

Figure 11.20 illustrates the use of graph splatting to visualize dependencies between modules of a software system. The first image (Figure 11.20(a)) shows a classical force-directed layout of the dependency graph produced using the GEM layout software [GEM 07]. Edge colors emphasize the dependency relation direction, which goes from a module (black) to the other modules this depends on (bright green). Node colors show the number of dependencies a module has using a rainbow colormap. Blue nodes have few dependencies, whereas red ones have the most dependencies in the system. This visualization is quite complex due to the high number of relations. Figure 11.20(b) shows the graph splatting applied to this dataset, visualized using a rainbow colormap. Here, the node importances (f_i in Equation (11.5)) are equal to the number of dependencies of the respective nodes. Hence, red colors indicate either tight clusters of modules or modules with many dependencies. Three "hot spots" have been labeled with the names of the representative modules they contain: Main, GUI, and Reader. These are high-level components of the considered system that consist of strongly connected modules or modules with many dependencies. In a real application, such information could be displayed interactively as the user sweeps the rendered graph splatting with the mouse. This technique, called *brushing*, is a frequently-used design element of both scivis and infovis applications.

Several other exploration scenarios can be used in conjunction with graph splatting. Isolines can be displayed to explicitly outline the "hot spot" regions in the visualized graph. Different weights derived from the graph attributes can be used together with the Gaussian splats to emphasize different patterns in the data. Graph splatting can be used with different layouts besides force-directed ones. However, it is important to note that the usefulness of graph splatting is highly related to the capability of the underlying graph layout to group related nodes in spatially separated clusters. If the layout cannot separate such groups, e.g., due to a highly interconnected graph, or if the resulting groups do not have a clear semantics, the emerging graph splatting image will be of limited use.

Multidimensional scaling. Graph splatting can be applied in a more general context than the visualization of relational data. Consider, for example, a set of data points $D = \{p_i\}$, where every point p_i has a k-dimensional vector of attributes $(a_1^i, \ldots, a_K^i) \in A^K$ defined on some domain A. One task that frequently occurs in practice is to visualize the structure of the dataset D. Subtasks thereof are the identifications of groups, or clusters, of similar points, and discovering the patterns in which the points are

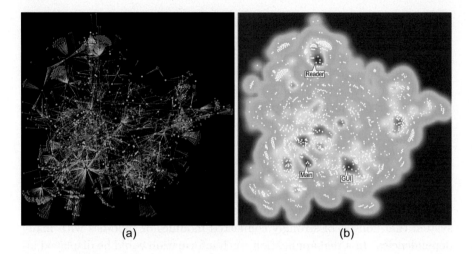

(a)   (b)

Figure 11.20. Software dependency graph visualized with (a) force-directed layout and (b) graph splatting (b). The splatting density is scaled by the number of dependent modules. Warm colors in (b) emphasize high-level system modules. The nodes, positioned identically to the layout shown in (a), are depicted by white dots.

distributed. For $K = 2$ or $K = 3$, we can simply draw the data points to obtain a scattered 2D or 3D plot where the patterns of interest will be visible. The problem becomes difficult for large values of K. In such a case, we must create a mapping between the K-dimensional space A^K where the points live and the two- or three-dimensional space where the visualization resides.

There are several ways to create such a mapping. One method is described next. Let us first assume that we have a distance function $d : A^K \times A^K \to \mathbb{R}_+$ over the attribute vectors. Such a distance can be computed, for example, based on the distance $\delta : A \times A \to \mathbb{R}_+$ between two attribute values, as follows:

$$d(a_1, \cdots, a_K, b_1, \ldots, b_K) = \sqrt{\sum_{i=1}^{K} \delta(a_i, b_i)^2}. \tag{11.6}$$

In case of numerical attributes, δ is the difference and d becomes the Euclidean distance in $\mathbb{R}^k$. For non-numerical attributes, one must design a distance δ that reflects the similarities of interest for the problem at hand. Given the distance d, we shall compute a position $q_i \in R^k$ for every data point i, with $k \in \{2, 3\}$. This computation, which associates a low-dimensional position to a high-dimensional attribute value, is known as *multidimensional scaling* [Borg and Groenen 97, Cox and Cox 01, Mead 92]. The name reflects an important property of the computation: the distances between data points in the low-dimension k should reflect the distances between the same points in the original high-dimension K. In the ideal case, we would like the two distances to be proportional to each other. If this can be achieved, then we can detect data patterns in the high-dimension K by looking at a scattered plot done using the low-dimensional positions q_i. This principle works also if there is not a strict proportionality relation between the distances in the two spaces, as long as the distances are highly correlated.

Multidimensional scaling can be computed in a variety of ways. A simple, though not very high-performace way is to use force-directed layouts. Consider a graph in which every data point i is a node, and every distance relation $d(i, j)$ is an edge between the corresponding nodes i and j. The edge stiffness is set to be inversely proportional to the distance between its nodes. Performing a force-directed layout on this graph will bring points that are highly similar in K-dimensional space close to each other in the k-dimensional layout space. In practice, several refinements must be applied to this basic idea to make it usable. Edges corresponding to high distance values are not created, as these have a negligible impact on the layout. Reducing the number of edges also considerably accelerates the layout process. Furthermore, more sophisticated layouts than the basic force-directed method and more complex distance functions can be used to obtain a better reflection of the K-dimensional distances in the computed k-dimensional layout.

After the layout is computed, the graph edges are discarded and the data points are visualized as a k-dimensional scattered plot. Here, graph splatting can be effectively used to emphasize dense point clusters, especially when many such points are drawn. In this context, graph splatting provides a simple but very effective instrument for visualizing multidimensional data in an easy-to-understand way.

11.6   Multivariate Data Visualization

Let us reconsider the task described in the previous section in the context of multidimensional scaling. We are given a set of data points $D = \{p_i\}$, where every point p_i has a k-dimensional vector of attributes $(a_1^i, \ldots, a_K^i) \in A^K$ defined on some domain A. Such a dataset is called *multivariate*, as there are several variables, or attributes, per data point. We want to visualize the dataset D such that correlations, outliers, clusters, and trends in the data become visible. We have seen that multidimensional scaling, implemented for example in the form of graph splatting, can be used to emphasize groups of data points that are close in the space A^K.

However useful, visualizations based on multidimensional scaling do not show the individual variables, or dimensions, of the data, but just the overall distances between data points. In some cases, we are interested in examining the correlation and distribution of the individual values of the various dimensions, as well as the overall distances between the data points. One technique that allows us to perform such investigations is the *parallel coordinate* plot [Inselberg and Dimsdale 90, Wegman 90]. This technique is described in this section.

To easier understand the way parallel coordinate plots work, let us consider an example.[10] The dataset contains around 400 data points. Each data point describes a car via $K = 7$ attributes: miles per gallon (MPG), number of cylinders, horsepower, weight, acceleration, manufacturing year, and origin (Europe, US, or Japan). Besides the latter, which is ordinal, and the number of cylinders, which is an integer, all other attributes are real numbers.

These data tuples can be seen as data points in a $K = 7$-dimensional space. Since we cannot directly render into seven dimensions, we must find ways to map this space onto two or three dimensions. One way to do this is to consider the dimensions as the columns of a data table, and each point as a table row. Such a visualization has already been described in Section 11.4. The parallel coordinates also map each dimension to a separate vertical axis. However, instead of corresponding to a horizontal row, each data point p_i is now mapped as a polyline that connects the points on the vertical axes whose ordinates (y values) equal the point attributes a_i.

---

[10]The visualizations in this section are created with the *parvis* open-source software. The software and example dataset are available from [Lederman 07].

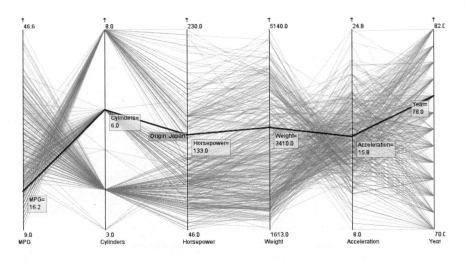

Figure 11.21. Parallel coordinate plot showing six attributes (miles-per-gallon, cylinders, horsepower, weight, acceleration, and manufacturing year) for about 400 cars. A selected car is shown in the image as a red polyline with the individual attribute values displayed as labels

Figure 11.21 illustrates the parallel plot technique for the car dataset. There are six axes, corresponding to the first six data attributes. Each axis is scaled individually to show the full range of its attribute value. Although the different axes have different ranges, this does not reduce the usefulness of the parallel coordinate plot, which shows correlations of attribute value distributions rather than the absolute values. Each polyline represents a different car of the several hundred in the dataset. The polylines are drawn with a certain amount of transparency using additive blending (see Section 2.5). In this way, areas covered by many lines, i.e., where the data are correlated, appear darker on the plot. The red line and associated labels show the details of the car record under the mouse pointer: a six-cylinder vehicle weighing 3410 lbs manufactured in 1978. The "origin" attribute is shown only for the selected data point, and not for all data points on a separate axis, as it is of ordinal type. For the selected car in the image, its value is "Japan."

This visualization already shows a number of facts. Clusters of lines that run parallel indicate similar data points. Lines widely spread apart along an axis show a large variation of that data attribute. We quickly

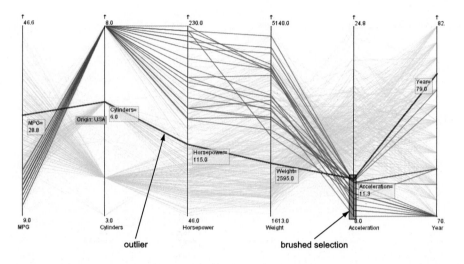

Figure 11.22. Using brushing to select the low-acceleration cars. The selected cars are shown in red. An interesting outlier is highlighted further.

see, for example, that most cars have 4, 6, or 8 cylinders, and there are a very few with 3 or 5 cylinders. There is a strong inverse correlation between the number of cylinders and the MPG rating, which is easily understandable. The fan-out of the lines going from the "Cylinders" to the "Horsepower" axis (right next to it) is quite strong. This shows that the number of cylinders does not determine the horsepower value. The lines from "Horsepower" to "Weight" run mostly parallel, which indicates a strong proportionality of the two attributes. Finally, the similar bundles of lines emerging from the "Year" axis (rightmost) indicate that there are similar numbers of cars produced every year, and that they come in all acceleration categories.

Adding interaction to the preceding basic visualization further supports our queries. Using brushing (point-drag-click with the mouse on the axes), we can select ranges of attribute values. Figure 11.22 shows the visualization after selecting a "low acceleration" attribute range. The polylines corresponding to all data points falling within the selected range are drawn in red. This shows us that cars with a low acceleration are also the heaviest, have powerful engines, are quite fuel-inefficient (low MPG), originate mostly from the early years of the considered period (1970), and all have

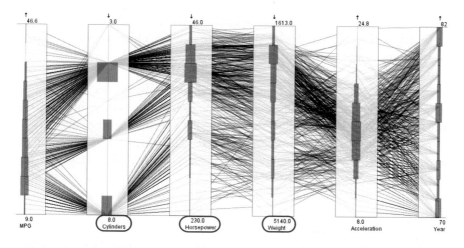

Figure 11.23. Enhancing parallel coordinates. The orientation of the axes whose labels are marked in red has been swapped as compared to Figure 11.22. Histograms show the attribute value distribution over 10 equally sized ranges for each axis.

the maximum number of cylinders (8). These are probably trucks or vans. We also find an outlier, shown by the selected thick red line with labels. This is a low-acceleration car, produced later (1978), which is quite light and low-power, has six cylinders, and an average MPG.

Many additional interaction and visual enhancements can be built on top of the basic concept of parallel coordinates to further support investigation tasks. Figure 11.23 illustrates several possibilities. Here, the orientation of several axes ("Cylinders," "Horsepower," and "Weight") has been swapped as compared to the previous examples. This reduces the number of line crossings, since inversely correlated axes become, after the orientation swapping, directly correlated. A second addition is the overlay of axes with histograms that show the number of data points within a number of fixed value range intervals. This figure uses 10 intervals for each axis. The histograms show how all attribute values are distributed along each axis, while the lines connecting them show high correlations between different ranges. For example, we see that most cars have four cylinders, and of those most have a low horsepower, low weight, and high MPG. The histogram of the "Year" axis shows that this dataset contains roughly the same number of entries for each manufacturing year. Such findings were in principle possible also by looking at the number of lines connected to a certain range of an axis, but the histogram displays make them easier and more accurate.

Several extensions have been proposed to the basic design described here. Hierarchical clustering and display techniques help reduce clutter when visualizing large datasets with parallel coordinates [Fua et al. 99]. Various brushing mechanisms can be added to help selecting more complex patterns than possible by simple axis range selection [Hauser et al. 02]. Parallel coordinate plots can be integrated with other techniques, such as scatter plots and statistical analysis tools, to facilitate the combination of different exploration tasks [Ward 94]. For more details, we refer the reader to a survey on this topic [Inselberg 98].

However useful, parallel coordinate plots also have their limitations. For large, complex datasets with many attributes, they can produce cluttered images that are hard to understand. The ordering of axes is also very important. Correlations are easier to find between axes that are (direct) neighbors than between axes placed far away from each other. In practice, this means a fair amount of interaction such as brushing and axis swapping and reordering is needed to understand complex datasets. Finally, parallel coordinates are abstract and novel for many users and may require a certain amount of training.

11.7   Text Visualization

As explained in Section 11.3.3, text is an important attribute in infovis datasets. The question is: how can we visualize text? To answer this question in detail, let us first consider the types of information contained in a text document. This information can be structured into three categories: content, structure, and metadata. The *content* describes the information contained in the text itself. The typical way to comprehend this information is apparent to the reader who reads these very lines: text content can be understood by reading it. On the next level, *structure* characterizes how the text is organized hierarchically into several levels of abstraction, such as paragraphs, sections, chapters, or elements of a document collection. The table of contents of a book can be seen as a basic form of visualization of the document structure. However, getting further insight into large document sets requires different visualization methods beyond plain reading, as the task now is to comprehend the document organization rather than its minute contents. Finally, *metadata* describes all types of information related to the text that are not contained in the text itself. Typically, metadata stores information about the document itself rather than information about the document content. Metadata includes cross-references, keywords, and indexes, as well as information on the document author, publisher, and publication date. Visualization methods that target metadata should provide insight in the metadata itself, but also ways to correlate metadata with the document content and structure.

A different dimension of text visualization concerns the *origin* of the data. All types of text-related information (content, structure, and metadata) can be already present in the document to visualize, or can be computed using various text-analysis methods in order to support a certain task. For example, document-retrieval systems, such as the engines internally used by the Google search tool, analyze documents to generate information used for classification and indexing. This process falls within the data-enrichment step of the visualization pipeline (see Section 4.1.2). Text analysis is an extremely wide topic, including techniques that range from neural networks and statistical analysis to lexical, syntactic, and semantic analysis and natural-language processing.

Just as for other visualization applications, methods for visualizing text should be scalable. An efficient text-visualization technique should support the user in understanding the structure and contents of a text document, as well as in finding specific details, in a shorter time than one would need to read the entire document.

Several visualization methods have been devised to cope with the tasks of quickly, scalably, and flexibly getting insight into text documents. These visualizations differ as a function of both the type of document, e.g., narrative text or software source code, and the type of task, e.g., getting a structural overview, comparing several documents or several versions of the same document, or answering precise, application-specific questions. In the following sections, we shall illustrate a few examples of text visualization methods encountered in practice.

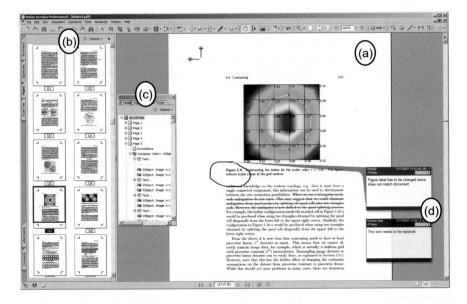

Figure 11.24. Visualization of an electronic (PDF) version of this book in the Adobe Acrobat system. Four design elements are emphasized. (a) The document's detailed content. (b) A page-level overview. (c) The document structure. (d) Annotation metadata.

11.7.1 Content-Based Visualization

A natural way to visualize a text document is to display its content using the document's "natural" layout, which is used when reading and printing the document. In addition to the document content, its structure and metadata can be shown. Since the visualization's main target is the document content, we call these methods *content-based* visualizations.

Figure 11.24 illustrates how such techniques are used in the Adobe Acrobat document management system [Adobe Systems Incorporated 07] to view an electronic PDF version of this very book. Several design elements that are often used in text-visualization tools are visible in this image. The main view shows the document content (text and images) in full detail (a). The level of focus here is a single page. The document context of the page in focus, consisting of the neighboring pages, is shown by means of a set of thumbnails (b), which are essentially downscaled versions of the renderings of the actual pages. The thumbnail of the page in focus is shown outlined in red. This context-and-focus visualization lets the user see all the details on the page in focus and also examine the context of the information in focus via the thumbnails. Navigation in the document can be done both linearly, e.g., by scrolling the main or thumbnail views, but also in a random-access fashion, e.g., by clicking on the page of interest in an overview displaying all thumbnails together. The structure view (c) shows the hierarchical, tree-like structure of the document, consisting of several levels of containment: pages, paragraphs and images, embedded objects, lines of text, down to the individual characters. This view is basically a browser for all syntactic elements in a PDF document and helps answer several technical questions about these elements. Finally, annotation views (d) can be used to both create and display user annotations on the document. Two such annotations are shown in Figure 11.24: a graphical red mark drawn by a user and a deleted piece of text, marked in blue, both with side boxes displaying annotation comments, author, and date. The annotation view allows one to create and visualize metadata that supports tasks such as collaborative document creation and review.

The main power of the text visualization described here resides in its simplicity. All views use simple and familiar two-dimensional layout and mapping techniques, such as the direct rendering of the document pages, at full or diminished size, and the tree-browser metaphor. The semantics of colors are also very intuitive. These represent either actual data in the document or user choices in the annotation process. Combined with simple navigation and interaction, these techniques can be quickly learned and used by a wide range of users.

11.7.2 Visualizing Program Code

In addition to plain narrative text, many other types of text documents exist. An important example in infovis is *source code*, written by humans but essentially targeted to be read and interpreted by computer tools. Source code is the fundamental asset of the software industry. "Our civilization runs on software," said Bjarne Stroustrup, the creator of C++, the most widely used programming language nowadays [Stroustrup 04]. Efficiently understanding source code is, hence, an important problem in software engineering. Modern systems have increasingly large sizes as measured in lines of code (LoC). New software components and libraries are created every day and distributed for use, while old ones are continuously modified. New programming languages and methodologies emerge, so that software systems are often written using a combination of these. Developer team composition also changes dynamically, with new people joining existing projects and people familiar with the software leaving. Given this situation, it is not surprising that a major part of the effort invested in software development is dedicated to understanding source code. Studies over 20 years, from Standish to Corbi, show that understanding software code accounts for more than half the development effort [Standish 84, Corbi 99].

Given this high prominence and complexity of source code in the software industry, it is natural to consider how visualization can aid its comprehension. Source code has several particular properties, including the following:

- exact: source code is written in programming languages that have strictly defined grammars with nonambiguous semantics.

- large-scale: the source code of modern software systems has tens or thousands up to millions of lines of code.

- relational: source code contains many kinds of relations, such as the types of variables, members and parents of classes, dependencies of packages, clients of services, and interfaces of modules.

- hierarchical: source code contains many types of hierarchies, such as the package-file-class-method-statement hierarchy or hierarchies of data structures.

- heavily attributed: source code entities have many attributes that express their semantics, such as access rights for interface members, comments that decorate specific statements, and signatures of functions.

Visualizing software source code is at the crossroads of software and document visualization. On one hand, the targets of such visualizations are defined by the software engineering context. On the other hand, source code is typically written and maintained by humans as text documents. Hence, it is reasonable to consider visualizing source code using the actual layout of the code text. However, displaying the text itself does not scale to

Figure 11.25. Visualization of C source code using the SeeSoft tool. Color shows the code age. Red depicts recently modified code, while blue shows code unchanged for a long time. The smaller window in front shows detail for a region in focus in the form of actual source code text.

more than a few hundred lines of code. If one is interested in discovering and correlating facts spread over a large code base of several tens of thousands of lines or more, we need a visualization capable of displaying all this code at the same time.

This can be achieved by using the same text-mapping method as in the table lens (see Section 11.4) and document thumbnails (see Section 11.7.1) visualizations. The principle is to "zoom out" and reduce each line of code to one pixel line, keeping the same line layout. This allows us to display several files containing tens of thousands of lines of code in total on a single screen. The zoom level is now too small to show actual program text. Instead, the pixel lines can be colored to depict various attributes of interest of the source code.

Figure 11.25 shows a C source code visualization based on the previous model. This visualization is constructed with SeeSoft, one of the first tools to use the technique of mapping text lines to pixel lines [Eick et al. 92]. The image shows several tens of files containing over five thousand lines of code in total. Color shows code age for each line: red shows recently

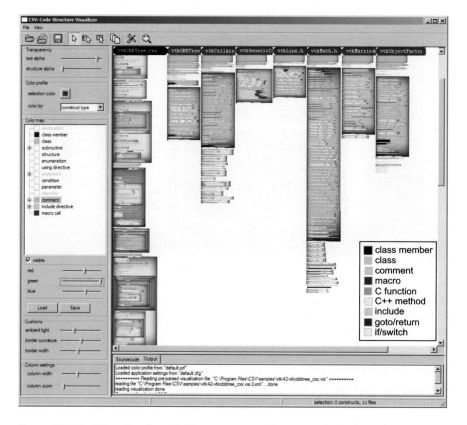

Figure 11.26. Visualization of C++ source code using shaded cushions. Color shows the occurrence of selected construct types. The cushion luminance profiles emphasize the syntactic nesting of structures.

modified lines, while blue shows lines unchanged for a long time. This type of visualization shows several facts about the code base. First, we get an overview of the relative sizes of all files in the project. Second, we quickly locate stable pieces of code that have not been changed for a long time, as well as recently changed code. Let us further make the plausible assumption that code fragments changed nearly simultaneously contain related functionality. By correlating such fragments, we can thus obtain insight in how cross-cutting concerns are distributed over the entire code base.

Figure 11.26 shows the use of the same technique to gain a different type of insight into C++ source code. Just like in the visualization shown in Figure 11.25, the layout of the original source code is used in a zoomed-out fashion. However, instead of mapping every code line to a pixel line, we now map syntactic structures of the target language (C++) to their geometric outlines. The process works as follows. The user selects a number of syntactic structures of interest, such as functions, methods, classes, macros, includes, and conditional and jump statements, and assigns custom colors to them. For every such structure present in the source code, its outline is computed. This is a shape identical to what one would see in a text editor when selecting the text contained in the respective structure. Every outline is next rendered using a generalization of the shaded cushions used for depicting treemaps (see Section 11.5.1), colored with the color of the respective syntactic construct.

The source code visualized in Figure 11.26 is part of the VTK class library [Schroeder et al. 04]. Each column depicts a separate file. In this example, the leftmost column shows one source file, whereas the other columns show all headers included by this file. Using this technique, we can discover several facts. The visual nesting of the shaded cushions, combined with the cushion colors, shows the nesting of the syntax structures. For example, in the lower part of the leftmost file, we detect a complex code fragment consisting of conditional (cyan) and iterative (light purple) structures nested several levels deep within a method (yellow). The headers (all columns except the leftmost one) have a different composition. In each header, we notice a similar comment block (green) at the beginning, followed by one large class declaration (orange). After this declaration, several short methods (yellow) are present. Closer inspection reveals that these are inline methods of the previous class. The large number of green lines contained in the class declaration indicate that the headers are generously commented. We see no tall shaded cushion contained within the class declarations, which indicates that there are no complex inline methods or nested classes declared within such a class scope. Finally, constructs that can indicate potential bad coding style, such as C macros, are colored red. This lets us see that there are few macros within the considered code, with the exception of a relatively large macro block concentrated in the class declaration contained in the third header, i.e., fourth column, from left.

The source-code visualizations discussed here are, together with the table lens and cushion treemap techniques, an instance of the dense pixel display method. The main advantages of showing source code in this way is the high scalability of the method and its intuitiveness given by using the original code layout. However, in contrast to the graph-based visualizations of source code discussed in Section 11.5.2, relations such as dependencies between code elements are not explicitly shown. In practice, a combination of dense pixel displays for showing code details and graph-based methods to show relational information can be a highly effective solution to the quest of understanding source code.

11.7.3   Visualizing Software Evolution

Text documents are not immutable. Documents are continuously changed, either by individuals working in teams or by automated computer tools. Getting insight into the *evolution* of a text document can sometimes be as important, or even more important, than understanding the information contained in the latest version of that document. Consider again the example of the set of text documents represented by all source code files in a software project. These documents are typically organized in a hierarchical fashion as files in folders. For a medium or large project, there are thousands of files containing millions of lines of code, continuously modified by tens of programmers over periods of many years.

For such a code base, several questions arise in the software industry in practice:

- how can we get insight into the overall structure?

- how can we see changes undergone by a specific document?

- how can we see who changed what?

- how can we see how or whether changes to different documents relate with each other?

- how can we see whether there is a trend in the performed changes, and if this trend is positive or negative?

These questions are typical infovis questions. They cannot be answered by a single, precise query, and even if this were possible, the answer is so information-rich that it justifies the need for a visual presentation. Answering such questions efficiently and accurately is important for the software industry. Software is modified as part of four types of maintenance activities: perfective (improving the product), corrective (removing bugs), preventive (change to prevent foreseen problems), and adaptive (changing environments, e.g., porting to another platform). The costs of maintenance have steadily increased in the last three decades from a mere 30% to more than 80% of total software development costs [Pfleeger et al. 05]. Of the maintenance costs, at least half are dedicated to the process of understanding the software code base [Standish 84, Corbi 99].

Software evolution visualization methods are an increasingly popular answer to the questions and problems. The main goal of these methods is to capture, in a visual presentation, the dynamics of the changes undergone by software as it evolves in time. Given its dynamic aspects, it is tempting to consider visualizing software evolution in terms of an animation of the source code content, structure, and metadata. However, even small-scale projects contain such a large number of data elements and changes that an animation becomes too complex to follow. A more effective way to convey the evolution dynamics is to map the time axis to a spatial dimension, so that the evolution can be graphed using appropriate layouts.

How can we visualize the evolution of a software project? First, we must make several choices as to what the unit of evolution is, based on the task and goals to be achieved. For example, in a software project, these units can range from specific lines of code, functions, or files, to the complete set of files of the entire project. After the unit of evolution have been chosen, we must define what we consider to be a *change*. For example, if our unit of interest is a file then we can say it has changed whenever an editing operation modifies its contents. However, this can produce a large set of change events, of which not all have the same importance. If we are interested in high-level modifications, such as the removal of bugs from code or additions of new features, then only a subset of the file content modifications will be perceived as actual change events. Next, we must decide how to *measure* change. Several possibilities are available here, ranging from a boolean measure (the file has been changed or not) to a continuous change metric (a certain percentage value of the file has changed). Besides the line or file level, we can measure the change of different aspects of software, such as structure, object-oriented design quality, or maintainability. To do

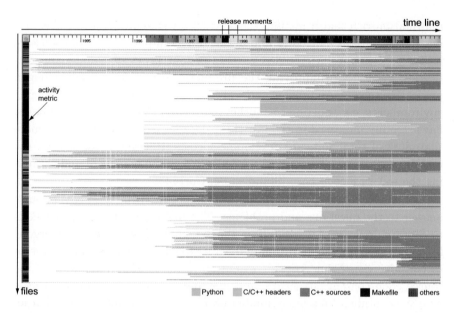

Figure 11.27. Visualization of the evolution of the VTK software project. Files are shown as horizontal pixel strips colored by file type. File strips are stacked on the vertical axis in the order they appear in the directories. Yellow dots indicate the file modification events.

this, we must first map these aspects to measurable quantities called *software metrics* [Lanza and Marinescu 06], followed by a measurement of the metrics' changes. Again, the right choice here is determined by the task at hand.

After the unit of change, change definition, and change metric have been established, the actual visualization must be designed. The challenge here is to find the best visual mapping of change units and change values that effectively and scalably conveys insight into the software evolution questions. Just as for the other information visualization cases discussed in the earlier sections, a good answer is a combination of understanding of the task and user group, intuitive and scalable visual representations, and simple but effective user interaction.

One possibility to visualize software evolution is shown in Figure 11.27. This visualization depicts the evolution of the VTK code base [Schroeder et al. 04] during the period from 1994 to 2001. The code base contains more than 2700 files modified by 41 developers, also called *authors*. The raw data for visualization is acquired by analyzing the CVS software repository containing the VTK code project using the freely available visualization tool CVSgrab [Voinea 07]. The visualization in Figure 11.27 has a simple structure. A two-dimensional layout is used, where the x-axis represents the time during which the code has changed, and the y-axis the files in the project. Every file in the code base is mapped to a horizontal pixel line, partitioned in several segments. These pixel stripes can be stacked in several orders along the y-axis. In Figure 11.27, the order follows a depth-first traversal of the code base. Hence, pixel strips close along the y-axis correspond to files situated at a small distance in terms of their directory paths.

Each segment of a given file strip represents the file between two consecutive modifications, or what in the terminology of software repositories is called a file *version*. The color of each file strip, or each segment, shows an attribute of the respective file or file version. In Figure 11.27, each file strip is colored to show its type, as indicated by the file extension in the color legend below the image. The pixels separating consecutive file segments are colored in yellow. These pixels indicate the location in time of the file modification events, or *commit* events in the terminology of software repositories. Along the left side of the main view, a metric bar shows the project activity, measured as number of modifications per file, encoded using a rainbow colormap. A different metric bar is shown atop of the main view, displaying the 1994–2001 timeline using a ruler metaphor and the so-called *release* dates when new software releases have been made available to the public. The releases are displayed by rendering shaded cushions with different hues over the intervals between consecutive releases.

This image tells us several facts about the evolution and composition of the VTK code base. Looking at the colors, we see that the VTK code base consists of roughly 40% Python files, 40% C and C++ source files, 15% C/C++ headers, and a small number of files of other types. We also see two large compact groups of Python files that have been committed at almost the same moments and are close along the y-axis. Closer inspection reveals that these are Python examples, which have been committed in bulk to the repository after being presumably developed offline. Looking at the horizontal release bar at the image top, we find that no system release was performed before 1996, even though the repository exhibits activity

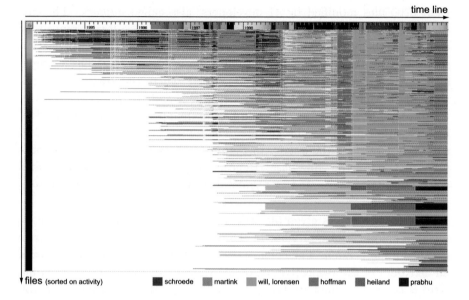

Figure 11.28. Visualization of author contributions in the VTK software project. The file versions are colored by the author who modified them. File strips are stacked on the vertical axis in decreasing order of activity, with the most modified files shown at the top.

since 1994. The release frequency after 1996 shows at least one release per year with no clear increasing or decreasing trend, which suggests a stable project and development process. The 1996 release also coincides with the introduction of the first large amount of Python code in the repository. Looking at the vertical activity bar and the commit yellow dots, we notice that the Python files are among the least modified, even though they come in large numbers. In contrast, C and C++ sources show a high activity, which suggests intense maintenance activity.

Figure 11.28 shows a different visualization scenario. Here, the files have been sorted along the y-axis in decreasing order of activity, as outlined also by the colors in the vertical activity metric bar. Each file version is colored to show the ID of the author who committed that version to the repository, i.e., who was responsible for the respective file changes. This color mapping lets us quickly discover who were the most active authors.

The respective authors are listed in the color legend below the image. We discover a correlation between the authors and the project structure and evolution. During the first third of the monitored period, until roughly one year after the first release, *schroede* (purple) was clearly the main contributor. His activity gets gradually interleaved with that of *martink* (orange). Starting from the second half of the project, and especially during the last third of the time line, *will* and *lorensen* (green) also become important contributors.[11] Vertical color patterns, such as the one ascribed to *hoffman* (blue), indicate projectwide changes executed by the same person at the same time. These are typical signs for important code refactoring or code beautification activities, such as a change in the copyright notice contained in all source files. Even though the previous findings are not significantly deep, they illustrate well the power of visualization. Obtaining the insight described previously about the evolution of the VTK project took practically less than five minutes, and involved studying two images and no complex user interaction or parameter setting. Obtaining a similar level of insight into the same repository would have clearly taken considerably longer using classical methods, such as browsing the repository via text-based web clients such as ViewVC [ViewVC 07] or Tortoise [TortoiseeSVN 07]. These observations about the effectiveness of visual analysis in terms of quickly discovering interesting facts in large datasets hold also for the table lens visualization (see Section 11.4), the map-of-the market and file system treemap visualizations (see Section 11.5.1), and the dense pixel source code visualizations (see Section 11.7.2). Visualizations that focus on relational data, such as the various graph and tree layouts described earlier, are arguably less effective. They take more time to configure and interpret the results, and are less scalable. All in all, this outlines once more the difficulty of efficiently and effectively visualizing relational data, which is one of the grand infovis challenges.

11.8 Conclusion

In this chapter, we have provided a succinct and inherently limited incursion in the field of information visualization, or infovis. Given the explo-

---

[11] It is interesting to consider these findings in the light of the names of the three main authors of the VTK toolkit: Will Schroeder, Ken Martin, and Bill Lorensen.

sion of data sources in the modern society, infovis is a rapidly growing field where applications and techniques emerge literally on a daily basis. Infovis inherits the same main goal from scientific visualization of providing insight to users into complex data. Yet, the infovis field is confronted with a number of specific challenges: The task of making abstract data visible, the challenge of high dimensionality, a richer set of attributes including noninterpolable types such as text and relations, and the quest for effective interaction mechanisms with the information space. Last but not least, many end users of infovis applications are not engineers or scientists who have a formal mathematical training, but individuals who require insight in an intuitive, easy-to-digest manner, and want fast and clear answers to their domain-specific problems.

As already mentioned, infovis is an extremely large field, and this chapter can only give a narrow overview of its developments. There are several good books on information-visualization topics, ranging from more theoretical works on human perception and cognition to more practical ones that overview several types of information visualization applications.

For a good start in exploring the various facets and applications of information visualization, the book by Card, Shneiderman, and Mackinlay [Card et al. 99] is a must. This book presents a collection of articles that discuss many aspects of the concrete use of infovis in various application areas, and also an overview of the main design elements of the infovis exploration process and applications.

A different, but equally useful reference is the book by Colin Ware on perception for design of infovis applications [Ware 04]. In this book, many issues related to the way humans perceive information by means of structure, color, shape, and other visual attributes are discussed. This material can help considerably in the process of choosing the right type of visual encoding and interaction techniques when designing an infovis application.

A recent book in the field by Robert Spence also targets the task of teaching how to design effective information-visualization applications [Spence 07]. To help readers understand the various, often subtle, issues that influence the effectiveness of an infovis application, a large set of applications are discussed in the text, along with a number of videos that illustrate these applications in action. This book is especially well suited as a teaching material for undergraduate and master's level courses in a wide range of study directions, as it assumes only a minimal mathematical background.

For guidelines and examples on how to design a good graphical display for visualizing information, we refer to the classic books by Tufte [Tufte 83, Tufte 90, Tufte 97], Bertin [Bertin 83], and Cleveland [Cleveland 85]. These books contain a wealth of information, in particular elements of graphics design, that can be directly used by the practitioner in the fields of infovis and scivis in the design of effective visualizations. An interesting element related to this field is the work of Mackinlay on the automated design of visualizations [Mackinlay 86].

For the technical topics of graph layout and drawing, a comprehensive starting point is the classic book by Di Battista et al. [Di Battista et al. 99]. This book covers both the theory and implementation of a large number of graph-drawing techniques. From a more practical perspective, the book edited by Jünger and Mutzel [Jünger and Mutzel 03] provides a comprehensive review of graph layout and graph-drawing software tools, and is a good guide for the practitioner in the field who is interested in weighing the pros and cons of using one of the many graph-drawing software systems. A survey of graph-visualization techniques from an information visualization perspective is provided by Herman et al. [Herman et al. 00].

To get acquainted with the extensive research in the graph-drawing area, one of the best ways is to browse the proceedings of the International Symposium of Graph Drawing, which have been published in Springer's series of Lecture Notes in Computer Science since 1992.

Software visualization is one of the fastest growing and most diverse branches of information visualization. For the readers interested in exploring the field of software visualization, a good starting point is the book by Diehl [Diehl 04], which presents an overview of several established techniques in software visualization such as source code visualization, algorithm animation, and the use of graphs in software visualization. In a recently published second book [Diehl 07], Diehl further explores the field of software visualization by presenting newly emerging topics such as visualizing the behavior and evolution of software systems. This book provides a comprehensive overview of the state-of-the-art in software visualization at the current moment.

As a final word: just as for scientific visualization, the best way to learn and understand the theory and techniques behind infovis is to apply them, first as a user of the many software tools available, and next as a developer of existing or new techniques. Only this path, where one combines the roles of critical end user and dedicated application developer, can make one fully understand the real problems, challenges, and the true meaning of the phrase "effective solution" in visualization.

Chapter 12

Conclusion

WE have arrived at the end of our incursion into the field of data visualization. In the previous chapters, we have presented a number of the most important theoretical and practical ingredients involved in the design of visualization methods and applications. As we have seen, designing an efficient and effective data visualization application is a complex process. This process involves representing the data of interest, processing the data to extract relevant information for the problem at hand, designing a mapping of this information to a visual representation, rendering this representation, and combining all this functionality in an easy-to-use application.

Visualization is a highly dynamic field. As the complexity, diversity, and size of datasets generated by current applications increase, new methods and tools emerge every year at a high pace in order to provide more effective and efficient ways to understand such datasets. As these methods and tools mature and become better known by the public, they are applied to an increasing range of application domains and eventually find their way into established commercial products. If we look at the different subfields of visualization, such as scientific visualization, medical visualization, information visualization, and software visualization, to name just those that have been discussed in this book, we see a number of evolution trends and patterns.

Scientific visualization (scivis) is arguably the oldest and most mature branch of data visualization. It is based on a firm mathematical foundation, has its roots in the experiments done in engineering and physics, and has taken advantage of extensive field testing in many types of applications. The complex simulation applications, in conjunction with which scivis has been developed and has grown as a field, have triggered the development of highly scalable data manipulation and rendering techniques. New scivis methods and techniques keep being created in response to the generation of new types of data, such as produced by diffusion tensor imaging (DTI) scanning techniques. There exist also a number of old problems, such as the visualization of time-dependent, three-dimensional flow fields, that are not yet considered to be fully solved. Although new scivis methods emerge on a constant basis, it is fair to say that a considerable number of techniques concerning visualizing scalar, vector, and tensor fields have been designed and tested to a level satisfactory for direct and efficient application in practice. This is reflected in the large number of stable and established scivis software systems, both commercial and open source (Appendix A). For further information on the latest advances in scientific visualization, we recommend the reader consult the several available books that provide more specialized overviews of the state-of-the-art of the field [Nielson et al. 06, Post et al. 03a, Hansen and Johnson 04], as well as the collection of proceedings of the IEEE Visualization conference.

Information visualization (infovis) shows a somewhat different picture. Infovis is a newer field, roughly half the age of scivis. Although the last 10 years have witnessed many developments in infovis, there are still several unsolved problems. It can be argued that infovis is, in some sense, a broader field than scivis, as it deals with data of more diverse structure and attribute types. Due to this diversity, infovis data cannot be easily fit into a uniform mathematical framework such as in the case of scivis. Infovis applications are also more diverse than scivis ones, and target a wider public that goes beyond the engineering and scientific audiences. But probably the most difficult and challenging aspect of infovis is the need to make inherently abstract, multidimensional data entities visible such that insight is effectively conveyed to the user. Many techniques for visual data representation and interaction are already widely accepted and used in infovis applications, such as tree and graph layouts, treemaps, scatter and parallel coordinate plots, and focus-and-context navigation techniques. Along with these, we witness a sustained stream of new techniques for visual data representation and interaction being created in this field. Given the growing interest and need for understanding multidimensional abstract datasets, we expect many additional techniques to be created and refined in the coming years.

Scientific and information visualization are not two clearly separate branches of the same field that evolve in parallel. In recent years, an increasing number of researchers have shown interest in applying infovis techniques and principles to the design of applications targeting scivis data. Many infovis techniques become interesting in a scivis context in situations when one needs to visualize multidimensional datasets, or in cases when the actual spatial data distribution is less important than understanding the relations between the data values themselves. Moreover, studies performed in an infovis context on perceptual issues such as the usage of color, shape, and texture to convey data, or interaction techniques for large information spaces, are immediately relevant in the context of designing effective scivis applications. Conversely, scivis techniques have also been applied in the context of infovis applications. An example is a number of hierarchical layout methods for very large graphs based on numerical techniques such as algebraic multigrid [Harel and Koren 00, Koren et al. 03] that were originally developed in the context of accelerating numerical solvers for partial differential equations for typical scientific simulations [Trottenberg et al. 01, Griebel and Schweitzer 06]. We foresee an increasing number of cross-fertilizations between the two fields of visualization, driven by the need to visually represent and navigate increasingly complex, abstract, and large datasets coming from multidisciplinary applications.

However, despite all developments in the field of visualization, or maybe just because of the rapid proliferation of a wide variety of visualization techniques and applications, there exist also signals that such developments need to be pursued with care and without forgetting the main goals and purpose of the visualization field. A strong message was sent in 2004 by one of the pioneers of the field in a paper titled "The Death of Visualization— Can It Survive Without Customers?" [Lorensen 04]. The title conveys the main message quite clearly: the visualization discipline needs to focus on providing solutions to concrete problems raised by customers in the field. This requires detailed understanding of the various specifics of the customer, such as the problem to be solved, accepted ways of working, and the complementary techniques beyond the scope of visualization that are to be integrated to yield a complete, usable solution. Without this tight and dynamic feedback from the customers, there may be a risk for visualization to become an academic discipline with a diminished impact in the real world. Similar reflections appeared in the context of the actual effectiveness of visualization used in the context of software engineering [Reiss 05].

Given the previous messages, what is a good path for visualization? A number of answers to this question are presented by another pioneer in the field in his recent paper, "The Value of Visualization" [van Wijk 05]. It is acknowledged that there is a growing gap between the providers (researchers) and the consumers (users) in the field. Following an economical model, a visualization method, technique, or tool is considered to be useful if it is *effective*, i.e., it answers a concrete question or helps solving a concrete problem of a given user, and *efficient*, i.e., it does so with a limited usage of resources, including but not limited to computational power, cost of equipment, and time spent by the user. Although not a direct answer, this provides a set of guidelines for assessing the value of a visualization technique or tool, whether existing or newly developed, as well as of an image produced by such a tool or technique. If using the technique or tool leads to taking decisions that demonstrably save costs and/or lead to increased profits then the tool is useful.

Since visualization is to be effective and efficient, we need ways to measure this. This implies that we must know a number of elements. First and foremost, we must be able to qualitatively, but also quantitatively, describe the problem to be solved or questions to be answered. This involves having a good amount of domain-specific knowledge, or working together with domain experts [Lorensen 04, van Wijk 05]. Second, we must be able to quantify the cost of using a certain visualization method. Measuring the actual computational resources involved is relatively easy and can be done by using various benchmarks involving processor speed, memory, and throughput. Measuring the user effort needed to gain a certain amount of insight is more difficult, and can be reliably done only by performing extensive user studies. However difficult and time-consuming, the need for such user studies at all points of the visualization process (requirement gathering, method design, testing, validation, and concrete usage) is increasingly viewed as a mandatory component of the design of a good visualization.

Visualization can only become accepted when developed and deployed for, and together with, its users. On one hand, this involves working together with domain experts and end users to design and validate the proposed techniques and tools. On the other hand, such visualization techniques and tools rarely work only by themselves. Integration of visualization methods, either for presentation or exploration needs, with complementary methods used for automated analysis such as data and pattern mining, can provide much stronger solutions than using either of these methods in isolation. This situation is reflected by the recent developments in the new field of *visual analytics*, which advocates the combination of visualization and data-mining techniques for integrated problem solving [Thomas and Cook 05].

As a last word, we conclude by repeating our statements from Section 1.2 of the introduction: visualization is a dynamic, growing field located at the crossroads of design, technology, science, and art. We consider our goal to be accomplished if we have, with the material presented in this book, awakened the interest and taste of the reader to further explore this exciting domain by studying the existing literature, but, first and foremost, by trying to use and design visualization methods and tools to solve concrete problems.

Appendix A

Visualization Software

O NE important element of the five-dimensional classification model for visualizations presented in Section 4.3 was the *medium*, or type of drawing canvas that the rendering takes place on. There are many examples of early visualizations that use paper as the medium [Spence 07]. Modern architectural blueprints can also be seen as visualizations that use a printed medium. Yet, by far the largest class of visualization applications described in this book have one thing in common: they use the computer screen as a medium.

Using the computer to do data visualization is a natural choice from several points of view. First, many visualization scenarios are, by their very nature, *explorative*. This makes interactive visualization tools the best instruments for such cases. Second, the datasets to visualize usually come in electronic form. Third, the large amounts of data, or dynamically changing datasets, make computer-based visualization tools again the natural choice.

In this appendix, we provide an overview of a number of issues concerning visualization software. First, we discuss how visualization software can be classified from an architectural perspective (Section A.1). Next, we provide a list of several representative visualization systems for scientific, imaging, and information visualization data, in order to illustrate the various flavors of systems available to practitioners.

A.1   Taxonomies of Visualization Systems

Visualization software tools are central to creating successful visualizations. Besides the provided functionality, such systems have also to cover several nonfunctional requirements in order to be effective. Relevant attributes in the latter group include the following:

- efficiency: the software should produce visualizations quickly. This can mean minutes for some applications, but fractions of a second for others, such as interactive applications.

- scalability: the software should be able to handle large datasets within given performance and resource bounds.

- ease of use: the software should provide an easy-to-learn-and-use interface for its intended user group.

- customizability: the software should allow a simple and effective way to customize it for specific tasks, scenarios, problems, or datasets.

- availability: the software should be available to its intended user group under specific conditions (e.g., license and platform).

Modern visualization applications are complex software systems containing tens or hundreds of thousands of lines of code organized on several layers. With respect to this layered application architecture, the users can have different *roles*. One such classification identifies three roles: end users, application designers, and component developers [Ribarsky et al. 94]. End users are the final customers of a visualization application, and use it to obtain insight into a given dataset, typically by means of customized user interfaces that support domain-specific tasks. Such applications are also known as *turnkey systems*. Application designers construct turnkey systems for the end users, typically by assembling a set of premade software components and providing them with the needed configuration and user-interface elements. Finally, component developers program software components that implement visualization algorithms and datasets, and provide these to application designers as ready-made visualization software packages or libraries.

From this perspective, visualization software can be classified into three classes: libraries, application frameworks, and turnkey systems. Libraries provide application programmer interfaces (APIs) that contain the data types and operations that constitute the basic building blocks of a visualization application, such as the ones presented in Chapter 3. At the other end of the spectrum, turnkey systems provide custom user interfaces, presets, and configurations designed to support specific tasks. Application frameworks fall between these two extremes. They encode a set of fixed domain-specific rules, operations, and functions as a backbone to which an open set of components can be added. The components use the backbone to interact and provide functionality at a higher level, and in a more compact way, than bare libraries. Several mechanisms exist for adding components to the framework and composing them in. A popular design metaphor presents the components to the application designer in a visual, iconic form. Applications are constructed by interactively assembling these iconic component representations. This allows nonprogrammers to quickly and easily prototype new applications without programming. The AVS, ParaView, and VISSION applications illustrated in Figures 4.5, 4.6, and 4.7 in Chapter 4 are examples of application frameworks.

In the next sections, we give several examples of visualization software systems used in practice. Instead of using an architectural taxonomy into libraries, frameworks, and turnkey systems, we have opted for a domain-centered taxonomy into three classes: general scientific visualization systems (Section A.2), medical and imaging systems (Section A.3), and information visualization systems (Section A.4). Given the size of the field and the rapid rate at which new software is produced, the list of systems presented here is definitely not exhaustive and limited in choice. However, we believe that this list can serve as a useful starting point for the interested reader in search for a given visualization software tool or component.

A.2   Scientific Visualization Software

The systems listed in this section fall in the category of general-purpose *scientific visualization* software. The target of such systems is primarily the visualization of datasets defined as two- and three-dimensional grids of various types with scalar and vector attributes, such as created by scientific simulations or data-acquisition processes. The main application domains targeted are engineering, mechanics (both in research and in the industry), and weather and geosciences. However, some of the systems provide also support for medical imaging, tensor visualization, and information visualization.

The Visualization Toolkit (VTK)

Type: Class library (written in C++)

Availability: Open source

Address: http://www.kitware.com/vtk/

Description: VTK is a set of class libraries written in C++. Classes come in two main flavors: datasets and algorithms. Dataset classes range from low-level containers, such as lists and arrays, to full-fledged uniform, rectilinear, structured, and unstructured grids. Several hundred algorithm classes provide grid manipulation, slicing, interpolation, contouring, streamlines, image processing, polygonal and volume rendering, and more. VTK is arguably one of the leading data visualization libraries at the moment.

Utilization: Applications are built by assembling dataset and algorithm class instances into a pipeline. This is done either via the native compiled C++ API or its wrappings in interpreted languages, such as Python, Java, and Tcl. The basic VTK building blocks offer a wide functionality. Yet, constructing a complete visualization application requires a fair amount of programming effort and knowledge of the VTK API and its programming paradigms.

AVS/Express

Type: Application framework

Availability: Commercial

Address: http://www.kitware.com/vtk/

Description: AVS/Express is an application framework for development of high-end scientific visualization solutions. AVS/Express provides more than 800 visualization building bricks (algorithms) that cover scalar, vector, and tensor visualization on several types of grids, much like VTK. Several extensions of AVS/Express provide support for parallel processing and high-end virtual-reality visualizations. Some extensions also target information visualization (OpenViz toolkit), operational industrial monitoring (the PowerViz toolkit), and scientific presentation graphics (the Gsharp toolkit). A snapshot of the AVS tool in action is shown in Figure 4.7.

Utilization: Applications are built by assembling premade components into a pipeline, somewhat similar to the VTK paradigm. This can be done programmatically in C or C++, or interactively, via a point-and-click visual application designer. The visual editor allows rapid application prototyping, user interface construction, and application steering. The AVS/Express components are less fine-grained than VTK classes, for example.

IRIS Explorer

Type: Application framework

Availability: Commercial

Address: http://www.nag.co.uk/welcome_iec.asp

Description: IRIS Explorer is an application framework for development of high-end scientific visualization solutions. Its user group and philosophy is quite similar to AVS/Express. The provided visualization functionality covers application domains as varied as life sciences, chemistry, medical imaging, geology, financial modeling, and aerospace engineering. IRIS Explorer builds its versatility on top of several major software components, such as the well-known Open Inventor 3D and ImageVision graphics libraries and the NAG numerical libraries. IRIS Explorer is particularly attractive for users who wish to combine numerical simulation code with visualization facilities.

Utilization: IRIS Explorer provides a visual application builder based on a dataflow application architecture, much like AVS/Express. Modules can be developed in C, C++, and FORTRAN, but also in a proprietary scripted language called SHAPE, which offers an easier way to manipulate complex n-dimensional datasets. Modules are next visually assembled in so-called maps, which are essentially dataflow networks.

SCIRun

Type: Application framework

Availability: Open source

Address: http://software.sci.utah.edu/scirun.html

Description: SCIRun is an application framework developed for the creation of scientific visualization applications. SCIRun is very similar in aim and scope to AVS/Express. It provides a set of modules for scientific data visualization that can be connected into so-called networks, following a dataflow application architecture. SCIRun has been used to construct visualization applications for several domains such as finite element numerical simulations, (bio)medical imaging, and computational steering.

Utilization: Similar to AVS/Express, SCIRun allows applications to be constructed visually, by editing the dataflow network, or programmatically. Once constructed, applications can be packaged into so-called PowerApps. These are dataflow networks provided with custom user interfaces into turnkey applications that facilitate specific exploration scenarios. Several such PowerApps are available for different domains, such as segmentation (Seg3D), tensor visualization (BioTensor), volume visualization (BioImage), and finite element problems (BioFEM). All in all, SCIRun is a mature environment that covers most needs and requirements of the users of a scientific visualization framework.

ParaView

Type: Turnkey system/application framework

Availability: Open source

Address: http://www.paraview.org/

Description: The ParaView system can be used as an end-user tool for visualizing scientific datasets. The main operations for data filtering, selection, mapping, and rendering are provided, such as slicing, isosurfaces, streamlines, and interactive viewing. ParaView provides an intuitive and simple graphical user interface that allows one to both prototype a visualization application and set its various parameters interactively. ParaView is built on top of the VTK class library. The user interface layer is written in the Tcl/Tk scripted languages. Most of the illustrations used in this book were created using ParaView, unless otherwise specified in the text.

Utilization: ParaView operates mainly as an end-user system. The application design freedom is considerably less involved, but also easier to learn, than AVS/Express, for example. ParaView makes an excellent system for learning the basics of scientific visualization without having to be a programmer. Only the core VTK functionality is exposed in the user interface. However, developers can add new modules to the ParaView user interface using a mix of Tcl, C++, and XML wrappers.

MayaVi

Type: Turnkey system/application framework

Availability: Open source

Address: http://mayavi.sourceforge.net/

Description: The MayaVi system is an end-user tool for visualizing scientific datasets. Its architecture, provided functionality, and intended user group are very similar to ParaView's. MayaVi is also built as an interactive front-end on top of the VTK class library. However, in contrast to ParaView, MayaVi uses Python as a scripted (interpreted) language to bind user interface functions to the compiled C++ libraries.

Utilization: MayaVi operates mainly as an end-user system, similar to ParaView. The user interface is structured differently. A relatively greater emphasis is put on executing operations by writing Python commands at a user prompt than via the user interface itself. The user interface exposes more of the VTK implementation details and is relatively lower-level than the one of ParaView. Overall, although MayaVi and ParaView are quite similar in intention, we find ParaView easier to learn and use and more mature than MayaVi.

A.3 Medical Imaging Software

In this section, we list a number of imaging software systems. By "imaging," we refer to several functionalities related to the manipulation and visualization of 2D and 3D image datasets. Such datasets occur frequently in medical practice as the output of the various scanning technologies, such as computed tomography (CT) and magnetic resonance imaging (MRI). Image datasets can contain scalar, vector, and tensor data. Imaging operations cover a wide range of tasks, such as basic data handling and manipulation, basic image processing, image segmentation and registration,

shape recognition, image visualization, and volume rendering. Just as for
the other types of software systems listed in this appendix, it is not possible
to cover all aspects and variants of such systems, so we limit ourselves to
a small selection of representative systems.

The Insight Toolkit (ITK)

Type: Class library (written in C++)

Availability: Open source

Address: http://www.itk.org/

Description: ITK is a set of class libraries written in C++. The main function-
                 ality targeted by the ITK toolkit is divided into three categories:
                 image processing, segmentation, and registration. As such, ITK
                 does not provide visualization (rendering) and user interface facil-
                 ities. However, ITK can be combined with other toolkits, such as
                 VTK, in order to construct complete visualization applications.

Utilization: The software structure of ITK bears a number of similarities to
                 VTK, which is not surprising given the fact that a large number
                 of common organizations and people have been jointly involved in
                 the development of both toolkits. ITK comes with a considerable
                 amount of documentation in the form of books, courses, online
                 material, examples, and demos. Also, the source code of several
                 medical imaging applications built on top of ITK is available for
                 downloading from the ITK site. However, just as for its older
                 cousin VTK, using ITK to construct an imaging application re-
                 quires a nonnegligible amount of effort, given the sheer size and
                 complexity of the toolkit APIs.

3D Slicer

Type: Turnkey system/application framework

Availability: Open source

Address: http://www.slicer.org/

Description: 3D Slicer is a freely available, open-source application framework
                 for visualization, registration, segmentation, and quantification of
                 medical data. 3D Slicer supports a wide array of tasks, ranging
                 from the investigation and segmentation of volumetric CT and

MRI datasets to providing the basic mechanisms for more complex applications, such as guiding biopsies and craniotomies in the operating room and diagnostic visualizations. 3D Slicer can handle scalar, vector, and tensor data attributes. In particular, several functions for visualizing diffusion tensor images, such as principal component analysis, tensor color coding, tensor glyphs, and hyperstreamlines are supported. 3D Slicer is supported by a large number of organizations, and is used in a large number of research projects, as well as in clinical studies and actual applications in the medical practice. Several images created with the 3D Slicer tool are shown in Section 7.6.

Utilization: 3D Slicer has an architecture consisting of an end-user front end and a framework that manages a set of application libraries. The front end provides user interfaces and direct mouse-based manipulation of the data, such as picking, probing, and interactive streamline seed placement. The application framework allows one to add new plug-ins in order to provide custom-developed functionality. The 3D Slicer architecture was designed to facilitate adding a wide variety of plug-ins, ranging from standalone binaries (executables and shared libraries) to modules based on the VTK and ITK toolkits and even shell, Tcl, and Python scripts. Although this makes learning the software architecture of 3D Slicer more complex than that of other toolkits such as VTK or ITK, it also makes 3D Slicer more flexible in interfacing with a broad spectrum of third-party software components.

Teem

Type: Turnkey/libraries

Availability: Open source (written in C)

Address: http://teem.sourceforge.net/

Description: Teem is a set of coordinated libraries representing, processing, and visualizing scientific raster data. Teem provides functions that support a wide range of operations on n-dimensional raster data (uniform grids) of m-dimensional attributes. The functions of Teem are provided as a set of standalone executables designed much like UNIX filters, which are parameterized by command-line options. The generic data model of Teem, together with the modular decomposition of operations in terms of several filters, allows many complex operations on image volumes to be specified easily and compactly. The set of basic operations provided by Teem include convolution, slicing, resampling, interpolation, statistics, principal component analysis for tensors, color mapping, volume rendering, and tensor glyph visualizations. Several images created using the Teem software are shown in Section 7.5.

Utilization: Data-processing and visualization tasks are typically written as shell scripts that construct and execute a dataflow pipeline by cascading the Teem basic filters. This is the easiest and most rapid way to use Teem to produce visualizations. If desired, Teem can be also used in terms of libraries providing APIs. Teem is not end-user software. As such, it does not provide user interface or interaction functions present in complete visualization applications. However, its generic, modular, and coherent API design allow such applications to be built on top of it. For example, the SCIRun and 3D Slicer applications integrate the functionality of Teem to provide high-level imaging capabilities.

A.4   Information Visualization Software

Compared to scientific visualization systems, information visualization systems come in a larger variety. There are fewer "generic" systems in this category that can be compared to frameworks such as AVS/Express, SCIRun, or IRIS Explorer. One reason is arguably the higher diversity of the application domains, data types, and end user groups for information visualization systems. Consequently, the selection of information-visualization systems presented next has even fewer pretensions to be exhaustive than our selection of scientific-visualization systems. The considered domains for this selection are graphs and trees, multivariate data, and table data.

The Infovis Toolkit (IVTK)

Type: Class library/application framework

Availability: Open source (written in Java)

Address: http://ivtk.sourceforge.net/

Description: IVTK is a general-purpose toolkit for developing information-visualization end-user applications and components. IVTK comes as a set of Java class libraries implementing a number of core infovis methods, such as scatter plots, time series, parallel coordinates, matrix plots, and several types of graph and tree layouts.

Utilization:	Developing applications with IVTK and VTK is quite similar. Both are class libraries, so building an application requires programmatically combining instances of the necessary datasets and visualization algorithms. One of the features of IVTK is that it uses a generic dataset model. All datasets (including relational ones) are represented as tables. IVTK provides efficient representations for these tables both in terms of memory and access time. However, just as for VTK, constructing a full-fledged end-user application with IVTK requires a fair amount of work and understanding of the toolkit design. Moreover, compared to VTK, IVTK is relatively newer and less developed toolkit, which provides only a small number of basic versions of the many infovis algorithms that exist for the supported data types (e.g., tree and graph layouts).

Prefuse

Type:	Class library / application framework
Availability:	Open source (written in Java)
Address:	http://prefuse.org/
Description:	Prefuse is a toolkit for constructing information-visualization applications, and is quite similar to IVTK. The toolkit comes as a set of Java class libraries that provides support for representing the main types of datasets used in information visualization, such as trees, graphs, and tables. Together with these, a number of fundamental algorithms for constructing infovis applications are provided, such as graph and tree layouts, glyphs, dynamic queries, brushing, search, database connectivity, and animation.
Utilization: ·	Prefuse is both a class library and an application framework. Functionality and data representation are provided in terms of classes. Programming interaction, correlation between multiple views, and application execution is provided by means of framework services. In this respect, prefuse is similar to the VTK and IVTK toolkits. However, the architectures and internals of the two toolkits are quite different. A VTK application is structured like a dataflow pipeline. In prefuse, the accent is laid more on connecting data and processing items via actions and events. All in all, prefuse is a good start to learn experimenting with information-visualization concepts and algorithms via prototyping. However,

the toolkit does not yet have a wide palette of implemented algorithms, which is similar to IVTK. Also, the scalability and efficiency of the implemented algorithms cannot yet cope with truly large datasets.

GraphViz

Type: Library and turnkey system

Availability: Open source (written in C)

Address: http://www.graphviz.org/

Description: GraphViz is a high-quality library for computing and displaying graph layouts. GraphViz implements several popular graph-layout algorithms such as rooted and radial trees, hierarchical directed acyclic graph layouts, and force-directed layouts. In addition to layout, GraphViz offers advanced control of the mapping and rendering of graph nodes and edges, including annotations, spline edges, and nested graphs. An extensive set of options allows one to specify the finest details of the layout and mapping. Its robustness, scalability, simplicity of use, and availability have made GraphViz one of the best-known toolkits for laying out graphs and quickly producing quality graph visualizations. Several graph visualizations created with the GraphViz software are shown in Section 11.5.2.

Utilization: GraphViz is structured as a set of separate executables. These read and write graph specification files in various formats. These executables can be easily used as turnkey systems to load, lay out, and draw graphs. In addition to these, GraphViz also provides an API that allows more flexible access to the layout functionalities. This allows one to use GraphViz as a layout library on behalf of other applications.

Tulip

Type: Library and turnkey system

Availability: Open source (written in C++)

Address: http://www.tulip-software.org/

Description: Tulip is a framework for the manipulation and visualization of large graphs. At the core of the Tulip system is an efficient data representation that allows manipulation of graphs with more than one million elements. The Tulip framework contains a core library and an end-user visualization tool. The library provides graph data representation and so-called algorithms. The algorithms include several layout engines (rooted, radial and bubble trees, treemaps, and force-directed) and rendering engines that allow one to parameterize the node and edge glyphs by graph data attributes. Apart from these, several graph data manipulation algorithms are provided, such as editing, clustering, decomposition, and computing statistics on graphs. Several tree visualizations created with the Tulip system are shown in Section 11.5.1.

Utilization: Tulip can be used either as a C++ class library or as a turnkey system. In the first case, developers build their application on top of the core Tulip graph data and algorithm classes. In the second case, end users can use the Tulip visualization front-end to interactively import, navigate, edit, lay out, and render graphs in a variety of ways. The functionality of the Tulip front-end, although not covering all the functions of the core library, is rich and customizable enough to allow one to use this application as a full-fledged viewer for complex graphs in real applications. Similar to ParaView and MayaVi, the Tulip front-end can be customized via a plug-in mechanism to load additional functionality developed on top of the core libraries.

Treemap

Type: Turnkey system

Availability: Open source for non-profit uses (written in Java)

Address: http://www.cs.umd.edu/hcil/treemap/

Description: Treemap is a customizable turnkey system for the visualization of large multivariate datasets using the treemap layout. Treemap implements several layout algorithms (slice and dice, squarified, and strip) and allows one to parameterize several elements of the mapping process, such as size, color, borders, and labels of the treemap nodes by the data attributes of the underlying tree. Several interactive navigation and filtering mechanisms support a wide range of structure and attribute-based user queries. Treemap also allows one to construct tree hierarchies from data dynamically using a mechanism called flexible hierarchies. Given a set of multivariate data points, trees can be built level-by-level by successively grouping the points by different user-defined criteria on the data attributes.

Utilization: Treemap comes as a turnkey system that can be customized by
                    means of its user interface. Treemap accepts many data formats
                    as input. Also, Treemap can be configured to monitor "live" data
                    that changes dynamically in time. Its many options can be saved
                    as presets, called feature sets, which allows relatively easy cus-
                    tomization without the need for programming. All in all, Treemap
                    is quite easy to use as a customizable turnkey system, but an im-
                    portant limitation is that it cannot be used as a library via an
                    API, e.g., for developing third-party applications.

XmdvTool

Type: Turnkey system

Availability: Open source (written in C/C++)

Address: http://davis.wpi.edu/xmdv/

Description: XmdvTool is a general-purpose visualization tool for the interac-
                    tive exploration of multivariate datasets. As such, XmdvTool im-
                    plements several visualization methods: scatter plots, star glyphs,
                    parallel coordinates, and dimensional stacking. These visualiza-
                    tion methods come in a "flat" and a hierarchical variant. The
                    flat variant visualizes all data points separately. The hierarchical
                    variant first groups the data points in a tree, based on some sim-
                    ilarity metric defined on the data attributes. Next, tree nodes,
                    which represent data clusters, are visualized using color and shad-
                    ing to map different cluster attributes. XmdvTool is implemented
                    in C++ using OpenGL for the graphics and Tcl/Tk for the user
                    interface functionality.

Utilization: XmdvTool comes as a turnkey system that can be directly used
                    to visualize multivariate data coming in a number of different for-
                    mats. The user interface is relatively easy to learn. A strong
                    feature of XmdvTool is the provision of many interaction mech-
                    anisms that allow several types of brushing in screen, data, and
                    structure spaces; zooming and panning; display distortion tech-
                    niques; and masking and reordering of the axes (dimensions). All
                    these mechanisms make XmdvTool a versatile tool that can be
                    used relatively easily to get a first look into a given multivariate
                    dataset. However, just as Treemap, the functionality of XmdvTool
                    is not available as an API or library, which makes its applicability
                    limited in some contexts.

Bibliography

[AbsInt 07] AbsInt. "aiSee: Graph Visualization." Available online (http://www.absint.com/aisee/), 2007.

[Adobe Systems Incorporated 07] Adobe Systems Incorporated. "Adobe Acrobat Family." Available online (http://www.adobe.com/products/acrobat/), 2007.

[AGD 06] AGD. "AGD: A Library of Algorithms for Graph Drawing." Available online (http://www.ads.tuwien.ac.at/AGD/), 2006.

[Ambardar 06] A. Ambardar. *Digital Signal Processing: A Modern Introduction.* Toronto: Thomson Engineering, 2006.

[Arya et al. 98] S. Arya, D. M. Mount, N. S. Netanyahu, R. Silverman, and A. Wu. "An Optimal Algorithm for Approximate Nearest Neighbor Searching." *J. of the ACM* 45:6 (1998), 891–923.

[Auber 07] D. Auber. "Tulip Graph Visualization Software System." Available online (http://www.tulip-software.org/), 2007.

[AVS, Inc. 06] AVS, Inc. *AVS/Express Developer's Reference.* Waltham, MA: Advanced Visual Systems, Inc., 2006.

[Bajaj and Xu 03] C. L. Bajaj and G. Xu. "Anisotropic Diffusion of Surfaces and Functions on Surfaces." *ACM Transactions on Graphics (TOG)* 22:1 (2003), 4–32.

[Banks and Singer 95] D. C. Banks and B. A. Singer. "A Predictor-Corrector Technique for Visualizing Unsteady Flow." *IEEE Transactions on Visualization and Computer Graphics* 1:2 (1995), 151–163.

[Bederson and Shneiderman 03] B. Bederson and B. Shneiderman. *The Craft of Information Visualization: Readings and Reflections.* San Francisco, CA: Morgan Kaufmann, 2003.

477

[Bederson et al. 02] B. Bederson, B. Shneiderman, and M. Wattenberg. "Ordered and Quantum Treemaps: Making Effective Use of 2D Space to Display Hierarchies." *ACM Transactions of Graphics* 21:4 (2002), 833–854.

[Bellard 06] F. Bellard. "The FFmpeg Multimedia System." Available online (http://ffmpeg.mplayerhq.hu/), 2006.

[Belytschko et al. 96] T. Belytschko, Y. Krongauz, D. Organ, M. Fleming, and P. Krysl. "Meshless Methods: An Overview and Recent Developments." *Computer Methods in Applied Mechanics and Engineering* 139:1 (1996), 3–47.

[Bentley 75] J. L. Bentley. "Multidimensional Binary Search Trees Used for Associative Searching." *Comm. of the ACM* 18:9 (1975), 509–517.

[Bentley 90] J. L. Bentley. "K-d Trees for Semidynamic Point Sets." In *Proc. 6th Ann. ACM Symposium on Computational Geometry*, pp. 187–197. New York: ACM Press, 1990.

[Bergman et al. 95] L. D. Bergman, B. E. Rogowitz, and L. A. Treinish. "A Rule-Based Tool for Assisting Colormap Selection." In *Proc. IEEE Visualization*, pp. 118–125. Los Alamitos, CA: IEEE Press, 1995.

[Bern and Eppstein 92] M. Bern and D. Eppstein. "Mesh Generation and Optimal Triangulation." In *Computing and Euclidean Geometry*, pp. 23–90. River Edge, NJ: World Scientific, 1992.

[Bertin 83] J. Bertin. *Semiology of Graphics*. Madison, WI: University of Wisconsin Press, 1983.

[Bitter et al. 00] I. Bitter, M. Sato, M. Bender, K. T. McDonnell, A. Kaufman, and M. Wan. "CEASAR: A Smooth, Accurate and Robust Centerline Extraction Algorithm." In *Proc. IEEE Visualization*, pp. 45–52. Los Alamitos, CA: IEEE Press, 2000.

[Bloesch 93] A. Bloesch. "Aesthetic Layout of Generalized Trees." *Software—Practice and Experience* 23:8 (1993), 817–827.

[Blum 67] H. Blum. "A Transformation for Extracting New Descriptors of Shape." In *Models for the Perception of Speech and Visual Form*, pp. 362–380. Cambridge, MA: MIT Press, 1967.

[Boardman 00] R. Boardman. "Bubble Trees: The Visualization of Hierarchical Information Structures." In *Proc. ACM CHI*, pp. 315–316. New York: ACM Press, 2000.

[Borg and Groenen 97] I. Borg and P. J. F. Groenen. *Modern Multidimensional Scaling: Theory and Applications*. New York: Springer, 1997.

[Brandenburg 03] A. Brandenburg. "Computational Aspects of Astrophysical MHD and Turbulence." In *Advances in Nonlinear Dynamics*, edited by A. Ferriz-Mas and M. Nú nez, pp. 269–337. Taylor and Francis Group, 2003.

[Brewer and Harrower 07] C. Brewer and M. Harrower. "ColorBrewer." Available online (http://www.colorbrewer.org/), 2007.

[Bruls et al. 00] M. Bruls, K. Huizing, and J. J. van Wijk. "Squarified Treemaps." In *Proc. VisSym*, pp. 33–42. Berlin: Springer, 2000.

[Bürkle et al. 01] D. Bürkle, T. Preusser, and M. Rumpf. "Transport and Diffusion in Time-Dependent Flow Visualization." In *Proc. IEEE Visualization*, pp. 61–68. Los Alamitos, CA: IEEE Press, 2001.

[Cabral and Leedom 93] B. Cabral and L. C. Leedom. "Imaging Vector Fields using Line Integral Convolution." In *Proceedings of SIGGRAPH 93, Computer Graphics Proceedings, Annual conference Series*, pp. 263–270. New York: ACM Press, 1993.

[Card et al. 99] S. Card, J. Mackinlay, and B. Shneiderman. *Readings in Information Visualization: Using Vision to Think.* San Francisco, CA: Morgan Kaufmann, 1999.

[Castleman 96] K. R. Castleman. *Digital Image Processing.* Englewood Cliffs, NJ: Prentice Hall, 1996.

[Chamberlin and Boyce 74] D. D. Chamberlin and R. F. Boyce. "SEQUEL: A structured English query language." In *Proc. International Conference on Management of Data (ACM SIGFIDET) Workshop on Data Description, Access and Coontrol*, pp. 249–264. New York: ACM Press, 1974.

[Chen and Carroll 00] S. J. Chen and S. D. Carroll. "3-D Reconstruction of Coronary Arterial Tree to Optimize Angiographic Visualization." *IEEE Transactions on Medical Imaging* 19:4 (2000), 318–336.

[Chi 00] E. H. Chi. "A Taxonomy of Visualization Techniques using the Data State Reference Model." In *Proc. IEEE InfoVis*, pp. 69–75. Los Alamitos, CA: IEEE Press, 2000.

[Chi 02] E. H. Chi. *A Framework for Visualizing Information.* Human-Computer Interaction Series, Amsterdam: Elsevier, 2002.

[Clarenz et al. 04] U. Clarenz, M. Rumpf, and A. Telea. "Surface Processing Methods for Point Sets using Finite Elements." *Computers and Graphics* 28:6 (2004), 851–868.

[Cleveland 85] W. S. Cleveland. *The Elements of Graphing Data.* Monterey, CA: Wadsworth Advanced Books and Software, 1985.

[Cline et al. 88] H. E. Cline, W. E. Lorensen, S. Ludke, C. R. Crawford, and B. C. Teeter. "Two Algorithms for the Three-Dimensioal Construction of Tomograms." *Medical Physics* 15:3 (1988), 320–327.

[Coffman and Graham 72] E. G. Coffman and R. L. Graham. "Optimal Scheduling for Two-Processor Systems." *Acta Informatica* 1:3 (1972), 200–213.

[Cohen et al. 96] J. Cohen, A. Varshney, D. Manocha, G. Turk, H. Weber, P. Agarwal, F. Brooks, and W. Wright. "Simplification Envelopes." In *Proceedings of SIGGRAPH 96, Computer Graphics Proceedings, Annual Conference Series*, pp. 119–128. Reading, MA: Addison Wesley, 1996.

[Cohen et al. 07] J. Cohen, A. Varshney, and G. Turk. "Simplification Envelopes Software." Available online (http://www.cs.unc.edu/~geom/envelope.html), 2007.

[Corbi 99] T. A. Corbi. "Program Understanding: Challenge for the 1990s." *IBM Systems Journal* 28:2 (1999), 294–306.

[Cormen et al. 01] T. H. Cormen, C. E. Leiserson, R. L. Rivest, and C. Stein. *An Introduction to Algorithms, Second edition.* Cambridge, MA: MIT Press, 2001.

[Cornea et al. 05] N. D. Cornea, M. F. Demirci, D. Silver, A. Shokoufandeh, and S. Dickinson. "3D Object Retrieval using Many-to-many Matching of Curve Skeletons." In *Proc. Shape Modeling and Applications (SMI'05)*, pp. 368–373. New York: ACM Press, 2005.

[Costa and Cesar 01] L. Costa and R. Cesar. *Shape Analysis and Classification.* Boca Raton, FL: CRC Press, 2001.

[Cox and Cox 01] T. F. Cox and M. A. A. Cox. *Multidimensional Scaling.* Boca Raton, FL: CRC Press, 2001.

[Cuisenaire and Macq 97] O. Cuisenaire and B. M. Macq. "Applications of the Region Growing Euclidean Distance Transform: Anisotropy and Skeletons." In *Proc. ICIP*, pp. 200–203. Washington, D.C.: IEEE Computer Society, 1997.

[CUMULVS 07] CUMULVS. "CUMULVS Visualization System." Available online (http://www.csm.ornl.gov/cs/cumulvs.html), 2007.

[Danielsson 80] P. E. Danielsson. "Euclidean Distance Mapping." *Computer Graphics and Image Processing* 14:3 (1980), 227–248.

[de Berg et al. 00] M. de Berg, M. van Krefeld, M. Overmars, and O. Schwarzkopf. *Computational Geometry: Algorithms and Applications, Second edition.* Berlin: Springer-Verlag, 2000.

[Dey and Sun 06] T. K. Dey and J. Sun. "Defining and Computing Curve-Skeletons with Medial Geodesic Function." In *Proc. Symposium on Geometry Processing*, pp. 123–152. Aire-la-Ville, Switzerland: Eurographics Association, 2006.

[Di Battista et al. 99] G. Di Battista, P. Eades, R. Tamassia, and I. G. Tollis. *Graph Drawing: Algorithms for the Visualization of Graphs.* Englewood Cliffs, NJ: Prentice Hall, 1999.

[Diehl 04] S. Diehl. *Software Visualization: International Seminar, Dagstuhl Castle, Germany, May 20–25, 2001, Lecture Notes in Computer Science 2269.* Berlin: Springer, 2004.

[Diehl 07] S. Diehl. *Software Visualization: Visualizing the Structure, Behaviour, and Evolution of Software.* New York: Springer, 2007.

[Eades 84] P. Eades. "A Heuristic for Graph Drawing." *Congressus Numerantium* 42 (1984), 149–160.

[Eick et al. 92] S. G. Eick, J. L. Steffen, and E. E. Sumner. "Seesoft—A Tool for Visualizing Line Oriented Software Statistics." *IEEE Transactions on Software Engineering* 18:11 (1992), 957–968.

[Engel 02] K. Engel. "Interactive High-Quality Volume Rendering with Flexible Consumer Graphics Hardware." In *Eurographics State-of-the-Art (STAR) Reports*, 2002. See also the software available at http://www.vis.uni-stuttgart.de/~engel/pre-integrated.

[Fisher et al. 96] R. Fisher, S. Perkins, A. Walker, and E. Wolfart. *Hypermedia Image Processing Reference.* New York: J. Wiley and Sons, 1996.

[Foley et al. 95] J. D. Foley, A. van Dam, S. K. Feiner, and J. F. Hughes. *Computer Graphics: Principles and Practice in C, Second edition.* Reading, MA: Addison-Wesley Professional, 1995.

[Frick et al. 94] A. Frick, A. Ludwig, and H. Mehldau. "A Fast Adaptive Layout Algorithm for Undirected Graphs." In *Proc. of Graph Drawing*, pp. 388–403. New York: Springer, 1994.

[Friedman et al. 77] J. H. Friedman, J. L. Bentley, and R. A. Finkel. "An Algorithm for Finding Best Matches in Logarithmic Expected Time." *ACM Transactions on Mathematical Software* 3:3 (1977), 209–226.

[Frigo 07] M. Frigo. "Fast Fourier Transform C Software Library." Available online (http://www.fftw.org/), 2007.

[Fruchterman and Reingold 91] T. M. J. Fruchterman and E. M. Reingold. "Graph Drawing by Force-Directed Placement." *Software—Practice and Experience* 21:11 (1991), 1129–1164.

[Fua et al. 99] Y. Fua, M. O. Ward, and E. A. Rundensteiner. "Hierarchical Parallel Coordinates for Visualizing Large Multivariate Data Sets." In *Proc. IEEE Visualization*, pp. 43–50. Los Alamitos, CA: IEEE Press, 1999.

[Gansner et al. 93] E. R. Gansner, E. Koutsofios, S. C. North, and K. P. Vo. "A Technique for Drawing Directed Graphs." *IEEE Transactions on Software Engineering* 19:3 (1993), 214–230.

[Garland and Heckbert 97] M. Garland and P. Heckbert. "Simplification using Quadric Error Metrics." In *Proceedings of SIGGRAPH 97, Computer Graphics Proceedings, Annual Conference Series*, pp. 209–216. Reading, MA: Addison Wesley, 1997.

[Garland 99] M. Garland. "Multiresolution Modeling: Survey and Future Opportunities." In *Eurographics'99 State-of-the-Art (STAR) Reports*. Aire-la-Ville, Switzerland: Eurographics Association, 1999.

[Ge and Fitzpatrick 96] Yaorong Ge and J. Michael Fitzpatrick. "On the Generation of Skeletons from Discrete Euclidean Distance Maps." *IEEE Trans. Pattern Anal. Mach. Intell.* 18:11 (1996), 1055–1066.

[Geist et al. 97] G. A. Geist, J. A. Kohl, and P. M. Papadopoulos. "CUMULVS: Providing Fault-Tolerance, Visualization and Steering of Parallel Applications." *International Journal of High Performance Computing Applications* 11:3 (1997), 224–236.

[GEM 07] GEM. "Graph Embedder (GEM) Software." Available online (http://i44ftp.info.uni-karlsruhe.de/pub/papers/frick/gem1.0a.tar.gz), 2007.

[GIMP 06] GIMP. "GIMP—The GNU Image Manipulation Program." Available online (http://www.gimp.org/), 2006.

[Gonzalez and Woods 02] R. C. Gonzalez and R. E. Woods. *Digital Image Processing, Second edition*. Englewood Cliffs, NJ: Prentice Hall, 2002.

[Gonzalez et al. 04] R. C. Gonzalez, R. E. Woods, and S. L. Eddins. *Digital Image Processing using MATLAB*. Englewood Cliffs, NJ: Prentice Hall, 2004.

[GPGPU 06] GPGPU. "General-Purpose Computation Using Graphics Hardware." Available online (http://www.gpgpu.org/), 2006.

[GraphViz 06] GraphViz. "The GraphViz Graph Visualization Software." Available online (http://www.graphviz.org/), 2006.

[Griebel and Schweitzer 06] M. Griebel and M. A. Schweitzer. *Meshfree Methods for Partial Differential Equations*. New York: Springer, 2006.

[Griebel et al. 04] M. Griebel, T. Preusser, M. Rumpf, M. A. Schweitzer, and A. Telea. "Flow Field Clustering via Algebraic Multigrid." In *Proc. IEEE Visualization*, pp. 35–42. Los Alamitos, CA: IEEE Press, 2004.

[Grivet et al. 04] S. Grivet, D. Auber, J. P. Domenger, and G. Melançon. "Bubble Tree Drwing Algorithm." In *Proc. International Conference on Computer Vision and Graphics (ICCVG)*, pp. 633–641. Berlin: Springer, 2004.

[GTS 06] GTS. "The GNU Triangulated Surface Library." Available online (http://gts.sourceforge.net/), 2006.

[Hansen and Johnson 04] C. Hansen and C. J. Johnson. *Visualization Handbook*. Amsterdam: Elsevier, 2004.

[Harel and Koren 00] D. Harel and Y. Koren. "A Fast Multi-Scale Method for Drawing Large Graphs." In *Proc. 8th International Symposium on Graph Drawing (GD00)*, pp. 183–196. Berlin: Springer, 2000.

[Hauser et al. 02] H. Hauser, F. Ledermann, and H. Doleisch. "Angular Brushing of Extended Parallel Coordinates." In *Proc. IEEE Visualization*, pp. 127–135. Los Alamitos, CA: IEEE Press, 2002.

[Heckbert and Garland 97] P. Heckbert and M. Garland. "Survey of Polygonal Surface Simplification Algorithms." In *SIGGRAPH'97 Course Notes on Multiresolution Surface Modeling*. New York: ACM Press, 1997.

[Heckel et al. 99] B. Heckel, G. H. Weber, B. Hamann, and K. I. Joy. "Construction of Vector Field Hierarchies." In *Proc. IEEE Visualization*, pp. 19–25. Los Alamitos, CA: IEEE Press, 1999.

[Henderson 04] A. Henderson. *The ParaView Guide*. Clifton Park, NY: Kitware, Inc., 2004.

[Herman et al. 00] I. Herman, G. Melançon, and M. S. Marshall. "Graph Visualization and Navigation in Information Visualization: A Survey." *IEEE Transactions on Visualization and Computer Graphics* 6:1 (2000), 24–43.

[Holten 06] D. H. R. Holten. "Hierarchical Edge Bundles: Visualization of Adjacency Relations in Hierarchical Data." *IEEE Transactions on Visualization and Computer Graphics (Proc. InfoVis 2006)* 12:5 (2006), 741–748.

[Hoppe et al. 92] H. Hoppe, T. DeRose, T. Duchamp, J. McDonald, and W. Stuetzle. "Surface Reconstruction from Unorganized Points." 26:2.

[Hoppe 97] H. Hoppe. "View-Dependent Refinement of Progressive Meshes." In *Proceedings of SIGGRAPH 97, Computer Graphics Proceedings, Annual Conference Series*, pp. 189–198. Reading, MA: Addison Wesley, 1997.

[Hoppe 98] H. Hoppe. "Efficient Implementation of Progressive Meshes." *Computers & Graphics* 22:1 (1998), 27–36.

[Hoppe 99] H. Hoppe. "New Quadric Metrics for Simplifying Meshes with Appearance Attributes." In *Proc. IEEE Visualization*, pp. 59–66. Los Alamitos, CA: IEEE Press, 1999.

[InfoWiki 06] InfoWiki. "The Information Visualization Community Platform." Available online (http://www.infovis-wiki.net/), 2006.

[Inselberg and Dimsdale 90] A. Inselberg and B. Dimsdale. "Parallel Coordinates: A Tool for Visualizing Multidimensional Geometry." In *Proc. IEEE Visualization*, pp. 361–378. Los Alamitos, CA: IEEE Press, 1990.

[Inselberg 98] A. Inselberg. "A Survey of Parallel Coordinates." In *Mathematical Visualization*, pp. 167–179. New York: Springer, 1998.

[Jain and Murty 99] A. K. Jain and M. N. Murty. "Data Clustering: A Review." *ACM Computing Surveys* 31:3 (1999), 264–323.

[Jain et al. 95] R. Jain, R. Kasturi, and B. G. Shunck. *Machine Vision*. New York: McGraw-Hill, 1995.

[Jain 89] A. Jain. *Fundamentals of Digital Image Processing.* Englewood Cliffs, NJ: Prentice Hall, 1989.

[Jankun-Kelly et al. 06] M. Jankun-Kelly, M. Jiang, D. Thompson, and R. Machiraju. "Vortex Visualization for Practical Engineering Applications." *IEEE Transactions on Visualization and Computer Graphics* 12:5 (2006), 957–964.

[Jansing et al. 99] E. D. Jansing, T. A. Albert, and D. L. Chenoweth. "Two-Dimensional Entropic Segmentation." *Pattern Recognition Letters* 20:3 (1999), 329–336.

[Jobard and Lefer 97] B. Jobard and W. Lefer. "Creating Evenly-Spaced Streamlines of Arbitrary Density." In *Proc. EG Workshop on Visualization in Scientific Computing*, pp. 43–56. New York: Springer, 1997.

[Johnson and Shneiderman 91] B. Johnson and B. Shneiderman. "Tree-Maps: A Space-Filling Approach to the Visualization of Hierarchical Information Structures." In *Proc. IEEE InfoVis*, pp. 284–291. Los Alamitos, CA: IEEE Press, 1991.

[Jünger and Mutzel 03] Michael Jünger and Petra Mutzel. *Graph Drawing Software.* New York: Springer, 2003.

[Kamada and Kawai 89] T. Kamada and S. Kawai. "An Algorithm for Drawing General Undirected Graphs." *Information Processing Letters* 31:1 (1989), 7–15.

[Kindlmann 04a] G. Kindlmann. "Superquadric Tensor Glyphs." In *Proc. EG/IEEE Symposium on Visualization (VisSym'04)*, pp. 147–154. Aire-la-Ville, Switzerland: Eurographics Association, 2004.

[Kindlmann 04b] Gordon Kindlmann. "Visualization and Analysis of Diffusion Tensor Fields." PhD thesis, School of Computing, University of Utah, 2004.

[Kindlmann 06] G. Kindlmann. "The Teem Tensor Visualization Software Package." Available online (http://teem.sourceforge.net/), 2006.

[Kitware, Inc. 04] Kitware, Inc. *The VTK User's Guide.* Clifton Park, NY: Kitware, Inc., 2004.

[Kitware, Inc. 06] Kitware, Inc. "VTK Home Page." Available online (http://www.kitware.com/vtk/), 2006.

[Koike 93] H. Koike. "The Role of Another Spatial Dimension in Software Visualization." *ACM Transactions of Information Systems* 11:3 (1993), 266–286.

[Koren et al. 03] Y. Koren, L. Carmel, and D. Harel. "Drawing Huge Graphs by Algebraic Multigrid Optimization." *Multiscale Modeling and Simulation* 1:4 (2003), 645–673.

[Lanza and Marinescu 06] M. Lanza and R. Marinescu. *Object-Oriented Metrics in Practice.* New York: Springer, 2006.

[Laramee et al. 04] R. S. Laramee, H. Hauser, H. Doleisch, B. Vrolijk, F. H. Post, and D. Weiskopf. "The State of the Art in Flow Visualization: Dense and Texture-Based Techniques." *Computer Graphics Forum* 23:2 (2004), 203–221.

[Larkin and Simon 87] J. Larkin and H. Simon. "Why a Diagram Is (Sometimes) Worth 10,000 Words." *Cognitive Science* 11 (1987), 65–99.

[Lederman 07] F. Lederman. "parvis parallel coordinates visualisation." Available online (http://home.subnet.at/flo/mv/parvis/), 2007.

[Levoy 88] Marc Levoy. "Display of Surfaces from Volume Data." *IEEE Computer Graphics and Applications* 8:3 (1988), 29–37.

[Linsen and Prautzch 01] L. Linsen and H. Prautzch. "Local versus Global Triangulation." In *Proc. Eurographics*. Aire-la-Ville, Switzerland: Eurographics Association, 2001.

[Lorensen and Cline 87] W. E. Lorensen and H. E. Cline. "Marching Cubes: A High Resolution 3D Surface Construction Algorithm." *Proc. SIGGRAPH '87, Computer Graphics* 21:4 (1987), 163–169.

[Lorensen 04] B. Lorensen. "On the Death of Visualization." In *Proc. NIH/NSF Fall Workshop on Visualization Research Challenges*. Los Alamitos, CA: IEEE Press, 2004.

[Lotufo et al. 00] T. Lotufo, A. Falcao, and F. Zampirolli. "Fast Euclidean Distance Transform using a Graph-Search Algorithm." In *Proc. of the 13th Brazilian Symp. on Comp. Graph. and Image Proc.*, pp. 269–275. Washington, D.C.: IEEE Computer Society, 2000.

[Low and Tan 97] K. L. Low and T.S. Tan. "Model Simplification using Vertex Clustering." In *Proc. ACM Symposium on Interactive 3D Graphics*, pp. 75–82. New York: ACM Press, 1997.

[Luebke 01] D. Luebke. "A Developer's Survey of Polygonal Simplification Algorithms." *IEEE Computer Graphics & Applications* 21:3 (2001), 24–35.

[Mackinlay 86] J. D. Mackinlay. "Automating the Design of Graphical Presentations of Relational Information." *ACM Transactions on Graphics* 5:2 (1986), 110–141.

[Majda et al. 01] A. J. Majda, A. L. Bertozzi, and D. G. Crighton. *Vorticity and Incompressible Flow*. Cambridge, UK: Cambridge University Press, 2001.

[Manzanera et al. 99] A. Manzanera, T. Bernard, F. Preteux, and B. Longuet. "Medial Faces from a Concise 3D Thinning Algorithm." In *Proc. ICCV 99*, pp. 337–343. Los Alamitos, CA: IEEE Press, 1999.

[Marcus et al. 03] A. Marcus, L. Feng, and J. I. Maletic. "3D Representations for Software Visualization." In *Proc. ACM SoftVis*, pp. 27–36. New York: ACM Press, 2003.

[Mao et al. 98] X. Mao, Y. Hatanaka, H. Higashida, and A. Imamyia. "Image-Guided Streamline Placement on Curvilinear Grid Surfaces." In *Proc. IEEE Visualization*, pp. 135–142. Los Alamitos, CA: IEEE Press, 1998.

[MathWorks, Inc. 07] MathWorks, Inc. "MATLAB." Available online (http://www.mathworks.com/products/matlab), 2007.

[McCormick et al. 87] B. H. McCormick, T. A. DeFanti, and M. D. Brown. "Visualization in Scientific Computing." *Computer Graphics* 21:6.

[McReynolds and Blythe 99] T. McReynolds and D. Blythe. "Advanced Graphics Programming Techniques using OpenGL." In *SIGGRAPH '99 Course Notes*. New York: ACM Press, 1999. Available online (http://www.opengl.org/resources/code/samples/sig99/).

[Mead 92] A. Mead. "Review of the Development of Multidimensional Scaling Methods." *The Statistician* 33 (1992), 27–35.

[Mebarki et al. 05] A. Mebarki, P. Alliez, and O. Devillers. "Farthest Point Seeding for Efficient Placement of Streamlines." In *Proc. IEEE Visualization*, pp. 479–486. Los Alamitos, CA: IEEE CS Press, 2005.

[Meijster et al. 00] A. Meijster, J. Roerdink, and W. Hesselink. "A General Algorithm for Computing Distance Transforms in Linear Time." In *Mathematical Morphology and Its Applications to Image and Signal Processing*, pp. 331–340. Dordrecht: Kluwer, 2000.

[Morse et al. 02] E. Morse, M. Lewis, and K. A. Olsen. "Testing Visual Information Retrieval Methodologies Case Study: Comparative Analysis of Textual, Icon, Graphical, and 'Spring' Displays." *Journal of the American Society for Information Science and Technology* 53:1 (2002), 28–40.

[Mount 06] D. M. Mount. "ANN Programming Manual." Available online (http://www.cs.umd.edu/~mount/ANN/Files/1.1/ANNmanual_1.1.pdf), 2006.

[Mullikin 92] J. Mullikin. "The Vector Distance Transform in Two and Three Dimensions." *CVGIP: Graphical Models and Image Processing* 54:6 (1992), 526–535.

[Myler and Weeks 93] H. R. Myler and A. R. Weeks. *Computer Imaging Recipes in C*. Englewood Cliffs, NJ: Prentice Hall, 1993.

[NLM 06] National Library of Medicine. "The Insight Segmentation and Registration Toolkit (ITK)." Available online (http://www.itk.org/), 2006.

[Nielson et al. 06] G. M. Nielson, G.-P. Bonneau, and T. Ertl. *Scientific Visualization: The Visual Extraction of Knowledge from Data*. New York: Springer, 2006.

[O'Donnel and Westin 05] L. O'Donnel and C.-F. Westin. "White Matter Tract Clustering and Correspondence in Populations." In *Proc. Medical Image Computing and Computer-Assisted Interventions (MICCAI'05), Lecture Notes in Cmoputer Science 3749*. Berlin: Springer-Verlag, 2005.

[Ogniewicz and Kubler 95] R. L. Ogniewicz and O. Kubler. "Hierarchic Voronoi Skeletons." *Pattern Recognition* 28:3 (1995), 343–359.

[Ohtake et al. 03] Y. Ohtake, A. Belyaev, M. Alexa, G. Turk, and H. P. Seidel. "Multi-Level Partition of Unity Implicits." *Proc. SIGGRAPH '03, Transactions on Graphics* 22 (2003), 463–470.

[Okabe et al. 92] A. Okabe, B. Boots, and K. Sugihara. *Spatial Tessellations: Concepts and Applications of Voronoi Diagrams.* Chichester, UK: John Wiley & Sons, 1992.

[OpenCV 07] OpenCV. "The OpenCV Computer Vision Library." Available online (http://opencvlibrary.sourceforge.net/), 2007.

[Palagyi and Kuba 99] K. Palagyi and A. Kuba. "Directional 3D Thinning using 8 Subiterations." In *Proc. DGCI 99, Lecture Notes in Computer Science 1568*, pp. 325–333. London: Springer-Verlag, 1999.

[Perona and Malik 90] P. Perona and J. Malik. "Scale-Space and Edge Detection using Anisotropic Diffusion." *IEEE Transactions on Pattern Analysis and Machine Intelligence* 12:7 (1990), 629–639.

[Pfleeger et al. 05] S. L. Pfleeger, C. Verhoef, and J. C. van Vliet. "Analyzing the Evolution of Large-Scale Software." *Journal of Software Maintenance* 17:1 (2005), 1–2.

[Pierpaoli and Basser 96] C. Pierpaoli and P. J. Basser. "Toward a Quantitative Assessment of Diffusion Anisotropy." *Magnetic Resonance in Medicine* 36:6 (1996), 893–906.

[Plaugher et al. 00] P. J. Plaugher, A. Stepanov, M. Lee, and D. R. Musser. *The C++ Standard Template Library.* Englewood Cliffs, NJ: Prentice Hall PTR, 2000.

[Post et al. 02] F. H. Post, B. Vrolijk, H. Hauser, R. S. Laramee, and H. Doleisch. "Feature Extraction and Visualization of Flow Fields." In *EUROGRAPHICS 2002 State of the Art Reports*, pp. 69–100. Aire-la-Ville, Switzerland: Eurographics Association, 2002.

[Post et al. 03a] F. H. Post, G.-P. Bonneau, and G. M. Nielson. *Data Visualization: The State of the Art.* New York: Springer, 2003.

[Post et al. 03b] F. H. Post, B. Vrolijk, H. Hauser, R. S. Laramee, and H. Doleisch. "The State of the Art in Flow Visualization: Feature Extraction and Tracking." *Computer Graphics Forum* 22:4 (2003), 775–792.

[Preim and Bartz 07] B. Preim and D. Bartz. *Visualization in Medicine: Theory, Algorithms, and Applications.* San Francisco, CA: Morgan Kaufmann, 2007.

[Press et al. 02] W. H. Press, S. A. Teukolsky, W. T. Vetterling, and B. P. Flannery. *Numerical Recipes in C++, Second edition.* Cambridge, UK: Cambridge University Press, 2002.

[Preusser and Rumpf 99] T. Preusser and M. Rumpf. "Anisotropic Nonlinear Diffusion in Flow Visualization." In *Proc. IEEE Visualization*, pp. 323–332. Los Alamitos, CA: IEEE Press, 1999.

[Prewitt and Mendelsohn 66] J. M. S. Prewitt and M. L. Mendelsohn. "The Analysis of Cell Images." *Annals of the New York Academy of Science* 128:3 (1966), 1035–1053.

[Rao and Card 94] R. Rao and S. K. Card. "The Table Lens: Merging Graphical and Symbolic Representations in an Interactive Focus+Context Visualization for Tabular Information." In *Proc. ACM Conference on Human Factors in Computing Systems (CHI)*, pp. 318–322. New York: ACM Press, 1994.

[Reddy 93] J. N. Reddy. *Introduction to the Finite Element Method, Second edition*. New York: McGraw-Hill, 1993.

[Reinders et al. 99] F. Reinders, F. H. Post, and H. J. W. Spoelder. "Attribute-Based Feature Tracking." In *Proc. Data Visualization (VisSym'99)*, pp. 63–72. New York: Springer, 1999.

[Reinders et al. 00] F. Reinders, M. Jacobson, and F. Post. "Skeleton graph generation for feature shape description." In *Proc. Data Visualization (VisSym'00)*, pp. 73–82. Aire-la-Ville, Switzerland: Eurographics Association, 2000.

[Reiss 05] S. P. Reiss. "The Paradox of Software Visualizaton." In *Proc. 3rd Intl. Workshop on Visualizing Software for Understanding and Analysis (VIS-SOFT'05)*, pp. 59–63. Los Alamitos, CA: IEEE Press, 2005.

[Rezk-Salama et al. 99] C. Rezk-Salama, P. Hastreiter, T. Christian, and T. Ertl. "Interactive Exploration of Volume Line Integral Convolution Based on 3D-Texture Mapping." In *Proc. IEEE Visualization*, edited by David Ebert, Markus Gross, and Bernd Hamann, pp. 233–240. Los Alamitos, CA: IEEE Press, 1999.

[Ribarsky et al. 94] W. Ribarsky, B. Brown, T. Myerson, R. Feldmann, S. Smith, and L. Treinish. "Object-Oriented, Dataflow Visualization Systems—A Paradigm Shift?" In *Scientific Visualization: Advances and Challenges*, pp. 251–263. New York: Academic Press, 1994.

[Robertson et al. 91] G. Robertson, J. D. Mackinlay, and S. K. Card. "Cone Trees: Animated 3D Visualizations of Hierarchical Information." In *Proc. ACM Conference on Human Factors in Computing Systems (CHI)*, pp. 189–194. New York: ACM Press, 1991.

[Roettger 06a] S. Roettger. "V^3: The Versatile Volume Viewer." Available online (http://www.stereofx.org/volume.html), 2006.

[Roettger 06b] S. Roettger. "The Volume Library." Available online (http://www9.informatik.uni-erlangen.de/External/vollib/), 2006.

[Rossignac and Borrel 93] J. Rossignac and P. Borrel. "Multi-Resolution 3D Approximations for Rendering Complex Scenes." In *Geometric Modeling in Computer Graphics*, pp. 455–465. New York: Springer, 1993.

[Sakamoto and Takagi 88] M. Sakamoto and M. Takagi. "Patterns of Weighted Voronoi Tessellations." *Science on Form* 3:2 (1988), 103–111.

[Samet 90] H. Samet. *The Design and Analysis of Spatial Data Structures*. Reading, MA: Addision-Wesley, 1990.

[Schalkoff 89] R. Schalkoff. *Digital Image Processing and Computer Vision*. New York: John Wiley & Sons, 1989.

[Schneider and Seifert 06] O. Schneider and B. Seifert. "WinDirStat—Windows Directory Statistics." Available online (http://windirstat.info/), 2006.

[Schroeder et al. 92] W. Schroeder, J. Zarge, and W. Lorensen. "Decimation of Triangle Meshes." *Proc. SIGGRAPH '92, Computer Graphics* 26:2 (1992), 65–70.

[Schroeder et al. 04] W. Schroeder, K. Martin, and B. Lorensen. *The Visualization Toolkit: An Object-Oriented Approach to 3-D Graphics, Third edition.* Englewood Cliffs, NJ: Prentice Hall, 2004.

[Schroeder 97] W. Schroeder. "A Topology-Modifying Progressive Decimation Algorithm." In *Proc. IEEE Visualization*, pp. 205–212. Los Alamitos, CA: IEEE Press, 1997.

[SCIRun 07] SCIRun. "SCIRun: A Scientific Computing Problem Solving Environment, Scientific Computing and Imaging Institute (SCI)." Available online (http://software.sci.utah.edu/scirun.html), 2007.

[Sethian 96] J. A. Sethian. *Level Set Methods: Evolving Interfaces in Geometry, Fluid Mechanics, Computer Vision, and Materials Science*. Cambridge, UK: Cambridge University Press, 1996.

[Shepard 68] D. Shepard. "A Two-Dimensional Interpolation Function for Irregularly Spaced Data." In *Proc. 23rd ACM International Conference*, pp. 517–724. New York: ACM Press, 1968.

[Shewchuk 02] J. R. Shewchuk. "Delaunay Refinement Algorithms for Triangular Mesh Generation." *Computational Geometry: Theory and Applications* 22:1–3 (2002), 21–74.

[Shewchuk 06] J. R. Shewchuk. "Triangle Project Home Page." Available online (http://www.cs.cmu.edu/~quake/triangle.html), 2006.

[Shirley and Morley 03] P. Shirley and R. K. Morley. *Realistic Ray Tracing, Second edition*. Natick, MA: A K Peters, Ltd., 2003.

[Shneiderman 92] B. Shneiderman. "Tree Visualization with Treemaps: 2-D Space-Filling Approach." *ACM Transactions on Graphics* 11:1 (1992), 92–99.

[Shneiderman 96] B. Shneiderman. "The Eyes Have It: A Task by Data Type Taxonomy for Information Visualizations." In *Proceedings of IEEE Symposium on Visual Languages*, pp. 336–343. Los Alamitos, CA: IEEE Press, 1996.

[Shneiderman 06] B. Shneiderman. "Treemaps for Space-Constrained Vsualization of Hierarchies." Available online (http://www.cs.umd.edu/hcil/treemap-history/index.shtml), 2006.

[Shreiner et al. 03] D. Shreiner, M. Woo, J. Neider, and T. Davis. *The OpenGL Programming Guide: The Official Guide to Learning OpenGL*. Reading, MA: Addison-Wesley Professional, 2003.

[Shreiner 04] D. Shreiner. *OpenGL Reference Manual*. Reading, MA: Addison-Wesley Professional, 2004.

[Sillion 94] F. Sillion. *Radiosity and Global Illumination*. San Francisco, CA: Morgan Kaufmann Inc., 1994.

[Slicer 06] Slicer. "3D Slicer." Available online (http://www.slicer.org/), 2006.

[SmartMoney 07] SmartMoney. "Map of the Market." Available online (http://www.smartmoney.com/marketmap/), 2007.

[Sobel and Feldman 73] I. Sobel and G. Feldman. "A 3×3 Isotropic Gradient Operator for Image Processing." In *Pattern Classification and Scene Analysis*, edited by R. Duda and P. Hart, pp. 271–273. New York: John Wiley & Sons, 1973.

[Spence 07] R. Spence. *Information Visualization: Design for Interaction, Second edition*. Englewood Cliffs, NJ: Prentice Hall, 2007.

[SQL 06] SQL. "SQL Database Reference Material." Available online (http://www.sql.org/), 2006.

[Standish 84] T. A. Standish. "An Essay on Software Reuse." *IEEE Transactions on Software Engineering* 10:5 (1984), 494–497.

[Stasko et al. 98] J. T. Stasko, J. Domingue, M. H. Brown, and B. A. Price. *Software Visualization: Programming as a Multimedia Experience*. Cambridge, MA: MIT Press, 1998.

[Stasko et al. 00] J. Stasko, R. Catrambone, M. Guzdial, and K. McDonald. "An Evaluation of Space-Filling Information Visualizations for Depicting Hierarchical Structures." *International Journal of Human-Computer Studies* 53:5 (2000), 663–694.

[Stone 03] Maureen Stone. *A Field Guide to Digital Color*. Natick, MA: A K Peters, Ltd., 2003.

[Stroustrup 04] B. Stroustrup. *The C++ Programming Language, Third edition*. Reading, MA: Addison-Wesley, 2004.

[Strzodka and Telea 04] R. Strzodka and A. Telea. "Generalized Distance Transforms and Skeletons in Graphics Hardware." In *Proc. EG/IEEE VisSym*, pp. 221–230. Los Alamitos, CA: IEEE Press, 2004.

[Sugiyama et al. 81] K. Sugiyama, S. Tagawa, and M. Toda. "Methods for Visual Understanding of Hierarchical Systems." *IEEE Trans. Syst. Man Cybern.* 11:2 (1981), 109–125.

[Telea and van Wijk 99] A. Telea and J. J. van Wijk. "VISSION: An Object-Oriented Dataflow System for Simulation and Visualization." In *Proc. VisSym*, pp. 309–318. New York: Springer, 1999.

[Telea and van Wijk 02] A. Telea and J. J. van Wijk. "An Augmented Fast Marching Method for Computing Skeletons and Centerlines." In *Proc. Data Visualization (VisSym'99)*, pp. 251–258. New York: Springer, 2002.

[Telea and van Wijk 03] A. Telea and J. J. van Wijk. "3D IBFV: Hardware-Accelerated 3D Flow Visualization." In *Proc. IEEE Visualization*, pp. 31–38. Los Alamitos, CA: IEEE Press, 2003.

[Telea and Vilanova 03] A. Telea and A. Vilanova. "A Robust Level-Set Algorithm for Centerline Extraction." In *Proc. Data Visualization (VisSym'03)*, pp. 185–194. Aire-la-Ville, Switzerland: Eurographics Association, 2003.

[Telea 04] A. Telea. "An Image Inpainting Technique Based on the Fast Marching Method." *Journal of Graphics Tools* 9:1 (2004), 23–34.

[Thiel and Montanevert 92] E. Thiel and A. Montanevert. "Chamfer Masks: Discrete Distance Functions, Geometrical Properties and Optimization." In *Proc. of 11th IAPR International Conference on Pattern Recognition*, pp. 244–247. Los Alamitos, CA: IEEE Press, 1992.

[Thomas and Cook 05] J. A. Thomas and K. A. Cook, editors. *Illuminating the Path: Research and Development Agenda for Visual Analytics.* Los Alamitos, CA: IEEE Press, 2005.

[TortoiseSVN 07] TortoiseSVN. "TortoiseSVN." Available online (http://tortoisesvn.tigris.org/), 2007.

[Tory and Möller 04] M. Tory and T. Möller. "Rethinking Visualization: A High-Level Taxonomy." In *Proc. IEEE InfoVis*, pp. 151–158. Los Alamitos, CA: IEEE Press, 2004.

[Trottenberg et al. 01] U. Trottenberg, C. Oosterlee, and A. Schüller. *Multigrid: Basics, Parallelism and Adaptivity.* Amsterdam: Elsevier, 2001.

[Tufte 83] E. R. Tufte. *The Visual Display of Quantitative Information.* Cheshire, CT: Graphics Press, 1983.

[Tufte 90] E. R. Tufte. *Envisioning Information.* Cheshire, CT: Graphics Press, 1990.

[Tufte 97] E. R. Tufte. *Visual Explanations.* Cheshire, CT: Graphics Press, 1997.

[Turk and Banks 96] G. Turk and D. Banks. "Image-Guided Streamline Placement." In *Proceedings of SIGGRAPH 96, Computer Graphics Proceedings, Annual Conference Series*, pp. 453–460. Reading, MA: Addison Wesley, 1996.

[Tutte 01] W. T. Tutte. *Graph Theory.* Cambridge, UK: Cambridge University Press, 2001.

[van Liere and de Leeuw 03] R. van Liere and W. de Leeuw. "Graphsplatting: Visualizing Graphs as Continuous Fields." *IEEE Transactions on Visualization and Computer Graphics* 9:2 (2003), 206–212.

[van Liere and van Wijk 96] R. van Liere and J. J. van Wijk. "CSE: A Modular Architecture for Computational Steering." In *Proc. EG Workshop on Scientific Visualization*, pp. 257–266. Berlin: Springer, 1996.

[van Liere et al. 07] R. van Liere, J. Mulder, K. Sharoudi, and J. van Wijk. "Computational Steering Environment." Available online (http://www.cwi.nl/projects/cse/cse.html), 2007.

[van Walsum et al. 96] T. van Walsum, F. H. Post, D. Silver, and F. J. Post. "Feature Extraction and Iconic Visualization." *IEEE Transactions on Visualization and Computer Graphics* 2:2 (1996), 111–119.

[van Wijk and van de Wetering 99] J. J. van Wijk and H. van de Wetering. "Cushion Treemaps: Visualization of Hierarchical Information." In *Proc. IEEE InfoVis*, pp. 73–78. Los Alamitos, CA: IEEE Press, 1999.

[van Wijk 91] J. J. van Wijk. "Spot Noise Texture Synthesis for Data Visualization." In *Proc. ACM SIGGRAPH*, pp. 309–318. New York: ACM Press, 1991.

[van Wijk 02a] J. J. van Wijk. "Image Based Flow Visualization." *Proc. SIGGRAPH '02, Transactions on Graphics* 21:3 (2002), 745–754.

[van Wijk 02b] J. J. van Wijk. "Image Based Flow Visualization Supplemental Material." *Proc. SIGGRAPH '02, Transactions on Graphics* 21:3. Available online (http://www.win.tue.nl/~vanwijk/ibfv/ibfv_sample.pdf).

[van Wijk 03] J. J. van Wijk. "Image Based Flow Visualization for Curved Surfaces." In *Proc. IEEE Visualization*, pp. 17–24. Los Alamitos, CA: IEEE Press, 2003.

[van Wijk 05] J. J. van Wijk. "The Value of Visualization." In *Proc. IEEE Visualization*, pp. 79–86. Los Alamitos, CA: IEEE Press, 2005.

[van Wijk 06] J. J. van Wijk. "The SequoiaView File System Visualization Tool." Available online (http://www.win.tue.nl/sequoiaview/), 2006.

[Verma et al. 00] V. Verma, D. Kao, and A. Pang. "A Flow-Guided Streamline Seeding Strategy." In *Proc. IEEE Visualization*, pp. 163–170. Los Alamitos, CA: IEEE Press, 2000.

[ViewVC 07] ViewVC. "The ViewVC CVS Repository Browser." Available online (http://www.viewvc.org/), 2007.

[Vilanova et al. 99] A. Vilanova, A. König, and E. Gröller. "VirEn: A Virtual Endoscopy System." *Machine Graphics and Vision* 8:3 (1999), 469–487.

[Voinea 07] L. Voinea. "The CVSgrab Software Evolution Visualization System." Available online (http://www.win.tue.nl/~lvoinea/VCN.html), 2007.

[Walton 04] J. P. Walton. "NAG's IRIS Explorer." In *Visualization Handbook*, edited by C. R. Johnson and C. D. Hansen. New York: Academic Press, 2004.

[Wan et al. 01] M. Wan, F. Dachille, and A. Kaufman. "Distance-Field Based Skeletons for Virtual Navigation." In *Proc. IEEE Visualization*, pp. 239–246. Los Alamitos, CA: IEEE Press, 2001.

[Ward 94] M. O. Ward. "XmdvTool: Integrating Multiple Methods for Visualizing Multivariate Data." In *Proc. IEEE Visualization*, pp. 17–21. Los Alamitos, CA: IEEE Press, 1994.

[Ware 04] C. Ware. *Information Visualization: Perception for Design, Second edition*. San Francisco, CA: Morgan Kaufmann, 2004.

[Wattenberg 99] M. Wattenberg. "Visualizing the Stock Market." In *Proc. Conference on Human Factors in Computing Systems (CHI)—Extended abstracts*, pp. 188–189. New York: ACM Press, 1999.

[Wegman 90] E. J. Wegman. "Hyperdimensional Data Analysis using Parallel Coordinates." *Journal of the American Statistical Association* 411:85 (1990), 664–675.

[Weickert 98] J. Weickert. *Anisotropic Diffusion in Image Processing*. Stuttgart: Teubner-Verlag, 1998.

[Wendland 06] H. Wendland. *Scattered Data Approximation*. Cambridge, UK: Cambridge University Press, 2006.

[Westin et al. 97] C. F. Westin, S. Peled, H. Gubjartsson, R. Kikinis, and F. A. Jolesz. "Geometrical Diffusion Measures for MRI from Tensor Basis Analysis." In *Proc. of the 5th Annual Meeting of the ISMRM*, p. 1742. Berkeley, CA: International Society for Magnetic Resonance in Medicine, 1997.

[Williams et al. 95] J. G. Williams, K. M. Sochats, and E. Morse. "Visualization." *Annual Review of Information Science and Technology (ARIST)* 30 (1995), 161–207.

[Wolfram Research, Inc. 07] Wolfram Research, Inc. "Wolfram Mathematica." Available online (http://www.wolfram.com/products/mathematica/index.html), 2007.

[Ye et al. 05] X. Ye, D. Kao, and A. Pang. "Strategies for Seeding 3D Streamlines." In *Proc. IEEE Visualization*, pp. 471–478. Los Alamitos, CA: IEEE Press, 2005.

[Zhou and Toga 99] Y. Zhou and A. W. Toga. "Efficient Skeletonization of Volumetric Objects." *Transactions of Visualization and Computer Graphics* 5:3
(1999), 210–225.

[Zhou et al. 98] Y. Zhou, A. Kaufman, and A. W. Toga. "Three-Dimensional
Skeleton and Centerline Generation Based on an Approximate Minimum
Distance Field." *The Visual Computer* 14:7 (1998), 303–314.

Index

advection, 183, 190, 192, 195–204

algebraic multigrid (AMG), 209–212, 459

ambient coefficient, 22, 23, 25, 26

AMG, *see* algebraic multigrid

anisotropy

    and diffusion, 210, 216, 237, 274, 291–292

    and distance metrics, 322

    and tensors, 227–228

    fractional, 230, 234, 238

    relative, 229–230

attenuation, 358–359, 361

attributes

    basic, 43, 68–81

    color, 69–74, 80, 113, 126, 136, 278

    metadata, 440

    non-numerical, 77–78, 126, 385, 389, 435

    of nodes and/or cells, 80, 97–98

    relational, 395, 426

    scalar, 44, 68, 78, 93–95, 156, 203, 278

    tensor, 74–77

    types, 68

    vector, 69, 73, 78, 94, 162

basis functions

    constant, 46, 55, 154, 209, 213, 255

    gridless, *see* basis functions, radial

    linear, 47, 55–58, 179, 210–211

    quadratic, 59–60

    radial, 101, 258–264, 432–433

    reference, 48, 77, 82

blending

    and OpenGL, 32–36, 199–201, 437

    and splatting, 247, 261–264, 312–315

    equation, 33, 313

    volumetric, 204, 367, 371–373

bricking, 246–275

brushing technique, 433, 438–440

C++, 16, 73, 122, 303, 344, 383, 412, 424, 427, 443, 447, 451

carpet plots, *see* elevation plots

Cauchy criterion, 41, 326

cells

    definition, 46

    hexahedron, 58, 150

    line, 55

    quad, 56, 147

    quadratic, 59

    reference, 48–49, 55, 82–83